THE TOWER AND THE RUIN

OTHER BOOKS BY Michael D.C. Drout

Drout's Quick and Easy Old English

Tradition and Influence in Anglo-Saxon Literature: An Evolutionary, Cognitivist Approach

Poems from the Edge of the World

Beowulf Unlocked: New Evidence from Lexomic Analysis

How to Learn How to Think: What the Liberal Arts Are Good For, Anyway

AUDIO COURSES BY Michael D.C. Drout

Tolkien and the West: Recovering the Lost Tradition of Europe

The Norsemen: Understanding Vikings and Their Culture

From Here to Infinity: An Exploration of Science Fiction Literature

Bard of the Middle Ages: The Works of Geoffrey Chaucer

EDITED BY Michael D.C. Drout

J.R.R. Tolkien Encyclopedia

Tolkien Studies: An Annual Scholarly Review (Volumes 1–21)

The TOWER *and the* RUIN

J.R.R. Tolkien's Creation

Michael D.C. Drout

W. W. NORTON & COMPANY
Independent Publishers Since 1923

Printed in the United States of America
First Edition

For information about special discounts for bulk purchases, please contact W. W. Norton Special Sales at specialsales@wwnorton.com or 800-233-4830

Manufacturing by Lake Book Manufacturing
Book design by Marysarah Quinn
Production manager: Lauren Abbate

ISBN 978-1-324-09388-6

W. W. Norton & Company, Inc.
500 Fifth Avenue, New York, NY 10110
www.wwnorton.com

W. W. Norton & Company Ltd.
15 Carlisle Street, London W1D 3BS

Authorized EU representative: EAS, Mustamäe tee 50,
10621 Tallinn, Estonia

1 2 3 4 5 6 7 8 9 0

TO MY FATHER

David Irving Drout
1946–2020

AND TO MY SON

Mitchell David Cornel Drout
2004–2022

And the ship went out into the High Sea and passed into the West, until at last on a night of rain he smelled a sweet fragrance on the air and heard the sound of singing that came over the water. And then it seemed to him that the grey rain-curtain turned all to silver glass and was rolled back, and he beheld white shores and beyond them a far green country under a swift sunrise.

—*The Return of the King*

CONTENTS

THE TOWER AND THE RUIN

INTRODUCTION:

Son and Father

MY FIRST INTEREST IN J.R.R. Tolkien was apparently caused by the infamous Barbara Remington artwork used for the covers of the Ballantine mass-market editions. When my father bought his paperback copies of *The Lord of the Rings* at the Cornell University bookstore in 1969, the three volumes came with a free poster of the Map of Middle-earth, also illustrated by Remington. That map somehow ended up taped on the wall of the spare room in my grandmother's house. According to family lore, one day I stood up in my crib, pointed to the "Black Riders" at the bottom of the picture, and kept repeating "What that? What that?"

I had to wait a few years for an explanation. But although I now know what a Black Rider is, to this day I do not understand what the three salamanders riding on a flattened frog, the pointed-nosed lizard-thing leaping from the water, the lion-maned dragon-snake, or the angry dog-monster have to do with *The Lord of the Rings*.* Tolkien was also confused, although he seemed more exercised by the emus and the

---

* And yet, just a month or so before my daughter was born, I stayed up until 2 a.m. bidding frantically on a copy of the poster that had come up for sale on eBay, eventually spending, to my wife's great irritation, over $300 so that I could hang the Map of Middle-earth over Rhys's crib. It is still in her childhood bedroom.

tree with bulbous pink fruit on the covers of *The Hobbit* and *The Fellowship of the Ring.**

For me, engaging with Tolkien's work began with trying—and failing—to figure things out, to synthesize fragmented, disjointed, and contradictory material into some coherent whole. That sounds like an inauspicious beginning to either a lifetime of loving Tolkien's work or a career as a literary historian, but in fact it is the same experience—although perhaps with a bit less failing—that every first-time reader of *The Hobbit* has when trying to make sense of something called a "hobbit" whose mother was "the famous Belladonna Took," an experience that recurs throughout the course of reading *The Hobbit* and is even more common in *The Lord of the Rings.*[1]

One of the central claims of this book is that the mental effects of the small gaps, contradictions, and inconsistencies in Tolkien's work contribute substantially to readers' experiencing it as somehow different than other pieces of literature. I will also argue, however, that this was not originally Tolkien's conscious intention but rather arose out of the long and tortuous composition-history of Tolkien's works. I do not intend in any way to disparage Tolkien's genius—a word I use in the most old-fashioned, naïve, unironic sense possible—as both writer and scholar, and I will not be focused on nitpicking apparent "flaws." Instead, my intention is to show both what Tolkien did and how he did it. We will be examining what Tolkien called "the course of actual composition," and I will not pass up noting that, at times, he worked his way from what is, in retrospect, a terrible concept (the Ring is "not very dangerous, if used for a good purpose"), or name

* With regard to the cover design of *The Hobbit* for the Ballantine paperback edition: "Can any member of the T[olkien] S[ociety of] A[merica] tell me what a lion and emus are doing in the vignette, or what is the thing with pink bulbs in the foreground?"; *Letters*, #276, 503. Tolkien spoke with a representative from the publishers: "With regard to the pink bulbs she said as if to one of complete obtusity: 'they are meant to suggest a Christmas Tree.' Why is such a woman let loose? I begin to feel that I am shut up in a madhouse"; *Letters*, #277, 507.

To be fair, Barbara Remington had been under extreme time pressure and had not read the books, but worked from a summary. After she did read the books, she became "enthralled" and sent Tolkien a letter of apology, "along with a literal olive branch" (TCG Letter #2248 [from Barbara Remington to J.R.R. Tolkien, November 1, 1967], *Tolkien Collector's Guide*, accessed August 17, 2024).

(Teleporno was the king of the elves of Lothlórien; Frodo was Bingo Bolger-Baggins), or plot-point (Bilbo stabbing the dragon "with his little knife"), to what became a great work of literature that has the power to engage an immense range of readers, engage them more deeply, and, most importantly, engage them in fundamentally different ways than its predecessors, contemporaries, or imitators.[2] This last point is far more important to me than the others. Trying to explain popularity is an exercise in sociology or marketing and therefore, in my view, a waste of the literary historian's time.* But trying to explain what about Tolkien's books may lead people to treat them differently than other texts is another story. *The Lord of the Rings* is over 600,000 words long; it contains many poems in various forms; it uses hundreds of unfamiliar names; there are untranslated passages written in invented languages; and the book depicts multiple scenes of terror and violence, including the mutilation of the protagonist—*of course* we should read it out loud to our six-year-old . . . and people do.

The first actual memory I have of anything related to Tolkien is my father reading "In a hole in the ground there lived a hobbit" while I struggled to stay awake in our stuffy and always overheated New York apartment on the ninth floor of 435 East 70th Street, one of our cats curled up at the foot of my bed, and my younger brother, a toddler, already asleep in his crib a few feet away. It was therefore late 1973 or early 1974, and I was five and a half years old. For the next two years, at bedtime my father would read me *The Hobbit*, then *The Lord of the Rings*, and when we reached the end of *The Return of the King*, we would go back to the beginning of *The Hobbit*. Often my father would start to doze while he read, so his voice would slur a bit and his New Jersey accent would become more pronounced. Half a century later, when reading the books silently, I sometimes hear his voice and his mispronunciations, /Le-gÓ-las/, /SAR-on/, /THEE-o-den/.[3]

* When I began writing this book, one of the notes I put on my monitor was: *NO amateur Sociology.*

Feelings of comfort and happiness accompany these memories, but there is also sadness and stress and, in retrospect, a foreboding darkness. My father was completing his internship and residency at New York Hospital at a time when physician-training hours had not yet been scaled back to humane levels. He worked not only every day, but also every other night for weeks at a time,* so his being home when both he and I were awake felt like a special privilege. There was also illness and fear: My brother and I both struggled with asthma exacerbated by the tight quarters, two pet cats, every adult smoking, and a building infested with cockroaches. The asthma attacks and occasional pneumonia were exhausting, and worse, frightening, because my father, a figure of calm mastery whenever we saw him at the hospital, could not hide the worry on his face when either of us was sick.

There was also some darkness around the edges of our lives, although I was too young to name it. Poverty, even the temporary poverty of medical school and internship, is hard for any family; there were also familial and marital tensions that I sensed even if I did not understand; and the city around us could be harsh and frightening. Sometimes we heard gunshots at night, and one day, in Carl Schurz Park, my friend and I found a man lying unmoving inside the spiral slide in the playground. As she hustled us away, my friend's mother said the man was sleeping, but I had seen that his eyes were open. A similar kind of darkness sometimes shadowed *The Hobbit*, beginning with Bilbo's inexplicable (to five-year-old me) panic at the thought of a dragon coming to the Shire and continuing with the hushed mentions of the Necromancer, the glimpses of the ruined castles on the journey to Rivendell, the laments of the Lake-men for their burned homes—hints of far more deep and serious fears that felt distinctly different

* I have a vivid memory of looking at the calendar and being filled with joy when I saw my father's schedule being every third night for two weeks in a row one month. Alas, it was not meant to be, as one of the other interns got sick and he had to cover. It is hard to imagine how anyone could work a thirty-six-hour shift, have twelve hours off, then work a twenty-four-hour shift, then have twelve hours off, then work a thirty-six-hour shift, repeating without letup for weeks at a time.

from the scary excitement of the trolls, goblins, wargs, and the Spiders of Mirkwood.

The Hobbit and its literary effects are thus for me inextricably tangled up with early memories from a time when much was confused. Or, perhaps more accurately, particular qualities of *The Hobbit* entered deeply and permanently into my psyche, entwined with memories of warmth and safety, of being comforted and protected, and also with flashes of terror: of struggling with all my strength to draw in one breath and then starting the struggle again for the next one; of watching my brother's lips turn blue and my father suddenly sweep him into his arms and dash out to the emergency room; of overhearing whispered, frightened conversations with words that I did not understand but knew to fear: *arterial blood gasses, cystic fibrosis, intubate.*

These circumstances could perhaps account for the vividness of my memories of those first glimpses of Middle-earth: Fever and illness can intensify perceptions; minor traumas can fix memories; and there may also be some echo of Tolkien's own severe illnesses in the rhythms of the narrative—more than once Frodo's pain and suffering leads to clouded vision, exhaustion, and eventual unconsciousness, followed by a peaceful awakening under clean sheets with the morning sun pouring through a window. But why is it, then, that *The Hobbit* and *The Lord of the Rings*—and not the many other books my father or mother read to me in that same period—have shaped my perception of my own life and the lives of my children? More importantly, why do so many other readers, in utterly different situations, have similar experiences with Tolkien's work? Dumb luck might explain me—perhaps I encountered Tolkien's work at just the right stage of intellectual development—but all of those other readers, too? Impossible. Another explanation could be simply the high quality of the work: It is a well-crafted story written in an engaging style. But even taken together, these reasons are insufficient. Many different books must end up being read at just the right age (whatever that is) out of the millions of children being read to by their caregivers, and although Tolkien's writing is of high quality (indeed, higher than was acknowledged by many critics for several decades), it is not transcendently superior to that of every other writer.

No one thing makes *The Hobbit* different from the other children's literature of the same time period. A constellation of qualities combine to make the book produce its unique effects, and perhaps the only one that is utterly unique is that it is followed by *The Lord of the Rings*. The experience of reading that great work changes the reader and, in so doing, retrospectively reshapes *The Hobbit*. What might have been just an engaging children's story becomes also a set of hints, allusions, and glimpses, the early experiences of learning about a larger world, the first steps in the process of creating a reader of *The Lord of the Rings*. And that reader, over the course of *The Lord of the Rings*, has learned along with and in the same ways as the viewpoint characters as they discover more of their world, actively synthesizing scraps of information into an ever-richer and more complete model, coming to understand Middle-earth in the same way we come to understand our world—by figuring it out on our own.

Whether understanding Tolkien's works is a goal worth pursuing has not always been obvious—at least to many scholars. In December 1996, when I was a PhD student interviewing for my first professor job, I was counselled not to make too much of my enthusiasm for Tolkien lest I seem "frivolous" or "childish," or "not a serious person." How widespread the attitude implied by that advice once was is why nearly every scholarly book about J.R.R. Tolkien begins with some kind of apology for or defense of Tolkien. The author compiles a list of stupid things that have been said about Tolkien (and there are many), refutes them (which is not difficult), and then makes a heartfelt argument for why Tolkien is actually worth studying (usually some variation of "his work actually is consistent with or similar to something the critical establishment *does* respect"). It is almost a template to be followed for the successful Tolkien book.

I don't think we need to do this anymore. There was a time when Tolkien absolutely needed defending. Even as recently as 2000, when Tom Shippey's *J.R.R. Tolkien: Author of the Century* was published, Tolkien studies occupied a very precarious position in academia. Most of the best work was being done by researchers with no institutional support, few college courses were dedicated to Tolkien,* and those professors who published on Tolkien, for the most part, did not specialize in his work: Except for a noble few, scholars interested in Tolkien kept their heads down and did not advertise their expertise in their departments or make it part of their professional identities.[4]

But those days are now long past. Although some scholars—and probably more self-appointed critics in journalism or on the internet—still raise eyebrows or snicker at the idea of studying Tolkien's works, there are now enough courses, lectures, journals, books, articles, academics, and students to allow us to conclude that the field of Tolkien studies has as much of a toehold in contemporary academia as any specialization in the humanities. Peter Jackson's massively successful film trilogies had more than a little to do with this state of affairs, but Tolkien studies could not have capitalized on that pop-culture success if the pioneering scholars who knew that Tolkien was "worth studying" had not built such a strong intellectual foundation for the subdiscipline.[5]

The most credit goes to Shippey, whose 1982 *The Road to Middle-earth* deserves to be recognized as doing for Tolkien studies what Tolkien's 1936 essay "*Beowulf*: The Monsters and the Critics" did for the study of *Beowulf*: arguing so effectively for the literary value of an object of study that, in a real sense, it opened up a new era of scholarship. Tolkien's essay had shown how *Beowulf* could be studied as a poem in its own right, and subsequent critics have universally accepted that the literary value of the poem has been proven. I believe that the same is true of *The Road to Middle-earth*, which has made the case for the literary value of Tolkien's work so well (and also, like "The Monsters and the Critics," demonstrated *how* to understand the work) that the defense no longer need be made. Shippey's *J.R.R. Tolkien: Author of the Century* (2000) makes the same argument, but in more detail and with a more rhetorically forceful tone, practically daring those scholars he critiqued to try to refute its arguments. No one ever did, so now scholars need not

* Since *The Lord of the Rings* is so long, it is almost impossible to include it in a course not solely devoted to Tolkien because reading and discussing it simply uses up too large a portion of the semester.

include the previously obligatory *apologia* for Tolkien, but can simply proceed to scholarship and criticism, invoking Shippey if needed.

Thus this book does not bother to defend Tolkien, or Tolkien's works, or the study of Tolkien. However, even though I have just asserted that Shippey demolished the arguments of the most significant anti-Tolkien critics, I also think that those critics were on to something. Tolkien's works *are* in some way different from the works of literature (primarily from the twentieth century) to which critics were comparing them. But Tolkien was not trying to write the next great modernist novel, and so evaluating his work according to criteria developed to rank modernist novels inevitably produces meaningless results.*

"Philosophy will clip an Angel's wings, Conquer all mysteries by rule and line," wrote Keats. "Empty the haunted air, and gnoméd mine—Unweave a rainbow, as it erewhile made, The tender-person'd Lamia melt into a shade." Tolkien's version of this lament could be Gandalf's response to Saruman when the latter says that white light can be broken. Gandalf replies: "he who breaks a thing to find out what it is has left the path of wisdom."[6] If my experience with students and other readers is any guide, although the academic study of Tolkien may no longer need a defense, the scholarly approach to Tolkien does worry a significant subset of nonacademic readers and fans, who fear that the supposed dissections of academic study will kill the awe and joy, or are concerned that the growing professionalization of Tolkien studies will displace the very people who laid the intellectual foundations for the present success. Such fears are not entirely unfounded. Knowing that nearly all of the names of the kings of Rohan are Anglo-Saxon words for *king* is for me both a light jest and a deeper comment by Tolkien about the ways that descriptions evolve into proper names, but other readers may not want to know the background, enjoying the web of words solely as Tolkien has spun it, not in its extratextual engagement with other words and things.[7] I respect that feeling, but for me (and, I hope, for many others), the rainbow is *more* beautiful when I know

* Thus indicating that what the critics were claiming as somehow "universal standards" were actually completely parochial, ex post facto justifications of what those individual critics liked (or, more likely, what the groupthink of their social set thought they should like)—which is fine, but why not be honest about it?

that it is made by the bending of the light, when my sensory joy and my cerebral knowledge interact. Similarly, understanding Tolkien's art intellectually and technically increases my pleasure in the text and in my personal exploration of how it creates its effects. One hesitates to contradict Tolkien (or Gandalf), but the "broken" white light *can* be mended simply by letting it pass through reversed prisms. Understanding does not inevitably displace joy.

Indeed, part of the joy of reading Tolkien's work, like the joy of being a literary scholar, is "the pleasure of finding things out," of seeing how different elements in a work combine to produce emotional and aesthetic effects.[8] This pleasure is common to the study of all literature. You find it when teasing apart the chronology of events in Toni Morrison's *Beloved,* or using a map of Joyce's Dublin to follow *Ulysses,* or tracing the family trees in Faulkner's *Absalom, Absalom!* The pleasure is further heightened when studying Tolkien's works because the imagined world is very different from Ohio, or Dublin, or Yoknapatawpha County. Morrison, Joyce, and Faulkner could rely on their audience's shared knowledge of real history, physics, botany, geology, and economics. Tolkien had to invent not only his stories, but the world behind them (even though there are parallels with the real northwest of the Old World).[9]

Some of the pleasure of studying Tolkien is figuring out how that world works, untangling the complex culture, history, theology, politics, and even biology of Middle-earth. One scholar calls this effort "Middle-earth studies"; game-designers call it "Lore."[10] Regardless, understanding the larger world is absolutely essential for understanding each work. Although some scholars may have tried examining only the published text of *The Hobbit* and *The Lord of the Rings* (sometimes even skipping the appendices) and ignoring the posthumous material, such interpretations are nearly always impoverished. Galadriel's lament in *The Fellowship of the Ring,* for instance, makes sense only if we know that she is an exile and why she was exiled, knowledge that we can only get from reading *The Silmarillion* and *Unfinished Tales.* Similarly, the tale of Aragorn and Arwen resonates much more deeply if we know the full Beren and Lúthien story, not merely the compressed abstract we get in *The Lord of the Rings.* "Tolkien studies" doesn't work without Middle-earth studies, but lore without literacy is likewise undesirable.

In its most extreme form, this approach would disallow our reading the language of the Rohirrim beyond what can be inferred from the text alone: *Wes thu hal* would be some kind of greeting, but we could not import from the extratextual world the meaning of the Old English words, "be you well." I know of no scholar or fan who has actually taken the approach to this extreme, but that is the reductio ad absurdum of the idea—widespread on the internet and elsewhere—that identifying Tolkien's sources and influences somehow ruins the effect of Middle-earth by breaking the illusion. True, it is not particularly illuminating to reduce Tolkien's invention merely to its sources. There are things about the Rohirrim that are different from the historical Anglo-Saxons, and it is important to keep the two distinct. But there is an additional level of knowledge that comes from knowing both the source and what Tolkien transformed it into, thus being able to understand not only what the author is saying about Middle-earth but also what he is saying about the historical world.[11] Ideally literacy and lore support each other, untangling the complexities of Middle-earth while at the same time relating them to things beyond the covers of Tolkien's books. In this book their relative proportion varies from chapter to chapter, but both are essential.

That Tolkien did not complete his Silmarillion or finish making it harmonious with the published *The Lord of the Rings*, and that Tolkien's conceptions of Middle-earth continued to evolve even after certain details had been crystalized in the published *The Hobbit* and, later, *The Lord of the Rings*, creates more opportunities for interpretation and the endlessly fascinating game of trying to make every detail fit, to iron out every seeming inconsistency. Tolkien himself loved this game. At one point Gandalf says that Treebeard is the oldest living thing in Middle-earth.[12] But Tom Bombadil says that *he* is eldest, that he saw the first acorn and the first raindrop.[13] Another author, upon noticing this contradiction, might have silently revised it out of the story. Tolkien let the text stand, treating his own novel like the medieval works he studied: assuming that beneath the apparent contradiction on the surface there was a consistent vision that should not simply be ignored by the later editor. In the twelfth century Snorri Sturluson wrote that in Old Norse tradition there were light elves, dark elves, and dwarves. Scholars—even those as eminent as Jacob Grimm—were not right to assume that Snorri was somehow confused and that dwarves and dark elves were two names for the same creatures. Perhaps Snorri knew stories, now lost, of dark elves who were distinct from the dwarves.[14] Similarly, seeming contradictions or ambiguities in Tolkien's work can sometimes be explained by more subtle analysis.

This approach, however, can also be taken to the extreme, where it becomes a form of *ret-conning* (creating *retroactive continuity*), devising overly ingenious and elaborate explanations for contradictions. Tolkien may not have removed the apparent problem in the comparative ages of Bombadil and Treebeard, but he did change the bridle of Glorfindel's horse to a headstall after a reader pointed out that he had claimed that elves ride without bridle or bit.[15] He might have revised out other contradictions if he had noticed them, or he might have let them stand but then invented explanations for the apparent discrepancies. The difficult job of the critic is to judge when a contradiction is just a contradiction (or an error) and when our reading needs to be more subtle. These problems are compounded by the great variation within Tolkien's works. Although *The Lord of the Rings* and *The Hobbit* were substantially revised by the author and the basic forms of the texts can be assumed to be for the most part what he intended, important subtleties are not always consistent and must therefore be discussed individually. Just one seemingly trivial example: Is *Elven* a proper adjectival form for something relating to the elves? Tolkien almost never used the word as a stand-alone adjective, hyphenating it nearly every time it appears in his work. Should we then emend the few times *Elven* appears by itself and use the much more common adjective *Elvish*?

These sorts of problems are even greater for *The Silmarillion*, the 1977 volume that is only a selection out of the mass of incredibly complex Silmarillion texts, composed over decades and often inconsistent or contradictory.[16] Christopher Tolkien's publication of the voluminous source material in the twelve-volume *The History of Middle-earth* has shown us how tangled a textual web Tolkien wove and how difficult it can be to tease out any single strand. That there is not really a canonical Silmarillion is a challenge for scholars, but not a challenge unprecedented in literary study: Similar problems afflict many medieval texts,* and scholars have developed various methods for dealing with such texts that can be adapted to the specific problems posed by Tolkien's works.

THE BASIC PREMISE of this book is that J.R.R. Tolkien's writings are qualitatively different from most other works of twentieth-century literature. In what follows, I seek to identify the particular qualities that make Tolkien distinct, explain how these characteristics affect readers both emotionally and intellectually, and so come to better understand the significance of his works. At the heart of the argument is the observation that reading feels Tolkien often like entering a world rather than just reading another book. This experiential quality—along with more tangible characteristics like the rich complexity of Middle-earth, the phonaesthetic beauty of Tolkien's languages, the intricacy of the narrative, and the sophistication of the moral vision—is a major contributor to his works' popularity, cultural influence, artistic success, and, above all, the greater personal significance they hold for many readers over other secular texts.

I am hardly alone in believing that Tolkien's work is qualitatively different from most (or all) other comparable literary texts from the same general period. Indeed, over the past twenty years I have had hundreds of conversations with people who feel the same way. Audience members at lectures, students in classes, people who send emails or letters or who post comments online all seem, independently, to agree that there is something special (and therefore different) about Tolkien's works. It is not just that Tolkien is very popular, which by itself proves little, but that for a remarkable number of readers, his work is not merely

* *Piers Plowman*, for example, was heavily revised twice, and the second revision radically changes parts of the poem, possibly because William Langland was horrified that leaders of the Peasants' Revolt of 1381 were quoting it.

entertaining but profoundly meaningful, moving them in ways that few other books do. This phenomenon is worth trying to explain both in and of itself and because of the implications it may have for our more general understanding of how literature works.

This book represents my attempt to synthesize what I have learned in my fifty-year engagement with Tolkien's works, bringing some order to the insights I began to acquire as a child first listening to my father read *The Hobbit* aloud and continued to develop through the later stages of my life: secret teenage enthusiast, undergraduate imitator, reluctantly fascinated graduate student, scholarly researcher, teacher, editor, supposed "expert," video-game consultant, TV talking head, fan, tour leader, and—most importantly—parent reading Tolkien's remarkable creations to my own children. My goal is to explain, as best I can, how Tolkien's stories work, both in their internal functioning and in the ways they affect their readers. My hope is that any insights I have might enable others to find even more in Tolkien's remarkable literary achievement. This book is also, I hope, useful for aspiring worldbuilders—that is, would-be writers of fantasy. No one has matched Tolkien's achievement as an author of fantasy literature, and perhaps no one ever will.* But there is much any writer can learn from this close look at Tolkien's works: What qualities make *The Hobbit* and *The Lord of the Rings* unique? Which characteristics are essential? How did Tolkien figure it out? Answers to these questions, even provisional ones, should be useful to the next generation of fantasy writers.

Although *The Tower and the Ruin* presupposes some familiarity with Tolkien's major works, and I have not oversimplified or diluted the research upon which I base the argument, readers do not need to have studied the previous scholarship on Tolkien to understand the book, which I hope can be read profitably even by those relatively new to Middle-earth. That said, this is a book aimed at dedicated readers of Tolkien. I do not pretend that it will be an easy book, even for them—but then, any serious book on Tolkien will of necessity challenge the

---

* Only Ursula K. Le Guin has come close.

reader. I have done my best to avoid testing the patience of nonacademic readers while still providing scholars with the details they need for their own work, so footnotes are limited to explanatory material of general interest; full citations and technical and historiographical notes are at the end of the book. I have also avoided using abbreviations in the main text, restricting them to the notes even though this meant typing "*The Lord of the Rings*" 269 times.

I approach Tolkien's works primarily as a literary historian, so I focus less on his biography and personal beliefs and more on the texts he read and studied and his processes of writing and revision. My goal is to explain how Tolkien's works came to have their unique characteristics and how these influence the experiences of readers, so the book begins with some of Tolkien's earliest works before turning to his mature masterpieces. Chapter 1, "Origins," examines three of Tolkien's earliest compositions, in which he experimented with techniques developed by Victorian writers H. Rider Haggard and William Morris in an effort to reproduce some of the ineffable qualities he found in *Beowulf*, the Finnish *Kalevala*, and other works of medieval literature from the North of Europe. The key to producing that "something in the air," it turns out, was not to replicate the original forms or styles, but to reproduce the sense of textuality of the early works. This textuality is reinforced by Tolkien's use of frame narratives—the focus of Chapter 2, "Frames"—which produce the impression that even new compositions are the culmination of long processes of compilation and transmission. Chapter 3, "Texts," discusses yet another quality of Tolkien's works that creates the impression that they are somehow older and more authentic than the printed volumes the readers hold in their hands: the variability and seeming inconsistency, at multiple levels, of their language and style.

Chapter 4, "Patterns," examines the ways in which the architectonics and rhythms of the narratives, as well as Tolkien's subtle use of focalization, help produce the sense of experientiality that characterize *The Hobbit* and *The Lord of the Rings*. "Emotions" are the subject of Chapter 5, both the unrelenting sorrow and loss of *The Silmarillion* and the more complex emotions of *The Lord of the Rings*, which is permeated with the sense of *Heimweh,* the German word for "pain for the lost home" felt by exiles (and we are all in some way exiles due to the relentless flow of time). Heimweh is never absent from *The Lord of the Rings,* but by the end of the book, perhaps it has been transmuted into a sadness that we can accept because we understand the shape and texture of that sorrow.

Chapter 6, "Threads," examines how some of Tolkien's secondary themes help shape the narratives of *The Silmarillion* and *The Hobbit* and thus the intellectual experiences of their readers. The evil caused by the Elvish racial hierarchy in *The Silmarillion* and the dialogic relationship between the epic and bourgeois worlds in *The Hobbit* both support and call into question aspects of the main themes of these works, making them much richer and more nuanced than other works of fantasy. The thematics of *The Lord of the Rings* are even more complicated, and the "Tapestry" that Chapter 7 investigates is produced by the intertwining of multiple subthemes, so that Tolkien's comparison of the cultures of Gondor and Rohan leads us to larger and larger issues: from responses to seemingly hopeless situations to the workings of the Ring and the morality of dominating other wills. This thematic complexity and sophistication is one of the reasons why readers from an enormous range of ideologies all interpret *The Lord of the Rings* as being consistent with their beliefs, as it creates the impression that Tolkien's work is in some fundamental way true, making it that much easier for readers to integrate it into their own worldviews.

Throughout the book I have interwoven my personal experiences with Tolkien's works as a way of showing some of the ways these literary masterpieces effect the perceptions and worldview of at least one identifiable reader. In the conclusion to *The Tower and the Ruin* I go one step further, discussing the ways that Tolkien's writings have shaped my own understanding of grief, loss, beauty, and hope.

Tolkien wrote:

> A man inherited a field in which was an accumulation of old stone, part of an older hall. Of the old stone some had already been used in building the house in which he actually lived, not far from the old house of his fathers. Of the rest he took some and built a tower. But his friends coming perceived at once (without troubling to climb the steps) that these stones had formerly belonged to a more ancient building. So they pushed the tower over, with no little labour, in order to look for hidden carvings and inscriptions, or to discover whence the man's distant forefathers had obtained their building material. Some suspecting a deposit of coal under the soil began to dig for it, and forgot even the stones. They all said: "This tower is most interesting." But they also said (after pushing it over): "What a muddle it is in!" And even the man's own descendants, who might have been expected to consider what he had been about, were heard to murmur: "He is such an odd fellow! Imagine his using these old stones just to build a nonsensical tower! Why did he not restore the old house? He had no sense of proportion." But from the top of that tower the man had been able to look out upon the sea.[17]

In this famous allegory, *Beowulf* is the tower, built by the poet out of the ruins of old tales.[18] Climbing the tower—reading what he himself had written?—allowed the poet to look upon the sea, an open symbol that can be filled by whatever the reader longs for: transcendent vision, unreachable frontiers, moral certainty, personal desires, immortal life.

The image of the tower appears throughout Tolkien's works, from the very earliest Silmarillion writings to the philosophical essays composed toward the end of his life. Minas Tirith, Orthanc, Minas Ithil, Cirith Ungol, Barad-dûr, Elostirion . . . the list is very long. Towers are achievements, visible expressions of design and knowledge, technology and labor. They show the creative spirit triumphing over gravity, over entropy. Elves and Númenóreans build towers and from them watch the stars or look upon the sea. But evil beings also rear towers to assert their dominion. Morgoth throws up the threefold peaks of Thangorodrim, higher than any masonry tower, and Sauron, in imitation and flattery, erects the Barad-dûr. Towers, then, are not *intrinsically* good or evil but rather ideas given solid form, representations of power. Towers can be taken away from the good—as when Sauron captures Minas Ithil, the Tower of the Moon, and turns it into the evil city of Minas Morgul—and a tower not taken can still be toppled, like the tower of Turgon in Gondolin, the Dome of the Stars in Osgiliath, or even Barad-dûr, Sauron's Dark Tower, which falls in ruin at the destruction of the Ring.

In Tolkien's work almost all towers end this way, and afterward, their ruins endure. From the empty castles that Bilbo and the dwarves spy on their journey to Rivendell, to the fallen tower of Amon Sûl on Weathertop, to the collapse of Barad-dûr, the remains of fallen towers litter Middle-earth's landscape. The theme of *Beowulf*, wrote Tolkien, is "that man, each man and all men, and *all their works shall die*."[19] Within time, all towers are cast down or fall, but their ruins can remain in the landscape. When Frodo reaches Weathertop, Amon Sûl has been destroyed for 1,043 years. Osgiliath fell into ruin more than 544 years before Pippin glimpses it in the distance. There are 4,763 years between the time the stones of Eregion were thrown down and when the Fellowship walks upon them. The tower is the glorious achievement, but the ruin is the permanent memory. What initially falls to entropy may still endure, *awa to aldre, æ mun uppi* [as long as people live], and beyond; of the long-departed elves the stones themselves lament: "deep they delved us, fair they wrought us, high they builded us; but they are gone."[20] The memory that surrounds the ruin may be imperfect, fragmented, or failing—merely scattered stones but it persists.

A ruin preserves the memory of what has been at the cost of making it impossible not to recognize the permanence of the loss. This melancholy, a longing for the unrecoverable past, is the dominant emotion in all of Tolkien's works, an important reason why they affect readers so strongly. Recall that heimweh describes a particular kind of pain that comes from the loss of home. In Tolkien's writings this pain is both acute and enduring, an ache that begins when Frodo looks down at Hobbiton and wonders if he will ever look back on that valley again, and never stops, even in the last line in the novel, when Sam's "Well, I'm back," leaves unstated but evident the pain of his separation from Frodo even in the joyful moment of reunion with his wife and daughter.[21] Along with heartbreaking sorrow, there is a grandeur to this view of human life, to the ruin persisting long after the tower is gone, preserving the memory that something once was there. Tolkien's vision is deeply and essentially true, and it gives shape and meaning to the grief and loss that is our common and inescapable inheritance as humans incarnate in time.

CHAPTER 1

Origins

IT SEEMS ENTIRELY APPROPRIATE that Tolkien's works of fiction have multiple origin stories. The most famous is the one in which the professor, marking examination papers for extra income during the summer, came across a page that a student had left blank and wrote: "In a hole in the ground there lived a hobbit."[1] And while that now-lost exam page is undoubtedly *an* origin of *The Hobbit* (and hence of the publication-history of Tolkien's prose fiction), it was certainly not the very beginning of his imaginative writing, which had started more than two decades before he penned the famous opening sentence.[2]

The origin story told by Humphrey Carpenter, Tolkien's authorized biographer, begins not with *The Hobbit*, but with a prose work that Tolkien wrote in early 1917 while he was convalescing in Great Haywood, Staffordshire, where he had been evacuated after contracting trench fever during the Battle of the Somme. *The Fall of Gondolin* depicts the heroic but doomed efforts of the elves to defend their beautiful city against an overwhelming assault of orcs, balrogs, and dragons. *Gondolin* was the first story in what would become *The Book of Lost Tales*, which would eventually grow into the Silmarillion material and go on from there to form the "vast backcloths" of *The Hobbit* and *The Lord of the Rings*. But even this "origin" has its own origin-story, Carpenter acknowledges: The prose *Fall of Gondolin* evolved out of Tolkien's early poetry. In the summer of 1914 Tolkien had written a poem that began: "Earendel sprang up from the Ocean's cup / In the gloom of the mid-world's rim." This, Carpenter asserts, "was in fact the beginning of Tolkien's own mythology."[3]

Thus, we now have three origin-stories (two from the same biographer!) each of which appears to be the beginning of one aspect of Tolkien's writing career: "In a hole in the ground there lived a hobbit" is the origin of Tolkien's unprecedented publishing success; in Carpenter's view, *The Fall of Gondolin* is the origin of "Middle-earth" as an elaborated setting; and the Earendel poem is the origin of Tolkien's "mythology."* That is the trouble with origins: They all have origins themselves, and these, in some sort of infinite regress, all in turn have their own origins.[4] For example, despite Tolkien's protestations, the word *hobbit* probably did not occur to him ex nihilo: The *Denham Tracts*, a nineteenth-century collection of folk sayings from the north of England, includes *hobbits* along with *hobgoblins*, *hobhoulards*, *hobby-lanthorns*, and *hob-headlesses* in a list of supernatural creatures.[5] And the Earendel poem, as Carpenter notes, was inspired by lines 105–109 of the Old English poem *Christ I* from the Exeter Book manuscript of Anglo-Saxon poetry.[6]

> *Eala earendel, engla beorhtast,*
> *ofer middangeard monnum sended,*
> *ond soðfæsta sunnan leoma,*
> *torht ofer tunglas, þu tida gehwane*
> *of sylfum þe symle inlihtes!* (lines 104–8)[7]

[Hail! Earendel, the brightest of angels, sent to men over middle-earth, and true light of the sun, bright beyond the stars, you from your own self always illuminate all seasons].[8]

---

* *Middle-earth* is just a literal translation of Old English *middangeard*, cognate with Old Norse *miðgarðr* (often written *midgard*). The second <e> in Tolkien's coinage is not capitalized because the word is a compound; the hyphen is added in order to separate the <e> in *earth* from the <e> at the end of *Middle*. (Capitalization of the <e> in *earth* is one of the most predictable tells that a self-proclaimed expert has not spent enough time studying Tolkien's works.)

I have underlined the only words from *Christ I* that, translated into Modern English, appear in Tolkien's verse: the name *Earendel* and the compound "mid-world" (an adaptation of *middangeard* [middle-earth] in line 106).* Otherwise Tolkien's poem has little in common with *Christ I.* The Earendel poem does, however, share its meter and rhyme scheme with Percy Bysshe Shelley's "Arethusa," a lyrical mythological narrative drawn from Virgil and Ovid.[9] Although the two poems do not initially appear particularly alike, their deep similarity in form becomes apparent when they are read aloud. In both poems, the stanzas begin with a rhyming couplet in iambic trimeter. Shelly prints his as two short lines; Tolkien combines his into a single longer line with internal rhyme.[10] When the two poems are recited, their scansions and rhyme schemes (AABCCB) are indistinguishable.

Tolkien seems to have adopted only the poetic form of "Arethusa."[11] The primary metaphorical image at the center of Tolkien's poem—the ocean as a cup with the horizon as its rim—has nothing to do with either Shelley's "Arethusa" or *Christ I.* Its origin is line 1208b of *Beowulf*, which reads *ofer yða ful* [over the cup of the waves].[12] We now have another three potential origins to add to the three with which we began: the word *earendel*, the poem "Arethusa," and *Beowulf* line 1208b.

And the infinite regress continues (as infinite regresses are wont to do). Both the key half-line of *Christ I* and the enigmatic name *Earendel* have origins of their own. *Eala Earendel* is a translation into Old English of the Latin phrase *O oriens* [O light in the east; i.e., dawn], which occurs in the "O Antiphons," a set of short Latin chants sung as responses to the Magnificat hymn on the last seven nights of Advent leading up to Christmas.† Each antiphon is a metaphorical name for Christ (O King of the Nations, O Root of Jesse, O Key of David). *Christ I* is a somewhat free Old English translation and elaboration of

* Tolkien capitalizes his own *Middle-earth* because, being the name of a specific place, it is a proper noun. But Old English *middangeard* is a common noun, and in any event, conventions as to the capitalization of proper names had not yet evolved in Old English.

† "O oriens" is sung on December 21. The traditional Christmas carol "O Come, O Come, Emmanuel," is an adaptation and translation of another of the "O Antiphons."

the "O Antiphons," and in translating "O oriens," the Anglo-Saxon poet has rather substantially modified the sense of the Latin:

> *O Oriens, splendor lucis aeternae, et sol iustitiae:*
> *veni, et illumina sedentes in tenebris et umbra mortis.*

> [O, light in the east, splendor of light eternal and sun of righteousness:
> Come and illuminate those who dwell in darkness and the shadow of death.]

The Latin text only mentions the dawn, but there are two sources of light referred to in the Old English poem: "the brightest of angels" and the "true light of the sun." The latter of these is equated to Jesus in the Latin antiphon, so "Earendel," which must be the name of the angel, represents some other astronomical object, which Tolkien took to be Venus, the "morning star as it may be seen shining brilliantly just before the actual rising of the sun."[13] Why the Anglo-Saxon poet chose to depart from the literal text of the Latin antiphon is unknown, but a hint may be found in another Old English text, Blickling Homily 14, in which we read that *se niwa eorendel Sanctus Iohannes; and nu se leoma þære soþan sunna, God selfa, cuman wille* [the new "eorendel" is St. John the Baptist, and now the light of the true sun, God himself, will come].[14] The poet may have seen an opportunity to display his knowledge of astronomy, Christian doctrine, or both by noting that just as the brightest star, Venus, can appear just before the rising sun, so too did the lesser splendor of John the Baptist precede the full glory of Jesus.

Whatever the poet's reasons for adapting the antiphon in this way, it was clear to Tolkien that the word *earendel* was the name of both an astronomical object and a mythical figure associated with it. He does not, however, seem to have been particularly taken with the most developed story of the object's origin that has been preserved in Northern mythology. The name *Aurvandill* in Old Norse is certainly a cognate of Old English *Earendel* (although neither evolved directly from the other, they share a common ancestor). Snorri Sturluson, twelfth-century Icelandic poet and scholar, relates a seemingly traditional story that once upon a time, the god Thor carried a man named Aurvandill across the

Élivágar Rivers in a basket, but the poor man's toe was sticking out through the basket's weave and became badly frostbitten. Thor then snapped off the frozen toe and flung it into the sky, where it became the star known as *Aurvandils-tá* [Aurvandill's toe], which is usually identified as the planet Venus.*

This decidedly homely origin for the beauty of the Morning (or Evening) Star appears not to have resonated with Tolkien. His origin story for Venus seems instead to have been influenced by the philologically reconstructed Common Germanic word from which Old Norse *Aurvandill*, Old English *Earendel*, Old High German *Aurendil*, and Lombardic *Auriwandalo* could all be descended.[15] **Auzo-wandilaz* means "ray of light" or perhaps "bringer/carrier of light" (the asterisk indicates that the word is not actually recorded in any ancient or medieval text but is a reconstruction by philologists). In Tolkien's poem it is Earendel himself—rather than just his severed toe—that is the source of the light.[16]

But to take **Auzo-wandilaz* as the origin of Tolkien's fiction not only seems intuitively wrong, but perhaps more importantly, it also has little explanatory power. The idea of a figure with the name Earendel being a bringer of light does seem to have shaped the mythological story that Tolkien eventually developed, which is presented very elliptically in the "Eärendil was a mariner" poem that Bilbo recites in Rivendell; it is summarized very briefly in Appendix A of *The Lord of the Rings*, and is told in much more detail in the published *The Silmarillion*.[17] But the bare word **Auzo-wandilaz* is too distant and abstract.† "Eala Earendel"

---

* Some scholars claim that the reference is to Rigel, the brightest star in the constellation Orion, rather than Venus. Rigel does appear to be Orion's toe, and Orion is at its brightest in the winter (December 21, when "O oriens" is sung is often the winter solstice), but Rigel does not work as well as Venus in the comparison with John the Baptist in Blickling Homily 14.

† The asterisk is a convention developed by August Schleicher in the nineteenth century to indicate a word that was never recorded but that is reconstructed using principles of philology; Victor Golla, "Reconstruction," *Journal of Linguistic Anthropology* 9, no. 1/2 (1999): 208–11. The term *asterisk-reality* that Shippey coined in *Road* seems to be frequently misunderstood as being equivalent to what Tolkien in "On Fairy-Stories" called a "secondary world." It is not. Rather "asterisk reality" is something that "no longer existed but could with 100 per cent certainty be inferred" from the surviving evidence and the principles of language-change; *Road*, 19–23.

in *Christ I* itself has an origin, but "O oriens" appears insufficiently connected with Tolkien's story. To be the origin of Tolkien's literary works, it seems, a text or word or idea should precede Tolkien's Earendel poem, but when we look at that poem's sources and inspirations themselves, none seem sufficient.

I think we must therefore conclude that the origin of Tolkien's Legendarium is not any individual source or inspiration in and of itself. Instead, it was the act of linking the name *Earendel* with the image of the sea as a cup, the astronomical character of the word and its identification with the Morning Star, and the idea that the character named Earendel was himself a bringer of light. Out of this set of words, images, and ideas, Tolkien created a story, which he told in Modern English verse. The resulting poem makes sense on its own, accounts for the existing literary-historical evidence, and reconstructs or invents some cultural context for the original sources. This synthesis of scholarship and imagination—using imagination not just to solve scholarly problems but to create new and original stories or poems in form and language different from the inspirational sources—is one of the characteristics that makes Tolkien's work so distinct. *The true origin of Tolkien's creative works is the act of inventive synthesis.*

One of the most distinctive qualities of *The Hobbit* and *The Lord of the Rings* is the impressions these works give—despite their being the creations of a single, known, twentieth-century author—of having been composed and compiled by multiple writers in several time periods and of drawing upon a large variety of cultural traditions and textual materials. The mixture of languages, poetic forms, and prose styles, and the presence of apparent narrative and epistemological gaps and contradictions, all combine to create a particular aesthetic effect that is both broadly and in detail comparable to that produced by *Beowulf*, *Sir Gawain and the Green Knight*, or even *The Canterbury Tales*, not only because these works are very old, sometimes damaged, and occasionally incomplete, but because our knowledge of the cultural matrix in which they were created and read is so fragmentary. Tolkien's writings did not suffer the ravages of time, and they are not merely adaptations of the medieval texts he studied professionally, yet they give very similar impressions and generate some of the same effects in their readers as the very old texts that we might call *textual ruins*.

Just how these effects came to be produced is the subject of this chapter, which traces the "course of actual composition" of Tolkien's textual ruins from their primitive origins in his three earliest works.[18] The ways Tolkien drew upon and modified his sources in his first Earendel poem, in the prose *The Fall of Gondolin*, and in the *prosimetrum*—a mixture of poetry and prose—*The Story of Kullervo* show that although the creation of works with the characteristics of textual ruins was not Tolkien's initial aesthetic goal, his experiments with adapting various sources and reshaping and revising his writing ended up producing something very like the "something in the air" that he had found in *Beowulf*, the *Kalevala*, and other ruined works of medieval literature from the North of Europe.[19]

Identifying inventive synthesis as the origin of Tolkien's work may put a halt to the infinite regress of origin-hunting, but it is in some ways unsatisfying. Writing works of literature is not some kind of natural process that simply unfolds on its own once the proper materials are assembled. When we seek the origin of Tolkien's imaginative creations, we are not just looking for a specific poem or story; we are also hoping to identify when he decided that he would create these works, and, most of all, *why* he did so. My choice of the act of synthesis was not meant to frustrate this desire, merely to draw a distinction between origin and motivation. Why, when Tolkien read *Christ I* and *Beowulf* 1208b, did he write a synthesizing poem? Other responses—most obviously the purely scholarly work that was the focus of Tolkien's professional life—were certainly possible.

The consensus explanation that has developed in Tolkien studies over the past few decades is that the motivation for Tolkien's creative work was his desire to create "a mythology for England."[20] Carpenter's biography is the origin of this idea: He asserts that the last letter Tolkien received from his close friend G. B. Smith (who died from gas gangrene after being wounded in WWI) was "a clear call to Ronald Tolkien to begin the great work that he had been meditating for some time, a grand and astonishing project with few parallels in the history of literature. He was going to create an entire mythology."[21] Subsequent scholars picked up the idea from Carpenter and ran with it, developing a rather extensive literature on Tolkien's "mythology for England."

However, as multiple scholars have pointed out, there are many problems with this interpretation—possibly the least of which, but also the most obvious, is that Tolkien never used the phrase "mythology for England" that has so often been attributed to him.[22] But even if we set aside the very convincing argument that Tolkien's assertions about mythology in a 1951 letter to Milton Waldman were simply for the purpose of persuading Collins to publish *The Silmarillion* along with *The Lord of the Rings* and were no longer operative by the time he was completing his great work, we still have the problem that there is no evidence in either Carpenter's authorized biography or John Garth's *Tolkien and the Great War*, the two essential sources for biographical information, to suggest that, while an Oxford student, Tolkien felt that England's mythology was impoverished, much less that he was personally called upon to fill any putative gap.[23]

Carpenter argues that there were three major motivations for Tolkien's writing: his recognition that he needed to create an invented history for his invented languages; his desire to express "his most profound feelings in poetry," and "his desire to create a mythology *for England*. . . . He had hinted at this during his undergraduate days when he wrote of the Finnish national epic, the *Kalevala*: 'I would that we had more of it left—something of the same sort that belonged to the English.'"[24] But taking these words as indicating a desire for—much less a plan to create—a new mythology is entirely Carpenter's interpretation of the very little evidence that we have of Tolkien's motivations at that time in his life. Wishing that something like the *Kalevala* had survived in Old English is not at all the same thing as deciding that he needed to rectify this lamentable state of affairs by creating new works, much less an entire mythology, to fill the void.*

* It is remarkable how much of the agenda of Tolkien scholarship up to and even beyond the year 2000 was set by Carpenter's biography and surprising when we realize that Carpenter had little interest in fantasy literature (or literature in general) and was not a particularly insightful reader of Tolkien's literary works. See Douglas A. Anderson, "Obituary: Humphrey Carpenter (1946–2005)," *Tolkien Studies* 2 (2005): 217–24.

Several of Tolkien's early letters mention his pleasure in reading the *Kalevala* and his love of working on his "nonsense fairy language,"[25] but there is no mention of creating a "new mythology." Even in his most intense expression of the sense that he and his three closest friends had of being given a special gift (and hence a special responsibility), Tolkien never mentions mythology: The TCBS—Tolkien, Christopher Wiseman, R. Q. Gilson, and the aforementioned G. B. Smith—had been "granted some spark of fire . . . that was destined to kindle a new light, or, what is the same thing, rekindle an old light in the world" to "testify for God and Truth."[26] Even the 1955 letter to W. H. Auden, which Tolkien wrote in part to influence Auden's upcoming BBC talk about *The Lord of the Rings*—which thus has as its rhetorical purpose the shaping of public perception of the author—is not just a presentation of biographical facts.* Tolkien only notes the importance of the *Kalevala*, and the influence of Anglo-Saxon, Gothic, Finnish, and other languages on his "linguistic taste." There is nothing, even in retrospect, about creating a mythology, for England or anywhere else.[27] Finally, even in the 1951 letter to Waldman, immediately after saying that he once thought he wanted to create a "body of connected legend," which he would "dedicate simply to England; to my country," Tolkien says that "such an overweening purpose did not develop all at once. The mere stories were the thing."[28]

I think the simplest explanation for why Tolkien never says that creating a mythology was his motivation for his early writings is that his motivation was something else. What the "Earendel sprang up from the Ocean's cup" poem and Tolkien's adaptation of the Kullervo section of the *Kalevala* show is that even at this very early stage, he was attempting to create works of literary art, in contemporary forms and in Modern English, that would produce in their readers some of the same effects that the works of medieval literature produced in him and others who read them in their original languages and forms.

Now, although I believe this contention to be correct and, perhaps more importantly, useful in the sense that it explains qualities of Tolkien's creative works that are otherwise difficult to understand, there

---

* A rhetorical purpose not always remembered by scholars quoting it.

are a number of problems that cannot be ignored. First and most obvious, Tolkien never stated in writing that he wanted to re-create the effects of medieval literature in contemporary language and forms. If he had, the rickety edifice of "mythology for England" arguments would never have been constructed and analysis of Tolkien's works would start with a discussion of what the best comparisons to works of medieval literature would be.[29] Second, and perhaps more challenging, I am claiming, at first by implication but then explicitly, that Tolkien's works possess some quality or qualities that produce phenomenological effects in readers similar to those produced by certain works of medieval literature, which therefore also must have similar qualities. When put that abstractly, this contention seems difficult to substantiate. In its most abstract and weakest form, the claim would be something like: "These things are like each other because of the ineffable effects they produce as a result of their possession of certain ineffable qualities." The problem with ineffable things is that they are hard to describe. However, identifying two difficult-to-describe things as being in some ways similar without in advance specifying what their similar characteristics are is not necessarily an invalid procedure. In fact, it is an essential first step in both explaining the effects and identifying the key qualities of the works that produce them. But, at least in abstract terms, we have crept up quite close to circularity.*

I think the first problem, of the lack of an explicit statement by Tolkien, is handled fairly easily by inferring that Tolkien very likely did not articulate, even to himself, any specific single motivation for creating the *kinds* of literary works he created because he did not know in every detail what he hoped to create when he began. From his early letters and from the characteristics of his initial efforts, we can deduce that he was not working from some overarching plan (such as creating a

* One of my favorite examples of this approach is that of Joseph Pearce, who argues that some of the unique and difficult-to-explain effects of reading Tolkien's work are equivalent to some of the effects a devout Roman Catholic experiences when partaking in the Eucharist. Although this has every possibility of being *true*—and I am strongly inclined to believe that it is—it is not particularly *helpful* because describing one experience in terms of another experience that is so complex and difficult to explain that it is technically a "*Mystery* of the Church" can only enlighten a very particular subset of readers. Joseph Pearce, *Tolkien: Man and Myth—A Literary Life* (San Francisco: Ignatius Press, 1998).

new mythology) but was experimenting with multiple forms for various purposes. In the letter to W. H. Auden, Tolkien states that it was the Finnish language "that set the rocket off in story," because he was "immensely attracted by something in the air of the Kalevala . . . the beginning of the legendarium . . . was in an attempt to reorganize some of the Kalevala, especially the tale of Kullervo the hapless, into a form of my own."[30] The key point to notice here (the invocation of form will be important later in this argument) is that Tolkien is not suggesting that he wanted to use the *Kalevala* for some external purpose—such as creating a mythology or gaining fame and fortune as a writer. The implication is that by working to reorganize the Kullervo tale, he would be able to re-create the "something in the air" of the *Kalevala* that so attracted him. In other words, to make more of a thing that he desired—stories that had that ineffable something—by writing new ones. My assertion that Tolkien's motivation was *to create works of literary art in contemporary forms in Modern English that would produce in their readers some of the same effects that the works of medieval literature produced in contemporary readers who read them in their original languages* is therefore fully justified as long as we can accept that if we had perfect knowledge of Tolkien's thoughts, we might have to emend the statement to read "produce in *a* reader, Tolkien himself, some of the same effects . . . "

The tougher question is whether or not I am correct in concluding that the "something in the air" is in fact related to Tolkien's reading works of the medieval literature of northern Europe in their original languages. This is certainly my subjective experience. When I first learned Old English and translated the Anglo-Saxon poems *The Wanderer*, *The Seafarer*, and *Beowulf*, I found the same "something in the air" that I loved about *The Lord of the Rings*. It was not just that I now knew that *Westhu Theoden hal!* was *Wes þu þeoden hal* in Anglo-Saxon and meant "Be you, King, well," but that Tolkien's works and the Old English poems produced many of the same feelings in me, even if, at the time, I could not articulate what those were or which features of the texts produced them. That I read Tolkien first and Old English later perhaps helps remove some of the circularity of my argument, but it does not eliminate the problem entirely.

My solution is to hold off on analyzing the fully realized, mature works like *The Hobbit* and *The Lord of the Rings* and, in the next section of this discussion, focus on the development of particular features in several of Tolkien's very early works: The Earendel poem (the sources of which have been discussed already), *The Fall of Gondolin*, and *The Story of Kullervo*. Although the "something in the air" has not fully evolved in any of these texts, each contains some hints of it, so by looking closely at these early efforts and tracing the ways Tolkien interacts with, and innovates away from, the characteristics of his sources, we may be able to see, in embryo, the distinctive form and style of *The Hobbit* and *The Lord of the Rings*. We therefore turn from origin- and motivation-hunting to some more specific details of literary history, and from Tolkien's adaptation and expansion of the content he had encountered in the medieval works he studied to his use and modification of styles and forms he found in more recent literature.

Written "in hospital and on leave after surviving the Battle of the Somme in 1916," *The Fall of Gondolin* was, according to Tolkien's 1955 letter to W. H. Auden, "the first real story of this imaginary world [Middle-earth]."[31] First appearing as part of *The Book of Lost Tales Part II* in 1984 and republished in 2018, the story is the first instantiation of many content elements that would be further developed throughout Tolkien's legendarium.

When I first encountered *The Fall of Gondolin* in its context in *The Book of Lost Tales*, I did not appreciate just how much of the Silmarillion mythology appears in this relatively short prose work. In the *History of Middle-earth* volumes, *Gondolin* is printed toward the end of the second volume of the *Lost Tales*. Although this is the appropriate location based on in-world chronology rather than date of composition, this placement means that by the time readers reach the story, they have already encountered the Valar, Melko the Dark Lord (later Melkor and then Morgoth), the division between elves and men, enemies like orcs and balrogs, and the various regions of Beleriand, all of which were invented in *The Fall of Gondolin*. This familiarity tends to obscure the almost shockingly large fraction of the later-elaborated Silmarillion material that appears in this story from the very beginning.

Indeed, it was not until I read the stand-alone *The Fall of Gondo-*

lin volume in 2018 that I realized just how many features of Tolkien's decades-long development of the Silmarillion can be traced directly to this first story. The natural temptation is just to marvel, and I must admit that I must have been so dazzled by the sheer creativity that initially I did not notice that Tolkien was experimenting with form and style in *Gondolin* just as he had in the Earendel poem. Indeed, I imagined him in the dramatic Victorian setting of Harrogate Spa, propped up in bed in the Grand Hotel, which had been converted into Furness Auxiliary Hospital, while the welter of images, characters, and ideas leapt into his mind and onto the page—possibly assisted by the undulant fever caused by his *Bartonella quintana* infection.[32] Some bit of this may be the way things did happen: The obvious error is not in my imagination but in my assumption that because *Gondolin* seems so inspired, Tolkien must have been merely transcribing his muse's dictation. A closer look at *The Fall of Gondolin* shows very clearly that Tolkien, even as he developed his unique imaginative content, was trying out various elements of prose style that he drew from established and familiar literary sources.

The most visible and telling of these experiments, and thus the focus of this section of the argument, is Tolkien's use of what is called the *historical present tense* (discussed in detail later in this chapter). This experiment is visible because Tolkien does it inconsistently and also because the technique is utterly out of favor in contemporary prose and therefore stands out to a twenty-first-century reader. It is telling because it indicates unequivocally the influence of H. Rider Haggard's 1891 novel, *Eric Brighteyes*.[33]

H. Rider Haggard (1856–1925), wrote adventure novels, including the famous and best-selling *She*, *Ayesha*, and *King Solomon's Mines*. He is one of the few modern writers Tolkien explicitly acknowledged as an influence. After an 1888 visit to Iceland, Haggard wrote *Eric Brighteyes*, a mash-up of multiple Old Norse saga storylines, characters, and names, combined into a fast-moving and dramatic story of a great hero brought low by implacable enemies and a conniving witch-woman.[34] In his introduction, Haggard states that the book "is cast in the form of modern romance of our own day, archaisms being avoided as much as possible," and that is a fair description as far as it goes.[35] But in contrast to Haggard's novels with settings in Africa, which use a very familiar Victorian adventure-yarn style (which, to be fair, is familiar because Haggard's works were successful and thus imitated), *Eric Brighteyes* is written in a pastiche of nineteenth-century English translations of Old Norse sagas mixed up with a dramatic style that seems more operatic than Icelandic.[36]

When I introduce my students to the Icelandic sagas, they are often surprised at how "modern" they seem. The narrative voice is laconic, the characters' speech is often deadpan, and even the most violent actions are described in matter-of-fact terms. But unlike the narrators of novels since the late eighteenth century—who are granted access to the thoughts and feelings of the characters and often know more about motivations and internal struggles than the characters themselves—saga narrators never discuss their characters' thoughts: Readers must infer psychological states from the characters' words and actions in the same way we must infer inner states from outward indicators in our real life interactions.[37] Drama arises not from purple prose, emotionally laden description, or elaborate explanatory characterization, but from the intrinsic, structural conflicts of the situations depicted. For example, when Egil Skallagrímsson is shipwrecked and must walk into the court of King Eric Bloodaxe in York, the narrator does not bother to remind the reader that Egil must be nervous because in the past he had frequently humiliated Eric and insulted his wife in addition to killing one of his sons and many of his retainers. There is also no description of Egil's emotional state as he nears the court and talks with his friend Arinbjorn; the author assumes that readers are well aware of the background and that from this knowledge and from Egil's words and outward actions, they can infer what the character may be feeling as he approaches King Eric and Queen Gunnhild.[38]

Such reticence about internal and emotional matters, however, is not a characteristic of *Eric Brighteyes.* Although Haggard, like his source, does not use the narrative voice to describe the interiority of the characters, his audience need not make the slightest effort to infer their thoughts, emotions, and motives, as these (and more) are communicated in great detail through extensive dialogue. *Very* extensive dialogue: *far* more elaborate than anything in the sources. With their one-liners and laconic comments in dramatic moments, saga heroes often sound like early Arnold Schwarzenegger characters: "Did that hit you or not?" asks Kolskegg in *Njal's Saga* when he hacks off Kol's leg. "This is what I get," says Kol, "for not shielding myself." "You've done what needed doing—that arm brought wounds and death to many a man," says Hrapp after his arm has been severed.[39] In marked contrast, the characters in *Eric Brighteyes* never hesitate to provide rich and exceedingly detailed contexts for their one-liners through long mono- or dialogues that explain the social situations, historical backgrounds, and their own dramatic emotions. Despite the saga-age settings, *Eric Brighteyes* is a very Victorian novel.

In his introduction, Haggard states that the sagas themselves are "undoubtedly difficult reading" due to "the archaic nature of the work, even in translation; the multitude of its actors; the Norse sagaman's habit of interweaving endless side-plots, and the persistence with which he introduces the genealogy and adventures of the ancestors of even unimportant characters." *Eric Brighteyes*, therefore, "is clipped of these peculiarities," in order to make the book more "to the taste of the modern reader." But although he modernizes his sources in all these ways, Haggard does adopt one of the most striking stylistic features of the sagas: their inclusion of passages in which the historical present tense is used rather than the ordinary simple past tense that makes up the vast majority of the prose narrative. In the passage that follows, I have underlined past-tense verbs and bolded verbs in the present tense (verbs in dialogue have not been marked):

> Now Ospakar shook his sword, laughing. . . . and he hurled a spear at him with all his might.
>
> But Skallagrim **catches** the spear as it **flies** and **hurls** it back. It **strikes** right on the shield of Ospakar and **pierces** it, ay and the byrnie, and the shoulder that is beneath the byrnie, so that Blacktooth was made unmeet for fight, and howled with pain and rage.
>
> "Go, bid Thorunna draw that splinter forth," **says** Skallagrim, "and heal the hole with kisses."
>
> Now Ospakar, **writhing** with his hurt, **shouts** to his men to slay the two of them, and then the fight **begins**.

> One **rushes** at Eric and **smites** at him with an axe. The blow **falls** on his shield, and **shears** off the side of it, then **strikes** the byrnie beneath, but lightly. In answer Eric **sweeps** low at him with Whitefire, and **cuts** his leg from under him between knee and thigh, and he **falls** and **dies**.
>
> . . .
>
> Then the fit **leaves** Skallagrim and he **walks** back, and they **are** alone with the dead and dying.
>
> Eric leans on Whitefire and **speaks**:
>
> "Get thee gone, Skallagrim Lambstail!" he said; "get thee gone!"[40]

The *historical present tense* (*praesens historicum*) is the use of the present tense to narrate events in the past.[41] It is a regular grammatical feature of Old Norse (as well as Ancient Greek) and also occurs in Latin, Middle High German, Old Irish, and Old English texts.[42] Some scholars have found it to be particularly prevalent in oral tradition.[43] In contemporary Modern English, historical present is commonly used in casual conversation in the context of retelling another person's story ("We were talking yesterday, and I say . . . and then we both go . . . and then he forgot . . . but she tells him that . . . "). Historical present tense was very frequently employed in Latin histories and has, on occasion been used for entire twentieth-century novels, including Margaret Atwood's *The Handmaid's Tale* and John Updike's *Rabbit, Run*.[44] In Old Norse the use of the historical present is far less extensive than in those two examples, but it is employed far more frequently than historical present is in most Modern English texts. An Old Norse narrative in the past tense will, without warning, shift to the historical present, stay in that tense for anything from a sentence to multiple paragraphs, and then abruptly switch back to the ordinary past-tense narration. Why this tense-shifting occurs in Old Norse narratives is not well understood. The various scholarly explanations of the function of the historical present tense in the Icelandic sagas are "inconsistent, contrary, and very often mutually exclusive," indicating that the evidence is complex and conflicting, most likely because the historical present was not particularly marked or distinctive to native speakers of Old Norse.[45]

But shifts to historical present are *extremely* distinctive to speakers of Modern English who are translating Old Norse, in part because such readers have not yet fully mastered the Old Norse verb system. You are working through a passage and just barely noting the past-tense forms of the verbs—since these are all consistent, and once you recognize a first past-tense verb, you assume that the rest of the passage is the same—when suddenly present-tense forms start appearing. My students, once they got past the confusion and accepted that the verbs really were present tense, often read historical-present passages aloud with greater emphasis (louder or faster—or both), under the assumption that the switch in tense is meant to highlight some dramatic action because to a Modern English reader, such a tense shift works to mark the sentences as being distinct and thus more important.* The problem, we inevitably discover, is that this is not always the case. Although the historical present tense is regularly used in the "framing of chapters . . . the connection of different episodes," and "the visualization of particularly dramatic episodes," its function varies—even from manuscript to manuscript of the same narrative (the fourteen earliest examples of *Njal's Saga*).[46] It is therefore unclear if shifting to the historical present was a widely shared discourse convention with a conventional meaning or just the individual practice of particular scribes (quite possibly because they were taking dictation). We therefore cannot conclude that using the historical present was definitely a stylistic technique for emphasizing dramatic action in the sagas—even though for Modern English readers translating the sagas, it certainly feels that way.

Shifts to historical present apparently made much the same impression on Haggard as they did on my students and me because he employs historical present tense only in dramatic contexts, scenes either of violent action or intense emotion:

> "Listen, Gudruda," Eric said at last. "Death draws near to us, and before it comes I would speak to thee, if speak I may."
>
> "Speak on," she **whispers** from his breast.

* I hope that the tense shifts in this paragraph show how the historical present can be used in a nonobtrusive manner. Reader, did you even notice?

> "This I would say, then: that I love thee, and that I ask no better fate than to die in thy arms."
>
> "First shalt thou see me die in thine, Eric."
>
> . . .
>
> And now Gudruda **sobs** and the tears **fall** fast from her dark eyes.
>
> "Nay, weep not. Dost thou, then, love me?"
>
> . . .
>
> And so these two kissed, for the first time, out in the snow on Coldback, and that first kiss was long and sweet.[47]

That Tolkien knew and liked *Eric Brighteyes* is well documented.[48] That his use of the historical present tense in *The Fall of Gondolin* is almost certainly derived from Haggard's novel has not, to my knowledge, been previously noted. Christina Scull and Wayne Hammond have determined that Tolkien read *Eric Brighteyes* around 1913,[49] thus before the composition of the Earendel poem or *The Story of Kullervo*, so the possibility of direct influence on the 1916–1917 *Fall of Gondolin* is not inconsistent with the chronology. Perhaps more significant is that Tolkien uses the historical present tense in much the same way Haggard does—to emphasize dramatic action—rather than in the inconsistent manner of the Icelandic sagas, which he read in the original Old Norse.*

The historical present tense appears a total of fifteen times in *The Fall of Gondolin*, usually for only a fraction of a given paragraph, though occasionally for longer passages.[50] The most common location of historical present is in the initial one or two sentences of a paragraph; only once is it employed in the terminal sentence without being used for the entire paragraph. The sprinkling of historical-present material does seem to be focused on moments of drama, particularly of surprise. For instance, the first use of historical present is the moment when, guided

* If the direct inspiration for Tolkien's use of historical present were the sagas, we might expect him to use the tense-shift in the same way those texts do rather than in the more restricted contexts in which Haggard employs it.

by the elf Voronwë, Tuor, the hero of the story, reaches the gates of the hidden city of Gondolin:

> Even so they came to the gates, Tuor in wonder and Voronwë in great joy that daring much he had both brought Tuor hither in the will of Ulmo and had himself thrown off the yoke of Melko for ever . . .
>
> Now there **is** a sally from the gates of Gondolin and a throng **comes** about these twain in wonder, **rejoicing** that yet another of the Noldoli had fled hither from Melko, and **marvelling** at the stature and the great limbs of Tuor, his heavy spear barbed with fish bone and his great harp.* Rugged was his aspect, and his locks were unkempt, and he was clad in the skins of bears . . . [51]

Historical present is not restricted to scenes of surprise, although a somewhat higher proportion of examples are moments of dramatic action (unexpected or not). The following passage, describing the battle between the forces of Morgoth and the people of Gondolin, is representative:

> Now it **is** that Tuor and the men of the Wing **fare** into the fight and **range** themselves beside Ecthelion and those of the Fountain, and the twain **strike** mighty blows and **ward** each many a thrust from the other, and **harry** the Orcs so that they **win** back almost to the gate. But **behold** a quaking and a trampling, for the dragons **labour** mightily at **beating** a path up Amon Gwareth and at **casting** down the walls of the city . . .
>
> Now the Orcs again **take** heart at the coming of the drakes, and they **mingle** with the Balrogs that **pour** about the breach, and they **assail** the Gondothlim grievously. There Tuor slew

---

* Here the pluperfect "had fled" is not a return to the narrative past tense but merely the use of a past tense within the historical present: They are rejoicing (present tense), about something that happened previously, which is therefore in the past tense. If the passage were recast in the narrative past, "had fled" would remain the same: "they rejoiced that yet another of the Noldoli had fled."

> Othrod a lord of the Orcs, cleaving his helm, and Balcmeg he hewed asunder, and Lug he smote with his axe . . . [52]

Note the switch from historical present to past tense *within* the paragraph. Tolkien uses historical present for one sentence on the following page and in several sections of paragraphs in the next four pages, but after that point the historical present becomes infrequent, and the tense is abandoned entirely after the city falls and the refugees reach the pass of Cristhorn: Even though this section of the story includes a battle between Glorfindel and a balrog, Tolkien employs only the ordinary past tense, and he continues to do so for the rest of *The Fall of Gondolin*.

It is tempting to conclude that, even before he reached a stopping point in *The Fall of Gondolin* (the tale is unfinished), Tolkien decided that the historical present tense failed to produce the effects he wanted and therefore he abandoned his experiment in imitating this aspect of Haggard's style, but we cannot be entirely certain. In all his many years of effort on the Silmarillion material, Tolkien never revised the majority of *The Fall of Gondolin*, so we have no way of knowing if Tolkien would have eliminated the historical present for the battle scenes if he had further developed the narrative.*

In the one section of the much later "Of Tuor and His Coming to Gondolin" that overlaps with one of the historical-present passages—when the elves of Gondolin challenge Tuor and Voronwë (quoted previously)—the later text uses only standard narrative past tense. However, because the scene is completely rewritten rather than just revised, the change from historical present to past tense is not as definitive a piece of evidence as we might desire. Still, that Tolkien never again employed the historical present tense in the subsequent decades of fiction writing at least strongly implies that such tense shifts did not produce the aesthetic effects he was seeking, and that the historical present tense in *The Fall of Gondolin* is a relic of an abandoned experiment.

Haggard's greatest effect on the style of Tolkien's works may best be

* To Christopher Tolkien's lasting dismay: "my father's profoundly saddening abandonment of the last version of the Tale at the moment when Tuor passed through the Last Gate of Gondolin," *Gondolin*, 17.

interpreted as a negative example than a direct influence. Tolkien not only abandoned the imitative technique of tense shifting for dramatic effect, but from the beginning he rejected Haggard's pastiche of the Old Norse sagas, instead telling his stories in his own evolving style and avoiding imitations of the grammar and—for the most part—the vocabulary of his medieval sources (though there are exceptions, particularly in the dialogue of aristocratic figures).

But although he did not adopt Haggard's stylistic techniques, Tolkien does seem to have followed the Victorian writer in his adoption of sophisticated, post-medieval narrative conventions such as interlaced subplots, consistent but shifting points of view, and the occasional use of an omniscient narrator rather than relying solely—as the sagas do—on exterior actions and speech to imply thoughts and emotions. However, it is difficult to point to Haggard's use of any of these techniques and be certain that Tolkien learned it from *Eric Brighteyes*. Haggard's influence is of a more general sort, in that he—like Walter Scott before him—showed that a medieval story could be told well using narrative techniques that had only evolved after the development of the novel.* Furthermore, because what works best in *Eric Brighteyes* is the plot—which is what Tolkien praised about the book—it seems likely that it was from Haggard that Tolkien learned ways of producing a story better than the medieval original by adapting, combining, augmenting, or manipulating the sources rather than trying to imitate their stylistic qualities.

The Earendel poem uses the form of Shelley's "Arethusa," which does not mark Tolkien's work as being fundamentally different than any other original composition by a twentieth-century poet. *The Fall of Gondolin*, although perhaps somewhat archaic in its prose style, is—with the exception of the small fraction of sentences in the historical

---

* I do not think we can attribute Tolkien's use of verse to Haggard, if only because verses are so much more prominent in Morris's and Haggard's sources in Old Norse sagas, which Tolkien knew firsthand. More likely candidates for being directly inspired by Haggard are the few explanatory footnotes that Tolkien sprinkles through *The Lord of the Rings*, such as "Elves (and Hobbits) always refer to the sun as she" (*FR*, I, ix, 172), which impart small tidbits of cultural knowledge. Compare Haggard's footnote explaining that "holm-gang" is fighting a duel "on an island—'holm'—within a circle of hazel-twigs" (41).

present tense—a straightforward prose narrative.* *The Story of Kullervo* is the only one of Tolkien's earliest works in which he experiments with a structure that marks the text as being in some way different from other contemporary works. And although this form, *prosimetrum*, is ultimately derived from medieval literature, Tolkien in fact adopted it from a nineteenth-century intermediary rather than directly from medieval works.

As noted previously, Tolkien credited his first encounter with the Finnish language with setting "the rocket off in story."[53] Finnish "quite intoxicated me," he wrote, and the experience of reading a Finnish grammar was "like discovering a complete wine-cellar filled with bottles of an amazing wine of a kind and flavour never tasted before."[54] The influence of Finnish was strongest on Tolkien's invented languages, but he was interested enough in some of the content of the *Kalevala* to attempt to transmute it into a work in Modern English.[55] In a 1914 letter to his fiancée Edith Bratt, Tolkien wrote that he was trying to turn one of the sections of the *Kalevala* into "a short story somewhat on the lines of Morris' romances with chunks of poetry in between"[56] *The Story of Kullervo*, along with two versions of an essay about the *Kalevala*, one delivered at Corpus Christi College, Oxford, in November 1914, the other at the Exeter College Essay Club in February 1915, were edited by Verlyn Flieger and published in *Tolkien Studies* in 2010 and as a stand-alone volume in 2015.[57]

Created in the early nineteenth century by the physician Elias Lönnrot out of his massive collection of traditional songs and oral tales from Karelia, the *Kalevala* is a large and somewhat loosely organized set of stories, all in trochaic tetrameter (hence octosyllabic) alliterative verse ("Kalevala meter").[58] The story of Kullervo is one of the major subcycles in the *Kalevala*, appearing in *runos* 31–36 (out of 50).[59] The

* Hindsight from after the subsequent rise and apotheosis of modernism makes Tolkien's vocabulary and prose style in *Gondolin* seem much more archaic than it actually was in the context of 1916–1917 popular writing. I cannot find much in the story that is substantially more archaic than the vocabulary and syntax of John McCrae's "In Flanders Fields," which was published in the very mainstream *Punch*, and there is no evidence that this poem was considered particularly old-fashioned; it only appears so after the overwhelming changes in style in English literature brought about by Woolf, Stein, Pound, Hemingway, Fitzgerald, Joyce, and the other Modernists, their imitators, and their successors.

supernatural strength, fierce temper, and less-than-dispassionate judgment of the eponymous protagonist interacts with the mendacity of an evil uncle (who had killed the father of the young man and raised him and his sister as serfs), and a remarkable run of misfortunes, to produce a terrible tragedy: rape, incest, and suicide.

The story of Kullervo was the original inspiration for what would eventually become Tolkien's multiple tales and poems about the hero Túrin in the Silmarillion. But in 1914, his reaction to this material was not to try to create a new story with a character similar to Kullervo, but instead to try to adapt the *Kalevala* material into a Modern English prose narrative with multiple passages of poetry interspersed—although this mixed form is not the same as the entirely poetic Finnish original. Just as Henry Wadsworth Longfellow did in his *Kalevala*-inspired "Song of Hiawatha" (1855), Tolkien adapted "Kalevala-meter" to English. Each octosyllabic line is made up of four trochees—a stressed syllable followed by an unstressed syllable*—but Longfellow's and Tolkien's poems lack the alliteration that characterizes the Finnish original, probably because it is extremely difficult to write alliterating trochaic tetrameter poetry in English.[60]

The distinctive, driving rhythm of the Finnish original is retained in the derived works, but unlike Longfellow, who structured his poem with end-rhyme, Tolkien limited himself to reproducing only the meter, adding no additional formal features to the verse. He follows W. F. Kirby not only in using *Kalevala* meter without alliteration or rhyme, but in his translations of individual lines. Indeed, many of the lines of verse in the published *Story of Kullervo* are nearly word-for-word matches with lines in Kirby, and the exact correspondences increase in frequency toward the end of the text.[61] We can therefore conclude that Tolkien's process of composition was to start with a passage from Kirby—perhaps even one copied verbatim—and, working

* An easy mnemonic is to note that "**T**EEN-aged MU-tant NIN-ja **T**UR-tles" is in **tro**chaic **t**etrameter, as each word follows the pattern of a stressed syllable followed by an unstressed syllable (trochee), and there are four words (tetra). Another potentially useful mnemonic (at least for readers of a certain age) is this rhyming couplet consisting of two lines of trochaic tetrameter: "HOLD the / PICK-le / HOLD the / LET-tuce | SPE-cial / OR-ders / DON'T up-/SET us."

line by line, progressively modify it until the translation became his own. There is no evidence that Tolkien's modifications were motivated by anything in the Finnish text. Indeed, when we compare the original *Kalevala* in Finnish with Keith Bosley's literal translation along with both the Kirby and Tolkien translations, we see that the latter two leave out a substantial fraction of the lines in any given section of the poem by compressing or deleting all the repetitive lines, so characteristic of oral-traditional materials, in the original. It seems likely that Tolkien was not able to read the original to any substantial degree and was therefore entirely dependent upon Kirby, whose verses he reorganized so that the content is presented in a more compressed form and logical order for contemporary readers. That this reorganization makes the translation less rather than more like the original is sufficient evidence that Tolkien's goal was not to imitate the *Kalevala* itself, but rather to develop the ineffable something he found (albeit imperfectly realized) in the Kirby translation.

Tolkien's decision to use the metrical form of *Kalevala* meter for his poetic passages implies that he wanted his composition to possess some qualities of the *Kalevala* beyond the plot. But while the simplest and most obvious approach to conveying various qualities of the original would have been for Tolkien simply to translate Lönnrot's long poem with a long poem of his own, he instead chose to structure his narrative as primarily prose with poetic passages mixed in. This decision strongly suggests that even at this early stage in his evolution as a writer he had concluded that exact replication of form was not the best way to convey to contemporary readers those qualities of the source material that were most important to him.[62] From this we can infer that the fully poetic nature of the text was not among the characteristics that produced the "something in the air" that Tolkien so valued and wanted to reproduce. Tolkien's verses are certainly very closely connected to the Kirby translation of the *Kalevala*, but the overall structure of *The Story of Kullervo* has nothing to do with the Finnish original because Tolkien adopted it from the prosimetrical romances of the nineteenth-century polymath William Morris.

Known as much for his art, textile design, and political activism as for his writing, Morris wrote epic poems, translated Icelandic sagas, and authored several romances in mixed prose and poetry inspired by medieval sources and containing many elements of what we now see as fantasy literature. Tolkien had used some of the money from his 1914 Skeat Prize to purchase *The Life and Death of Jason*, *The House of the Wolfings*, and Morris's translation of *Völsunga Saga*. In yet another apparent infinite regress of origins, we must note that Morris got the general idea of not just retelling the medieval stories he loved, but trying to convey some of their nonnarrative qualities, from *his* great inspiration, Walter Scott, who—after beginning his career as a writer of long narrative poems—had, in his historical novels, developed the technique of relying on prose style, particularly with regard to historical speech, to transmit some of the qualities of his early sources without including significant quantities of poetry in the text.

That Tolkien chose to use a mixture of poetry and prose in his Kullervo adaptation shows that he had come to the conclusion, as Morris had in the 1870s, that retaining the exact form of a medieval text in a translation or adaptation was not the best way to enable contemporary readers to experience the most important effects of the text in the original language. However, because they included such a substantial quantity of verse in their hybrid works, both authors also seem to have rejected the possibility of ignoring the poetry altogether and producing a pure prose narrative like Tolkien's *The Fall of Gondolin*.

Although based in part on Old Norse poems from the Elder Edda, *Völsunga Saga* is a prose epic, but Morris's Modern English adaptation, *Sigurd the Volsung*, is written in anapestic hexameters arranged as rhyming couplets.[63] It appears that Morris thought that some key qualities of the Old Norse source could only be transmitted to nineteenth-century readers in the form of verse.[64] Similarly, his prosimetrical romances do not imitate actual medieval prosimetra, which usually use prose merely to string together long passages of poetry, the inverse of Morris's practice. Additionally, Morris's specific sources and inspirations for the prosimetrical romances were not themselves prosimetra, implying that Morris chose the form not for directly imitative purposes, but because in his nineteenth-century context, prose did not communicate the sense of the ornamentation, interlacement (of a kind that we would now probably identify as fractal), and beauty that he found in medieval literature and art. Morris thought that medieval texts were ornamented, so he used what Victorian readers would recognize as ornamentation for his faux-medieval works. Whether he was successful in this specific effort is not easy to determine, but the effect of his mixing poetry and prose produced texts that, at the very least, look and feel very different from other nineteenth-century works of literary art, and it is quite possible that this indication of difference was sufficient to accomplish his aesthetic purposes—certainly his prosimetrical romances were commercially successful and still popular when Tolkien read them in the early twentieth century.[65]

Both Tolkien and Morris concluded that the combination of poetry and prose was important to the aesthetics of their literary creations; Scott and Haggard, who shared with Tolkien and Morris the goal of reinventing medieval literature for their contemporary audiences, did not, and from this we can conclude that adapting a poetic source with a prosimetrum was not a forced move, though in Tolkien's case it seems to have been a good one. He incorporated poetry into *The Hobbit*, *The Lord of the Rings*, and (although to a much lesser extent) in the published *Silmarillion*. And while Morris's use of prosimetrum did not carry over to Haggard, Tolkien's became, for several decades, one of the fundamental formal characteristics of fantasy literature: Many of Tolkien's early imitators seem to have also felt the need to include poems—even terrible free-verse poems—in their works.*

Morris was a reasonably effective poet, and some of Tolkien's poems are very good indeed, but we cannot attribute the success and subsequent influence of Tolkien's blend of poetry and prose merely to superior poetic ability. It is not the poems themselves, but their interaction with the prose narrative that creates a substantial qualitative difference between Morris's and Tolkien's prosimetra. In Morris's romance, the shift to verse does not change very much about the narrative, which continues to advance at a consistent pace, and the verses themselves do not give the impression of being substantially different from the sur-

* It is difficult to imagine any literary form less medieval, epic, or fantasy-consistent (or readable) than the egregiously awful free-verse poems in Stephen R. Donaldson's *The Chronicles of Thomas Covenant* series, and Donaldson's works are hardly the only mass-market derivative fantasy to include bad poems.

rounding prose. For the most part, the same is true of Tolkien's verses in *The Story of Kullervo.*

The poems in *The Hobbit* and *The Lord of the Rings* work very differently. Tolkien's verses, and those in the Icelandic prose sagas, do much more than simply represent the characters' singing or reciting.[66] Some verses are used to authenticate information by indicating that it in some way precedes the prose narrative in which it is embedded, thus making the story more authoritative.* Other verses emphasize particularly important action by slowing the pace of the narrative or repeating descriptions of events in poetic form. Like the anonymous composers of the sagas, Tolkien used verse as a tool of narrative development and pacing more effectively than did Morris.

Additionally, and perhaps most importantly, Tolkien's poems—unlike Morris's, but like the saga verses—create the distinct impression that they are not all by the same author. The dwarves' "Far over the Misty Mountains" song is meant to be composed by them and thus communicate specific characteristics of their inner selves, the "desire of the hearts of dwarves" as the narrator summarizes.[67] Similarly, the harsh goblin songs both in the tunnels ("Swish! Smack!") and in the woods ("Fifteen Birds in Five Fir Trees") are intended be taken as expressions of the fundamental character of those creatures.[68] Indeed, it does not seem that any of the poems in *The Hobbit* are supposed to be interpreted as coming from the narrator, and only three—Bilbo's two sets of verses taunting the spiders, and "Roads Go Ever On,"—are said to be compositions of the protagonist.[69]

This heterogeneity of authorship is further developed in *The Lord of the Rings.* From the very first page of the text, with the Ring-verse that begins "Three rings for the Elven-kings . . . ," we see indications of composite authorship, although it is not until later in the story that we learn that the frontispiece poem was composed by the Dark Lord

* We therefore can infer that participants in or immediate inheritors of the oral tradition recognized that material in poetic form was more likely to preserve genuine old information than similar content in a prose narrative; see Gísli Sigurðsson, *The Medieval Icelandic Saga and Oral Tradition: A Discourse on Method* (Cambridge: Harvard University Press, 2004), and Michael D.C. Drout, *Tradition and Influence in Anglo-Saxon Literature: An Evolutionary, Cognitivist Approach* (New York: Palgrave MacMillan, 2013).

Sauron and has been translated out of the Black Speech of Mordor. As the narrative continues, we encounter not only verses that are said to be composed by various characters, but poems that are to be attributed to the folk-customs (hobbit walking, drinking, and bath songs), histories, and traditions of various peoples (elves, dwarves, Ents, several distinct nations of men); rhymes of lore or wisdom poems; incantations; prophetic verses, both ancient and recent; elegies; an epitaph; riddles, funeral laments; battle poetry, both inspirational and memorial; and panegyric and Psalm-like praise poetry.

Tolkien's use of prosimetrum thus creates a very strong impression that the verses in *The Hobbit* and *The Lord of the Rings* were not all composed by a single author but were collected from many different eras and writers—even though in point of fact they were all written by Professor Tolkien (and indeed, the verses in *The Hobbit* were "written in sequence with the manuscript of the book").[70] The poems' heterogeneity and their various in-text attributions—and lack of attributions—create the impression that Tolkien was a compiler of diverse materials that were not composed by him.* *The Hobbit* and *The Lord of the Rings* thus produce the impression of *textuality*, of having been created from a multitude of preexisting texts, which, readers are to infer, had different authors, purposes, biases, cultural matrices, and transmission histories.[71] Such a large variety of texts implies the existence of a world with a complex culture and a lengthy history.

For centuries now, texts have been produced as accurate mechanical copies of an original, which comes—perhaps with some mediation of editor and publisher—from an author. We assume, rightly, that one copy of *Portrait of the Artist as a Young Man* is fundamentally the same as every other copy of *Portrait of the Artist as a Young Man*, and that it represents what James Joyce, and James Joyce alone, wanted to

* The runes on *The Hobbit* dust jacket state that the book was "Compiled from his [Bilbo's] Memoirs by J.R.R. Tolkien." See Anderson, *Annotated Hobbit*, 378.

appear in the text.* This is not the case for manuscripts, whose production method—copying by hand—assures that no two will be precisely identical, even when scribes attempted to match the handwriting of their exemplars and produce absolutely accurate copies (and that sort of accuracy was only one of the goals of a medieval scribe). Information was lost, augmented, and modified. Materials from outside the main text were at times incorporated without comment. A text might be damaged and then recopied, the scribe guessing at what the original had been before the damage.

The unique nature of every manuscript, the distance in time between us and even the latest copies, and the complex histories of each text (often obscured by later copying) are mostly unfamiliar to readers of modern, mass-produced books. Even students who are studying medieval texts in published editions see a complete and finished product that has been created out of the mess of half-understood, miscopied, and deliberately changed texts from which we get most of the medieval literature that remains to us. Translators give to students and interested readers an authoritative edition, a single version with none of the chaos of the manuscripts. Students can pick up a copy of *Sir Gawain and the Green Knight* or *Beowulf* and simply read the book in front of them.

But this is very often not the experience of the scholar of medieval literature, who works within the confusion, damage, misreading, and obscure detail that makes up the medieval manuscript. Sometimes the confusion is immensely frustrating, when we know approximately what a text means but a specific word is impossible to make out. I had this problem deciphering some of Tolkien's handwriting, where I knew that what I had transcribed seemed wrong but could not come up with anything better that might fit the scribbles on the page.[72] But sometimes—and the frequency of these occurrences in part determines whether one becomes addicted to medieval studies or walks away without looking back after the first experience—the hidden logic of the page takes over,

* All of these assumptions are questionable, but to only a minor degree: There are variations in physical appearance between different printings, and there was likely some interaction between Joyce and his editors that influenced the text to some degree, but these are quibbles, and we can be reasonably confident that various copies of printed texts are for the most part the same and are attributable to the texts' authors.

and after a long stretch of wandering in a maze of detail and confusion, arguing about individual words, even individual letters, trying to bring order to parts of the text while at the same time becoming less sure what exactly the poet was saying, something clicks, and you solve the little problem in front of you—is that blob *nn* or *mi*?—and simultaneously get a glimpse of the big picture, of what the poet might have meant and how this fits into the web of other texts and ideas from the period.

The particular kind of textuality that Tolkien's mature works produce is extremely similar to the effects of medieval works of literature on modern and contemporary readers who, like Tolkien, other medievalists, and me, have struggled through the process of learning to read them in their original languages. Although some of these works—*Beowulf*, *The Canterbury Tales*, *Sir Gawain and the Green Knight*—are still part of the literary canon (in whatever form this still clings to life in 2025), most readers only engage with them in Modern English translation, usually in the form of inexpensive paperback editions or as sections of the *Norton Anthology of English Literature*. In these contexts, they appear pretty much like any other literary texts—not distinctively different from the works of Shakespeare, Milton, Pope, Wordsworth, Coleridge, and other long-established literary icons.

To students learning Old English, however, *Beowulf* presents a very different face than what appears in a contemporary translation. A page of the text looks fundamentally different than a page of any novel or long poem in Modern English. The center of each leaf is filled by a surprisingly small group of lines, numbered somewhat obtrusively. Below these sits a dense block of tiny agate type without paragraph breaks and thick with opaque abbreviations and unfamiliar names. Not only is the language of the poem unfamiliar, but several strange letters (*þ*, *ð*, *æ*) are used, as well as various obscure typographical conventions: seemingly random italics and square brackets, dots above letters and lines of dots below words, the occasional obelus. The edition itself is massively larger than just the main text, with pages and pages of explanatory material, line-by-line commentaries, glossaries, and sometimes more than one index.

The combination of these features gives a reader a very strong impression that the work being studied has a complex authorial, compositional, and transmission history. Quite obviously a *lot* of people were involved in the creating the text, thus completely dispelling a fundamental and nearly universal illusion about the modern novel: that it comes from the author to the reader without any substantial intermediation. To a student trying to work through one of these poems in the original language, it soon becomes evident that *Beowulf*, *Sir Gawain and the Green Knight*, *The Canterbury Tales*, *Piers Plowman*, the shorter Old English poems, and all the other monuments of medieval literature simply cannot be read without all the material that fills up the pages of the standard editions. Even if a manuscript somehow perfectly preserved the author's original creation, various features of the text no longer function as they used to: We do not know the meanings of certain words or allusions or references; we have trouble distinguishing hyperbole, litotes, and satire from straightforward narration; jokes go over our heads. The reader is therefore constantly engaging with the fundamental quality that all these works share among themselves: They are broken. We have not *Beowulf* itself, but the ruin of *Beowulf*.

A physical ruin often includes both fragments whose original purpose we cannot determine and features that are damaged but partially recognizable. There are tumbled blocks of stone, half-buried piles of rubble, ditches and mounds whose purpose can only be guessed. But then we recognize the right half of an arch, the foot of a broken column, a few steps leading to a gallery that was destroyed half a millennium ago. A textual ruin is likewise a mixture of the completely obscure and the partially understandable. There are lines in *Beowulf* that have been lost to fire damage, or blurred to illegibility by water, or that are missing entirely—we infer—because the scribe's eye skipped a line in the exemplar he was copying. And there are places in the poem where we recognize a word as a name but know nothing about its significance: Who was Yrmenlaf (besides being Æschere's younger brother)? What is the significance of gold being described as *icge*? What does the poet mean when he says that Grendel could not approach the gift seat—was the monster just particularly afraid of furniture? What was the name of King Hrothgar's sister who was married to Onela the Swede, and why did the scribe fail to copy it? These broken pieces are equivalent to the stairs going nowhere or the broken arches we see in physical ruins: We have a general idea of their purpose, but we must use our imaginations to integrate them into the whole, to rebuild in our minds that tower the ruin once was.

Before it became a ruin, there was a complete building in which each block of stone served a purpose: The archways opened into rooms, the stairways led to halls and balconies. Likewise there was once a culture in which people knew the names of Hrothgar's sister and Beowulf's mother, and some story about Yrmenlaf, and why Grendel could not approach Hrothgar's throne as each night he roamed the hall of Heorot. That culture was, of necessity, different from ours—or we would understand what is now obscure—and it was also extensive and sophisticated.

I have analyzed Tolkien's three early creations in such detail in order to support my contention that the textually ruined state of medieval works is the ineffable "something in the air" that attracted Tolkien to the *Kalevala*, the lost English Earendel story implied by the passage in *Christ I*, and *Beowulf*, and which, in turn, he ended up producing in his mature works.[73] The purpose of these analyses was not to trace the origin of every feature of Tolkien's mature work back to the most likely proximate source, but to identify in the first substantial examples of his creative work those qualities of the sources that became parts of the Tolkienian style in *The Hobbit* and *The Lord of the Rings*, and those, such as Haggard's use of the historical present tense, that did not.[74] The investigation certainly could be expanded further, but I hope that the point is made that out of Tolkien's various experiments in employing the techniques of nineteenth-century authors who also had tried to capture some of the ineffable qualities of medieval texts, the approaches he retained into his mature works are those qualities that are characteristic of a textual ruin.

Tolkien's Earendel poem displays an effort to invent a cultural context in which interpreting the ocean as a cup with the horizon as its rim and the Morning Star as the glowing emanations of a supernatural figure would be (1) reasonable in its own terms; (2) consistent with surviving evidence or known facts; and (3) beautiful.* The first two

* Or, if pedantry is desired: consistent with Tolkien's personal aesthetic preferences.

characteristics help produce the impression that the material is representative of a culture distinct and coherent but fundamentally different from the culture of the text's actual readers.* Although the supernatural actions the poem describes are not possible in the audience's world, we nevertheless can understand the inherent logic in them—Earendel is an agent performing actions that produce effects—basic intuitively understood principles of causation are not violated, and motivations can be inferred. That the invented material does not contradict and indeed may provide some kind of explanation for the surviving evidence connects the invented culture to our own world. Tolkien said that Middle-earth is not another planet or universe, but "the North-West of the Old World, east of the Sea," and this connection is emphasized by the integration of real-world material; even when most readers find the real-world words obscure, they still forge links to the imagined world by their consistency with other words and additional aspects of our culture and history.[75] The third quality, that the resulting story be beautiful, is an inference from Tolkien's rejection of the story of Aurvandill's frostbitten toe and his linking the appealing "ocean's cup" metaphor with the similarly appealing luminous-being idea in the Earendel poem.

After *The Fall of Gondolin*, Tolkien never again used Haggard's technique of abrupt shifts to and from the historical present tense.† This avoidance probably indicates that the aesthetic effects the tense shift produced were not those Tolkien particularly valued. Many other features of *Gondolin*—names, images, characters, plots, themes—evolved into the enormous Silmarillion mythology, but this very early piece is the last in which Tolkien adopted a prose style that was most definitely not found in Modern English.

Tolkien's original impulse for mixing verse and prose was to imitate

---

* Throughout I use *impression* rather than *illusion* to avoid the potential pejorative connotations of the latter.

† There is a least one possible minor exception in *The Hobbit*, when Smaug realizes that the cup is missing from his hoard, Tolkien writes, "His rage *passes* description—" (*H*, XII, 229; my emphasis), but the rest of the verbs in the paragraph are in the past tense. This does not appear to be a printer's error, as *passes* is the form in the draft version edited by John Rateliff, *The History of The Hobbit, Part Two: Return to Bag End*, 2 vols. (Boston: Houghton Mifflin, 2007), 507.

Morris's medieval romances. He was certainly not at this stage trying to reproduce any aspect or effect of a scholarly edition of a medieval text, and *The Story of Kullervo* is not in structure at all like the Finnish original or Kirby's translation of the *Kalevala*. However, *Kullervo* was Tolkien's first use of the prosimetrum form, which eventually—after he had extensively refined it—evolved into one of the most important characteristics of his literary works. *The Story of Kullervo* not only switches from prose to verse for songs by characters, but it also includes what appears to be a distinct charm for protecting cattle. This inclusion of traditional material, the origin of which is in nonnarrative discourse, foreshadows the ways that Tolkien used verses in *The Hobbit* and *The Lord of the Rings*. In *Kullervo* Tolkien had not yet thought to replicate the aesthetic effects of the damaged, reconstructed, and editorially conflicting incarnations of medieval works, but he had made the first big step of including verses not attributed to a character's singing or recitation.

Walter Scott, William Morris, and H. Rider Haggard had all tried to convey something of the *feel* of the medieval texts that had inspired them. In this effort they reproduced the elevated rhetoric, the poetry, the grammar, and the dialogue of their sources and inspirations, but they never thought to reproduce the gaps, contradictions, unknowns, and obscure references—most likely because they were unaware of them (only Morris made an effort to learn a medieval language). But even if they had known of the ways in which medieval works are ruined, it seems likely, perhaps even certain that, Victorians as they were, they would have rebuilt the ruin by filling in the gaps, eliminating the contradictions, smoothing the awkwardly abrupt transitions, and explaining away or deleting the obscurities.* The result might be aesthetically accomplished—certainly Morris's readers up to and including Tolkien had found his works based on or inspired by medieval sources to be beautiful—but it was so in a Victorian way. In rebuilding, they erased features of the sources that helped produce the ineffable qualities

* When I lead tours of Anglo-Saxon sites in England, I tell my groups "Victorian fake-medieval is the best fake-medieval": Buildings reconstructed in the nineteenth century look far more like our mental prototypes of medieval castles than the ruins that have not been "improved" in this way, and their roofs don't leak as much.

that they and Tolkien so valued, those which he, not they, succeeded in reproducing.

None of this is to say that by the time he stopped writing *The Fall of Gondolin*, Tolkien had developed his mature style. The next two decades would see his experimentation with long narrative poems in various forms, further development and massive expansion of his invented languages, elaboration of the imagined world of Middle-earth and its history, and the construction and abandonment of multiple frame narratives within which to present the growing Silmarillion legendarium. When the time came for Tolkien to compose *The Hobbit*, he had produced a massive textual archive of dizzying complexity, materials from which found their way into the narrative of the children's book he was trying to write.

It was in *The Hobbit* that Tolkien brought together the separate strands of experimentation from his three earliest works. It is probably not a coincidence that it was the incorporation of medieval-inspired material that got Tolkien writing again after he had become "stuck."[76] Beorn (from Old Norse *berserk* and medieval bear-lore), the Arkenstone (from *Beowulf* 1218, the same line as the "cup of the waves"), Smaug's name (from the Old English verb *smugan*), and the scene in which the theft of a cup infuriates a dragon (from *Beowulf*) are all examples of Tolkien doing what he did in the Earendel poem: solving cruces or clearing up obscure parts of medieval texts by inventing a story in which they made sense.

As he had done in *The Fall of Gondolin*, Tolkien invented for *The Hobbit* not only names, characters, and locations, but also their deep histories and legendary pasts. Bringing the pure invention of *Gondolin* into contact with the creative solutions to interpretive problems in medieval texts that he had first tried in the Earendel poem gave Tolkien sufficient freedom to invent his own geographies and cultures while simultaneously tying these creations to the real but partially lost cultures of our own world. Finally, incorporating poems into the narrative (as he had done in *Kullervo*) helped to produce the impression that even *The Hobbit* was to some degree a textual ruin, compiled and edited by Professor Tolkien, an impression only strengthened by the narrator telling readers that there were multiple and conflicting opinions about certain aspects of the story: Rumors of Bilbo's mother's ancestor's taking of a fairy wife existed, though they were "absurd"; no one knows where Gollum came from; the narrator knows Beorn has a backstory but not what it is. However, in *The Hobbit*, most of the gaps are filled and the rough patches smoothed away. If *Beowulf* is Whitby Abbey, then *The Hobbit* is Warwick Castle, fully reconstructed with tapestries on the walls, furniture in the rooms, and bright flags flying from the battlements—a place many children might find more appealing than bare stone ruins, no matter how beautiful. The impression of a textual ruin is more prevalent in *The Lord of the Rings*, and much stronger still in *The Silmarillion*, although, as we will discuss later, for different reasons.

If we did not have Tolkien's mature works, we would never notice the ways the three early compositions discussed in this chapter begin to create the impression of textual ruins, and so this effort is a kind of retrojection—projecting backward onto an antecedent qualities of the later work—an action that runs a very real risk of constructing a false literary history. I want to reiterate that I do not think that Tolkien in 1913–1917 was trying to create textual ruins. Indeed, I am not sure Tolkien *ever* consciously recognized that he was creating textual ruins.* What I am certain he consciously thought (because he said he did) is that he sensed some ineffable qualities, "something in the air," in medieval literary works—the Earendel passage in *Christ I*, *Beowulf*, the *Kalevala,* and others—and that (this next is a bit more of a strongly supported inference than a documented statement) he sought to write works of his own that would produce the same ineffable effects in the minds of those who read them. But because ineffable qualities are nearly as difficult to reproduce as they are to describe, he tried imitating various characteristics of the medieval works themselves and of the adaptations or reinventions of them by more recent writers.

Only a few of the characteristics of Tolkien's earliest writings are retained in his later work—the qualities of what I have been calling textual ruins, the very works that Tolkien spent his professional career studying. Note that when I claim that Tolkien ended up producing his

* Except, perhaps, when he was creating the "facsimile" pages of the damaged Book of Mazarbul for *The Fellowship of the Ring.*

own textual ruins, I am not asserting that *The Hobbit* or *The Lord of the Rings* is the equivalent of Friedrich Klaeber's *Beowulf and the Fight at Finnsburg*, or R. W. Chambers's *Widsith: A Study in Old English Heroic Legend*, or Tolkien and E.V. Gordon's edition of *Sir Gawain and the Green Knight*. Rather, I am claiming that Tolkien created something analogous to what is at the heart of each of those texts: the medieval work itself, the numbered lines in larger type in the middle of the page, distinct from the apparatus and explanatory notes and glossary. Analogous, but not equivalent, because what Tolkien created is written in Modern English and can be read without glossary or critical apparatus, which is among the reasons his works have been read by so many people, and many of those readers have felt "something in the air," some special and, yes, ineffable qualities of Tolkien's masterpieces that emotionally engage them in ways different than many other works of literature.

In my comparison of ruins, I mentioned those of Whitby Abbey because Tolkien, like many other poets and artists, and millions of ordinary people, and me, visited them, more than once, and experienced the beauty and the sorrow that they produce in those who stand in awe of the "bare ruin'd choirs," the stones thrown down by both violence and neglect, etched by wind and spray, and yet still there nearly five hundred years after the monks were disbanded and the Abbey abandoned to time and weather.[77] A ruin like Whitby is often beautiful in itself, and some minds can imagine additional beauty by reconstructing the tower it once was. Indeed what the mind reconstructs from a ruin may be more beautiful than the building ever was, as what is in the mind can lack the imperfections of the mere physical. But the greatest power of the ruin is not its ability to generate an imagined tower, or even the pure beauty of the colors of the stone, the shadows on the grass, the patina of great age, but is instead the doubled sense of loss and permanence that it forces upon us, simultaneously insisting upon its continued existence—real, material, heavy stones set firmly in the earth, here, now—and the enormous loss that it cannot but represent, all the light and song and lives that once filled it, swept away by Time's devouring wave.

The ruined text produces the same feeling of fragility and permanence: It comes to us broken beyond repair, confused, mangled, barely clinging to existence, but enduring and old, so much older than we can really understand, and yet the unmistakable work of an individual, of the one person who dipped a quill into ink and touched it to the parchment that we ourselves touch. Tolkien was neither the first nor the only person to feel this sense of entwined loss and endurance, but he was one of the very few to find a way to reproduce it.

CHAPTER 2

Frames

Late in 1916 or early in 1917, Tolkien, still classified as medically unfit for military service as a result of his trench fever, began to write what would become *The Book of Lost Tales.*[1] Previous to this he had been composing poems that in one way or the other touched upon his developing "mythology," and he seems to have decided that those poems needed to be contextualized in some way. The result, *The Cottage of Lost Play*, is the first of many frame narratives that Tolkien would experiment with over the next decades as he worked not only to create stories and poems but to connect them both to each other and to the history and geography of England.

A *frame narrative* is a story that wraps around the central story, giving it a context and, often, a reason for its existence. Frame narratives have a very long history in European literature.[2] They are a common feature of the medieval works Tolkien studied at Oxford. An imagined journey to Canterbury is the excuse for Chaucer's motley pilgrims to tell tales in various genres. Chaucer took this structuring idea from Boccaccio's *Decameron*, in which ten young people flee the Black Death in Florence, taking refuge in the mountains and entertaining each other by each telling one story per night for ten nights.[3] Dante's *Divine Comedy* uses the author's report of a dream as its frame narrative, as do several of Chaucer's shorter works and a number of the most-studied Middle English poems, including *Pearl* and William Langland's *Piers Plowman*. The context provided by a frame narrative often explains how the author of a work could have acquired the special knowledge or information being depicted, thus *authorizing* the story that is inside the frame, implying that it has a greater truth value than it would have if presented alone. This authentication is just one of the functions of frame narratives.

Tolkien's *The Cottage of Lost Play* introduces the character of Eriol, a mariner who arrives at the Lonely Isle of Tol Eressëa, in the center of which he finds a small cottage in which dwell Lindo and his wife Vairë. In the Room of Logs inside the cottage, the magic Tale-fire burns year-round, aiding storytellers with its powers. Eriol, who, over the course of the composition of the Lost Tales, acquires a variety of names, including *Ottor*, *Waéfre* [Old English: restless, wandering], and eventually *Ælfwine* [OE: Elf-friend],[4] asks to hear the history of "this goodly house and the fair company of maids and boys, for of all houses this seems to me the most lovely and of all gatherings the sweetest I have gazed upon."[5] The overarching frame narrative for the *Lost Tales* is thus the story of Eriol on Tol Eressëa listening to "The Lost Tales of Elfinesse" related by several speakers.[6] The histories and personalities of some of these are more developed than others, and we can infer that Tolkien intended each narrator to contribute some particular perspective to their tales: Some witnessed the events they related; others had connections to the characters in the tales.

Although Tolkien did not complete the Eriol frame narrative or all of the tales inside it, he seems never to have considered completely eliminating this frame. His unrealized "project for the revision of the whole work" retains the frame narrative, and Tolkien even prefaced the epilogue to the Lost Tales with a note: "The last words of the book of Tales. Written by Eriol at Tavrobel before he sealed the book." After the epilogue was in existence he made a note saying that the text still needed a "Prologue by the writer of Tavrobel [*i.e., such a Prologue is needed*] telling how he found Eriol's writings and put them together. His epilogue after the battle of Ladwen Daideloth is written."[7] The material in square brackets is Christopher Tolkien's interpretation, which is undoubtedly correct: Tolkien had already composed the epilogue and was, in this note, deciding he needed a prologue to go with it in order to set up the frame narrative. Much later, when Tolkien was taking a very different approach to the Silmarillion material and converting the events of the Lost Tales stories into historical-annal form, he wrote that the earliest Annals of Valinor were said to be translated in Tol Eressëa "by Eriol of Leithien, that is Ælfwine of the Angelcynn."[8] We can therefore conclude that Tolkien viewed a frame narrative (or narratives) as essential to his literary project, and this never changed, even for *The Hobbit* and *The Lord of the Rings*, though in these two works the frame narrative is more subtle and even, in *The Hobbit*, mostly hidden.

What did change over the course of the several decades in which he worked on the Silmarillion material was Tolkien's original conception of fitting the Lost Tales to early English history. Historical fiction was still in its early stages of development as an independent genre, so many of its conventions were not yet firmly established, but Tolkien nevertheless seems to be committed to the generally observed rule that the fictive history cannot contradict any of the relevant real history. It can fill in gaps, provide different motivations, depict actions that were peripheral to the accounts of historians, and show what is imagined to have been going on "off stage," but the factual—or generally accepted as factual—elements of real-world history must be respected.

The way this narrative requirement is worked out in Tolkien's writings is primarily through the connections between names from history and the Ælfwine or Eriol narrator. Ælfwine operates as an intermediary through whom Tolkien can transmit his mythology by presenting the legends as if he is discovering them (via Eriol), rather than just making them up. This relationship links the "outside" contemporary reader to the "inside" culture that generated the myths. Ælfwine is analogous to King Gylfi in Snorri Sturulson's *Gylfaginning*.[9] The king, who calls himself "Gangleri" [Wanderer], travels to Asgard, where he naïvely questions three lords who call themselves Hárr, Jafnhárr, and Þriði [High, Just-as-High, and The Third One] about the Norse pantheon. This frame narrative allows Snorri to retell many stories about the Norse gods and their adventures, preserving and transmitting pre-Christian oral traditions without giving the impression that he believes that the pagan gods were actually deities.* Snorri thus simultaneously communicates the idea that the stories he is telling about his poetic ancestors' beliefs are authentic while also implying that they are untrue.

The frame narrative of *The Cottage of Lost Play* works similarly, providing a reason for Tolkien's various narrators to relate the tales that make up his mythology while distancing the stories from his individual authorship: Readers are supposed to think that the stories are not inventions, but rather discoveries. The figure of Ælfwine, then, serves as a bridge between Tolkien's mythology and Anglo-Saxon history, authorizing the former by interlinking it with the latter. At the early stages of the composition of the *Book of Lost Tales* material, Ælfwine was named Eriol and also "Ottor, who called himself Wæfre," which could be taken as an Old English translation of *Gangleri*, since both words mean "Wanderer." Ælfwine's other name, Ottor, is equivalent to the Old English name Ohthere, the name of one of two voyagers who visited the court of King Alfred. Ohthere provided the king with information about the lands and peoples surrounding the North Sea.[10] An account of Ohthere's voyages and those of the other visitor, Wulfstan, was interpolated into the Old English translation of Orosius's *Historiae adversum paganos*.[11] In Anglo-Saxon history, therefore, Ohthere was a great voyager and mariner, attributes also held by Tolkien's Ælfwine/Eriol/Ottor figure.

Tolkien's Ottor's father is named Eoh, which means "horse" in Old English. He marries Cwén (Old English for "queen" or "woman") and has two sons, Hengest and Horsa (both names mean "horse" in Old English). Ottar ends up leaving Heligoland in the North Sea, where he has settled, and sailing west to Tol Eressëa, the Lonely Isle of the Elves,

* One of Snorri's goals is to explain poetic kennings to Christians who had not grown up with the traditional stories of the Old Norse gods; he therefore provides the stories that explain why, for example, gold is called the Hair of Sif, the Drops of Draupnir, or the Otter's Ransom, why earth is called the Flesh of Ymir, the Floor of the Hall of the Winds, etc.

where he weds a woman named Naimi who is also called Eadgifu (the Old English antecedent of the name Edith). Heorrenda is one of the sons of Ottor/Eriol/Ælfwine, who also adopts the name Angol, which "refers to the ancient homeland of the 'English' before their migration across the North Sea."[12]

This somewhat bewildering collection of names and historical and pseudo-historical tidbits can be disambiguated by relating it to what is known of the earliest English history, producing a coherent narrative that, while not fully supported by the historical evidence (in which immortal, seafaring elves and their kingdoms in the Western Isles do not play a large role) does make logical sense. The Venerable Bede claims that England was colonized by three Germanic tribes, the Angles, Saxons, and Jutes. This migration was led by two brothers, Hengest and Horsa.[13] In Tolkien's conception, then, the father of the leaders of the Anglo-Saxon migration was Ælfwine, who therefore must have originally come from the ancestral homeland of the Anglo-Saxons on the continent—in Tolkien's conception, somewhere in northern Germany or southern Denmark between the Flensburg Fjord and the river Schlei.[14] Ælfwine first left the continent for Heligoland in the North Sea, where Tolkien says he settled, and from there he traveled to the Elvish lands in the West: His sons returned to the continent and then led their people into England.[15]

Ælfwine's first wife Cwén, the mother of Hengest and Horsa, may also have links to the "Voyages of Ohthere and Wulfstan."[16] Ohthere described a tribe of northern Sweden called the Cwenas, who at times carried their ships overland to large lakes and then harried the Northmen on these waters.[17] In any event, Cwén may represent the union of the Anglo-Saxons' ancestors with another tribe and would thus explain the culture of the more distant north influencing a tribe from southern Denmark or northern Germany.

The figure of Hengest—the son of Cwén and Ælfwine—is particularly significant to our understanding of the interrelationship of Tolkien's imagined mythology and his Anglo-Saxon scholarship. In his posthumously published *Finn and Hengest*, Tolkien had developed a very complex argument as to the identity of the character Hengest, who appears in both the Finnsburg episode in *Beowulf* and the separate Finnsburg Fragment that tells the same story.* This Hengest was, Tolkien believed, the historical Hengest who led the migration to England with his brother Horsa.[18] Thus the original colonizer had also been a major participant in the heroic Finnsburg incident that Tolkien called the *Freswæl* [Frisian slaughter] in *Beowulf.* Tolkien believed that *Beowulf* preserved memories of "a tradition concerning moving *historical* events, the arising of Denmark and the wars in the islands," but *Beowulf* is primarily a work of literature, so identifying the Finnsburg Hengest as the Hengest who led the migration to England creates a variety of literary effects.[19] By making the Hengest in *Beowulf* the historical Hengest, Tolkien brings the story of *Beowulf* from Geatland (wherever in Scandinavia that is) to England, and he ties the legendary and mythical world of *Beowulf* to Anglo-Saxon historical culture. Interpreted this way, the character Hengest is a three-way link between *Beowulf,* the Migration of Germanic tribes after the Fall of Rome, and Tolkien's Ælfwine frame narrative.

Tolkien's original idea for the *Lost Tales* was that the Lonely Isle, Tol Eressëa, originally located far to the west of Europe in the Atlantic, was inhabited by the "Eldar." At some point these elves decided to return to the Great Lands (later Middle-earth, but in this early conception, equivalent to continental Europe) to rescue those of their kin who were still living there under the domination of a Dark Lord. As part of this great "Faring Forth," the island of Tol Eressëa is physically dragged to a point close to the continental coastline. Part of the island breaks off, and this remnant becomes known as Ireland, while the rest becomes England, from which a bridge is built to Rôs (Brittany), on the coast of France. The elves fight to rescue their kindred, but they are defeated and have to retreat back to the Isle. Evil men and monsters follow them over the bridge and are thus able to reach Tol Eressëa (England). Ælfwine, who has come to the Isle from the original homeland of the Angles on the north coast of the continent, and whose sons

* Several of my students over the years have called *Finn and Hengest* "the most frustrating book ever written," and I can't say they are wrong. The argument takes place entirely in notes in such a tangled fashion that it requires many readings before even experienced *Beowulf* scholars understand what is going on; I fear that even after years of study I have missed subtleties.

led the migration of the Anglo-Saxons to England, is a witness to "the devastation of Tol Eressëa by the invasion of men and their evil allies." As a result of this catastrophe, the elves begin their process of physical diminishment, and eventually they fade away.[20] In a second "Scheme for the Lost Tales," Ælfwine "does not arrive until all the grievous history is done. His part is only to learn and to record," and England is just England, with Tol Eressëa being a separate island far to the west.[21]

Regardless of whether Tol Eressëa is conceived of as being England itself or exists in the sea to the west of England, Tolkien uses his frame narrative not just to contain and authorize his tales of the Elves and their struggle with the original Dark Lord, but to join together his self-contained mythology with what little we know of the early history of England. This linkage helps create the effect that so many people report about Tolkien's work: that it seems like something traditional and historical rather than being the literary invention of a twentieth-century Oxford professor. Part of that effect is due to the simultaneous sense of consistency and distance that the connection to real history helps produce.

Far from inhibiting his creative powers, the restriction of not being able to contradict the known facts of Anglo-Saxon migration-era history seems to have been a productive constraint for Tolkien's frame narrative story. The names and relationships are, in their very natures, deeply interlinked because they were produced by real-world culture and history and therefore innately possess a sense of consistency and plausibility. At the same time, this history and culture are so distant from our own that Tolkien can fill many gaps with his invented stories. Thus even though the Ælfwine frame was eventually abandoned, the characteristics produced by the connections to Anglo-Saxon history still remained in the subtle qualities that the frame imparted to the stories inside it. The requirement to be consistent with—or at least not contradictory to—real-world history helps interconnect the material inside with the frame. We see emerging here both interlinking and consistency among the connections. The metaphorical parallels to physical ruins would be the columns that now support nothing, the broken stairs going nowhere: Although not useful in themselves, they provide shape and definition to the emptiness that remains, and their own locations are determined by things now absent.

Tolkien's frame narrative links his mythology to the Anglo-Saxon historical and cultural worlds not only through the character Hengest, but by inventing for him a brother Heorrenda (Ælfwine's son by Eadgifu). Although Heorrenda is not a historical Anglo-Saxon, his name is known to scholars of Old English literature. The eponymous narrator of the poem *Deor*, from the Exeter Book, is a poet, or *scop*, who has fallen on hard times. For years Deor had the love and respect of his lord, but recently a new *scop* named Heorrenda usurped his place, leaving Deor to lament *þæs ofereode, þisses swa mæg* [that passed away, this also may].[22] Tolkien interpreted this story as implying that Heorrenda was a better poet than Deor, and so in some Oxford lectures, he attributed *Beowulf* to the former.[23] Although Tolkien does not mention *Deor* or *Beowulf* in sketches or outlines for the frame narrative of the *Book of Lost Tales*, he does identify Heorrenda as an author in a title-page and a fragmentary prologue:

> The Golden Book of Heorrenda
> being the book of the
> Tales of Tavrobel
>
> ---
>
> Heorrenda of Hægwudu*
> This book have I written using those writings that my father Wæfre (whom the Gnomes name after the regions of his home Angol) did make in his sojourn in the holy isle in the days of the Elves; and much else have I added of those things which his eyes saw not afterward; yet are such things not yet to tell. For know . . .[24]

With the invention of "The Golden Book of Heorrenda," Tolkien arrived at the form of frame narrative that he would eventually perfect in *The Lord of the Rings*: an invented book that is a compilation of stories from multiple narrators. However, before reaching this point he would

---

* *Hægwudu* is just an Old English translation of Haywood. Starting in March of 1916, Tolkien's wife, Edith, lived in Great Haywood in Staffordshire. Until he was posted to France in June 1916, Tolkien would visit her when he had leave. He returned to Great Haywood in December 1916 and lived there with Edith until February 1917. *Chronology*, 96–99.

pursue several other experiments with framing narratives and narrators both in the abandoned *The Lost Road* (1938), and the abortive *Notion Club Papers*.[25] This latter, which Tolkien wrote some time in 1944–46, in the middle of the long composition process of *The Lord of the Rings*, was in part a response to some of the ideas in C.S. Lewis's "space" trilogy (*Out of the Silent Planet*, *Perelandra*, *That Hideous Strength*), but it ended up being instead a fuller development of a story initially presented in *The Lost Road*: the Downfall of Númenor, Tolkien's own version of the Atlantis myth.[26]

At least in its earliest form, *The Notion Club Papers* has more frame than story. The conceit is that in 2012 a stack of papers is found in the basement of the Examination Schools at Oxford. These turn out to be "the elaborate minute-book of a club, devoted to conversation, debate, and the discussion of 'papers,' in verse or prose, written and read by its members" from 1980–1990.[27] The Notion Club is a fictionalization of the Inklings (*notion* being a synonym for *inkling*), the informal group of Oxford writers that had coalesced around C.S. Lewis, including his brother Warren, Charles Williams, Hugo Dyson, John Wain, Tolkien, and at times his son Christopher.[28] The dramatized meetings inside the frame of the pseudo-edition create a second frame that consists first of a debate about whether "time and space travel is more or less believable in fiction than fairies and fantasy" and then a discussion of the possibility of tapping into the distant past through true dreams.[29] The material inside the second frame narrative would eventually become the Downfall of Númenor, and its invention was a significant contribution to Tolkien's being able to return to and complete *The Lord of the Rings*.[30]

Tolkien starts *The Notion Club Papers* almost exactly the same way a scholar would begin an edition of a medieval text, by describing the physical manuscript, its discovery, location, presumed context, paper, and handwriting. The opinions of eminent experts (imaginary) as to the possible history and purpose of the papers are presented, and in the first few meeting entries, occasional footnotes attributed to one of the characters provide additional information; these are occasionally augmented with material in square brackets that is attributed to the fictional editor. That invented frame narrator, Howard Green, identifies

The Notion Club Papers as being fragments of a larger work, since they were intended to cover twenty-five meetings of the club but bundles containing the minutes of multiple nights are missing.

From this description (and even more quickly by simple inspection of the text published in *Sauron Defeated*), *The Notion Club Papers* is quite clearly a textual ruin manufactured by Tolkien. The "papers" have all the characteristics of a modern edition of a very old text that requires a critical apparatus in order for it to be understood by contemporary readers. Tolkien emphasizes the necessity of this scholarly framework by inventing a very complex textual history: The edition of the text was published in 2014 (as a second edition) but was written in the 1980s, although, as noted by the two external experts, W. W. Wormald and D. N. Borrow of the Institute of Occidental Languages,* the dialogues are written in the idiom of the 1940s and possibly on paper from that era, thus perhaps indicating that the text was actually composed forty years before the handwritten manuscript, a conclusion scornfully rejected by the editor. Tolkien's seemingly quixotic decision to invent such an overly elaborate transmission-history is much more comprehensible if we see him as wanting to justify the presentation of the outer frame narrative as a scholarly edition.†

When I first read *The Notion Club Papers* it was very difficult for me to understand why Tolkien would abandon *The Lord of the Rings* at one of the most exciting parts—Frodo had been captured by the orcs and the other members of the fellowship were heading toward Minas Tirith

---

* Wormald is a surname with a long and illustrious history in medieval scholarship. D. N. Borrow has the feel of a joke, possibly relating to a library stamp ("Did/do not borrow"?), seeming to be a person's name, but I have not been able to track down a definite reference.

† One amusing detail that supports this interpretation is the footnote in which Wormald is said to have stated that "the use of a pen rather than a typewriter would indeed, in itself, already have been most unusual for a man of 1990, whatever his age." Half true, but Tolkien did not foresee the personal computer and dot-matrix printer the way he anticipated the "Great Storm" of 1987, which, in the mid-1940s, he predicted for June 12, 1987. As Christopher Tolkien notes, this "'prevision' was only out by four months," as the greatest storm in living memory devastated southern England on October 16, 1987; *Sauron*, 155–58, 211n1. For a powerfully evocative remembrance of this storm, see W. G. Sebald, *The Rings of Saturn*, trans. Michael Hulse (New York: New Directions, 1997), 265–68. For a more fictionalized depiction, see A. S. Byatt, *Possession: A Romance* (New York: Vintage, 1990), 534–51.

by various paths in preparation for a great battle—in order to compose this slow, digressive story that is for many pages just a group of friends sitting around and talking. Of all Tolkien's works, it is closest stylistically to "On Fairy-Stories," the insightful but incredibly frustrating 1939 essay that has long defied my attempts to understand it fully. In some ways *Notion Club* is even more frustrating, because the frame narrative dramatizes (in the loosest sense of that term) the tentative intellectual groping in the dark of a group of intelligent people trying to understand very complex and sophisticated new ideas. If supernatural phenomena had not started to intrude into the club's debates, it seems likely that this putative time-travel novel would have been abandoned even sooner. But as the long and complex narrative told by Michael Ramer goes on, such events do start to force their way from the deep past into the world of the characters in the club: first as partially recalled words and mental images, and then as the physical manifestation of the "Great Storm."[31]

In this way, through the storm and ideas of the drowning of the land by an enormous wave, the matter of *The Fall of Númenor*, which Tolkien had first developed in 1936–37, became the narrative inside the double frame of the Notion Club papers and the dialogues of the Notion Club members. Initially the focus, as it was in *The Lost Road*, is on words and incidents connected to Anglo-Saxon traditions,[32] but relatively quickly Tolkien's story of Númenor and the language he began inventing for it—then spelled Adunaic, without the circumflex accent on the <u>—becomes central to the story.[33] As Christopher Tolkien notes, "the Adunaic language emerged . . . with an abandoned but elaborate account of the phonology, and *pari passu* with *The Notion Club Papers* my father not only wrote a first draft of an entirely new version of the story of Númenor, but developed it through further texts: this is *The Drowning of Anadûnê*, in which all the names are in Adunaic." Tolkien seems to have been very focused on the development of these new and unanticipated Middle-earth materials for some time, expanding them substantially.[34] They certainly take over Part 2 of *The Notion Club Papers*, with the rather leisurely debate and dialogue of Part 1 being replaced by a much more focused discussion of not only abstract ideas (particularly about the nature of language), but specifics of the emerging Adûnaic language and the Númenor story.

"Why my father abandoned *The Notion Club Papers* I do not know," writes Christopher Tolkien. "It may be that he felt that the work had lost all unity, that 'Atlantis' had broken apart the frame in which it had been set."[35] I think this is correct but not quite complete. The need to keep returning from the rapidly expanding and ramifying Númenor story to the conversations among the Club members was unnecessarily retarding the pace of the story, which no longer needed the frame narrative to carry it. Originally intended to make plausible a sort of time-travel, in which certain people could recover memories of the ancient past, the frame narrative was now constantly interrupting the far more interesting inner story. That, at least, was my experience both in my initial reading of *The Notion Club Papers* years ago and my more recent return to the text. Although the ideas Tolkien starts to develop in the frame narrative are academically interesting, and the linguistic insights he gives to his characters are always worthwhile, the conceit of the edition of meeting-minutes rapidly becomes tedious. That frame could perhaps have been dropped for the majority of the story and picked up only at the end in the same way so many other authors using invented-source tropes unapologetically abandon their imaginary sources once the story has gotten going. Unfortunately for Tolkien, the structure he had developed at the beginning of the composition process precluded completely discarding the outer frame even as the inner frame began to dissolve into the story as the characters began to experience past events in the present.

Most people only ever encounter old and damaged texts through scholarly editions, so their constellation of textual features and stylistic characteristics serve as indicators of authenticity despite these aspects of the combined texts being absolutely modern. A pure facsimile of a manuscript (such as Tolkien's pages from the Book of Mazarbul) or the presentation of only the ancient material itself, paradoxically creates less of an impression of being truly old than does the same material surrounded by the trappings of a scholarly edition. Support for this contention comes from Jorge Luis Borges's leveraging the authority of academic style in multiple stories, including "Tlön, Uqbar, Orbis Tertius," or Vladimir Nabokov parodying it in *Pale Fire*.[36] Academic affectation and style understandably generate authority and authorization much better than purple prose, an author's direct insistence, or characters intensely testifying as to the truth of a story.

But a scholarly frame is not enough. One of the problems with *The Notion Club Papers* is that despite the detail of the outer frame, the well-realized characters of the inner frame, and the complexity, originality, and internal consistency of the Númenor material, there is not much to make the reader—as opposed to the characters in the inner frame—feel as if the central matter is in fact from a lost civilization. The majority of the text reads very much like someone's fictionalized recollection of some meetings of literary friends in Oxford in the 1940s (which makes sense, because that's what it is), and the impression generated by this inner frame narrative mostly outweighs the impression of great age and authenticity created by the consistency and detail of the Adûnaic language and the Númenor story. Although a faux scholarly edition frame-narrative can suggest that what is inside is a textual ruin, the inner material must itself possess some additional characteristics if readers are to interpret it as being old and authentic. In the case of the *Notion Club Papers*, the inner frame's conceit of connecting to the central narrative material via past-transmitting dreams and visions clashes with the textuality of the outer frame. Perhaps if the inner frame had been about Ramer and Lowdham finding old manuscripts in the bowels of Duke Humfrey's Library, the double-frame would have worked, but as it stands, the central story lacks textuality, and this was a fatal flaw.

The work that Tolkien returned to when he gave up on *The Notion Club Papers*, *The Lord of the Rings*, does not have this weakness, and neither do *The Hobbit* or *The Silmarillion*. Whether this was a conscious decision on Tolkien's part is impossible to determine. Nothing in the *Letters* suggests that he had recognized this particular problem with *The Notion Club Papers*, but the frame narratives in his masterpieces—where they exist—do not clash with the interior material, and the impression of textuality that they maintain is a major contributor to the illusion they present of age and authenticity.

The Lost Road, an unfinished work that, like Part 2 of *The Notion Club Papers*, explores the idea of ancient historical events presenting themselves as dreams in later-day people, had been written just after Tolkien finished *The Hobbit*. Present-day father and son Edwin and Elwin time-travel into the deep past by reliving the experiences of a series of father and son pairs, each of whose names means "Bliss-friend" and "Elf-friend" (*Eadwine* and *Ælfwine* in Old English). Although in its larger conception the first two chapters of *The Lost Road* were to function as a kind of frame narrative—in that they introduced the contemporary father-son pair and the phenomenon of information from the deep past coming into the present in the form of a character mysteriously learning or inventing languages—nothing in the chapters marks that function. They seem like parts of a work of ordinary twentieth-century semi-realistic prose fiction: A father and son discuss mundane matters such as studying and scholarships, and any fantasy material—the son's reception of unknown languages in his dreams—is treated in a matter-of-fact way.

The next two chapters, which are set in Númenor immediately before the downfall, are written in the same style, marked as fantasy rather than realism only by their content (most obviously the names in Tolkien's invented languages). If I did not know it was by Tolkien, I would classify *The Lost Road* as a bit of early- to mid-twentieth-century science fiction, as it employs the technique of normalization that had developed in that genre.[37] There is, deliberately, no sign that the characters are talking about anything unusual, and invented materials are introduced casually, as if the reader should be able to recognize them as easily as the characters do. Tolkien does use thee/thou pronouns for the conversation between father and son, but probably a large fraction of the imagined audience would understand these as a convention from Victorian romance, so we should not take them as being intended to defamiliarize anything about the setting. It is all quite similar in general feel to C.S. Lewis's *Out of the Silent Planet*: well written but in no way stylistically innovative, and fitting comfortably within the mainstream of 1930s science fiction.

The Hobbit and *The Lost Road* having no overt frames, *The Lord of the Rings*' frame being nonobvious, and the *Notion Club Papers* having two elaborate frames should not, I think, be interpreted as demonstrating some kind of linear evolution in Tolkien's frame narratives. I have not discussed in any detail the long narrative poems of the Beren and Lúthien and Túrin stories that Tolkien worked on before *The Hobbit* and *The Lost Road*, and for that matter, the frame narrative of

The Book of Lost Tales had not been definitively rejected when Tolkien began *The Hobbit*. All this continued experimentation with frame narratives should probably be interpreted as an indication that Tolkien had concluded that he could not get the effects he wanted by simply presenting his Silmarillion tales as bare stories but that he needed to connect them to the present-day world. It was only after the failure of both *The Lost Road* and *The Notion Club Papers* that he discovered that a subtle frame was more effective than a very explicit one and that directly and explicitly connecting his narratives to the present day was unnecessary.

Although I have said twice in this chapter that *The Hobbit* appears to have no frame, it does in fact have two, though neither is obvious, and the first is a feature of the text that Tolkien later wished he could remove: the intrusive narrator.* The beautiful and famous opening of the book—"In a hole in the ground there lived a hobbit . . . " ends with "He may have lost the neighbors' respect, but he gained—well, you will see whether he gained anything in the end," and this is just the first instance of the narrator directly addressing the reader to provide explanation, interpretation, or evaluation of the actions within the story.[38] This narrator is never characterized but is presented as having complete knowledge of the future course of the story, and this stance is maintained throughout the book via comments such as: "It was not the last time he wished for that!" and "Not for the last time!" said of Bilbo's desire to be back in his comfortable hobbit-hole, and "It was a turning point in his career, but he did not know it," said of Bilbo's finding the Ring.[39]

The narrator also has more knowledge about the world of the text than the implied readers. For example, in "The mother of our particular hobbit—what is a hobbit? I suppose hobbits need some description nowadays,"[40] the word *nowadays* implies the narrator's knowledge of the past, and *I suppose* distances the narrator from the implied readers, since the narrator does not know for certain what the readers know,

---

* In part, this is a deduction, since Tolkien only said that he regretted having written "'for children' in style or manner"; *Letters*, #165, 317. But the narrator's direct addresses to the reader and evaluative comments are the elements of the style that are most obviously "for children."

though at other times he knows enough to be able to describe in-world phenomena in real-world terms; for example, the goblins know their tunnels "as well as you [know the way] to the nearest post-office."[41] Additionally, knowledge that would be esoteric in the real world seems commonplace to the narrator: how trolls (even those with only one head each) really behave, the many terrible things goblins do and have done, and that "no spider has ever liked being called Attercop."[42] Finally, the narrator confidently makes synthesizing evaluative judgments such as "I don't suppose you would have done half as well yourselves in his place";* and "There it is: dwarves are not heroes, but calculating folk with a great idea of the value of money; some are tricky and treacherous and pretty bad lots; some are not, but are decent enough people like Thorin and Company, if you don't expect too much"; and "Now these were fair words and true, if proudly and grimly spoken." Taken together, these characteristics construct the narrator as a wise adult and the implied readers as children, which should not be the slightest bit surprising, since *The Hobbit* was intentionally written to be a children's book.[43]

What is perhaps less obvious is that this constructed relationship between the narrator and the readers—an adult speaking to children—is as much a frame narrative as The Golden Book of Heorrenda in *The Book of Lost Tales*, or *The Notion Club Papers*. The difference is that rather than being explicitly identified, the frame narrative of *The Hobbit* is constructed through rhetoric and implication. It is a storytelling session rather than a tome found in an Elvish cottage or a bundle of papers from an Oxford basement, but it is nevertheless a frame narrative and does the same work of contextualizing and authorizing the story inside it. Indeed, the implied frame is quite emotionally convincing, particularly when *The Hobbit* is being read aloud, because it is exactly the form that would result from an adult telling (or retelling) the story of

---

* I have been reading *The Hobbit* for fifty years, and studying, teaching, and writing about it for more than twenty-five, and the writing of this paragraph was the first time that I realized that the narrator addresses *readers* in the plural rather than *a* singular *reader*. This may be the only example of the narrator's direct addresses to the reader in which it is possible to tell if the addressee is singular or plural, because the second person is only differentiated between singular and plural in the reflexive form *yourselves*.

Bilbo Baggins's great adventure. Even the small features of the story that seem inconsistent with the world of *The Lord of the Rings*—the trolls' talking purse, the enormous stone giants who never reappear, Beorn's animals that walk on their hind legs and set the dinner table—are exactly the sorts of narrative elements that would be likely to be inserted by an adult narrator into a traditional story for children.

The Hobbit's subtle framing even does what Tolkien unsuccessfully tried in *The Lost Road* and *The Notion Club Papers*: Much more so than any imagined manuscript or edition could, *The Hobbit*'s story-telling session is, by implication, always happening at the moment the book is being read and is therefore in the present day of the reader, whenever that might be. This implied frame narrative is more effective even than the far more explicit tale-telling frame of *The Princess Bride* and similar works.[44] The risk of any frame is that it can distance readers even as it authenticates the inner story, but the implied frame of *The Hobbit* avoids this problem. It may not be a coincidence that when, in 1960, Tolkien set out to revise *The Hobbit* into the style of *The Lord of the Rings*, the results were unsatisfactory.[45]

Without the intrusive narrator, the narrative of *The Hobbit* would not quite work. The talking down to the implied reader that Tolkien seemed later to deplore turns out to be what permits the more whimsical elements of the narrative: the musical instruments of the dwarves that they must have brought from far away with much trouble but then abandon seemingly without a thought; the story about Bullroarer Took knocking the head of the goblin king Golfimbul off and down a rabbit hole, thus winning a battle and inventing the game of golf; the aforementioned talking purse; the goblins knowing the names of the two Elvish swords by sight alone; and others.[46] The intuitive response of the anonymous friend of Tolkien's who read the 1960 revision, "that's wonderful, but it's not *The Hobbit*," is apposite: Without the frame constructed by the putatively intrusive narrator, *The Hobbit* is not *The Hobbit* because the narrative loses the authenticating function of the implied tale-telling session.[47] This does not mean that a revised version of *The Hobbit* in the style of *The Lord of the Rings* would have necessarily failed, but removing or significantly modifying the narrator would have forced a cascade of downstream changes in everything from plot elements to nomenclature, as important elements of the plot that work well in the implied adult-to-child tale-telling context would have had to be made more plausible in order to function within a different frame narrative.*

There is also a second frame narrative for *The Hobbit*, easier to identify as a frame once noticed but harder to see at all, and far more limited in its effects than the implied frame we have been discussing. The early British edition had runes printed on the dust jacket.[48] To read them requires performing a little cryptology, first figuring out the phonetic values of the runes from the brief runic passage and translation that Tolkien provides inside the book, and then using the resulting table of equivalents to translate the runes on the dust jacket:

> The Hobbit or There and Back Again being the record of a year's journey made by Bilbo Baggins of Hobbiton compiled from his memoirs by J.R.R. Tolkien and Published by George Allen and Unwin LTD.[49]

Readers who translate the dust-jacket runes, however, would not find their experience of reading the book substantially different from that of the many readers who don't notice the runes or think of them as merely decorations. The conceit of this frame—that *The Hobbit* is a compilation and translation rather than an original composition in Modern English by Professor Tolkien—is not borne out by the text itself, which is consistent throughout in its colloquial and contemporary style.[50] This second frame narrative, then, which is almost certainly an afterthought, is primarily decorative. In itself it does nothing to change a reader's experience of the book because it is so well hidden, but also, and more importantly, because there are no characteristics or features of the text that would be explained or justified if the facts asserted by the frame were true. The dust-jacket runes create an *asserted* frame narrative. In general such frames have very little influence on readers' perceptions of

* Not merely small issues like the appearance and disappearance of the musical instruments, the talking purse, and Beorn's animals, but the more diffuse tone with regard to the Necromancer, the trolls and goblins, the geopolitical situation surrounding the Battle of Five Armies, etc.

a text, and in the case of *The Hobbit*, any such influence would be overwhelmed by the force of the rhetorically constructed implied frame of a story-telling session, a frame narrative that is consistently *demonstrated* but never baldly asserted.

That the two different types of frame narratives in *The Hobbit* produce such different effects (or, rather, one produces effects and one really does not) allows us to see how frame narratives work or fail. A frame that is not interlinked with the material inside the frame is essentially trivial because although it asserts something about the work, that assertion is not supported by the frame-internal material. I could put a frame narrative around this book by saying that it was dictated to me by my pet unicorn Clarence, but if nothing within the body of the text would be better understood by being the ideas of Clarence and not the words of Mike, the frame narrative will not substantially affect the ways readers experience the text.*

In contrast to a purely asserted frame, a frame narrative that is integrated with the material that it frames—such as Chaucer's *Canterbury Tales*—affects the audience's perceptions of the text to a much greater degree. In one of the rare instances in which the word *synergy* is appropriate, in such cases the interconnection between the frame and what is framed can work to authenticate and contextualize both. I have taught the *Canterbury Tales* for a quarter century, and every single time I read and discuss this work I constantly have to remind my students (and myself!) that the Pilgrims—the Knight, Miller, Wife of Bath, Summoner, Pardoner, and others—were not real people and, more importantly, did not write the tales they tell: The characters and their tales are all literary creations of Chaucer.† The illusion of character- and tale-independence is so powerful exactly because there are such substantial

* For the record: Clarence is not responsible for my errors and misunderstandings, which in his view are legion.

† The illusion is so strong that Chaucer even has the Wife of Bath highlight the disjunction between author and character with the rhetorical question: *Who peyntede the leon, tel me who?* [Who painted the lion, tell me who?] asked by a lion about a painting of a hunter slaying a lion. Yet we still talk about what the Wife of Bath thinks and what *she* is communicating through *her* prologue and tale; "The Wife of Bath's Prologue," line 692, in *The Riverside Chaucer*, 3rd ed., ed. Larry D. Benson (Boston: Houghton Mifflin, 1988).

differences of content and style among the tales, and this heterogeneity is perfectly explained by the frame narrative of the tale-telling contest during the Pilgrimage to Canterbury.

Nearly two decades after the publication of *The Hobbit* and ten years after the creation of *The Notion Club Papers*' double frame, Tolkien produced just such a fully integrated framed narrative in *The Lord of the Rings*. However, unlike Chaucer, or, to use an example chronologically closer, William Faulkner in *As I Lay Dying*, Tolkien does not create his frame to highlight the differing perceptions or experiences of his various characters, but to produce that "something in the air" that he had found in *The Kalevala* and in the medieval English works he studied: the sense that the text was old, traditional, and mythological, the production of a culture rather than the expressive creation of the single individual whose name is on the cover of the book.

The frame narrative of *The Lord of the Rings* might not be as hidden as that of *The Hobbit*, but it is still not particularly obvious unless one translates the runes that border the first few pages of each of the three volumes. The details of *The Lord of the Rings*' frame must be pieced together from the "Note on the Shire Records" at the beginning of *The Fellowship of the Ring* and Appendix F, section II, at the very end of *The Return of the King*. According to the "Note," by the end of the first century of the Fourth Age—thus about a hundred years after the events of *The Lord of the Rings*—there were several libraries in the Shire, and the most important item in their collections was the Red Book of Westmarch. This book was "in origin Bilbo's private diary," supplemented by Frodo, plus three volumes translated by Bilbo and a fourth containing commentaries, genealogies, and other matter written well after the War of the Ring. "The original Red Book has not been preserved, but many copies were made"; the most important of these was kept in Tookland but had been written in Gondor. It began as an exact copy, but "in Minas Tirith it received much annotation, and many corrections, especially of names and quotations in the Elvish languages."[51]

Many attentive readers of *The Lord of the Rings* have, after finishing the book, reread the "Note" and reasonably connected the Red Book of Westmarch to the "big book with plain red leather covers" that Frodo gives to Sam just before their journey to the Grey Havens. The tall pages of that book were almost completely filled, with the beginning written in Bilbo's "thin wandering hand," but the majority of the text is in Frodo's "firm flowing script." It was divided into chapters, but Chapter 80 was unfinished.[52] There are nineteen chapters in *The Hobbit*, twenty-two in *The Fellowship of the Ring*, twenty-one in *The Two Towers*, and nineteen in *The Return of the King*, for a total of eighty-one, which supports the deduction that Bilbo is the primary author of *The Hobbit*, that Frodo composed almost all of *The Lord of the Rings*, and that Sam wrote "The Grey Havens," Chapter 9 of Book VI in *The Return of the King*—this chapter describes Frodo's departure from the Grey Havens and so could not have been written by him (although there is regular postal service in the Shire, there is apparently none from the Uttermost West).[53] The frame narrative given in the "Note on the Shire Records" would therefore fit the published texts.

But this frame narrative is somewhat more complicated than simply the conceit that *The Hobbit* and *The Lord of the Rings* are the diaries of Bilbo and Frodo (and, to a lesser extent, Sam). It is always essential, when analyzing Tolkien's work, to pay close attention to the precise words he uses. In this case, the key words are *in origin* and *compiled.* In the "Note on Shire Records" and in various places in the appendices, Tolkien develops the idea of a complex chain of textual transmission, with multiple copies of the Red Book, one in particular being made in Gondor by Findegil, the King's Writer.[54] Findegil's copy included not only all the additions and corrections in Elvish, but the contents of all three volumes originally given by Bilbo to Frodo as a parting gift in Rivendell: "Three books of lore that he had made at various times, written in his spidery hand, and labelled on their red backs: *Translations from the Elvish by B.B.*"[55] In Appendix F, Tolkien says that he is "presenting the matter of the Red Book, as a history for people of today," adopting the pose that he is merely a translator rather than also being one of the compilers of the text.[56]

It is the conceit of the "translation" that creates the final, complete, and effective synthesis of external frame narrative, internal characteristics explained by that frame narrative, and overarching justification for why the book has the particular qualities is does. Taking *The Lord of the Rings* as a translation of some earlier text solves the problem—

common in all frame narratives that claim their central texts to be old or from different cultures—of the language and style of the inner text needing to be both distinct from that of the frame and easily accessible to the work's intended readers. In nearly all previous attempts to communicate the ineffable qualities, the "something in the air," of the medieval or medievalesque core material, writers from Scott to Morris to Haggard had imitated the grammar or style or diction of their medieval sources. Doing so, however, made the main matter of their works harder to read than the frame narratives surrounding them.

But if the frame narrative claims that the central matter has been translated by the actual author of the work from an older source, which was itself a compilation of multiple sources, the core material can be written in language familiar to—and thus readable by—readers of the time period in which it was written. Tolkien's particular conceit of representing Middle-earth languages by using real-world languages with the same approximate relationship—if the Common Speech is Modern English, the language of the Rohirrim would be Old English, and that of the Men of Dale Old Norse—also explains why different characters are represented as speaking with varying degrees of formality in everything from sentence structure to the use of the familiar forms of second-person pronouns (*thee* and *thou*). This variation among the Modern English pseudo-translations of the speech of characters from different imagined cultural and linguistic backgrounds contributes to the linguistic variation found throughout *The Lord of the Rings*. More importantly, what Tolkien says about translation in Appendix F serves to transform stylistic variations or inconsistencies in the text of *The Lord of the Rings* into support for the conceit of the frame narrative that the book is a translation of a compilation, which explains why the prose might vary from one section to another and from one implied narrator to another while being, in general, broadly consistent with other twentieth-century popular prose narratives.

The word *compiled* in the runes on *The Hobbit* dust-jacket, and the same idea being implied throughout Appendix F, indicates that the author wants readers to conceive of the book not as the unified creation of a single literary artist—which it in fact is, and which also has been the default presumption about literary works in English since the eighteenth century—but as the result of the cobbling together of disparate and perhaps contradictory texts. In the Middle Ages this process was called, unsurprisingly, *compilatio*. Twenty-first-century readers, inheritors of a Romantic tradition about the lonely, individual talent (and perhaps traumatized by poorly understood antiplagiarism rules in school), sometimes have trouble understanding that to medieval writers, *compilatio* was a strength, not a weakness: A text was more authoritative for being "a honeycomb gathered from different flowers."[57] There is even some evidence that medieval authors claimed to be quoting texts even when they were composing the material themselves (inverse plagiarism?) to augment their authority.

If it is a translated compilation, *The Lord of the Rings* would be expected to vary in multiple ways and at multiple scales across the whole text, but also to be broadly consistent in language through the homogenizing effect of a single translator. As we will see later in Chapter 3, the prose style of the text really does vary in these ways, helping to produce the convincing illusion that the work has a long and complex composition- and transmission-history rather than merely being the creation of a single Oxford professor in the twentieth century.

The composition-history of *The Lord of the Rings*, however, is not consistent with a conclusion that the work was composed with the frame narrative in mind, and there is evidence that, at least initially, the textual heterogeneity was unintentional. The components of the frame narrative—the "Note on Shire Records," the section of Appendix F, "On Translation," and the idea of *The Lord of the Rings* being an English translation of the Red Book of Westmarch—are all rather late additions to the work. The first reference to the Red Book appears in a draft of a prologue that eventually evolved into the "Foreword: Concerning Hobbits," and which was likely written in the summer of 1948, when Tolkien was composing the final chapters of the narrative.* In that draft, Tolkien wrote: "it has required several years to translate, select, and arrange the matter of the Red Book of Westmarch in the form in which it is now presented to the Men of a later Age, one no less darkling

* Chapters 6–9 of Book VI: "Many Partings," "Homeward Bound," "The Scouring of the Shire," and "The Grey Havens."

and ominous than were the great years of 1418 and 1419 of the Shire long ago."[58] In another scrap of writing from approximately the same time, part of what Christopher Tolkien believes to have been a draft of a "personal and dedicatory 'preface,'" Tolkien wrote that "This tale is drawn from the memoirs of Bilbo and Frodo Baggins, preserved for the most part in the Great Red Book of Samwise."[59] Although this text did not become the "Foreword: Concerning Hobbits," parts of it were used in both Appendix F and the Foreword of the 1954 first edition of *The Fellowship of the Ring* (but in no subsequent editions). The simplest conclusion would seem to be that Tolkien had not written *The Lord of the Rings* with the idea that the story would have a frame.

However, a subtle but telling piece of evidence suggests otherwise. To my knowledge it has not previously been noted that Bilbo's farewell speech at the Party Tree in Chapter 1, "A Long-Expected Party," is printed entirely in italics rather than being, like all the other speeches in *The Lord of the Rings*, composed of quotations set in Roman type between inverted commas.

> They could all see him standing, waving one hand in the air, the other was in his trouser-pocket:
>
> *My dear Bagginses and Boffins,* he began again; *and my dear Tooks and Bradybucks and Grubbs, and Chubbs, and Burrowses, and Hornblowers, and Bolgers, Bracegirdles, Goodbodies, Brockhouses and Proudfoots.* 'ProudFEET!' shouted an elderly hobbit from the back of the pavillion . . .
>
> *I wish to make an ANNOUNCEMENT.* He spoke this last word so loudly and suddenly that everyone sat up who still could. *I regret to announce that—though, as I said, eleventy-one years is far too short a time to spend among you—this is the END. I am going. I am leaving. NOW. GOOD-BYE!*
>
> He stepped down and vanished.[60]

In *The Lord of the Rings* Tolkien uses italics consistently for emphasis within dialogue, for the names of establishments (*The Ivy Bush, The Floating Log, The Forsaken Inn*), and for the titles of poems. Italics are also sometimes used for dialogue, or for quotation within dialogue, such as in Gaffer Gamgee's retelling of a conversation he once had with Sam, and in Gandalf's reading of the damaged Book of Mazarbul. On a larger scale, all poems and songs are printed in italics, as are both Gandalf's letter to Frodo and the text of Isildur's scroll as reported by Gandalf. Italics, therefore, are an indicator that the words being read are a quotation from somewhere else rather than simply being the speech of the character. The simplest explanation for the italicization of Bilbo's birthday speech, therefore, is that it is meant to also be an originally separate text inserted into the main body of the narrative. The implication is that Bilbo kept a copy of the birthday speech and brought it with him to Rivendell, where he included it in his memoirs.*

The inclusion of the birthday speech as an inserted text makes sense only within something like the eventual Red Book of Westmarch frame, which implies that Tolkien was thinking that he would eventually create a frame narrative in which Bilbo was one of the writers of *The Lord of the Rings.* Bilbo's speech being in italics dates all the way back to the second version of the opening chapter and is thus approximately a decade older than the first explicit reference to the Red Book of Westmarch. To put in perspective how early this is in the composition process of *The Lord of the Rings,* when Tolkien used italics for Bilbo's speech in this second revision of "A Long-Expected Party," the entire narrative had only reached the point of the post-party labeled gifts.[61] We can therefore infer that Tolkien had the frame narrative in mind for almost the entire writing history of *The Lord of the Rings.* That the inner narrative is never inconsistent with the frame narrative—despite the lack of prominence given to that frame (especially in comparison with the frame of *The Notion Club Papers*)—should therefore be no surprise.

Unfortunately, however, we do not have similarly direct evidence for the intentionality of the stylistic heterogeneity that subtly interweaves the framing and central narratives of *The Lord of the Rings.* It is possible that the interconnection of the frame with variations in the prose may merely be an epiphenomenon of the composition process

* This would be completely consistent with Bilbo's character in *The Lord of the Rings*: a touch of vanity combined with a view that his actions were in some way historical and thus should be documented.

rather than a consciously sought-after effect. If so, this is among the happiest accidents in literary history, for, as we will see, these variations in prose style contribute powerfully to the impression that *The Hobbit* and *The Lord of the Rings* are presentations of genuine old material rather than new, twentieth-century compositions.

There is no question that Tolkien recognized the importance—even the necessity—of frame narratives in his efforts to reproduce the "something in the air" of the medieval works he studied, possibly because he understood that every real textual ruin comes packaged in a frame narrative: the scholarly edition that surrounds it and provides the scaffolding upon which we mount the damaged text in order to use it. The last frame narrative he created, for the poetry collection *The Adventures of Tom Bombadil*, is explicitly scholarly, with a footnoted explanatory preface that adopts the conceit that there is information that the editor of the poems simply does not know.[62] One of the reasons Tolkien struggled to complete the Silmarillion to his satisfaction was that he had not devised a satisfactory framing narrative.

Verlyn Flieger argues that:

> It will not do to pursue too far the notion of *The Lord of the Rings* as serially written by Bilbo, Frodo, and Sam. Too many things will not fit comfortably into the concept—narrative voice, point of view, the amount of knowledge each of these "authors" could have had at any one time. If these are put together, the whole concept falls apart. It is best seen as an authorial conceit but not a substantial structural factor, an expedient way for Tolkien to collect his often narratively disparate material into one scheme.[63]

But the frame narrative shared by *The Lord of the Rings* and *The Adventures of Tom Bombadil*—the conceit that Tolkien is translating the Red Book of Westmarch, and that this imaginary text has a long and complex compositional and transmission history—makes an important contribution to the transformation of the ontological status of a set of twentieth-century mass-produced objects into something greater than just another made-up story. Even with their incomprehensible cover illustrations of emus and bulbous fruit, those cheap paperbacks that my father purchased out of a wire rack at the checkout line in Sloan's so that he could read them aloud to me were transformed into what felt like a recounting of things that, even if they had not happened in the real world, seemed to me to be true in some very important way.

I wasn't wrong about that.

CHAPTER 3

Texts

In 1978, possibly because the project gave us an excuse to sit in the back of our fifth-grade classroom and talk rather than do whatever it was the class was supposed to do, my best friend and I wrote an adapted play of one part of *The Lord of the Rings*. Carefully considering all the most exciting and iconic scenes of the great epic, we chose to dramatize . . . the Council of Elrond, a long meeting in which a variety of characters talk, a lot, about what to do with the Ring now that Frodo has brought it to Rivendell.

The chapter is not the most obvious choice for dramatization. Years ago, right after the first Peter Jackson film had been released, I was on a radio show when one caller, the owner of a bookstore in New Hampshire, said that "since the '60s" he had been advising customers to skip the first chapter of *The Fellowship of the Ring* and "The Council of Elrond," and that hundreds of people who had followed this advice came to love Tolkien's works! But although I know quite a few readers who could not get past the hobbit-banter and lack of action in "A Long-Expected Party," I have never spoken to anyone else who skipped "The Council of Elrond." I just do not see how the plot of *The Lord of the Rings* can make any sense without the information presented in this chapter. In fact, I think the chapter is so important that for years I have done an exercise in my Tolkien classes in which students represent the characters at the council—and some who were not invited, including Sauron, Gollum, Denethor, Saruman, and even Gwaihir the Eagle. The students are responsible for understanding their character's point of view and advocating for their interests in an unscripted debate about the geopolitics of Middle-earth in light of the finding of the Ring.* There have been some great moments in these exercises: In 2008 I asked the student representing Saruman, "What do you have to offer to Middle-earth?" and in an utterly deadpan voice he said, "Hope and Change." There was a short pause followed by mass laughter. In 2018, in response to the same question, the student representing Saruman said, "With the Ring I would build a BETTER Dark Tower! Some people say that I build the BEST Dark Towers, and mine would be the biggest, most beautiful Dark Tower in all of Middle-earth!" It took a few minutes for the class to stop laughing. And everyone, both times, got the point.

The Council made for a decent short play for some of the same reasons it requires an in-class exercise: There are a lot of characters (many classmates could participate), all the dramatic interaction is done through speech (no need for props, stunts, or special effects), and the speech is generally more in the form of set pieces to be recited than in turn-taking dialogue that might be beyond the limited skills of a group of ten- and eleven-year-olds. Indeed, looking over our script forty-five years later, I could make the case that we did a better job than Peter Jackson at communicating all the essential information without tedium or histrionics: At least Chipper and I never came up with anything as ridiculous as Gimli the dwarf trying to destroy the Ring by smashing it with a war-axe!

I begin this chapter with "The Council of Elrond" because it is by

* In one of my course evaluations, a student wrote: "Loved the 'Jerry Springer goes to Middle-earth' exercise we did on The Council of Elrond." For additional discussion, see M.D.C. Drout, "The Council of Elrond, All Those Poems, and the Famous F-ing Elves: Teaching the Hard Parts of Tolkien," in *Approaches to Teaching The Lord of the Rings and Tolkien's Other Works*, ed. Leslie A. Donovan (New York: Modern Language Association, 2015), 231–36.

far the most *multivocal* chapter in *The Lord of the Rings*. There are a least thirteen characters present, the speech of twenty-three are presented in quotation or paraphrase, and each of these speakers has a distinctive and distinguishable speaking style—even though Tolkien never describes characters as having accents and avoids nonstandard spelling (except in the case of Gaffer Gamgee's reported speech).[1] The chapter manages to explicate those aspects of the history, geopolitics, and metaphysics of Middle-earth that are required to justify the central plot device—that the Ring cannot be used, hidden, or thrown away, but must be carried into Sauron's stronghold in the land of Mordor and destroyed in the fires of Mount Doom—without being what my students would call an "information dump."

In "The Council of Elrond," Tolkien further develops some of the techniques he used in Chapter 2, "The Shadow of the Past," most importantly the trick of having his most knowledgeable characters being reluctant to share the knowledge they have, thus creating some minor tension as other characters try to extract that information. In both chapters, the reader comes to wish there was *more* background being given, as fascinating details about the forging of the Rings of Power and the subsequent history of Middle-earth are telescoped into a paragraph. Thus Tolkien can present an enormous quantity of information—almost all of it essential for understanding later plot developments—without boring readers or overwhelming them with a lecture.

Tolkien manages the information flow in the chapter by marking the provenance of various pieces of information, closely associating each story with both the character who tells it and the characters quoted within. As Shippey first noted, "language variation gives Tolkien a thorough and economical way of dramatizing ethical debate," and the interactions that are marked by this variation demonstrate the different kinds of rhetoric—and their relative powers—available to the characters.[2] Twelve of the characters present at the Council speak, and three of these tell stories in which they quote the speech of other characters not present.* In his story Glóin quotes both the messenger from Mor-

* Gimli, Glóin's son, attends the Council but does not speak.

dor and the Dwarf-king Dáin; in his story Boromir quotes the unknown voice that recites the prophetic poem in his dream; and Gandalf ventriloquizes for at least five characters, one of whom (Radagast) quotes another (Saruman).* All of this speech and reported speech produces a set of nested frame narratives, with the deepest embedding being Radagast's quotation of Saruman as reported in Gandalf's story.

I only have two things to add to the masterly explication of the Council in Shippey's *J.R.R. Tolkien: Author of the Century*. First, it is important to emphasize that in this chapter Tolkien relies upon a conceit of accurate reportage in all the quoted speeches. That is, he does not attempt to show characters imposing any of their own speaking style on the speeches they quote. We simply hear Gaffer Gamgee's, Radagast's, Saruman's, Denethor's, and the messenger from Mordor's voices without any signs of deliberate filtering by the speaker who is telling the particular tale. Second, not only does each character have a different and distinct "mode of speech," but the chapter includes multiple texts and references still others.[3] The "Seek for the sword that was broken" poem from Faramir's and Boromir's dreams, Bilbo's "All that is gold does not glitter" poem, Isildur's scroll, and the Ring inscription in the Black Speech and its translation into the Common Speech are all italicized, indicating that they—like Bilbo's birthday speech and the multitude of poems encountered to this point in the narrative—are meant to be taken as texts that have been inserted into the larger text of *The Lord of the Rings*. These inserted texts advance the plot, represent features of the characters, or enact the themes of the narrative—although perhaps not as much as the speech and reported speech in the chapter. Throughout, Tolkien's rhetorical skills are on full display, producing, as Shippey notes, a tour de force of speech variation that ranges from Gaffer Gamgee's impromptu malapropism ("changes for the worst" rather than "worse") to Saruman's highly polished rhetoric that manages to sound lofty while saying nothing at all, to Elrond's elegant, accurate, and sophisticated anachronism.

* Seven, if you count reciting the Ring inscription as quoting Sauron and reading Isildur's scroll as quoting Isildur.

However, nothing about Tolkien's adroit handling of speech variation, his masterful rhetoric, or his ability to avoid reader confusion while nesting speeches within speeches, is fundamentally different from what great modernist writers have done in their works. Associating each character with a distinctive speaking or narrating style is an utterly normal feature of twentieth-century works of literature, and, although he is certainly good at producing it, Tolkien neither invented nor perfected this kind of multivocality. Expanding "The Council of Elrond" to novel length and having each chapter be narrated by a different character would just be *As I Lay Dying in Middle-earth.* It is not Tolkien's multivocality that makes his mature works so distinctive, but his *heterotextuality.*

After brief descriptions of the characters who are present—ending with the introduction of the newly arrived Boromir—the Council proper begins with a comment from the narrator that "Not all that was spoken and debated in the Council need now be told. Much was said of events in the world outside, especially in the South, and in the wide lands east of the Mountains." The narrative appears to be focalized through Frodo, since that passage continues by noting that Frodo had heard rumors of these things, but the story of Glóin the dwarf, from the Lonely Mountain, was new to him. We might conclude, therefore, that Frodo is the narrator who says that not all the content of the Council is being reported in the chapter, particularly when his feelings of shame, fear, and trepidation at holding up the Ring are described, but this is never stated explicitly, and it is certainly possible that we are supposed to take the chapter as a joint production by Bilbo and Frodo (Bilbo, after all, says he tried to take some notes).[4] In either case, the reader must interpret the subsequent discussion—as extensive as it is—as only a partial transcript of all that was said. This seems reasonable if we take the first story presented, the tale of Glóin from the Lonely Mountain, as representative of the approximate narrative pace of the speakers and contrast this to the pace of the narration that actually occurs.

Immediately after Glóin has finished speaking, Elrond, acting, in Shippey's words, like a good committee chair, establishes the purpose of the meeting, sets the agenda for the subsequent debate, and then begins his own tale.[5] The pace of this narrative is markedly faster than that of Glóin's tidings, which had included quoted speech and descriptions of the quality of the voice and inference as to the state of mind of the messenger from Mordor, whose words "held both menace and deceit."[6] Elrond relates the deep history of Sauron and the Rings of Power, but his exact words (which are said to have taken most of the morning to speak) are not reported and instead the reader gets a single-paragraph summary of the forging of the Rings in the Second Age: "Then through all the years that followed he traced the Ring; but since that history is elsewhere recounted, even as Elrond himself set it down in his books of lore, it is not here revealed."[7]

This is a good, clear example of Tolkien's heterotextuality in the midst of the greatest density of multivocality in the chapter. The narrative implies a set of relationships between two sets of events (the discussion at the Council of Elrond and the history relating to the forging of the Rings of Power) and two or more texts (the chapter "The Council of Elrond" in *The Fellowship of the Ring*, and Elrond's books of lore). The text we are reading is identified as being incomplete in two ways: It does not contain a full transcript of the things said in the Council about events in the South and the East, and much of the history that Elrond related is "not here recalled" since it can be found in his lore-books.* Not only the existence of those books of lore is implied, but their accessibility, since it makes little sense for the narrator to explain that he is leaving out information because that material can be found elsewhere if it would be impossible for the reader to consult the necessary books (a dynamic that includes the reader in the world of the text's internal narrative). This more abstract heterotextuality is then augmented by the inclusion in the narrative of items marked typographically as textual: the poems, scroll, and Ring inscription. Although each of the italicized items might be thought of as existing within its own frame narrative (the frame for Isildur's scroll is the story Gandalf tells of finding it in Minas

---

* This latter point is what suggests that Bilbo may be one of the authors of "The Council of Elrond" chapter: He was in a much better position to know what is in Elrond's books of lore than Frodo ever would have been.

Tirith), Elrond's books of lore are *not* a frame narrative unless we want to infer that the brief summary of the Second Age that precedes mention of the books was actually drawn from them—which is not impossible but seems to be a bit of a stretch. The overall effect is to create the subtle impression that the text that the reader possesses is made up of other texts, all of which may have different authors and transmission histories. Note that this impression does not rely on the reader being aware of the existence of the frame narrative that *The Lord of the Rings* is a translation of the Red Book of Westmarch or even having read the introductory material that sets up that frame: "The Council of Elrond" chapter by itself creates the impression of heterotextuality.

Tolkien's heterotextuality is subtle: The reader is not required to sift through contradictory materials or piece together a narrative out of nonchronological fragments. There is just a slight impression that the narrative being read has been itself constructed out of other texts rather than being the perfectly consistent emanations of an Author-God. Heterotextuality is an essential component of the famous "impression of depth" that Tolkien's works create, the sense that behind the immediate text "there was a coherent, consistent, deeply fascinating world about which he had no time (then) to speak."[8] Tolkien himself identified this quality in works of medieval literature that had "deep roots in the past" that were "made of tales often told before and elsewhere, and of elements that derive from remote times, beyond the vision or awareness of the poet."[9] He believed that part of the attraction of *The Lord of the Rings* was "due to glimpses of a large history in the background: an attraction like that of viewing far off an unvisited island, or seeing the towers of a distant city gleaming in a sunset mist."[10]

Scholars have made significant progress in explaining the ways that Tolkien creates this impression of depth, attributing it to four major factors: (1) the vast size and intricate detail of the background Tolkien created for his imagined world; (2) the ways he refers to this background material through seemingly casual and incomplete allusion; (3) the logical gaps and apparent inconsistencies in the stories; and (4) the variations in style within given texts.[11] All four of these characteristics are, to a significant degree, effects of the tortuous composition-histories of the texts. Although Tolkien may not have set out to create a complex, multilayered textual archive as a background for subsequent work, once this resource existed he exploited it, and the ways in which he both drew upon and modified the archive created a textual patchwork whose heterogeneity in both content and style works in concert with the other factors to produce the impression of depth by implying that multiple and different written works were created in the imagined world.

THE PRESENCE OF a frame narrative implies the influence of at least two narrators, one for the frame and one for the story in the frame, even when the name of only one author—Geoffrey Chaucer, William Faulkner, Toni Morrison, J.R.R. Tolkien—is on the book's cover. Scholarly editions of old texts likewise imply the influence of both the editor (given credit on the cover) and the author of the text being edited (even when unknown and thus uncredited). The incorporation into a prose text of poems, maxims, precepts, songs, or wise sayings, or of passages identified as having separate sources, similarly implies the influence of more than one writer. Such multivocality has long been recognized as an important characteristic of a multitude of literary works, from medieval masterpieces such as *The Canterbury Tales* and Boccaccio's *Decameron* to modernist touchstones like Joyce's *Ulysses*, Faulkner's *As I Lay Dying* and *The Sound and the Fury*, and Alice Walker's *The Color Purple*.

At its most basic, multivocality is simply an assertion or implication that different sections of a text are the work of different narrators or fictionalized authors. The statement "Seven of the footnotes in this book were dictated to me by my pet unicorn, Clarence,"* could theoretically produce a sense of multivocality even if those footnotes were in no obvious way different in content or style from the rest of the text, indicating that the assertion of multivocality depends primarily upon established narrative conventions of text-attribution. With a nod to Walter Ong, let us note that *the writer's narrators are always a fiction*.[12] Support for

* This one wasn't—Clarence.

the near universality of this convention in over five hundred years of Western literature can be found in the complete absence of plagiarism charges leveled against the authors of multivocal texts: No one has gone in search of the "real" Wife of Bath, or Vardaman ("My mother is a fish") Bundren, or Quentin Compson, and no copyright lawsuits have been filed on behalf of Molly Bloom, or Nettie and Celia Harris. But despite the power of the convention—which allows us to attribute the same narrative to both Chaucer and the character the Wife of Bath—bare assertion is neither necessary nor always sufficient for production of an effective-enough illusion of multivocality. If the footnotes attributed to Clarence are not in some way different from those that are not, the assertion is unlikely to be enough to convince the reader, and if the footnotes have some characteristics that make them appear to be more likely to have been written by Clarence than by me, the assertion may be unnecessary. The key factor is the ability of one author to produce segments of text that, in their differences from their text-matrix, suggest that they were produced by a different author. However, producing a convincing-enough illusion—despite the aid of the narrative conventions—is not easy, which perhaps explains why the ability to write in different "voices" is one of the more highly praised characteristics of canonical authors. Part of what makes Chaucer or Joyce or Walker great is their ability to make different sections of a literary work have enough stylistic difference from one another that they appear to have been narrated by different characters.

And yet we still attribute a multivocal narrative to a single author: Absolutely no one questions the idea that the words of "Leopold Bloom," "Stephen Dedalus," and "Molly Bloom" were all written by James Joyce, whose identity provides an organizing principle for the text of *Ulysses*. The illusion, assisted as it is by narrative convention, is strong but not overpowering. To the best of my knowledge no one has suggested that Nora Barnacle (or anyone else) *really* wrote the words *Ulysses* indicates as being thought by Molly Bloom, and scholars and critics seem to be in agreement that the chapters attributed to Adie, Vardaman, Jewel, Darl, Anse, and Dewey Dell, or to Benjy, Quentin, Jason, and Dilsey, are all characteristically "Faulknerian" in style. Similarly, the letters attributed to Celie and those attributed to Nettie are both recognized as exhibiting the stylistic characteristics of Alice Walker, not some other writers. Thus we see that the narrative multivocality so celebrated in modernist and subsequent fiction is subordinated to the overarching organizational principle of the "Author Function" of a given work.* All stylistic and content variations are categorized under the author's name, and this process in an important way homogenizes them, transforming all the variation associated with each fictitious narrator into a single category: Joycean, Faulknerian, Walkeresque. Modernist and later texts, although proudly multivocal, remain textually homogeneous, interpreted by readers as the productions of a single author.

Tolkien's mature works operate quite differently. Rather than explicitly marking the changes in narrator—even those implied by or explicitly identified in his frame narratives—Tolkien obscures some of the multivocality of *The Hobbit* and in particular *The Lord of the Rings* behind the conceit of a translation preceded by a long transmission-history and a complex composition process. Although it is possible to make a good guess as to which chapters should be attributed to Bilbo, Frodo, and Sam, we cannot be entirely sure, and we have very little idea of what was added to the text by subsequent editors and redactors such as Findegil, the King's Writer. In contrast to the modernists, who greatly emphasized the stylistic variation among their narrators, Tolkien's prose style is generally consistent at the surface level, with no obvious stylistic markers for each implied narrator. We might assume that Bilbo would be responsible for the more playful tone of the first few chapters of *The Lord of the Rings*—"and the Hobbiton post-office was blocked, and the Bywater post-office was snowed under," the amusing labels on the items being given away after the party, and perhaps the confused thoughts of the itinerant fox—but there is no obvious stylistic differentiation between what we presume to be Frodo's narration and

---

* Old chestnuts Roland Barthes's "The Death of the Author" and Michel Foucault's "What Is an Author?" are still useful despite their limitations of being more than half a century old and all too obviously products of their time. Michel Foucault, "What Is an Author?" in *The Foucault Reader*, ed. Paul Rabinow (New York: Pantheon, 1984), 101–20; Roland Barthes, "The Death of the Author," in *Image, Music, Text*, trans. Stephen Heath (New York: Hill, 1977), 142–48.

the material that follows after the point at which Sam must have picked up the story in the final chapters.[13]

Nevertheless, there are subtle variations in cultural knowledge, prose style, and vocabulary throughout *The Lord of the Rings* and *The Silmarillion* and, to a lesser extent, *The Hobbit*, and these variations are consistent and coordinated with both explicitly and implied variations in narrators—as these are constructed by the frame narratives. Although Tolkien's works are not nearly as blatantly multivocal as the modernist classics noted previously, they produce a far more effective impression of being composed and transmitted by multiple writers and editors.[14] No one reading *The Sound and the Fury* believes that in the Benjy chapters Faulkner was somehow transcribing the moment-by-moment thoughts of a specific mentally disabled individual, or that the exact words of Molly Bloom's soliloquy occurred in any mind other than Joyce's. If modernist works do create an impression of reality (and this is endlessly debated), it is psychological-reality or sociological-reality or aesthetic-reality, not simple, brute, factual existence. Tolkien's mature works, in contrast, do produce a convincing illusion that they are translations of real texts that actually once existed. The reason for this surprising difference in effect is that modernist works, while multivocal, are textually homogenous, while Tolkien's are both multivocal and heterotextual.

"The allusions in *The Lord of the Rings* are not illusory," notes Christopher Tolkien.[15] Because the development of Tolkien's legendarium had begun as early as the winter of 1916–17, by the time he began to write *The Lord of the Rings*, soon after the publication of *The Hobbit*, Tolkien had created a great mass of interconnected stories, poems, and histories upon which the later work was able to draw.[16] The "songs and digressions like Aragorn's lay of Tinúviel, Sam Gamgee's allusions to the Silmaril and the Iron Crown, Elrond's account of Celebrimbor, and dozens more" were linked to stories in texts that physically existed. When Tolkien used the phrase "vast backcloths" to describe this material, the adjective was no exaggeration.[17] The sheer size of just the published record is staggering, including as it does *The Silmarillion*; *Unfinished Tales*; *The Book of Lost Tales, Part One* and *Part Two*; *The Lays of Beleriand*; *The Shaping of Middle-earth*; and sections of *The Lost Road*, *Morgoth's Ring*, *The War of the Jewels*, and *The Children of Húrin*. And because Tolkien's writing process regularly incorporated multiple revisions and reworkings, behind all the published material there are additional drafts, partially edited copies, riders, canceled pages, and even lost texts.[18]

For example, there are twelve published versions of Tolkien's story of the tragic hero Túrin (whose name is mentioned by Elrond at the end of the Council and referred to by the narrative voice in Sam's fight against Shelob) written over the course of approximately forty years. The earliest, "Turambar and the Foalókë," was composed between 1917 and 1919, and the last, parts of the *Narn i Chîn Húrin* and some Túrin material in the *Grey Annals*, was written in the 1950s.[19] These texts range from chronicles of differing lengths and levels of detail to poems, summaries, and elaborated, novelistic narratives—a network of revisions and rewritings in which each successive version draws on what came before, continuously evolving while retaining a core story.[20] The Túrin story is only one—and not the oldest—of the three "Great Tales" at the heart of the Silmarillion narrative, but its complex and reticulated textual history is characteristic.[21]

Thus by the time Tolkien eventually came to write *The Lord of the Rings*, he had created a massive textual archive. The size of these "backcloths," their detail and their existence as texts—in contrast to the apparently sketched, fragmentary, or purely imagined backgrounds of other works of fantasy—generates two major aesthetic effects. First, the references to the background are sufficiently diverse to create the impression that there is an extensive and heterogeneous archive.[22] Unlike, for example, H. P. Lovecraft, who repeatedly refers to a very small suite of imaginary texts and places, Tolkien invokes a great number of different stories, characters, events, and objects.[23] These references, scattered through the text and not possessing any obvious tight cohesion among themselves, can be invoked in a nonsystematizing way even though they, as a result of their development as a connected body of legend, possess an internal consistency of their own.[24] Second, the detail of the referenced background material produces the sense that the world extends both temporally and physically beyond the text. For example, two brief references to the ruined town of Tharbad imply both that the geography of Middle-earth is much more extensive than the landscape passed through by the characters and that there is a deep history beyond the main narrative.[25] The wood smoke that rises over Coombe that the hobbits and Strider see during their journey to Weathertop, even though that village is hidden from the view of the characters and plays no significant role in the story, implies that the world of the text is richly imagined even at the periphery of the narrative.[26]

When the Fellowship is deep in the Mines of Moria, Aragorn reassures the other companions by telling them that Gandalf "is surer of finding the way home in a blind night than the cats of Queen Berúthiel."[27] The flesh of Shelob was so tough that it "could not be pierced by any strength of men, not though Elf or Dwarf should forge the steel or the hand of Beren or of Túrin wield it."[28] The horn that Éowyn gives Merry "came from the Hoard of Scatha the Worm."[29] Shippey's approximation of similar references as "dozens" is probably conservative, even if we limit our count to those times when the characters or narrator mention people, places, things, or events that are entirely unknown to the reader. These references are not treated as invocations of arcana, nor do they usually become opportunities for historical lectures by a narrator; they are instead casual, offhand mentions of cultural material that the other characters in the conversation seem to understand, thus helping to create the impression that the characters are operating within a sophisticated historical culture that happens to be distinct from that of the readers.

A number of Tolkien's medieval sources and influences treat references similarly. In *Beowulf*, for example, the poet writes as if his audience has preexisting knowledge of the identity and significance of many characters, including Hygelac, Hrothulf, Éomer, and Onela.* Chaucer

---

* So, for example, the *Beowulf*-poet assumes that his readers know something about Éomer, the grandson of Offa, mentioned in line 1960, but this assumption was not even correct with regard to the scribe who around the year 1000 copied this part of *Beowulf*: He did not recognize Éomer as a proper name and so wrote "geomor" [mournful] in its place. Tolkien and other scholars concluded from this failure of understanding (among many other pieces of evidence) that the poem itself must antedate the scribe by more than a century. See KL4, 227.

refers to "Wade's Boat" and "Jakke Straw and his meynee" as if he assumes that his audience knows what these are, and the poet who wrote *Sir Gawain and the Green Knight* brings the evil sorceress Morgan le Fay into his story without ever explaining who she is or why she hates Queen Guenevere, presumably because the audience already knew.[30] These references were obviously not esoteric to the authors or their audiences—the assumption that readers would understand are probably not qualitatively different from a contemporary writer's assuming readers' knowledge of the name of the US president in a given year or the approximate distance from New York to Boston.

Both literary and ordinary discourse are filled with similar references, as writers and speakers presuppose an enormous amount of cultural background knowledge in their readers.* When they are correct in their assumptions about shared knowledge, references are useful because, through the phenomenon of *communicative economy*, they transmit more knowledge to the speaker than is contained in them alone by invoking information that had been acquired piecemeal and assembled in the minds of the audience over periods of time.[31] When the *Beowulf*-poet mentions Háma in line 1198, he is assuming that his audience already knows a story in which this character has something to do with King Eormenric and the marvelous Brosing necklace.[32] The poet does not have to retell the story but simply triggers the audience's recollection of it.

But when the shared cultural knowledge no longer exists, references cannot communicate more information than they themselves contain.[33] For readers whose cultural knowledge is substantially different than that of the original interpretive community, the reference is not a metonymic invocation of information external to the text but simply a noticeable

* It requires significant effort to compose a text of any length that does *not* include such references, which can come to seem alien (and alienating) in as little as a generation. For example, even in a relatively contemporary novel like Ken Kesey's *Sometimes a Great Notion* (1964), allusions to consumer products, political events, advertising campaigns, or popular music from as recent as the early 1960s can be incomprehensible to readers born after 1980, while to a reader born before 1970 these allusions do not even stand out as being cultural references. Anyone my age or younger who has had a child ask "what's a record?" after hearing the Dead or Alive song "You Spin Me Round (Like a Record)," or who has had to explain to a younger person why we say we "dial" a phone has firsthand experience with broken cultural references.

gap in knowledge. Because we no longer know the details of the stories behind the characters Éomer, Háma, and Unferth in *Beowulf*, there is a contrast between these references and their surrounding matrix. Such references, instead of transmitting information through communicative economy, now call particular attention to themselves for exactly the opposite reason: that the audience does not receive *any* knowledge from the references beyond their surface, denotative meanings.

These *broken references* are an inevitable effect of cultural change over time, so the presence of broken references in an artwork works to emphasize the distance between the reader and the author's original imagined audience.[34] The obscurity of references in medieval or ancient texts therefore produces a particular effect for the modern reader, the impression that, to repurpose Shippey's words, "there was a coherent, consistent, deeply fascinating" culture behind the text *and* that this culture is different from the one we inhabit.[35] We thus perceive simultaneously both the remarkable survival of these pieces of culture and their ruined and fragmentary nature. Tolkien reproduces this effect in *The Lord of the Rings* when his characters and narrator assume that other characters (and readers) know about Beren and Lúthien, the Silmaril and the Iron Crown, and many other references to Middle-earth's long history and complex cultures.

The effect is heightened by the casual manner in which characters employ references. Because the characters do not identify their references as unusual discourse, their invocation emphasizes an epistemological regime in which characters effortlessly understand the reference in detail while readers must rely on context and inference.* This unequal distribution of knowledge helps to generate the illusion that the background material in the story is of a historically factual kind, the sort of reference that a character would make without thinking it required explanation. For example, when Elrond says that, by accepting the quest of the Ring, Frodo has earned himself a seat among the great elf-friends, including "Hador and Húrin, and Túrin, and Beren himself," Elrond is not being deliberately abstruse, since obfuscation

---

* All a reader needs to understand the *denotative* meaning of Aragorn's reference is the common trope that cats see well in the dark.

would completely undercut his rhetorical aim of praising Frodo.[36] He is merely speaking in an idiom he expects to be understood, if not by the hobbit, then at least by the other elves at the Council, Gandalf, Aragorn, and perhaps Bilbo. Nevertheless, to the reader of *The Lord of the Rings*, the first three names in the list of elf-friends are at this point in the narrative entirely unknown. Their denotations are thus unavailable, and even any connotations beyond a generally positive notion of an "elf-friend" can only be interpreted in a local context.[37] The significance of the final elf-friend in the list, Beren, may be in part understood through Aragorn's earlier song and summary in "A Knife in the Dark," so by including this name, Tolkien implies that the accomplishments of the other elf-friends are similar in some way. But because the character making the reference apparently also understands the background of the stories of Hador, Húrin, and Túrin and acts as if he assumes that his hearers do also, readers must infer the existence of cultural information to which they are not privy. For them, Elrond's comparison is a broken reference that calls attention to itself exactly because it invokes a cultural context not available to the reading audience.

It is useful to draw some distinctions among the types of references. A simple broken reference at one time invoked a larger meaning in the minds of an audience but no longer does. Chaucer's mention of "Wade's Boat" is one such: Although the story is now lost to us, it appears to have existed for both Chaucer and his readers.* But authors can also feign the invocation of cultural knowledge by employing what appears to be a reference, but which in fact never referred to any particular cultural knowledge. This is a *pseudo-reference*. Chaucer's "Book of the Leon" may be an example, and Malory's "French Book" almost

---

* The Elizabethan scholar Thomas Speght, in his 1598 edition of *The Canterbury Tales*, certainly appears to have known about Wade's Boat; Larry D. Benson, ed., *The Riverside Chaucer*, 3rd ed. (Boston: Houghton Mifflin, 1988), 886. Speght's statement that he is passing over explaining Wade's Boat because everyone already knows the story makes me want to dig him up and beat him with his own femur. Wade's Boat is another example of a crux in medieval literature leading to Tolkienian literary production, in that Tolkien was apparently inspired enough by the fragmentary and enigmatic references to Wade and his boat *Guingelot* to try to incorporate them into his mythology via a reference to Wade of the Helsings (taken from the Old English poem *Widsith*) and by Eärendel's ship being named *Wingelot*; *Lays*, 142–44; *Peoples*, 371. And see John Garth, *Tolkien and the Great War: The Threshold of Middle-earth* (Boston: Houghton Mifflin, 2003), 86–87.

certainly is.[38] Closer to Tolkien's time, we find pseudo-references in early science fiction, fantasy, and horror, including the invented cryptic runic manuscript by Arne Saknussemm in Jules Verne's *A Journey to the Center of the Earth*, Lovecraft's *Necronomicon*, and Chambers's *King in Yellow*.[39] Although Tolkien was obviously not the first writer to invent such references, he was extraordinarily good at creating them, and the extent to which his many imitators have made it a cliché in fantasy literature indicates how effective the technique is in producing the impression of a large, lost cultural context.[40]

Note that there is no conscious experiential difference between a *reader's* perception of a pseudo-reference and one that is merely broken. That the *Beowulf* poet was referring to cultural knowledge that he assumed to be widespread, while Tolkien was drawing on background material he had written himself, is, in the case of any given reference, a difference in ontogeny rather than aesthetic effect.[41] Individual pseudo- and broken references will both be perceived in the same way by an audience that cannot access the requisite background information. In fact, Tolkien's references are almost all broken rather than pseudo-. According to three letters he wrote in 1956, only the cats of Queen Berúthiel did not already exist in the Legendarium when he wrote *The Lord of the Rings*.[42] The other pseudo-references, therefore, are at least in part an accident of publication history, since Tolkien originally intended to publish the Silmarillion material.[43] But whether originally intended or not, the seemingly broken links between individual references and their backgrounds generate the impression of significant cultural distance between the text and the contemporary reader.

However, because Tolkien had the Silmarillion material to draw upon, his references, while seeming broken to the audience, are coherent in their underlying stories. They thus have the logical consistency and lack of overt contradiction characteristic of real traditions. A similar overall coherence of background gives *Beowulf* much of its particular quality of feeling historically true, or as Tolkien put it, as taking place in "the named lands of the North," even though the poem includes trolls, sea monsters, and a dragon.[44] Linked to a coherent (if not textually stable) body of legends, the references possess a consistency that, while perhaps not obvious to the reader, nevertheless gives the impression that the world they refer to exists on its own so that the details are not ad hoc inventions of the author. Not every reference needs to be linked to a definite extratextual antecedent to produce this *Zusammenhang*, but the combination of many links with few overt contradictions produces the impression that another culture is both underlying and distant from the text.

At the very beginning of his composition of *The Lord of the Rings*, Tolkien may not have intended to produce this particular effect, but by 1938, according to Carpenter, he had mostly abandoned hope that the Silmarillion material would be published.[45] He therefore cannot have assumed that his readers would be able to identify the references and allusions in the evolving *The Lord of the Rings*.[46] Thus, because of the contingencies of publishing history, the references in Tolkien's works present some complicated problems. Tolkien was in a situation unlike that of either the *Beowulf* poet, who did not know his references would be broken, or Verne, Lovecraft, or Chambers, who knew that their references were entirely pseudo-. His references were unbroken for himself but pseudo- to his audience, which had no access to the referenced material, so he had to shape the references in *The Lord of the Rings* subtly so that some of their meaning could be reconstructed from context, thus allowing readers to experience the distancing effect of a broken reference without fatally compromising the information content of a given passage.[47] Readers who are familiar with *The Silmarillion* may have a richer understanding of the significance of the compliment Elrond is paying to Frodo by comparing him to Hador, Húrin, and Túrin, but even naive readers can still extract enough information from context to make general sense of the passage while at the same time experiencing the aesthetic effect of the broken references.

When a reference is decoupled from its background informational context but nevertheless continues to be replicated in its own surface form it can evolve into what scholars of oral tradition call a *traditional referent*.* Like a reference, a traditional referent invokes previously accu-

* It is unfortunate that "referen*ce*" and "referen*t*" are so similar, but the nomenclature has already been established for the former in literary studies and the latter in scholarship on oral tradition.

mulated information through communicative economy.* But unlike a reference, which is linked to *external* cultural information, a traditional referent is connected only to information *inside* the traditional discourse.[48] Repetition of particular phrases or formulas within a tradition creates links between individual instantiations and other appearances of the same words within the tradition, thus enabling a variant of communicative economy that invokes "a context enormously larger and more echoic than the text or the work itself," but still within the discursive tradition.[49] For participants in a tradition, then, the appearance of repeated phrases such as *korythaiolos Hektor*" [Hector of the Glancing Helm] or *glaukopis Athene* [Gray-Eyed Athena] in Homer's *Iliad* are able to invoke the entire traditional persona of a character even if the particular characteristics of a historical or literary antecedent have been completely lost.[50]

A broken reference becomes a traditional referent when it is replicated *in its own form* and can thus be lexicalized within the discourse.[51] Referents are therefore under substantial selection pressure to evolve formal features that contribute to mnemonic (and hence replicative) stability.[52] Traditional referents are thus often efficient ways of solving problems of the interlinking of form and content. *Beowulf maþelode,*

---

* The disassociation of the inferred denotative meaning of a reference from its original connotations is what enables semantic change. In *Beowulf,* "Háma" may have originated as a reference to a specific story about the acquisition of a necklace, but after enough cultural change the character's name might only be an archetype of a thief. When there has been sufficient cultural change in the audience of a referent, the surface features and literal meaning may even take on meanings that contradict the import of the original reference. For example, in the earlier Icelandic sagas in which he appears, Bjarni Brodd-Helgason, although called Víga-Bjarni [Killer Bjarni], is a peacemaker and a reluctant fighter who received his sobriquet not out of lust for murder but from a very complex family situation in which he reluctantly had to kill some relatives for reasons of both justice and self-preservation. Víga-Bjarni's *name,* however, appears to have influenced writers who were more temporally and physically distant from people who remembered him to depict the character as a blood-loving, death-dealing maniac: The influence of the name itself was too strong once its link to particular stories was broken. The conservation of the surface form leads to a significant change in meaning. This phenomenon may be called the Killer-Barney Effect; Michael D.C. Drout, "Reference and Referentiality," in *Tradition and Influence in Anglo-Saxon Literature: An Evolutionary, Cognitivist Approach* (New York: Palgrave MacMillan, 2013). For a much more detailed discussion of Bjarni Brodd-Helgason's treatment in various sagas, see Gísli Sigurðsson, *The Medieval Icelandic Saga and Oral Tradition: A Discourse on Method* (Cambridge: Harvard University Press, 2004), 146–57.

bearn Ecgþeowes [Beowulf made a speech, the son of Ecgtheow] fills out an entire metrical line, introduces the character, and reminds the reader of his heritage. *Korythaiolos Hektor* similarly meets a metrical need.[53] Such references are consistent with a tradition's poetic requirements and so remain stable as long as the tradition itself persists. The conservation of form leads to the well-studied phenomenon of traditional referents being marked linguistically with "poetic" features of a given language, features that are *tradition-dependent* and thus vary from one cultural context to another,[54] but that, in Modern English, would include a word or phrase's metrical profile, alliteration, and rhyme. Furthermore, because those elements of a discourse that are not fixed will of necessity change more rapidly than those that are, fixed elements like traditional referents are more likely to preserve archaisms. The interlinking of formal features with potential archaism contributes to the marked linguistic quality of the surface form of the traditional referent, which by its being broken is already marked in terms of content.[55] The combination of formal features and broken content makes the traditional referent stand out as being different from the surrounding text.[56]

A number of the references in *The Lord of the Rings* exhibit features of traditional referents. The formal patterning of Elrond's comparison of Frodo to heroes of the First Age can be made more obvious if we lineate the passage and underscore the vocalic alliteration, boldface the consonantal alliteration, and italicize the rhymes:

> elf-friends of old,
Hador
and ***H***_úrin_,
and *Túrin*,
and Beren **h**imself,
were assembled

The sentence is organized paratactically, without subordination. The repeated coordinating conjunction "and" is an example of anaphora, the repetition of words at the beginning of clauses for the purpose of emphasis.[57] This reference may not have fully become a traditional referent that would be repeated in precisely its own form (we cannot tell, because we only read it once), but it has many of the characteristics of one: It is a broken reference, and it is marked by the "poetic" linguistic features of anaphora, alliteration (both consonantal and vocalic), and rhyme. Poetic features are also found in the instances of name-epithet combinations where these appear in *The Lord of the Rings*. Note the repetition of the /h/ and /r/ sounds in "**H**ado**r** the Golden**hair**ed," of /e/ in "Elrond the Halfelven," or /k/ in the ***C**ats of* ***Qu**een Berúthiel.* Goldbe**rr**y's epithets "daughte**r** of the **R**ive**r**," "**R**ive**r**-daughte**r**," and "**R**ive**r**-woman's daughte**r**" not only include repetition of /r/ sounds but are metrical with near-rhyme on "river" and "daughter."[58]

Because they are a type of broken reference, traditional referents create the impression of depth in the same manner: by invoking a cultural context not possessed by the reader. But a traditional referent also produces the impression of a different kind of depth. Because the form of the referent is linguistically marked, readers interpret it as coming from a source or author different from that of the rest of the text. This phenomenon is most obvious when a character explicitly quotes an older work, as when Sam recites some lines from "Gil-galad was an Elven-king," or when someone employs a proverb, as when Théoden says "but it has long been said: *oft evil will shall evil mar.*"[59] But even when there is not an explicit in-text indication like "it has long been said," linguistically marked words or phrases imply that a character or narrator is referring to previously existing texts or oral traditional phrases. When Glorfindel says "Yet oft in lies, truth is hidden," readers do not think that the elf made up the saying on the spot but that he is repeating a bit of Elvish wisdom.[60]

Any text that is in some way culturally distant from a reader can include broken references, but only one that is also old is likely to contain traditional referents, whose inclusion creates the impression of a series of transmissions and therefore implies the existence of a tradition—the same way a smoothly polished pebble in a stream implies a long history of weathering. Traditional referents are therefore themselves markers of heterotextuality, as their existence implies lines of transmission of other stories, to other people, throughout a culture.

AKIN TO THE USE OF broken references and traditional referents, the absence of seemingly relevant information and the presence of apparent contradictions also help create the impression of a deep textual history. Readers know intuitively that a work of fiction, at least at the level of content, was under the absolute control of an author, who was able to eliminate inconsistencies and contradictions from the text by fiat through the act of revision. The presence of apparent contradictions, then, suggests that the text is not entirely under control of this God-like author but is instead a compilation of different discursive sources, of multiple minds and hands. Tolkien drafted, redrafted, and revised *The Lord of the Rings*,[61] so we know that he was not entirely averse to emending his text to eliminate contradiction. For example, when correspondent Rhona Beare pointed out that, although elves were said to ride horses without saddle, bridle, or rein, Glorfindel's horse in *The Fellowship of the Ring* was said to have not only a bridle, but a bit,[62] Tolkien acknowledged the apparent inconsistency in a letter and emended accordingly so that in later printings the texts reads "headstall."[63] However, he either did not catch or decided not to change the apparent contradiction in Glorfindel's saying that he would shorten the stirrups for Frodo, or that the hobbit's hand leaves the bridle and grips the hilt of his sword when confronted by the Black Riders.[64]

The conflicting stories of how Bilbo acquired the Ring from Gollum are perhaps the greatest inconsistency of all, though that inconsistency was originally external to *The Lord of the Rings* and differs depending upon which edition of *The Hobbit* has been read. In the original published version of *The Hobbit*, Bilbo had found the Ring lying on the floor of the goblin-tunnels and put it in his pocket, just as he does in the revised edition. But in that original text, Gollum had offered to give Bilbo a present (which turned out to have been the Ring) if the hobbit won the riddle-game. When Bilbo won via the questionable "What have I got in my pocket?" question, Gollum went back to his island to get the Ring and discovered that it was lost. Cringing and apologetic, he returned to Bilbo and explained the properties of the Ring he no longer had to give. Bilbo then insisted that instead of giving him the Ring, Gollum must show him the way out of the tunnels, and Gollum did. They parted amicably.

This original version of the story was a significant problem for Tolkien when he developed the plot of *The Lord of the Rings*, as Gollum's being willing simply to hand over the Ring contradicted Tolkien's thoughts about its power to make its owners immoderately possessive. Eventually, Tolkien hit upon the idea of revising *The Hobbit* to eliminate Gollum's willingness to give away the Ring. Although he did not expect his publisher to revise the original text, he rewrote the key passages in such a way that they could replace the older ones without necessitating re-typesetting the entire chapter. Then in 1951 Allen and Unwin unexpectedly printed an entirely new edition that silently incorporated Tolkien's revisions.

This solved one problem while creating another. How would readers who knew only the 1937–1950 *Hobbit*—and it is important to remember that in 1951, this was *all* the readers of *The Hobbit*, ever—understand the treatment of the incident in *The Lord of the Rings*? Tolkien's solution was to reveal in *The Lord of the Rings* that Bilbo had told the dwarves, Gandalf, and everyone else a false story that was intended to put the hobbit's claim to the Ring beyond question—although he eventually told the truth to Frodo. This solved the problem of the conflict between the pre-1951 versions of *The Hobbit* and *The Lord of the Rings*, but it spawned another problem, one that I remember being confused about and my father having no explanation for: What was Bilbo talking about when he said he had told another story? For readers who had read only the *post*-1951 *Hobbit*, Bilbo's admitting to having told a different version of the story made no sense because the version of the scene in that and subsequent editions of *The Hobbit* was fully consistent with what was said in *The Lord of the Rings*!

Tolkien's revisions thus produce an inconsistency around the story of Bilbo's acquisition of the Ring no matter which edition of *The Hobbit* one reads: Either the story will conflict with the story told in *The Lord of the Rings*, or it will not conflict with the story and will therefore conflict with the narrator's, Bilbo's, Gandalf's, and Frodo's assertions that the story in *The Hobbit* conflicts with the story as summarized in *The Lord of the Rings*. You could not find a better example of heterotextuality than this, particularly once it became unlikely that a reader would have read the pre-1951 version of the story: Not only is there a text behind the story in *The Lord of the Rings—The Hobbit*, which we can read for ourselves—but there must be two different *versions* of that text, since the one we have read does not have the same material in it as one we are being told about.

Similar—though perhaps less dramatic—inconsistencies are not unknown in other literary texts. In the notes to "*Beowulf*: The Monsters and the Critics," Tolkien had argued that "minor discrepancies" in *Beowulf* were not proof of composite authorship, arguing that:

> It is very difficult, even in a newly invented tale of any length, to avoid such defects; more so still in rehandling old and oft-told tales. The points that are seized in the study, with a copy that can be indexed and turned to and fro (even if never read straight through as it was meant to be), are usually such as may easily escape an author and more easily his natural audience. . . . Modern printed tales, that have presumably had the advantage of proof-correction, can even be observed to hesitate in the heroine's Christian name.*

But even while asserting that "minor" discrepancy is not proof of composite *authorship*, Tolkien points out that small discrepancies are the result of "rehandling" older material, and thus the presence of such apparent discrepancies would be characteristic of a text whose author is making use of previously existing discourses, "old and oft-told tales." And Tolkien in fact makes a virtue of what might originally have been error by not emending away other apparent contradictions in the text. Most famously, Tom Bombadil states: "Eldest, that's what I am. Mark my words, my friends: Tom was here before the river and the trees; Tom remembers the first raindrop and the first acorn," but when Gandalf prepares Théoden for his meeting with Treebeard, the wizard says that "Treebeard is Fangorn, the guardian of the forest; he is the oldest of the Ents, the oldest living thing that still walks beneath the Sun upon this

---

* A penciled note in the B-version of the lecture provides a hint as to why Tolkien may have noticed this particular discrepancy: "the heroine's very name changed from *Edith* to Ethel"; *B&C*, 432, my emphasis. *MC*, 46–47n28.

Middle-earth."[65] The seeming conflict between the two claims has led to a minor scholarly argument that has gone on for over thirty years.[66] Tolkien might have finessed the apparent contradiction, the way he said he could have with Glorfindel's horse's tack, explaining away the discrepancy, but instead he let it stand.[67]

Other minor inconsistencies also remain, although it is not always known if Tolkien was aware of them.[68] Among the most significant are the seeming loss of a full day from the chronology when Sam and Frodo are in Shelob's lair (a discrepancy that may or may not be intentional); Aragorn's claim that Sauron does not permit his name to be spoken being contradicted by the words of both the messenger to Dáin and the Mouth of Sauron; Gandalf's assertion at the Council of Elrond that the Nazgûl possess the Nine Rings seeming not to agree with either his earlier statement that Sauron gathered the Nine Rings to himself, and Galadriel's comment that Sauron "holds" the Nine.[69] Whether there are five or six ponies stabled at Crickhollow may be a contradiction or an unrevised error.[70] And there are other apparent inconsistencies in chronology and between information in the main body of the text and either the appendices or the posthumously published *Silmarillion*. For example, the writing on the Moria Westgate calls the home of the dwarves "Moria," but this name, which means the "Black Pit" in Sindarin, would not have been given until after the dwarf-kingdom there was destroyed, long after the doors were made.[71] When he meets the hobbits in the Shire, the elf Gildor introduces himself as being of the house of Finrod, although Finrod never married because he prophesied that he would have no kingdom to leave to a son.[72]

Tolkien also leaves gaps in the story, not just those in pseudo-references (like the cats of Queen Berúthiel), but also in unresolved plot points. The identity of the old man seen by Aragorn, Legolas, and Gimli at the eaves of Fangorn is never confirmed in material published during Tolkien's lifetime. Gandalf says it was not him, but the man is wearing a hat, not the hood that Saruman is said to wear.[73] The voice that says "Verily I come, I come to you!" could be Frodo or the Ring itself.[74] The tale does not tell us what eventually happens to Shelob, and although the Lord of the Nazgûl is defeated, the narrator only tells us that his voice was never heard again "in that age of the world."[75] The fate of the entwives is also not known from the text, with Treebeard at times seeming to assume that they are extinct but at others hoping for a reunion.[76]

Other inconsistencies arose when the larger context of a scene or phrase was radically modified in Tolkien's revision process but the original scene or image remained unchanged despite the new context. For example, Tolkien originally had the Ranger whom the hobbits meet in Bree be a hobbit himself. "Trotter" had suffered some sort of torture by Sauron.[77] The Black Riders, he tells the hobbits,

> "will come on you in the wild, in some dark place where there is no help. Do you wish them to find you? They are terrible!"
>
> The hobbits looked at him, and saw with surprise that his face was drawn as if with pain, and his hands clenched the arms of his chair. The room was very quiet and still, and the light seemed to have grown dim. For a while he sat with unseeing eyes as if walking in distant memory or listening to sounds in the Night far away.[78]

But the character of Trotter the wild hobbit became the man Aragorn, the heir of Isildur, and not only is there no evidence that he had ever encountered the Nazgûl before the attack on Weathertop, but such an interaction seems to be ruled out by the chronological material in Appendix B. Yet the passage in the published text remains close in spirit and takes imagery from the "Trotter" drafts of the chapter.[79] That Aragorn gives every impression of having distant memories triggered by the thought of the Black Riders, despite there being no narrative warrant for this, and the unexplained capitalization of Night both strongly suggest that part of this passage comes from another text that includes different information than is presented in the reader's copy of *The Lord of the Rings*.

In later stages of the composition of *The Lord of the Rings*, Tolkien decided that Sauron would not allow the flying Nazgûl to cross the Great River until much closer to the start of open warfare against Gondor, but he had not made this decision when he wrote "The Ring Goes South," in which we read:

> It was the cold chill hour before the first stir of dawn, and the moon was low. Frodo looked up at the sky. Suddenly he saw or felt a shadow pass over the high stars, as if for a moment they faded and then flashed out again. He shivered.
>
> "Did you see anything pass over?" he whispered to Gandalf, who was just ahead.
>
> "No, but I felt it, whatever it was," he answered. "It may be nothing, only a wisp of thin cloud."
>
> "It was moving fast then," muttered Aragorn, "and not with the wind."[80]

In the earlier draft of the passage printed in *The Return of the Shadow*, the narrator adds: "It did not sound as if he thought much of his own explanation."[81] Christopher Tolkien notes that "This incident was retained in *The Fellowship of the Ring*, but it is not explained. The Winged Nazgûl had not yet crossed the River."[82] This "mysterious passage of something against the stars" is never clarified, but if it is a high-flying flock of birds rather than a Nazgûl, why does Frodo shiver and Gandalf state that he felt something?[83] Like the scene of Strider shivering at the thought of the Black Riders, at this point in the narrative there is no visible contradiction—that only arises with additional information—but in retrospect this passage is also an inconsistency that can imply the existence of other texts that might make sense of the apparent contradiction.

Tolkien certainly could have revised away all of these seeming inconsistencies, but he did not: Some apparent contradictions he explained away in letters; others he ignored. Statements by authors that they do not know things inside their texts may be psychologically true, but the texts *are* fiction and thus, in a reader's mind, remain at a fundamental level under the author's ultimate control.[84] A compiler, however, has no such freedom, since he can at times lack important information because it was never recorded or has been lost. This imaginative stance justifies the appearance in Tolkien's work of "the inevitable flaws when plots, motives, symbols, are re-handled and pressed into service of the changed minds of a later time, used for the expression of ideas quite different from those which produced them," and the presence of these "flaws" implies both that behind the stories was a real history that their author was not at liberty to change and that the history itself existed in the form of stories and texts that might not include all the information desired by later readers.[85] Discrepancies and gaps contrast with the general consistency of the references in the text, but they end up contributing to the same impression of depth, making Tolkien's works seem as if they are not invented, but reported, not a new creation, but a continuation of a long tradition.*

The culture and history of Middle-earth that underlies *The Lord of the Rings* thus gives the impression of being mediated through texts, some of which are referred to in the body of the narrative itself; some, like the Red Book of Westmarch, invoked only in the book's apparatus; and some merely implied through variations in discourse or via the use of what appear to be traditional referents.[86] This textual depth makes Tolkien's works seem as though they are elements of a corpus "within a textual world" and accounts in part for their myth-like quality.[87] The impression of textual depth is created by the references to other, absent texts, which are, for the reader, broken references (and for the author may be, in some cases, pseudo-texts). For example, by having Sam recite lines that Aragorn identifies as being Bilbo's translation of *The Fall of Gil-galad*, "which is in an ancient tongue," Tolkien implies the existence of at least two texts that are not contained in *The Lord of the Rings*: the original lay and Bilbo's complete translation.[88] Similarly, Aragorn's recitation and retelling on Weathertop invokes both a poetic version of the Beren and Lúthien story written in "the mode that is called *ann-thennath* among the Elves" and also a written translation, unless Aragorn's comment that the poem's being "hard to render in our Common Speech," and his evaluation that his poem "is but a rough echo" of the original lay means that he is performing the remarkable compositional feat of translating poetry from one language into poetry in another in real time.[89] There are similar implications of textuality in the Túrin story, including the in-text statement that the version in the pub-

* I recognize that there is the potential for circularity in this argument, in that mere mistakes could end up being interpreted as clever, imaginative touches that produce the impression of depth (a similar problem plagues *Beowulf* criticism). But we can avoid circularity by noticing the difference in effect between simple mistakes—like the dropped lines noted by Christopher Tolkien in *The History of The Lord of the Rings* volumes—and the more complex contradictions noted in the preceding discussions.

lished *Silmarillion* is a compression of an originally much longer lay, the *Narn i Hîn Húrin*, which itself cannot be identical to the version of this text published in *Unfinished Tales*, since a lay would presumably be in poetry (written in Elvish by the Mannish poet Dírhaval), while the published *Narn* is in prose.[90] "The implication is that *Túrin* is a compressed *retextualization* of another text. This is where depth is again created by a claim of a[n] unknown text and a corresponding textual relation."[91]

The sense of cultural or textual depth is not solely generated by content. Variations in style also imply the influences of different authors or sources, thus giving the impression that a narrative has had an extensive textual history. The presence of a quotation indicates a source. An unattributed passage that sounds like it is a quotation implies almost as strongly that other texts are influencing an author. Sounding like a quotation, therefore, is one way that the prose style of one passage of a text can be detectably different from that of another. Segments of a text may differ in vocabulary (both of content- and of function-words), sentence length or structure, repetition or avoidance of rhyme and alliteration, and other linguistic features. A consistent variation of features between any two text segments gives the impression that a text has multiple authors or a history of compilation and transmission.[92]

In the published *Silmarillion* "styles change within units of text," with the "resulting disunity in the 1977 text producing a fitting effect"—the impression that *The Silmarillion* is a compilation of multiple sources.[93] "Tolkien succeeds in implying, merely by the stylistic differences, that the *Silmarillion* is indeed a compendious volume 'made long afterwards from sources of great diversity.' "[94] Tolkien's prose contains many instances of marked language, including anaphora, alliteration, rhyme, polysyndeton, parataxis, and repetition. "There are passages, short strings of sentences, individual sentences or even single clauses which read as if they were poetry adapted to prose," implying that the text as we have it was at some stage based on poetic texts that are unavailable to the reader in the "textual world."[95] The poetic language therefore creates the impression of heterotextuality and thus the same sorts of effects as the broken references or traditional referents, hinting to the reader that there is a much larger culture, possessed of long-standing traditions, behind the surface narrative.

Tolkien had composed several long poetic works, most significantly a version of the Túrin story in alliterative long lines and a long poem on Beren and Lúthien in octosyllabic rhyming couplets, as well as other, shorter poems on Middle-earth subjects.[96] A "relatively large number" of the apparently poetic passages in the Túrin chapter in *The Silmarillion* "go back explicitly to the verse *Túrin,*" such as: "**b**earing a **b**urden heavier than their **b**onds" and "that **gr**ief was **gr**aven on the **f**ace of Túrin and never **f**aded" and "he **w**alked as **o**ne **w**ithout **w**ish or purpose."[97] But there are no direct poetic sources for other, very similar passages in the same chapter, some of which come from parts of the narrative behind which there is verse, and others that appear not to have even any prose antecedents.[98]

These "poetic" passages that are not based upon the extant verse texts—such as "**t**all and **t**errible on that day looked **T**úrin, and the **h**eart of the **h**ost was up**h**eld as he **r**ode on the **r**ight hand of O**r**odreth"—are analogous to pseudo-references.[99] Just as pseudo-references produce in the reader the same effects as broken references, so too do both types of poetic interpolation signal the participation of the surface narrative in a textual tradition not immediately available to the reader whether or not there is an actual poem influencing the prose.

Features of the language that would not have been particularly unusual in poetry became marked when they were transferred into the prose narrative, making the interpolated material distinct from its surrounding matrix even when the text is not typographically distinct. Tolkien does something similar in *The Lord of the Rings* with the speech of Tom Bombadil, much of which, as Shippey notes, falls into "strongly marked two-stress phrases with or without rhyme or alliteration, usually with feminine or unstressed endings."[100] But Bombadil's poetic speaking is not lineated or printed in italics like the other poems in the text.

The stylistic heterogeneity in *The Silmarillion* is not entirely the result of the poetic origin of some of the passages, since other passages that appear to be just as "poetic" do not have their ultimate sources in poems. When we follow the evolution of the Túrin story word by word through its various textual incarnations, we find that language from the poems does not in general survive through multiple revisions, and many of the sections of the text that appear most markedly poetic "evolved sometimes suddenly, sometimes by slow steps of refinement, sometimes obviously by editorial action," rather than by being imported into the prose text from the poetry.[101] Furthermore, we see a concentration of poetic features in "central scenes, climaxes or privileged points in the narrative," passages that were, as examination of the textual history shows, extensively revised and reworked.[102]

The process of copying, revising, recopying, and converting a text from one genre to another—for example, from narrative prose to verse to annalistic prose and back to narrative prose—creates a textual tradition, where "with time the work incorporate[s] many layers and changes that are preserved or discarded according to the needs of the actual version worked on."[103] That the tradition was the production of a single author rather than of a distributed network of contributors does not prevent it from developing according to the dynamics of more "traditional" traditions; quite the opposite: That all the texts were written by Tolkien, that it was his single mind through which they passed and repassed as they were copied, revised, and reinvented, simply speeds up the cultural evolution that occurs in distributed traditions. Processes that might otherwise take a century or more could occur in decades, years, or even months. The iterative copying and revision of the text generates the same evolutionary pressures that shape traditional referents.[104] "Poetic" passages are more likely to be reproduced in their own forms than unmarked language with the same content because the linguistically marked passages are mnemonically superior and so less likely to be modified.[105] Even though Tolkien was producing written texts—presumably less labile than purely oral traditions—he was not forced to copy them verbatim. A text transferred from the page through the eyes to the brain and then through the hand and back to the page is shaped by various selection pressures. The form on the page has a certain inertia, but it may be that only selected features of that form remain after the passage through a mind: plot, perhaps, or theme, or a pattern of sounds.[106]

We see this evolution happening in the history of a short passage describing Túrin's tragic accidental killing of Beleg, his closest friend. Although the passage in *The Silmarillion* derives directly from the prose tradition, it has some formal links with the verse text:

> Then Túrin stood stone still and silent, staring on that **d**readful **d**eath, knowing what he had **d**one.[107]

> stone-faced he stood standing frozen
> on that **d**readful **d**eath his **d**eed knowing (ll. 1273–74).[108]

The particular alliterative sounds /s/ and /d/ have come through to the final version, as well as the pairing of "stone" with "stood" and "dreadful" with "death," but the precise wording has not been reproduced, demonstrating how an author's mind can transfer some formal patterns even in the absence of verbatim copying. Perhaps surprisingly, the later, prose version of the lines is more poetically effective than the original verse. The cliché "stone-faced" has been replaced by the descriptive (though still slightly clichéd) "stone still," a collocation that extends the alliteration to an additional word.

The evolution of traditional referents out of broken references and the appearance of pseudo-interpolations that cannot in their formal features be distinguished from broken interpolations late in the textual history of the Túrin story shows a purely textual creation of a single author following the same patterns documented for oral traditions (both living and historical).[109] Tolkien's works give the impression of depth not only because he consciously imitated the features of other texts that produce this same aesthetic effects—in their modern readers if not their original audiences—but because his writing process generated the same dynamics of replication, circulation, and adaptation as do distributed cultural traditions.[110]

Tolkien's complex and uneven revision process is also the source of an even deeper level of heterotextuality in *The Lord of the Rings*.[111] Newly developed "Lexomic" techniques of computer-assisted stylometry show that the distribution of vocabulary in Tolkien's great work is particularly heterogeneous, more like that of a multiauthored or multisourced work than a single-authored text.[112] The overall distribution of vocabulary in *The Lord of the Rings* follows Zipf's law, which states that the frequency of a word in any sufficiently large natural language corpus is inversely proportional to its rank in the frequency table. The most common words, therefore, are used exponentially more often than the rarer words.[113] In the English language, these are *function words* such as conjunctions, articles, prepositions, pronouns, and forms of the verb *to be*. In *The Lord of the Rings, the* and *and* are the two most common words, followed by *of* and *to*. It is not until we come to the fifteenth most frequently used word that we find an ordinary verb, *said*, and the first noun we encounter is the proper name *Frodo*, which is the thirty-sixth most commonly used word. Fluctuations in the frequencies of such common words are too subtle to be identified by the unaided eye and mind, so computer-assisted methods are required to identify any patterns.

The extent of the heterogeneity of vocabulary distribution can be visualized through the method of hierarchical agglomerative clustering.[114] If an electronic text of *The Lord of the Rings* is divided into separate chapters and all punctuation and other formatting is removed, cluster analysis using the Lexos software suite will produce a tree-diagram or *dendrogram* representing the relative similarity of the vocabularies of each chapter (see Figure 1 opposite).[115] Chapters are grouped based on overall similarity, with the distance to the branch-point indicating the amount of variation between each branch or group of branches.

A single-authored, unsourced text generally produces a flat, "stepwise" dendrogram, in which there are few subgroupings, and the distance between branch-points is very short.[116] *The Lord of the Rings,* however, generates a complex, hierarchical dendrogram with several large groupings and a few outliers, the most dramatic of which is Chapter 10 of Book I of *The Fellowship of the Ring*, "Strider," which is separate from all other clusters in the dendrogram.[117] Additionally the distance to its branchpoint, which is proportional to the difference in vocabulary between chapters or subclusters, is larger than those separating all the other high- and medium-level clusters combined. Less dramatic but still substantial are the differences between the rest of the text and the pairing of Chapters 23 and 29, and the five-leaved cluster that contains Chapters 49, 53, 57, 58, and 62.[118]

Not only is this dendrogram geometry characteristic of a multiauthored text, but it does not match up with any of the obvious divisions of *The Lord of the Rings*. Chapters from all six books are spread throughout the three large clusters, and the Frodo and Sam chapters

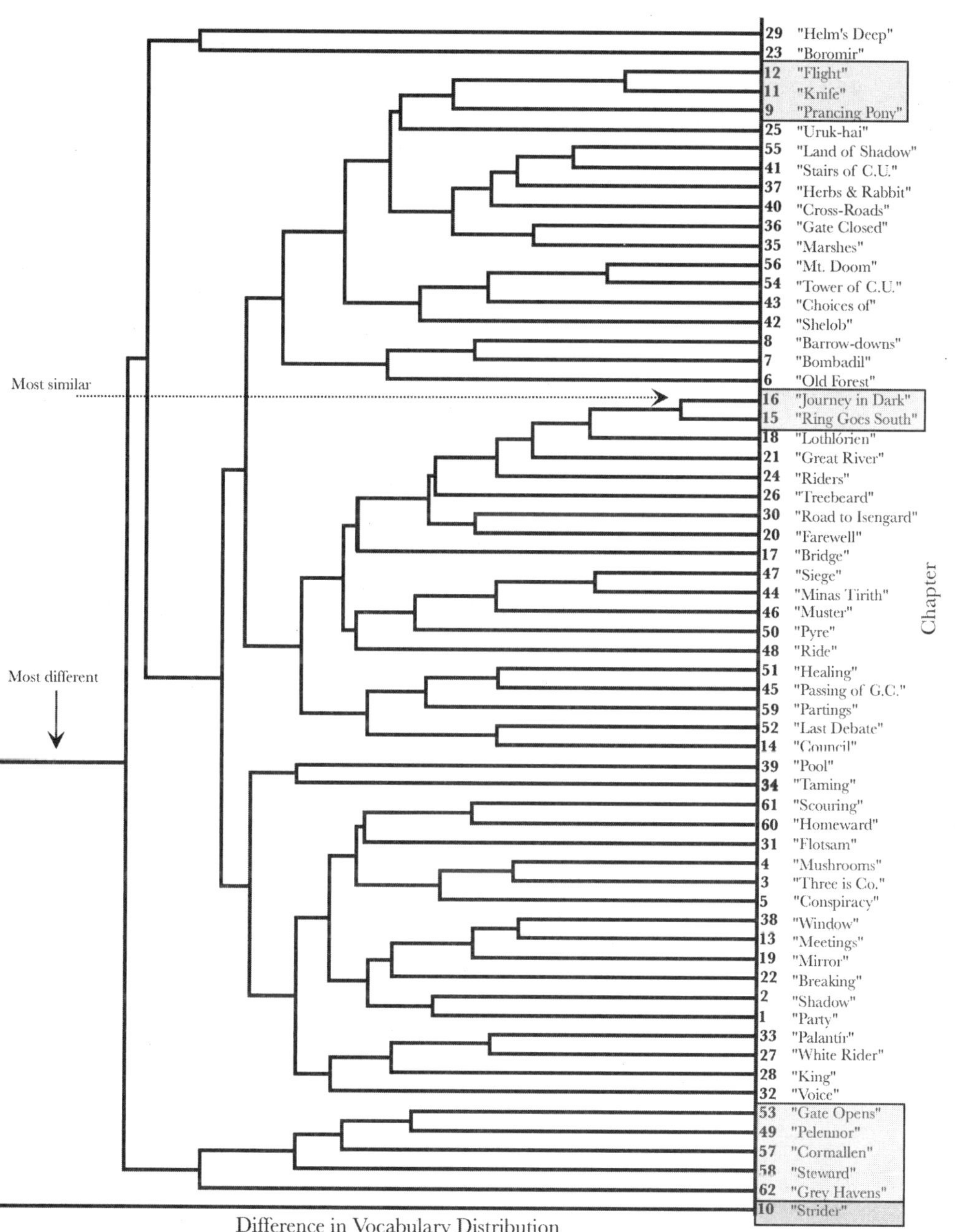

Figure 1. *Hierarchical clustering of the sixty-two chapters of* The Lord of the Rings.

are not distinct from those from the point of view of Merry and Pippin. The dendrogram geometry is also not correlated with chronology of the original composition: Early and late chapters are mixed together, and there is no obvious division between the chapters composed before and after Chapter 17, "The Bridge of Khazad-dûm,"[119] which is the point at which Tolkien had paused for over a year in his writing.[120]

The geometry of Figure 1, however, is correlated with the revision-history of *The Lord of the Rings*. As Peizhen Wu and I discovered, chapters cluster together in the places where Tolkien reported that the narrative "wrote itself" and therefore did not require much revision.[121] These chapters have a distribution of vocabulary very similar to the average across the entire work and thus can be seen as containing Tolkien's "natural" writing.[122] So, for example, Chapters 15 and 16, "The Ring Goes South" and "A Journey in the Dark," are the two most similar in the entire work, and Tolkien wrote these "ab initio as a full narrative; and this being so it is remarkable how much of its wording survived into the final form, despite the radical differences that Trotter was still the hobbit Peregrin and that neither Dwarf nor Elf was present."[123]

Christopher Tolkien explains that his father's writing of *The Lord of the Rings* proceeded "in a series of 'waves' or . . . 'phases,'" of vision and revision that were "always changing but always closely dependent on what preceded." For example, there are six main texts of the first chapter of *The Lord of the Rings*, "A Long-Expected Party," along with "a number of abandoned openings" that survive, and much of the rest of *The Fellowship of the Ring* went through as many as five phases of revision.[124] Most chapters of *The Fellowship of the Ring* were modified in at least two of these phases.[125]

All similar things are similar in the same way, but there are many ways of being different.* If little-revised chapters have very similar vocabulary distributions, then any of the revisions would be changes

* With apologies to Leo Tolstoy (*Anna Karenina*)—*Все счастливые семьи похожи друг на друга, каждая несчастливая семья несчастлива по-своему*, and Richard Dawkins, *The Blind Watchmaker*: "however many ways there may be of being alive, it is certain that there are vastly more ways of being dead, or rather not alive," Richard Dawkins, *The Blind Watchmaker: Why the Evidence of Evolution Reveals a Universe Without Design* (1986; repr. New York: W.W. Norton, 1996), 9.

from Tolkien's natural vocabulary distribution. However, the most-revised chapters do not all group together, and the amount of revision does not accurately predict the placement of a chapter in the dendrogram. The late chapters that cluster together outside the main groupings (49, 53, 57, 58, and 62) were hardly revised, but Chapter 10, "Strider," whose placement in the dendrogram indicates that its vocabulary distribution is substantially different from every other chapter of *The Lord of the Rings*, is one of the more heavily revised chapters. Even more strangely, "Strider" is not even paired with Chapter 9, "At the Sign of the Prancing Pony," even though these were originally a single longer chapter. In fact, Chapter 9 clusters closely with the very homogeneous pair of chapters, 11 ("A Knife in the Dark") and 12 ("Flight to the Ford") that follow "Strider." These kinds of seeming contradictions are usually signs of multiple authorship; here they show how heterogeneous in vocabulary distribution *The Lord of the Rings* really is.

Another Lexomic technique, *rolling window analysis*, enables us to trace the fluctuating frequencies of any letter, word, or phrase throughout the entire text, allowing us to locate concentrations or gaps.[126] Abrupt changes in the rolling average of features are frequently associated with changes in authorship, source, scribe, or quantity of revision.[127] Previous research indicates that plots of the most frequently used words in a text can be used to identify sections that have different authors or sources. Figure 2 (see below) is a plot of the frequency of *and*

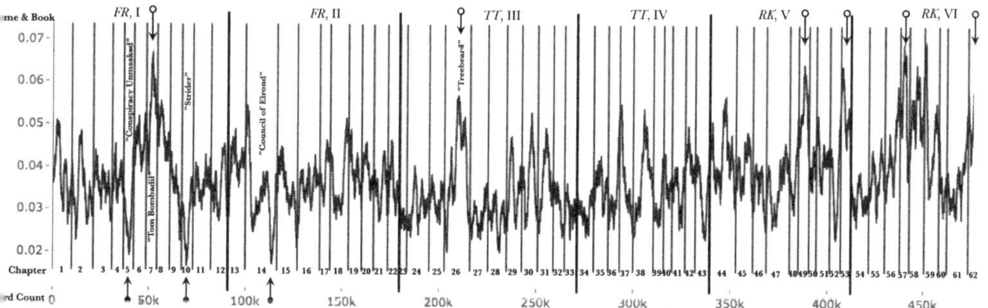

Figure 2. *Frequency of* and *in a rolling window of two thousand words in* The Lord of the Rings. *Book and chapter boundaries are indicated by vertical lines. Chapters discussed are identified with arrows.*

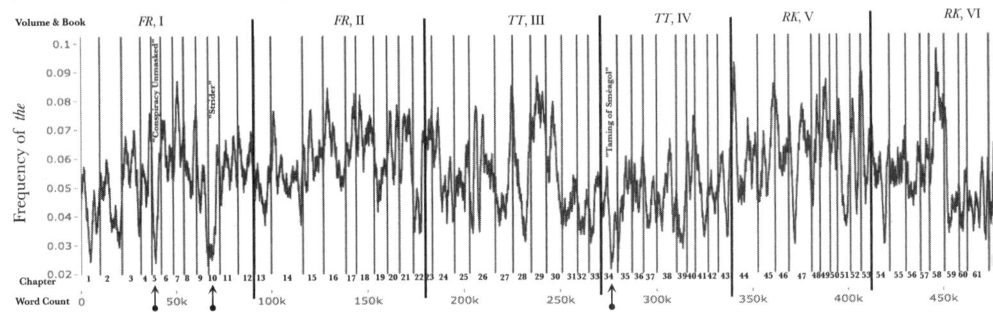

Figure 3. *Frequency of* the *in a rolling window of two thousand words in* The Lord of the Rings. *Book and chapter boundaries are indicated by vertical lines. Chapters discussed are identified with arrows.*

in *The Lord of the Rings*. Chapters 49, 53, 57, 58, and 62, which, as just discussed, were portions of the text that Tolkien did not revise substantially, contain some of the highest frequencies of *and*, and other peaks in *and* turn out to be chapters described by Christopher Tolkien as having been composed fluidly and without later changes; both "Treebeard" (Ch. 26) and "In the House of Tom Bombadil" (Ch. 7) seem to have been inspired in some way, as they hardly needed to be revised at all.[128]

At the other extreme, Chapter 10 has the lowest frequency of *and* in the text, with only Chapter 5, "A Conspiracy Unmasked," also one of the more heavily revised chapters of *The Lord of the Rings*, containing nearly as few instances of the word.[129] Chapter 10 also has the lowest frequency of *the*, also matched only by Chapter 5, and Chapter 34, "The Taming of Sméagol."[130] One of the most difficult chapters for Tolkien to write, "The Taming of Sméagol" was multiply revised, cut, rearranged, and restarted until Tolkien was finally able to extricate Frodo and Sam from the Emyn Muil.[131] From this rolling window analysis we can provisionally conclude that Tolkien's revisions tended to remove or replace *and* and *the* in the text, so the more times he revised, the lower the frequency of these two function words. We also must note, however, that the lower frequencies of *and* and *the* are not sufficient to move Chapter 10 to such a separate place in the dendrogram, and therefore the amount of revision alone does not explain the whole change in vocabulary distribution. It turns out that in addition to employing the most common conjunction and article at lower frequencies than elsewhere in the text, Chapter 10 also uses the first-person singular pronoun *I* massively more than any other chapter. It is the combination of differences that accounts for the dendrogram placement.

Chapter 10 was revised so much more and so differently from all the other chapters in *The Lord of the Rings* because it is a nexus of multiple plot strands that were very much in flux throughout the first few drafts of the work. The extremely complex details of the seven phases of the revision process are beyond the scope of this chapter, but in essence, Tolkien had to keep revising "Strider" due to the multiple changes in the subplots about the reason for Gandalf's failure to meet Frodo in the Shire and the evolution of the identity of the character who would eventually become Aragorn. With each revision, Tolkien increased the information density of the chapter, in great part by developing the personalities of the characters, particularly Strider, but also the minor character Barliman Butterbur, the innkeeper at the Prancing Pony. To make the characters' actions plausible and their motivations understandable, Tolkien had them tell their stories, and this substantially increased the frequency of the use of the word *I* over baseline. Increases in first-person sentences force increases in first-person verbs and a concomitant decrease in the other pronouns and verb forms that are more common elsewhere in the text, and all of these variations contribute to the anomalous placement of Chapter 10 in the dendrogram.

From this analysis we can draw several conclusions. The distribution of vocabulary in *The Lord of the Rings* is heterogeneous: The frequencies of the most common words vary among chapters rather than being consistent throughout the work or varying along a gradient of some sort. The cause of this heterogeneity is the uneven revision history of the text, and that uneven revision history was in part caused by the evolution of the plot. The textual heterogeneity that is produced by multivocality; broken-, pseudo- and ordinary references; gaps and inconsistencies; and variations in style is also present at the level of vocabulary distribution. This impression of heterotextuality, because it can be found at multiple levels of a nested hierarchy, is somewhat fractal in nature: The same pattern is repeated at smaller and larger scales, creating a rich texture of variation, like the grain in a wooden beam, the patina on a metallic surface, or the lichen covering an ancient stone.

At the end of the previous chapter I quoted Verlyn Flieger's argument that the notion that *The Lord of the Rings* was written by Bilbo, Frodo, and Sam was just a helpful organizing conceit, "not a substantial structural factor," since if a variety of narrative characteristics are brought together, "the whole concept falls apart."[132] But the rich heterotextuality of *The Lord of the Rings* pulls together and harmonizes the seemingly conflicting features that Flieger interprets as destroying the conceit that the work is a translation of the augmented and revised Red Book of Westmarch. Heterotextuality gives Tolkien's mature works—despite their being the creations of a single writer—their sense of being the product of a long and complex compositional and transmission history and thus being older and somehow more authentic than the printed volumes readers hold in their hands.

CHAPTER 4

Patterns

✣

MY FATHER READ *The Lord of the Rings* to me at least twice, probably three times. I read it aloud twice to my daughter and my son, and I have read Tolkien's masterpiece silently to myself approximately forty times. In not a single one of those readings—not even when I reread *The Lord of the Rings* specifically to prepare for writing this chapter—have I felt that I was just reading a book. Assuming you accept this description of my subjective experience—and you should, because I am not making anything up—you might attribute it to the ridiculous number of times I have read the work. After all, if we have a strange phenomenon (reading a book feeling like an experience) and a strange set of actions (more rereading than any normal human seems likely to do), it might make sense to see the two as being linked—as well they could be. I might even be inclined to accept the connection if not for two factors. First, the experiential feeling has been with me since that very first time my father read the books out loud, when, obviously, I had not yet read *The Lord of the Rings* dozens of times. If nothing else, I would be inclined to reverse the arrow of causality from the multiple readings causing the experiential feeling to the experiential nature of the book being the cause of my wanting to read it multiple times. Second, and possibly more significant: I am not alone in my perceptions. Since I began talking about this subjective experience more than twenty years ago in classes and public lectures, multitudes of students have raised their hands in class to agree; some have described their own similar perceptions; and it is a rare public lecture at which fewer than a half-dozen people come up to speak with me afterward and describe their own experiential reactions to Tolkien's masterpiece.

Indeed, a surprising number of people read Tolkien's work in an almost ritualistic way every year, starting *The Fellowship of the Ring* on September 22, or at the beginning of summer break, or on their late father's birthday. I now wish I had written down dates and numbers to provide some quantitative documentation of this phenomenon, although I find it difficult to determine how exactly that documentation could be converted into real sociological research. How would I create a comparison or control group? How would I determine if there were other books that provoked the phenomenon more or less than *The Lord of the Rings?* But a perusal of the enormous archive of the Tolkien Experience Project should alleviate any concern that my response is utterly idiosyncratic, even though it is not obvious how to test any claim that my subjective experience is in some way typical.[1]

Fortunately, for the purposes of this chapter it is not necessary to try to determine what fraction of Tolkien's readers find the book experiential because I am simply going to accept my subjective experience as something that has actually happened (as one does with experiences) and try to understand and explain it.[2] The full philosophical-literary-theoretical justification for this approach is beyond the scope of this book, but the gist of the argument is my conclusion that all "average reader" arguments are merely disguises for or displacements of the subjective impressions of the person performing the analysis, and so by discussing my personal experience as a reader, I am merely cutting out an awkward and imaginary abstract middle-man. There is, I aver, no method of literary studies that can in the abstract objectively determine how readers respond to a text or specify what the actual "horizon of expectations" is for a given work of literature.[3] A critic could try to adapt sociological or anthropological or psychological methods—survey readers, or interview some representative cohort about their subjective experiences, or wire them up to various machines and observe what happens in their brains when they are reading—but to the best of my knowledge, these kinds of approaches have never been applied to literary texts. And while the results of such studies would be fascinating, it seems unlikely that they could resolve a question like "Is reading *The Lord of the Rings* more like having an experience than like reading a book?"

So how then do I avoid solipsism in the analysis that follows? What is to stop my interpretation from being utterly idiosyncratic and personal? The short answer would be: Nothing at all—except that my readers would surely be unconvinced if I did not supply evidence and convincing arguments. A less flip reply would be that an idiosyncratic and purely personal interpretation of a text would only be interesting if it explained how and why the interpretation arises from the material, in which case it would no longer be overly idiosyncratic or personal. That the final five hundred lines of *Beowulf* always make me think of the death of my uncle is trivial, and so of no interest to readers. That certain characteristics of the final five hundred lines of *Beowulf* can give shape to otherwise inchoate grief and loss, like that which many feel upon the death of a beloved relative, and that I reached this conclusion based in part on my experience participating in a complete recital of *Beowulf* in Old English the night my uncle was passing away, may be interesting.* Transforming this discussion from an accurate description of my personal experience to the imagined experience of some abstract "average reader" adds nothing to the argument; it merely conceals, in an effort to make conclusions appear authoritative or universal, the specific phenomena that actually (rather than hypothetically) occur: the experiences of the individual reader upon whose perceptions the argument is based.

* My mother's brother, with whom I was very close, died in 1993 in the second wave of the AIDS epidemic. The night he passed away happened to be when Professor John Miles Foley, who taught me Old English at the University of Missouri–Columbia, was hosting our graduate seminar for a reading of all of *Beowulf* in Old English. When I had stopped home to get my copy of Fr. Klaeber's edition of the poem, I listened to an answering-machine message from my mother telling me that my uncle was unconscious and would likely not survive the night, so I should prepare to come home for the funeral. Through the entire three hours and seventeen minutes of the reading of the poem, I was thinking about him and his kindness and bravery and suffering. Hearing and reciting *Beowulf* this way helped me to withstand the grief and loss, and so forever afterward, reading the end of *Beowulf* brings back both the memory of those feelings and the effect of the poem on them.

❦

ALTHOUGH IT WAS Tolkien's original intention that *The Lord of the Rings* be published in one large volume rather than as a trilogy, the cost of paper in postwar England necessitated a division into three volumes, each of which contains two books. The titles of the volumes are reasonable indicators of their contributions to the narrative: The first is about the formation and adventures of *The Fellowship of the Ring*; the second is structured around the now separated members of the Fellowship in their interactions with the powerful antagonists who occupy *The Two Towers* of Isengard and Barad-dûr; and the final volume depicts the events that lead to *The Return of the King* of Gondor and Arnor as a result of the destruction of the Ring and the consequent downfall of the Dark Lord. Originally the six books into which *The Lord of the Rings* was divided were given their own names: *The Return of the Shadow*, *The Fellowship of the Ring*, *The Treason of Isengard*, *The Journey to Mordor* (or *The Two Towers)*, *The War of the Ring*, and *The Return of the King*. These names were removed when the decision was made to publish the work as a trilogy (although they were resurrected by Christopher Tolkien for volumes in *The History of Middle-earth*). Each book includes between nine and twelve chapters, the numbering for which restarts with every book.

There are an enormous number of ways to conceptualize and diagram the architectonics of a narrative. In high school, we were taught Freytag's Triangle, in which the narrative begins with Exposition, then complications are introduced to produce the Rising Action, which eventually reaches a Climax, after which the Falling Action ultimately leads to the Resolution, or as my teacher had us call it, "Conclusion or Denouement" (always phrased that way; never just one or the other). You can find narrative schemas as old as Aristotle or as new as the most recent volumes of the journals *Narrative*, *Storyworlds*, *Journal of Narrative Theory*, and *Frontiers of Narrative Studies*.[4]

I am not going to use any of these approaches directly, because in this discussion I am interested only in those features of the narrative architecture that contribute to the ways *The Lord of the Rings* produces the effect of experientiality. For our purposes we can radically simplify narrative forms into two very general categories: the *linear*, the flow of narrative from the beginning of the work to the end, and the *cyclical*, in which patterns are repeated. Obviously everything in every written narrative is linear because we read words and sentences sequentially, and a narrative is just a very long string of words, but linear narrative can also contain cyclical subsections, since at the very least subdivisions of the text (chapters, books, volumes) are repeated, and each of these abstract categories has more than one member. These trivial senses of the terminology, however, are uninteresting, and we can also ignore highly philosophical objections that even verbatim repeats are not truly repetitions, since the linear nature of the narrative means that each putative repetition occurs in a different context due to its placement in the linear stream.[5] More significant is that the architectonics of *The Lord of the Rings* combine linear and cyclical features in the form of an *interlace*. In 1967 Richard West characterized the work this way: He argued that "the narrative line is digressive and cluttered, dividing our attention among an indefinite number of events, characters, and themes, any one of which may dominate at any given time, and it is often indifferent to cause and effect relationships."[6] The "apparent meandering" of the interlaced plot serves to "mirror the ebb and flow" of events, but it can also show "purpose of pattern behind change."[7] West does not link Tolkien's work to the interlace patterns of Anglo-Saxon and Celtic art of the seventh and eighth centuries, but instead he finds the closest parallels to be thirteenth century romances, including Arthurian material well known to Tolkien—this is why West, and Shippey, who follows him, often use the French term *entrelacements*.[8]

Careful study of the evolution of the plot in *The History of Middle-earth* volumes leads me to agree with West in one sense: There does not seem to be deliberate and conscious borrowing of form from either medieval romances or Anglo-Saxon art, and it is probably relevant that Tolkien had very influentially described the structure of *Beowulf* as "static" and argued that it paralleled the form of the Old English alliterative poetic line, which is nothing like an interlace.[9] Nevertheless, the combined linear and cyclical qualities of the architectonics of *The Lord of the Rings* sounds very much like the putative interlace structure of *Beowulf*: "verbal braids in which allusive references from the past cross and recross with the present subject" produce "a complex structure of great technical skill, but . . . woven with relatively few strands." The narrative form "reveals the meaning of coincidence, the recurrences of human behaviour, and the circularity of time . . . it allows for the intersection of narrative events without regard for their distance in chronological time . . . the significance of the connections is left for the audience to work out."[10] This description actually fits *The Lord of the Rings* somewhat better than it does *Beowulf.*

Shippey says that Tolkien's *entrelacement* represents the "fundamental character of reality."[11] Although due to their limited knowledge of the other events occurring elsewhere, the characters experience the world as operating chaotically, there are in fact large-scale chains of cause-and-effect relationships: "The world is a Persian carpet and we are ants lumbering from one thread to the other and observing that there are no patterns in the colours."[12] Shippey also points out that interlacement allows Tolkien to maneuver through a set of apparent paradoxes, the obvious and ever-present problem of balancing between free will and fate in a story-world in which there are accurate prophesies, and the clash between the narrative requirement that evil be an active force and Tolkien's expressed philosophical position that evil is an absence of good and cannot create creatures with free-will.[13] In his later *Author of the Century*, Shippey takes this idea a step further by arguing that "there is a pattern in Tolkien's story, but his characters can never see it (naturally, because they are in it)."[14] This disconnect, which, Shippey notes, often applies to the readers as well as the characters, produces a kind of "anti-irony, as one slowly realizes that the characters' frustration, gloom, even approach to despair is at once natural and justified, and also needless and falsified."[15] All of these observations are true. What links them to the main argument of this chapter is Shippey's summary conclusion that the architectonics of *The Lord of the Rings* produce a "a profound sense of reality, of that being the way things are."[16]

This evaluation appears paradoxical. No person looking at an interlace would imagine, even for a moment, that it was a pattern from nature: Even the most primitive woven basket immediately identifies itself as a work of human hands, and any reasonably elaborate interlace is obviously and undeniably artful, and hence artificial. Yet Shippey is absolutely correct about the "sense of reality" produced by *The Lord of the Rings*; the apparent logical inconsistency allows us to recognize a distinction between this sense of reality and what we are accustomed to think of as "realism" in twentieth-century novels, and to understand why this distinction exists. The realism in novels inheres in the impression they give of being precise in their description of sensory detail and accurate in their reproduction of speech and behavior. It is essential to realize, however, that the sense of realism produced by works like those of John Steinbeck, Edith Wharton, or Upton Sinclair is entirely a product of art rather than the result of these works being in any quantifiable way closer to physical reality than literature that follows different sets of conventions.

The sense of reality of *The Lord of the Rings* arises from patterns at higher levels of abstraction. The interlaced architectonics of the narrative create repetitions at varying scales, each of which is more abstract than the concrete sensory details that are among the conventions of literary realism. These repetitions help produce the impression that many patterns of human behavior, and even time itself, are cyclical, and this impression is interlinked with the experiences of the reader incarnate in the world through the parallel rhythms of nature and culture: the seasons and human response to them, the dynamics of the processes of illness and recovery, the patterns of music and movement.

Only partly in jest, I tell my students that J.R.R. Tolkien kept writing the same scenes over and over with just enough differences between them that readers do not notice they are reading the same scenes over and over (but their subconscious minds do). For example, Tolkien repeatedly describes characters entering and exiting caves or tunnels, or walking through an unknown forest.[17] In all cases the atmosphere and description are unique, but the pattern of entrance and traversal of a dark or wild place, in which powers other than those of the characters are dominant, underlies the individual scenes. Repetitions with variation create expectations and fulfill them: After an instance of fear or suffering, the hobbits repair to a safe haven, a "homely house,"—the elves' outdoor "hall" in the Woody End, the Crickhollow house, the house of Tom Bombadil, the Prancing Pony, Elrond's Last Homely

House, the sojourn in Caras Galadhon. The pattern even holds when, on the fences of Mordor, Frodo and Sam encounter Faramir and are brought to Henneth Annûn for a short rest.[18] Repetitions also allow for the contrast produced by the frustration of expectations: The hobbits are trapped underground in the barrow, only to be rescued by Tom Bombadil; the Fellowship is nearly trapped in Moria, only to be saved by Gandalf; Frodo and Sam are trapped in Shelob's Lair, but no one comes to save them, so they have to save themselves.[19] Repetitions can also heighten contrasts: The three hobbits slowly strolling through the rural beauty of the Shire in perfect, warm autumn weather in "Three's Company" is paralleled by Frodo, Sam, and Gollum dragging themselves through the dank chill of the Dead Marshes and the Noman Lands outside Mordor.[20]

Among the more obvious patterns that make up the interlaced architectonics of *The Lord of the Rings* are the symmetries between the two books of the *Fellowship of the Ring.* As Shippey notes, the second chapter of each book "is largely explanation of the past building up to decisions about the future—and ending with much the same decision, that Frodo has to take the Ring to the Cracks of Doom." The two books also contain "much the same number of scene-shifts and scenes of threat."[21] In fact, the two books are even more symmetrical in terms of narrative patterning than Shippey discusses, and this symmetry occurs at multiple levels of abstraction. Not only is the second chapter of each book primarily historical, but the initial chapters are generally lighthearted and full of hobbit-banter until a scene of tension—related to the Ring—introduces a jarring note of conflict that, although soon resolved, cannot be forgotten and is directly connected to the events of the next chapter. In "A Long-Expected Party" this is the tense interaction between Gandalf and Bilbo immediately after the elderly hobbit's birthday party. Back inside Bag End after vanishing at the end of his speech, Bilbo prepares to set out on his journey, even donning the travel-stained green cloak and hood from his original adventure. At the last moment, instead of setting an envelope containing the Ring and some documents on the mantelpiece for Frodo to find, he impulsively puts it in his pocket. But before he can leave, Gandalf arrives and questions him, eventually pressuring the hobbit to leave behind the Ring: "You agreed to that, you remember." Bilbo, surprisingly, becomes angry and defensive, saying of the Ring "It is mine, I tell you. My own. My precious. Yes, my precious."[22] As frightening as Bilbo's unexpected use of Gollum's old expression is, the tension is soon resolved by Bilbo moving to set the envelope containing the Ring on the mantel and Gandalf placing it there after the hobbit accidentally drops it. Bilbo recites his "The Road Goes Ever On" poem and departs. The chapter ends with the amusing depiction of the post-party aftermath at Bag End, including Bilbo's snarky gift labels, the interaction between Frodo and Lobelia Sackville-Baggins, and Frodo and Gandalf's conversation.

The structure of "Many Meetings" is generally parallel, with the chapter beginning with Frodo's waking in the House of Elrond after nearly dying from the wound of the Morgul-knife. Gandalf's relating the events at the Ford of Bruinen and then Frodo's reunion with Sam, Merry, and Pippin are all generally lighthearted and positive, as is the conversation with Glóin at the feast (Glóin notes that Bombur is now so fat he needs six young dwarves to move him from couch to table), and the feast itself is a scene of happiness and beauty. Then Frodo has a moment of pure joy when he finds Bilbo sitting in the Hall of Fire. Their reunion, however, is briefly marred by Bilbo asking to see the Ring. Frodo shows it to him, but when Bilbo stretches out his hand, "to his distress and amazement [Frodo] found that he was no longer looking at Bilbo; a shadow seemed to have fallen between them, and through it he found himself eyeing a little wrinkled creature with a hungry face and bony groping hands. He felt a desire to strike him."[23] Again, comity is soon restored: Frodo puts away the Ring, and the chapter concludes with Bilbo's "Eärendil Was a Mariner" poem, some additional lighthearted banter, and a brief conversation among Bilbo, Frodo, and Sam.

Although none of the initial chapters in Books III, IV, V, and VI can possibly be seen as lighthearted, Books IV and VI both contain scenes that echo those first instances of tension caused by the power of the Ring. In "The Taming of Smeagol," long passages of conversation between Frodo and Sam, which include some banter, are interrupted by the encounter with Gollum, which finally resolves when the miserable creature promises to serve Frodo and lead the hobbits to Mordor. To affirm his promise, Gollum asks to swear "on the Precious" (i.e., to touch the Ring physically when swearing his oath. Frodo does not allow this and instead: "For a moment it appeared to Sam that his master had grown and Gollum had shrunk: a tall stern shadow, a mighty lord who hid his brightness in grey cloud, and at his feet a little whining dog."[24] Similarly, in "The Tower of Cirith Ungol," when Sam tells Frodo that the orcs did not take the Ring but that he, Sam, has it, Frodo snatches away the Ring on its chain and has a vision in which Sam appears to be a slavering orc.

Possible parallels in Books III and V are less obvious. In "The Departure of Boromir," the only possible echo of the Ring-caused scene of tension would be when Boromir says "I tried to take the Ring from Frodo. . . . I am sorry. I have paid," invoking the awful transformation in Boromir in the final chapter of *The Fellowship of the Ring*, "The Breaking of the Fellowship," in which "his pleasant and fair face was hideously changed; a raging fire was in his eyes."[25] In "Minas Tirith," the opening chapter of *The Return of the King*, Denethor says that "Yet the Lord of Gondor is not to be made the tool of other men's purposes, however worthy. And to him there is no purpose higher in the world as it now stands than the good of Gondor; and the rule of Gondor, my lord, is mine and no other man's unless the king should come again."[26] The action that Boromir confesses to was a result of the Ring's power to make people desire it, the same power that is at the root of the obviously parallel scenes in Books I, II, IV, and VI. Denethor's statement is his subtle way of telling Gandalf that he rejects the decision not to use the Ring in the defense of Minas Tirith and thus that he desired (and still desires) to possess Isildur's Bane. Thus the oblique parallelism of the openings of Books III and V with the openings of the other books serves both to link the Steward of Gondor to his son (implying that Denethor would have done what Boromir tried to do) and to other characters negatively affected by the power of the Ring: Bilbo, Frodo, Gollum, and Sam. The structural repetition in the initial chapters of Books I and II creates expectations—albeit likely unconscious ones—

for what will be found in subsequent openings of books, thus allowing the latter to be informed by the former and producing a sense of structural familiarity and cyclical time.

Other repeated patterns in the narrative include the motif of a departure from a pleasant house followed by a journey that reaches a crisis point when the hobbits are threatened by a hostile entity from which they are rescued by the intervention of a benevolent stranger, after which they sojourn in a different safe and welcoming house. As Shippey notes, "Frodo has to be dug out of no less than five 'Homely Houses' before his quest is properly launched.[27] I would add Farmer Maggot's house to that list, and I interpret the pattern slightly differently than Shippey does: not so much as the quest not getting started until Frodo leaves Rivendell, but as the departure from Rivendell being just the most important of the interlacements of this particular cyclical pattern within the linear narrative that begins with Bilbo leaving Bag End and ends with Sam returning there.[28] Each of the small cycles reinforces the pattern, producing both expectations and resonances in the minds of readers. The cyclical time emphasized by the repetitions of the patterns is complemented with the steadily growing tension and danger of each hostile interaction, as the stakes are continually raised until what is perhaps the climax (in the old-fashioned, Freytag's Triangle sense) of *The Fellowship of the Ring*: the loss of Gandalf at the Bridge of Khazad-dûm. The trauma of Gandalf's fall is greatly emphasized by the apparent breaking of the heretofore consistent pattern: No previous benevolent rescuer has died in the effort. Gandalf's return as the White Rider removes this source of architectonic tension, as the pattern is restored when we learn that the rescuer has not in fact been destroyed, but for a sizable segment of the narrative the pattern seems to have been broken.

Additionally, each of these miniature cycles includes a small-scale version of the "eucatastrophe," the unexpected positive turn, that is the defining feature of the full narrative.[29] The unexpected appearances of Gildor and the elves, Bombadil, Strider, Glorfindel, Treebeard, Gandalf, and Gandalf with Erkenbrand, primes the reader for the greater eucatastrophes—the Horns of Rohan, Aragorn in the Black Ships of the Corsairs, "The Eagles are coming!"—and the greatest, the destruction of the Ring.

The linear increase in tension occurs not only from one cyclical repetition to the next, but within the cycles as well. Each engagement with the hostile entities is bipartite, in that a frightening initial encounter that the hobbits survive on their own is followed by a far more dangerous encounter that requires the assistance of the benevolent rescuer. The first Black Rider merely sniffs and rides away, while the second appears to get down from his horse to seek Frodo (who feels a compulsion to put on the Ring, perhaps indicating that the Rider senses the Ring or that he is closer to Frodo than before), only to be frightened away by the song of the wandering Elves.[30] Old Man Willow tips Frodo into the water, but he escapes, only to discover Merry and Pippin trapped in the willow cracks from which only Bombadil's power can rescue them.[31] All of the encounters with hostile entities in *The Fellowship of the Ring*, and most of those in the other two volumes, fit the pattern. The only exceptions are the depictions of warfare, in which the interactions are more complex. Elements of this narrative pattern are also repeated at different scales, the architectonics of individual scenes or chapters being echoed in larger narrative units. For example, the pattern of doubled hostile interactions, with the first one less severe than the second, can be seen at the level of the entire narrative of Book I: The journey from the Shire eventually leads to the Barrow-wight's temporary capture of the hobbits (first and lesser hostile encounter), ended by Tom Bombadil, followed by the even more damaging attack by the Ringwraiths and their near killing of Frodo, which is foiled only by the intervention of multiple benevolent characters (Strider, Glorfindel, Elrond commanding the river, and Gandalf adding his own touches to the flood). After this second crisis, the hobbits are able to rest and recuperate in the safe and welcoming confines of the Last Homely House.

Similarly, the narrative structure of much of Book I, Chapter 3, "Three Is Company," maps onto the larger narrative of Book I and the first two chapters of Book II. The small farewell birthday party at Bag End matches up with the enjoyable meal and conversation at the Prancing Pony, the initial trek through the familiar parts of the Shire with the hobbits' journey with Strider from Bree to Weathertop. The first appearance of the "Roads Go Ever On" poem is paralleled by Strider's recitation of the poem about Beren and Lúthien, and each poem is soon followed by the appearance of a Black Rider or Riders. Additional journeying pauses for a comic poem—respectively "Ho! Ho! Ho! To the Bottle I Go" and Sam's Troll song—which is soon followed by a second encounter with Black Riders, from whom the hobbits are rescued. Elvish feasting and poetry follows, and the pattern is completed by elf-counsel at the Council of Elrond.

This parallelism of structure at different levels reinforces the sense of cyclic time.* As the line of the narrative twists, winds, and interlaces itself into similar repeated patterns, resonances and rhythms build. Repetitions with variations that make a scene both new and a recapitulation of a previous scene are the stuff of our own memory-narratives as we categorize our day-to-day experiences according to the larger patterns into which they fall: a typical day, a slow week, a relaxing holiday, a sorrowful parting, a joyful reunion. When narrative patterns resonate with the rhythms of our internal categories, the experience of reading the text activates memories and emotions in ways that just reading a book does not.

One of the most distinctive patterns that is consistent with the rhythms of readers' lives is that of illness and recovery, which Frodo experiences multiple times in the narrative, beginning with the wound inflicted by the Morgul-knife of the Lord of the Nazgûl in the dell under Weathertop. After initially recovering consciousness, and while being comforted and tended to by his friends, Frodo has difficulty staying awake, dozing "though the pain of his wound was slowly growing and a deadly chill was spreading from his shoulder to his arm and side."[32] Aragorn's healing efforts using the herb *athelas* help to a degree, as Frodo "felt the pain and also the sense of frozen cold lessen in his side," but he is still injured and ill and experiences the self-directed recriminations so common among people who have suffered either injury or sudden illness for which they in some way blame themselves: "He bitterly regretted his foolishness, and reproached himself for weak-

* It is very tempting to employ the overused term *fractal*, but as it is not obvious that there are similar repetitions at even larger or smaller scales, I will resist doing so.

ness of will."[33] During the worsening illness caused by the Morgul-knife, Frodo tries to hide his suffering from his companions—"before the first day's march was over Frodo's pain began to grow again, but he did not speak of it for a long time."[34] Eventually he reaches a point in which "the cold and wet had made his wound more painful than ever, and the ache and sense of deadly chill took away his sleep," so that he has visions or hallucinations, and when he finally does sleep, he dreams that "he walked on the grass in his garden in the Shire, but it seemed faint and dim, and less clear than the tall black shadows that stood looking over the hedge."[35] This sense of clouded vision, familiar to those who have suffered long-lasting high fevers, expands from dreams into waking: "Frodo threw himself down, and lay on the ground shivering.[36] His left arm was lifeless, and his side and shoulder felt as if icy claws were laid upon them. The trees and rocks about him seemed shadowy and dim." And even in the brighter morning "every now and again a mist seemed to obscure his sight, and he passed his hands over his eyes."[37]

The brief respite of improved feeling that comes with the discovery of the petrified trolls and the subsequent arrival of Glorfindel soon gives way to a rapid decline in Frodo's condition: "Ever since the sun began to sink the mist before his eyes had darkened, and he felt that a shadow was coming between him and the faces of his friends. Now pain assailed him and he felt cold."[38] Frodo's illness is reaching the stage, recognized since Hippocrates, of *crisis*, the inflection point, the moment of greatest danger after which the patient will either recover or die.[39] The external crisis of the attack of all nine Black Riders mirrors this internal struggle, and when Frodo collapses on the far shore of the ford after a hallucinatory image of roaring waters turning into horses, the reader cannot be sure whether the crisis has been survived, just as the patient in the moment of health crisis often loses consciousness.[40]

After this confused and dramatic scene, the description of Frodo's finding himself lying on a comfortable bed with patches of sunlight playing on the wall and having the sense that a long unpleasant dream is fading from his memory is so precisely parallel to the experience of waking up recovered after having gone to sleep very sick—more common in childhood, but not unknown later in life—that it feels like a specific memory of one or more of Tolkien's many illnesses.* The conversation with Gandalf, in which the wizard recounts recent events that Frodo had been too ill to remember, tells him of the treatment he required, and gives him the news of what his friends have been doing while he was incapacitated, will also be familiar to anyone who has suffered a serious illness. Frodo's becoming sleepy after only a short conversation but finally waking up in the early evening to find that he "no longer felt in need of rest or sleep, but had a mind for food and drink, and probably for singing and story-telling afterwards," and his somewhat bemused perusal of his thinner self in the mirror are also familiar experiences.[41] Finally, Sam's responding with excitement to Frodo's being awake, his touching of the injured part of Frodo's body, and his subsequent slight embarrassment are all actions that caregivers of the injured or the seriously ill regularly perform:

> At that moment there was a knock on the door, and Sam came in. He ran to Frodo and took his left hand, awkwardly and shyly. He stroked it gently and then he blushed and turned hastily away.
>
> "Hullo, Sam!" said Frodo.
>
> "It's warm!" said Sam. "Meaning your hand, Mr. Frodo. It has felt so cold through the long nights."[42]

My own memories from the patient side of this sort of interaction are of my mother touching my forehead again and again, just to confirm

---

* *Bio*, 85. The trench fever that Tolkien suffered is now rarely seen in the developed world, but during the 1970s my father saw cases among homeless people in New York City. He described the symptoms to me as "high-powered Lyme disease," characterized by extremely high—and thus disorienting—fevers. He wondered how many of Tolkien's later health troubles were sequelae of the trench fever infection, particularly if it was never fully cured. Current treatment guidelines imply that the disease cannot be cured without antibiotics, which were not discovered until 1928; G. M. Anstead, "The Centenary of the Discovery of Trench Fever, an Emerging Infectious Disease of World War 1," *Lancet Infectious Disease* 16, no. 8 (August 2016):164–72. Tolkien's injuries and illnesses can be somewhat reconstructed from the long list of references under the heading "Tolkien, J.R.R., *Health*" in the index to *Letters*. At one time or another Tolkien suffered from concussion, arthritis of the knees, fibrositis and neuritis of the arm, arthritis of the left hand, a torn Achilles tendon, appendicitis, catarrh, dysentery, leg injury, gastric flu, bronchial virus, laryngitis, lumbago, sciatica, gall-bladder trouble, and throat trouble; *Letters*, 700–701.

that my fever was finally gone after I endured a life-threatening bout of pneumonia that lasted over a week. Similarly, when my son finally recovered from very bad Lyme-disease-caused edema of his knee, which required a month-long treatment of IV antibiotics, I noticed my wife frequently touching and gently palpating the knee for a few days after the swelling had finally gone down.

This initial dynamic of illness and recovery is repeated in micro after Frodo is hit in the side by the Moria-orc's spear. Because he is protected by the hidden *mithril* coat, he is only bruised, but Aragorn nevertheless tends his and Sam's wounds with *athelas*. "Of Herbs and Stewed Rabbit" includes a scene with similar dynamics. Although Frodo is not injured, he is exhausted and demoralized after the long and seemingly futile trek to the Black Gate and then south through Ithilien. Sam does not heal him medically, but the stewed coneys and sweet herbs and the long sleep do restore Frodo's energy and morale, as does the evening meal and rest later in Henneth Annûn.

I hope that the fourth parallel scene is not one that resonates with the personal experiences of the readers of this book, but the inversions that transform a pleasant and healthy waking into a nightmare demonstrate the sort of emotional effects that are enabled by the interlacement of repeated motifs and reinforce the impression that the pattern of illness, injury, and unconsciousness followed by healthy waking into sunlight is the natural one.* Frodo, who after being poisoned by Shelob's venom had seemed dead to Sam, was carried by the orcs to the topmost room in the Tower of Cirith Ungol. When he awakens there he is stripped of everything and questioned by Shagrat and Gorbag until a quarrel over the *mithril* coat leads to internecine fighting that kills almost every orc in the tower. Nevertheless, Frodo is barely conscious. Although he replies to Sam's song with his own weak singing (which attracts the attention of Snaga the orc, who leads Sam to the hidden room), his initial interaction with Sam is parallel to the slight confusion

* Uglúk's orc-healing of Merry's scalp wound during the Uruk-hai's march through Rohan could also been seen as another inversion of the patterns of recovery after injury, with the drinking of the ent-draughts at Wellinghall being the re-establishment of the healing pattern, but the parallels are much less exact.

upon waking that occurs in two of the three previous iterations of the illness and healing scene:

> "Am I still dreaming?" he muttered. "But the other dreams were horrible."
>
> "You're not dreaming at all, Master," said Sam. "It's real. It's me. I've come."
>
> "I can hardly believe it," said Frodo, clutching him. "There was an orc with a whip and then it turns into Sam! Then I wasn't dreaming after all when I heard that singing down below, and I tried to answer? Was it you?"
>
> "It was indeed, Mr. Frodo. I'd given up hope, almost. I couldn't find you."
>
> "Well you have now, Sam dear Sam," said Frodo, and he lay back in Sam's gentle arms, closing his eyes, like a child at rest when night-fears are driven away by some loved voice or hand.
>
> Sam felt that he could sit like that in endless happiness, but it was not allowed. It was not enough for him to find his master, he had still to try and save him. He kissed Frodo's forehead. "Come! Wake up Mr. Frodo!" he said, trying to sound as cheerful as he had when he drew back the curtains at Bag End on a summer's morning.[43]

The references to feeling like a child comforted by touch and to the memory of sunlight coming through a window both link this scene with the previous iterations of the pattern and emphasize the horror of the actual circumstances. The squalid room, lit by a single torch and the red light of the Fiery Mountain in the distance, the pile of filthy rags in which Frodo is lying, and the clothing Sam scavenges from dead orcs are all disturbing inversions of the sunlight on the wall and the clean bedsheets and clothes at the House of Elrond.[44] Even more horrible is the breaking of the pattern of a consoling conversation that had been so important in all three of the previous scenes of recovery. When Frodo learns that Sam had taken the Ring to continue the quest, he reacts not with gratitude or understanding, but with something close to violence,

"'Give it to me!' he cried, standing up and holding out a trembling hand. 'Give it to me at once! You can't have it!'" Frodo then snatches the Ring away and angrily rejects Sam's offer to share the burden: "'No you won't, you thief!' He panted, staring at Sam with eyes wide with fear and enmity . . . Sam had changed before his very eyes into an orc again, leering and pawing at his treasure, a foul little creature with greedy eyes and slobbering mouth."[45]

The inversion of key features in this fourth scene of recovery after injury not only emphasizes the horror of Mordor and the ability of the Ring to contaminate interpersonal interactions, but also greatly increases the emotional power of the later scene at the Field of Cormallen, in which the pattern of healing after injury is restored. After the darkness and filth of the Tower of Cirith Ungol, the sunlight seems brighter, the conversation happier, and the clean linen whiter. That this last scene is given from the newly awakened Sam's point of view rather than Frodo's also works to universalize the repeated pattern by making it applicable to more than one character.

Even if some readers do not respond to the specific patterns just discussed, lower-level rhythms in the narrative resonate more generally with human life. As Ursula K. Le Guin (in my view, the only fantasy writer the equal of Tolkien) notes in "Rhythmic Patterning in *The Lord of the Rings*," the base rhythm of the narrative "is as simple as a rhythm can be: two beats. Stress, release. Inbreath, outbreath. A heartbeat. A walking gait."* Le Guin locates this rhythm in repetitions of "words and phrases, images, actions, moods, and themes." Each stress, she argues, is followed by a release, "a dark event in the story [is] likely to be followed by a brighter one (or vice versa) . . . when the characters had exerted terrible effort, they then [get] to have a rest . . . each action

---

* I read Le Guin's essay over two decades ago and then not again until I had written most of this chapter. I am chagrined to find that so much of what I have done here (and in my teaching over two decades) is really just a substantiation and elaboration of Le Guin's original conceptions. She published this essay in a nonscholarly collection and seems to have worked within constraints of space because she does not extensively document the evidence for her conclusions or even attempt to explain the structure of the narrative as a whole. And yet, in a few pages, she manages to illuminate more of Tolkien's narrative technique than any article or chapter previously written. Greatness understands greatness. Ursula K. Le Guin, "Rhythmic Pattern in *The Lord of the Rings*," in *Meditations on Middle-earth*, ed. Karen Haber (New York: St. Martin's Press, 2001) 101-16.

brought a reaction, never predictable in nature . . . but more or less predictable in kind, like day following night, and winter after fall."[46]

Le Guin's description is certainly accurate at the chapter level. The narrative patterns of two hostile encounters with a short respite after the first, and recovery in a safe location after the second, is just a slightly larger rhythm built up of two stress-and-releases. This, and the patterns of image, word, and actions that Le Guin discusses in her analysis of "Fog on the Barrow-Downs," shows that the two-beat rhythm underlies scenes as well. It does not appear that the pattern presents consistently at even smaller scales (inside sentences or even within words), but such low-level patterning would convert the prose into poetry. Le Guin also explains how the two-beat rhythm at lower levels works to produce some of the effects at the higher levels of the complete narrative, noting that the walking rhythm "carries the whole narrative straight through from beginning to end, from There to Back Again, without faltering . . . One, two, left, right, on foot, all the way. And back."[47] It seems to me that the steady walking rhythm at the level of the scene and chapter drives the story through its slow and gentle interlacing twists and curls in *The Fellowship of the Ring* and then sustains the ramifying narrative in the final two volumes in the same way that a musical composition has an underlying rhythm (indicated by its time signature) and a fundamental set of regular repetitions upon which all the larger-scale variations and elaborations depend.[48]

That "unstressed" or "released" is half of the fundamental rhythm of the narrative also contributes to the sense that reading *The Lord of the Rings* is more like having an experience than reading just another book. As Le Guin notes, "unrelieved psychological or emotional stress or tension, and a narrative pace racing without a break from start to climax characterize much of the fiction of" the mid-twentieth century.[49] These characteristics, although not explicitly marked, would certainly be familiar to readers, shaping their expectations of a book. Failure to meet these expectations causes the experience of reading *The Lord of the Rings* to be mentally categorized differently than the experience of reading other books: It *feels* like something else. The natural, human-centered rhythms of the text and the resonances these create with the patterns of the lived experiences of the readers can cause that "something else" to be "having an experience," going through life, albeit a more vivid, beautiful, terrible, and emotionally powerful part of life than most of our regular day-to-day experiences.

THE FREEDOM THAT writers of fantasy and science fiction have to invent alternate worlds imposes on them a task of explanation that writers who work in more constrained genres can generally avoid. Writers of realistic fiction, detective novels, or spy thrillers do not need to explain the basic geography of a world, nor the various kinds of plants, animals, and sentient beings that inhabit it, nor the workings of physics or magic there, because the minds of their readers already have a sufficiently complete idea of our mundane world and its workings. In contrast, writers of fantasy and science fiction have the challenging task of depicting their imagined world and explaining how it works. Readers come to a story lacking sufficient information about the world in which the story operates, and indeed, one of the pleasures of reading science fiction and fantasy is identifying differences from the mundane world and inferring the rules of the story-world.

But the vast majority of works of fantasy and science fiction are not abstract *Gedankenexperimente*; they are novels and short stories that follow most of the conventions of these forms. Writers of fantasy and science fiction almost never present a list of or disquisition on those specific features of their imagined world that differ from the mundane world.[50] Instead, they interweave essential information into their narratives in such a way that their readers can piece together knowledge sufficient for understanding the story. The experience of doing the cognitive work required to understand a work of fantasy or science fiction is probably the most distinctive characteristic of these two genres,* and the amount of cognitive effort required to infer the rules of the invented world is a substantial component of a reader's experience of any given work of fantasy or science fiction.

* Whether or not a reader understands the need for and enjoys experiencing this required cognition is probably what separates those who enjoy these genres from those who do not.

The more explication there is in a narrative, the less cognitive effort is required of the reader, but explication also distances the reader from the characters and interrupts the flow of the narrative, making it less emotionally engaging. Conversely, although the free-flowing narratives enabled by essential information being interwoven rather than explicated are generally more engaging, the increased cognitive effort required by this approach can distract and therefore distance the reader. Every work strikes its own balance among these complex tradeoffs.

The unnamed narrator of *The Lord of Rings* is able to communicate what any character is thinking or feeling, to view scenes or objects not immediately visible to characters, and to present historical background information of which the characters are unaware.* The global point of view is thus third-person fully omniscient. The narrative of *The Lord of the Rings* does open with this non-associated point of view, but by the middle of the second page, the point of view switches to that of Sam's father, old Gaffer Gamgee, who is used to communicate the general opinions well-disposed hobbits have about Bilbo. His point of view is then used for most of the rest of the chapter—although there is one multi-paragraph and one shorter passage in which the omniscient narrator summarizes the goings-on at Bilbo's birthday party, and the chapter finishes off from Frodo's point of view. "The Shadow of the Past," starts off with a few pages of general omniscient explication, although some of this is said to be information that Frodo had gathered, but the rest of the chapter is firmly associated with one or another character's point of view, indeed, there is not another long passage of pure omniscient explication until Chapter 5, "A Conspiracy Unmasked":

> Long ago Gorenhad Oldbuck, head of the Oldbuck family, one of the oldest in the Marish or indeed the Shire, had crossed the river, which was the original boundary of the land eastwards. He built (and excavated) Brandy Hall, changed his name to Brandybuck, and settled down to become master of what was

* For example, describing what the road or river did after it went out of the sight of the characters behind a hill or bend, or describing what Isengard had looked like before Saruman defiled it; *TT*, III, viii, 159–60.

> virtually a small independent country. . . That was the origin of Buckland, a thickly inhabited strip between the river and the Old Forest, a sort of colony from the Shire.[51]

This omniscient historical point of view is relatively rare in *The Lord of the Rings* and is used primarily in two contexts: providing the historical background of Isengard, Dunharrow, Minas Tirith, and the various towers and fortresses of Mordor; and narrating the large-scale action of battles that a single character would not be able to perceive.

Obviously this third-person fully omniscient point of view was available to Tolkien, and as is evident from the quoted paragraph, it is very effective at giving the reader a great deal of information about the world of the story. Nevertheless, Tolkien did not use it for the vast majority of the narration. Instead, there is in every chapter a character or small group of characters through which the narrative is focalized, and readers are informed directly of the mental and emotional states of only the focalized character. For example, we are told how Frodo feels in the journey through the wilderness after he is wounded by the Morgul-knife, but the hunger, cold, fear, exhaustion, and concern for their friend that are surely felt by Sam, Merry, Pippin, and Aragorn are only communicated through external actions or statements. This sophisticated technique enables Tolkien to create the impression that the action takes place in an enormous, detailed landscape with a deep history without losing the intimacy that is generated by a strictly limited-omniscient point-of-view. Indeed, the intimacy that arises from limited omniscience is at times enhanced rather than broken when Tolkien is presenting the "vast backcloths" of Middle-earth and its history.[52]

It has long been recognized that much of the particular character of the narratives of both *The Hobbit* and *The Lord of the Rings* results from the story being mediated through the points of view of the hobbits: "In the former, Bilbo works as the link between modern times and the archaic world of dwarves and dragons. In the latter, Frodo and his Shire companions play a similar part, though the world they move in has also and in more complex ways been 'mediated.' "[53] Almost from the moment of their introduction as hole-dwellers in the first paragraphs of *The Hobbit*, hobbits are depicted as being uninterested in the world beyond the borders of the bucolic Shire. They are the least-traveled people in Middle-earth, know little of the world's extensive and complex history, have seemingly no commonly held geographical lore, and are not part of any social networks outside of their Shire. Tolkien's using hobbits as mediators, therefore, allows him to provide essential information about Middle-earth to readers in an organic form that does not break the flow of the narrative in the ways that long passages of authorial explication would: The hobbit characters need knowledge about the world as much as readers do, and supplying information in this way—as the answers to hobbit questions or explanations for the benefit of the hobbits—maintains the consistency of the narrative.

Shippey and many others have seen the mediation of the hobbits as one of Tolkien's greatest innovations—as indeed it is—because it allows him to present the epic or heroic world to readers without adopting the awkward and off-putting (to many twentieth-century readers) methods discussed earlier in Chapter 1. The mediation of the hobbits allows Tolkien to avoid a heavy-handed frame narrative or stylistic imitation of old literature, or any awkward time- or space-travel machinery that would transport a modern observer into Middle-earth.

But the sheer effectiveness of Tolkien's narrative technique has perhaps obscured a more abstract principle. Although the narrative of *The Lord of the Rings* is mostly focalized through hobbit characters, not all focalizing characters are hobbits.* Much of Book III is focalized through Aragorn, Gimli, and Legolas, and in other portions of the narrative, Gandalf, Faramir, Gollum, the band of Black Riders who attack the Crickhollow House, the Lord of the Nazgûl, and even a somewhat confused fox also serve as focalizing characters. Although to readers swept along by the story it may seem that the narrative is always from the point of view of one or another hobbit, in fact Tolkien tells the story very consistently through the point of view of the *least knowledgeable character*—who very often happens to be a hobbit. This is a subtle but important distinction.

The narrative is focalized through a character who *is* knowledgeable

* Frodo is the primary focalizer in Books I and II. In Books IV and VI it is both Frodo and Sam, with the latter taking an increasingly large role as the story progresses. Merry and Pippin are the major focalizing characters in most of Books III and V.

only when the true least-knowledgeable character is unconscious (or when there is only one character in the scene). For example, in "Many Meetings" the narrative is briefly from the point of view of Gandalf when the Wizard looks at newly awakened Frodo in Rivendell and wonders if he will completely recover from his wound. The beginning of "The Departure of Boromir" is from Aragorn's point of view as the Ranger is alone, running back to Parth Galen looking for the hobbits. These focalizations are not a violation of the least knowledgeable character principle, since although Gandalf and Aragorn are very knowledgeable in general, in these two scenes they do not know, respectively, if Frodo will be fully healed or where the hobbits have gone.

Focalizing the narrative through the point of view of the least knowledgeable character allows Tolkien to communicate in an organic way all the information about Middle-earth that the reader needs in order to understand the story. The character's quest for that information is a natural result of his lack of knowledge about the world, and as the character receives new information, so does the reader. Tolkien is thus able to provide substantial quantities of information about geography and history without interrupting the experiential flow: Hobbits ask questions, and hobbits and readers receive answers. More knowledgeable characters inform the hobbits about something, so readers become informed. Information can thus be presented as dialogue and broken up into more manageable pieces, and the in-world significance of that information can be openly stated—an approach that is relatively rare in interwoven fantasy and science fiction stories, which often must rely on rather gimmicky ways of explicating key features of the world. For example, in Chapter 2, Tolkien needs to introduce readers to the idea that there is more than one wizard in Middle-earth, so when Gandalf is starting to explain the significance of the Ring, he says:

> "I might perhaps have consulted Saruman the White, but something always held me back."
>
> "Who is he?" asked Frodo. "I have never heard of him before."
>
> "Maybe not," answered Gandalf. "Hobbits are, or were, no concern of his. Yet he is great among the Wise. He is the chief

of my order and the head of the Council. His knowledge is deep, but his pride has grown with it, and he takes ill any meddling. The lore of the Elven-rings, great and small, is his province. He has long studied it, seeking the lost secrets of their making; but when the Rings were debated in the Council, all that he would reveal to us of his ring-lore told against my fears."[54]

The in-story reason for Frodo needing to ask this question is the insularity of the hobbits, who have never heard of Saruman despite his living in the tower of Orthanc for the past 250 years and having been in Middle-earth for centuries before that.[55] Frodo needs this information to understand his circumstances, and readers need it in order to understand the later plot, but Gandalf delivers it as the answer to a question in a natural dialogic form: He says that Saruman is "the chief of my order" without explaining what this order is and "head of the Council" without explicitly naming the "White Council," which earlier in the same paragraph Gandalf had said "drove the dark power from Mirkwood."[56] It is up to readers to infer that Saruman is a Wizard, because Gandalf never uses the word.

Instead of distancing readers from the narrative by making them endure a lecture on the history or geography of Middle-earth, this technique draws them more deeply into the story. I am certain that many readers experience the same hungry frustration I felt when my father first read me "The Shadow of the Past" (the most explanation-heavy chapter in *The Lord of the Rings*). It seemed as if Frodo had to drag important information out of Gandalf piece by piece, and still the wizard did not tell as much of the history of the Ring and about Gil-galad and Elendil overthrowing Sauron as I wanted to hear.[57] By the time the narrative reaches the end of "Three's Company" and there have been multiple frightening and enigmatic encounters with Black Riders, readers' emotions are fully aligned with Frodo's when the hobbit's frustration at the difficulty of getting information from more knowledgeable characters boils over in his speech with the elf Gildor: "I cannot imagine what could be more terrifying than your hints and warnings."[58] But Gildor does not really relent, and neither does Tolkien: Essential information comes out in dribs and drabs and is not always in the form that would be most efficient for either the least knowledgeable character or the reader. For example, although the multiple speakers at the Council of Elrond are focused on the decision of what to do with the Ring, the information that they—and readers—need comes within complex stories focused around the knowledge and interests of the characters telling them. It is up to the reader to synthesize, which is perhaps why, as discussed previously, this chapter has a reputation for being particularly challenging. Nevertheless, even in "The Council of Elrond," the least knowledgeable character point of view is maintained throughout the chapter, aligning readers and characters in both their learning of new information and their desire for more.

There are, however, several places in *The Lord of the Rings* in which the point of view is not that of the least knowledgeable character in a given scene but is also not the long-range historical point of view discussed earlier. The most dramatic of these is the beginning of "The Battle of the Pelennor Fields" in Book V:

> But it was no orc-chieftain or brigand that led the assault upon Gondor. The darkness was breaking too soon, before the date that his Master had set for it: fortune had betrayed him for the moment, and the world had turned against him; victory was slipping from his grasp even as he stretched out his hand to seize it. But his arm was long. He was still in command, wielding great powers. King, Ringwraith, Lord of the Nazgûl, he had many weapons. He left the Gate and vanished.[59]

At first glance this paragraph appears to follow the same rules as the majority of the text: Despite his age, power, and knowledge, The Lord of the Nazgûl is the only, and hence the least knowledgeable, character in the scene. It is not impossible that the Lord of the Nazgûl wonders if "the world has turned against him" but stiffens his resolve by reminding himself that he is "King, Ringwraith, Lord of the Nazgûl," but that seems at best awkward, and interpreting these lines along with the opening description of what he is not, the assertion that "victory was slipping from his grasp," and the statement that he "vanished" is more consistent with a fully omniscient point of view.

Further support for this interpretation comes in the next paragraph, which seems initially to be from Théoden's point of view but also turns out to be a fully omniscient narrator, as the king's consciousness cannot focalize what the character cannot see when he is crushed under his horse as the fell beast ridden by the Lord of the Nazgûl descends upon the Rohirrim.[60] It is only after three long paragraphs of action that the narrative becomes focalized through a character, Merry, who sees Éowyn's victory over the Black Rider and then has words with the dying Théoden. The story then proceeds to subtly shift from Merry's point of view to that of the omniscient narrator since Merry cannot possibly see all the things happening in the massive battle—no one character could—so despite this brief focalization through a least knowledgeable character, full omniscience is by far the chapter's dominant point of view: The verses on Snowmane's Howe, which could only be carved after the battle, and the assertion that "green and long grew the grass" there necessitates an omniscient narrator, as does the statement that few of the Easterlings or Haradrim ever returned eastward.[61]

However, even when the storytelling necessitates a fully omniscient point of view, Tolkien finds spaces in which he can link the narrative to the perceptions of particular characters. The brief focalization through Merry and two equally short section of the chapter in which readers get some of Éomer's thoughts, first when he sees his sister Éowyn lying among the slain, and then when he recognizes the vulnerability of the Rohirrim after their initial charge through the hosts of Mordor, connect readers to the points of view of the characters. Even in these very small instances, the least knowledgeable character principle holds: Merry is the least knowledgeable of the three actors in the scene of Éowyn's combat with the Lord of the Nazgûl because he is external to their interaction until the very end. Éomer is least knowledgeable when he first sees Éowyn seemingly dead in a battle when he had believed her to be in Dunharrow because Merry knows why she is present. Éomer is no less knowledgeable about the significance of the black sails, but he does not know any more, either.[62] Indeed, even the omniscient narrator claims not to have all possible knowledge: "No few had fallen, renowned or nameless, captain or soldier; for it was a great battle and the full count of it no tale has told."[63]

THE NARRATIVES OF *The Hobbit* and *The Lord of the Rings* are tightly oriented not only to what the least knowledgeable characters know, but also what they perceive. Subjectively, Tolkien seems to spend more time on the physical description of geography and the characters' orientation within it than on any other feature of his narrative. Passage after passage of detailed prose describes the appearance of the land, the foliage, the flowing of water, and, most of all, the topography. Even something as apparently simple as the meeting with the elves in the Woody End includes nearly a full-page description of both the general lay of the land in that part of the Shire and the details of the specific location.[64] Tolkien spends more words on the physical layout of Helm's Deep and the Hornburg than he does on the initial combat of Aragorn, Éomer, and Gimli against the orcs and Dunlendings. Gimli's rapturous description of the Glittering Caves is longer than the entire battle at daybreak.[65]

Part of Tolkien's genius is his ability to blend traditions of the epic with the techniques of the modern novel, and nowhere is that kind of realism more apparent than in the description of landscape, in which Tolkien's simple, unornamented—but by no means bland—style is put to its best effect. We walk with the characters for hundreds of miles, oriented in space the same way they are and seeing the same things they see. As Le Guin notes, Tolkien consistently and frequently provides compass directions so that readers are aware of not just the relative, but the absolute directions in which the characters are moving. Because they are so clearly realized and straightforward, the descriptive passages are not boring: There are very few metaphors at all and no purple prose, just images of landscape, geology, and flora that can be easily visualized. I think that is a key point: Because Tolkien moves us through the landscape as the characters would perceive it rather than from other viewpoints, the images unroll before us in an experiential manner. We may not be physically seeing what is being described, but we read about it in the same order we would see it if we were in Middle-earth rather than if we had a God's-eye view. This consistent focalization contributes to making *The Lord of the Rings* experiential.

❦

EVERY LITERARY WORK produces and operates within what is called an *epistemic regime*, a particular distribution of knowledge among the author, characters, and readers. An epistemic regime in which the reader knows more than the characters produces irony; this is the most common situation in most literary works and is in some ways unavoidable: At the very least readers know that they are reading a book with a particular title and a certain length. But in some works the ironic relationship is inverted to various degrees, and characters are more knowledgeable than readers about their own emotions, thoughts, or histories. In science fiction and fantasy, characters may also know a great deal more about their world and its rules than readers do, forcing readers to synthesize scattered hints into an understanding of how the world of the book works that is sufficiently detailed for the plot to make sense.

One of the effects of an anti-ironic epistemic regime is the reduction of the assumed readerly—and authorial—superiority that is an important component of many modernist and post-modernist works. Anti-irony can dislodge readers from their accustomed position of privilege and may therefore push them away from an emotional engagement with the text, particularly when they must perform cognitive work to understand a world that the characters understand without effort. Tolkien's use of the least knowledgeable character point of view substantially reduces this readerly alienation by aligning the learning experiences of the focalizing characters with those of readers. Thus despite *The Lord of the Rings* being set in a different world than the mundane world of the reader, both character and reader end up learning essential information at the same time. This experience of learning is a major contributor to the overall experiential sense of *The Lord of the Rings*.

Learning, I contend, is a qualitatively different reading experience than most (or all) of the other emotions or sensations that are invoked by literature. Only in the act of learning are the character and the reader experiencing *the same mental processes at the same time*. When we read about a character being sad, we may feel a concomitant sadness, but we are not necessarily experiencing the emotion in exactly the same way. A character's sadness is based on in-world situations or actions; our sadness is based on what we *read* about the character's emotions. The same is true for hunger, exhaustion, anger, comfort, warmth, or joy: Despite the ability of art to invoke feelings in us, our cognitive experiences are not the same as the characters'. No reader, one hopes, is having the same experience as Frodo when Gollum bites off his finger. We can imagine the pain, and we may even feel some of it vicariously, but we do not feel the *same* pain because ours is at least one remove via the text. However, when a character learns and the reader learns the same information, the reader is experiencing at least some of the same things that the character is experiencing.* The cognitive processes taking place in the reader and those imputed to the character are as close to being the same as is possible, so for moments of learning, the reader and character are closely aligned. Tolkien's use of the least knowledgeable character point of view thus transforms the presentation of essential information from an unfortunate necessity to a strength. Rather than being distanced from the narrative while essential information is being imparted by an omniscient narrator or through interwoven material that requires extra cognitive work on the part of the reader (work that world-knowledgeable characters do not themselves perform), readers' and least knowledgeable characters' mind-states are synchronized by the shared, simultaneous experience of learning.

The importance of the anti-ironic epistemic regime to the narrative helps to explain some features of one of the more complex and difficult passages of *The Lord of the Rings*: Frodo and Sam's conversation about stories and Gollum's missed opportunity for redemption, both of which occur in "The Stairs of Cirith Ungol," in *The Two Towers*. While he and Frodo are resting in a dark crevice partway through their long climb, Sam suggests that the heroes of old tales probably had not sought out adventures but had "been just landed in them," and had many chances of turning back that they did not take. Comparing his and Frodo's plight to that of Beren and Lúthien, Sam suddenly realizes that "we're in the same tale still! It's going on. Don't the great tales

* There is always the inescapable mediation that readers are aware that they are reading a book; we should not imagine that the characters and readers are experiencing precisely the same mental processes, as the information learned would have different associations and contexts, but in the case of learning there are surely more cognitive processes in common than in other situations.

ever end?" After Frodo's pessimistic assessment that "our part will end later—or sooner," Sam continues:

> Still, I wonder if we shall ever be put into songs or tales. We're in one, of course; but I mean: put into words, you know, told by the fireside, or read out of a big book with red and black letters, years and years afterwards. And people will say: "Let's hear about Frodo and the Ring!" And they'll say: "Yes, that's one of my favourite stories. Frodo was very brave, wasn't he dad?" "Yes, my boy, the famousest of the hobbits, and that's saying a lot."[66]

Verlyn Flieger correctly identifies this passage as "the most-self-referential and post-modern moment in the entire book,"[67] but, probably because it is so obvious, she does not specify what makes it post-modern: the fully ironic epistemic regime. Here we have an example of the reader not just knowing more than the characters in some general sense, but knowing the answers to the specific questions the characters are asking—that Frodo's and Sam's story did indeed get "put into words" not just in an in-world book (about which we do not find out until much later in the narrative), but in the book that the reader is now holding and reading. This violation of the otherwise consistently unironic epistemic regime is perhaps why other critics have balked at the passage.[68]

What, to my knowledge, has not previously been noted is how vigorously Tolkien wrenches the epistemic regime back to being anti-ironic in the passage that follows almost immediately. Frodo and Sam had fallen asleep soon after finishing their conversation,

> And so Gollum found them hours later, when he returned, crawling and creeping down the path out of the gloom ahead. Sam sat propped against the stone, his head dropping sideways and his breathing heavy. In his lap lay Frodo's head, drowned deep in sleep; upon his white forehead lay one of Sam's brown hands, and the other lay softly upon his master's breast. Peace was in both their faces.
>
> Gollum looked at them. A strange expression passed over

> his lean hungry face. The gleam faded from his eyes, and they went dim and grey, old and tired. A spasm of pain seemed to twist him, and he turned away, peering back up towards the pass, shaking his head, as if engaged in some inner debate. Then he came back, and slowly put out a trembling hand, very cautiously he touched Frodo's knee—but almost the touch was a caress. For a fleeting moment, could one of the sleepers have seen him, they would have thought that they beheld an old weary hobbit, shrunken by the years that had carried him far beyond his time, beyond friends and kin, and the fields and stream of youth, an old starved pitiable thing.
>
> But at that touch Frodo stirred and cried out softly in his sleep and immediately Sam was wide awake. The first thing he saw was Gollum "pawing at master," as he thought.[69]

The first paragraph is focalized through the least knowledgeable character, Gollum: The narrative is made up of what he sees, hears, and thinks. But in the second sentence of the second paragraph the point of view shifts abruptly to a different focalization, but not that of the fully omniscient or historical narrator who is otherwise used in situations in which characters are unconscious. Gollum cannot see his own expression or the dimming of the gleam in his eyes, so the focalization cannot be through him, but the narrator does not know if Gollum actually feels pain or even if he truly had a spasm (it "seemed to twist him"). The narrative moves into the subjunctive—"as if engaged in some inner debate," and "could one of the sleepers have seen him,"—yet despite not having access to Gollum's thoughts, the narrator does know what the two sleeping hobbits "would have thought." The next paragraph snaps back to focalization through the suddenly wide-awake Sam.

That this very complex set of point-of-view shifts occurs immediately after the anti-ironic epistemic regime has been broken by Frodo's and Sam's meta-fictional conversation perhaps indicates how important anti-irony is to the overall effect of *The Lord of the Rings*. For Tolkien to avoid slipping fully into an ironic—and hence modern or postmodern epistemic regime—he needed to avoid creating instances of readers knowing more than characters, but at the same time he needed to narrate a scene absolutely essential to some of the major themes of the book—and which was so emotionally important to him that, he reported, he wept when he wrote it.[70] A least-knowledgeable-character focalization through Gollum works for the first paragraph, but if Tolkien had retained that point of view or adopted that of a fully omniscient narrator, he would have had to reveal *what* Gollum was inwardly debating when he was shaking his head, and from that point on readers would know more than Frodo and Sam about Gollum's plan to betray them—a fully ironic epistemic regime that would have interfered with the experientiality of the narrative. To avoid this, Tolkien briefly creates a non-omniscient narrator who can nevertheless observe Gollum's external behavior, speculate about his internal states, and then project hypothetical reactions onto the sleeping hobbits. Although these rapid and unsignaled shifts in point of view are sufficiently cognitively demanding to have generated a mismatch between the singular antecedent "one of the sleepers" and the plural pronoun "they," the narrative contortions do restore the briefly disturbed anti-ironic epistemic regime. Readers do not know that Gollum has decided to abandon the hobbits in Shelob's Lair in hopes that he will be able to recover the Ring after the monster has killed and eaten them, so the knowledge of the focalizing characters and the readers is again aligned.

The experiential quality of *The Lord of the Rings* is not *caused* by its being anti-ironic, but this epistemic regime works in concert with other features of the narrative, especially the least knowledgeable character point of view. Resisting the modernist and post-modernist impulse to emphasize readerly—and hence writerly—superiority, Tolkien instead maintains an arrangement of knowledge that causes his readers to learn along with his least-knowledgeable characters, creating a shared experience of Middle-earth.

IN ALMOST EVERY even-numbered year since 1998 I have taught my J.R.R. Tolkien course in the Holman Room of Mary Lyon Hall, the oldest classroom in the oldest building at Wheaton College, with twenty-foot-high coffered ceilings, ornate trim and fixtures, and a 175-year tradition of classes being held there.* There is a platform at the front of the room where the lectern, blackboard, and professor stand several steps higher than the desks, and from this vantage point I have an excellent view of everyone in the class when, on the first day, I ask my students about their previous engagement with Tolkien's work. Since the initial release of the Peter Jackson *Lord of the Rings* films in the early 2000s, more than 90 percent of the students have raised their hands when I ask if they have seen one of the movies. This is not surprising, given the immense popularity of the films and their ubiquitous presence as reruns on various networks. It is also not surprising that between 60 and 70 percent of the students have read at least one of Tolkien's books: Even though they are not school set-texts, Tolkien's works are still extremely popular.† What regularly surprises me is the response to my third question: "How many of you had any of Tolkien's works read aloud to you?" Year after year, from before the first Jackson film was released to fully two decades after *The Return of the King* was in theaters, more than half of the students in the class have raised their hands, and there are usually others nodding their heads. All of these students—around 350 over the course of 27 years—had at least *The Hobbit* read to them, and probably two thirds of these listened to the entire *Lord of the Rings* read by a parent, grandparent, older sibling, or other caregiver.‡

As far as I can tell, in the English-speaking world in the twenty-first century, no other text of comparable length and reading difficulty is so frequently read aloud to children. On principle I avoid sociological research performed by literature professors, but I would make an exception for a study of the reasons people give for reading *The Hobbit*, and, in particular, *The Lord of the Rings*, to their children. On the surface very little about Tolkien's great works would seem to recommend them for bedtime reading: The books are long, complex, and filled with unfamiliar names; they include poems in a variety of forms, and there

* You can see the Holman Room and even the exact chalkboard I use in some scenes of the 2017 film *Professor Marston and the Wonder Women*.

† Although *The Hobbit* may be becoming one for middle-grade readers.

‡ Or, in more recent years, as an audiobook.

are phrases and even whole passages in invented languages; there are many scenes of violence; beloved characters die; other characters suffer terribly; and in the end the protagonist has been so traumatized physically and mentally that he cannot live happily ever after. Yet in multiple families, the reading aloud of Tolkien's masterwork has reached its third generation, and, if my students' responses are any guide, a non-negligible fraction of that younger generation intends to pass on this tradition to their own children.

I would welcome sociological research on this topic because I myself do not have a thoroughly convincing explanation for the phenomenon. I will note that, based on about seventeen years of reading books of fantasy and science fiction aloud to both of my children, *The Hobbit* and *The Lord of the Rings* are the very easiest to read—in the words of my daughter when she was seven years old—"The *right* way. With *voices*." Tolkien always makes it clear which characters are speaking, so that you do not start in on a piece of mono- or dialogue with the wrong adopted voice.* He also provides a great deal of geographical description so that you are always clear where you are oriented in space, and his poems are both charming and easy to read or sing. Lloyd Alexander's *The Chronicles of Prydain*, Susan Cooper's *The Dark Is Rising*, and Ursula Le Guin's original Earthsea trilogy, while they do not all possess exactly the same qualities as Tolkien's works, are nevertheless reasonably close to being as effective as read-aloud books. However, in my informal surveys only a tiny fraction of the students report being read those works of fantasy aloud even though they, unlike *The Lord of the Rings*, were written specifically for an audience of children. It seems plausible that the experiential qualities of the works that are discussed in this chapter may contribute to the desires of people to want to pass Tolkien's works on to their children as directly as possible, not merely as a physical book, but as the gift of many hours of reading aloud.[71]

Whatever their reasons for doing so, by reading Tolkien's works

---

* This clarity is in contrast to a book like Frank Herbert's *Dune*, in which it is possible to read almost an entire page before realizing that the speech you thought was being made by Gurney Halleck was actually spoken by Duncan Idaho, and thus you have used the wrong voice for the whole thing. Don't think my daughter didn't notice and ask for the entire giant paragraph to be reread in the correct voice.

aloud to their children, people have caused those children to have an experience of *The Hobbit* and *The Lord of the Rings* that is qualitatively different from that of those who only read the works silently to themselves. As noted above, my own introduction to Tolkien was my father reading the books aloud to me when I was five or six years old. During his internship and residency years at New York Hospital, on the nights he was home, he read me *The Hobbit*, then *The Lord of the Rings*, and when we reached the end of *The Return of the King*, we started again on *The Hobbit*. This repeated until I finished second grade. I actually cannot remember my father reading me any other book (although he must have).*

Even before my children were born I knew I would be passing on the experience and trying to create a tradition. In the winter and spring of 2005 I read *The Lord of the Rings* to my daughter, who was then four and a half. We started very soon after Christmas and finished on Easter, which comes reasonably close to mirroring the journey of the Fellowship from Rivendell (they departed on December 25) to Mount Doom (the Ring was destroyed on March 25). We read just about every night. A few characters had special voices—Gimli got my attempt at a Yorkshire accent, which I had used for Thorin in *The Hobbit*; I tried to do a West Midlands accent for Sam, and Treebeard and Gollum were easy and fun—but mostly I just read in my "regular voice," as she called it.† When we reached the end of *The Return of the King*, we stopped, as she wanted new books. But only a few years later my son, four years younger than his sister, was ready for *The Hobbit* and *The Lord of the Rings*. He wanted more rather than fewer voices when I read the books to him at age five, and he even insisted that I sing the poems. My daughter then insisted on a second reading because, she said, she did

---

* Except for an abortive attempt at T. H. White's *The Once and Future King* that failed because—I now realize—I could not understand how "Wart" could be a nickname for "Art," because in my and my father's dialect the first word is pronounced to rhyme with "port" while the second rhymes with "cart." Not understanding that joke—and no one in the family being able to explain it—bothered me enough that, to my father's disappointment, I asked him to go back to *The Lord of the Rings*.

† A result of my having listened obsessively to the 1974 four-record set of *The Hobbit* by Nicol Williamson who, among other roles, played Merlin in the film *Excalibur*.

not remember the first one, and so she and I worked our way through the books again when she was about eight years old. To my surprise, my children were not in the slightest bit bored listening to passages of landscape descriptions—they never asked me to speed up or skip ahead the way they did when I was reading Saruman's speeches or toward the end of some of the longer conversations with Treebeard.* Adopting distinctive voices for the characters or singing the poems, which can only occur in oral performance of Tolkien's work, quite obviously makes them more experiential (for both reader and hearer) than reading them silently. Likewise, orally presented or aurally received passages of landscape description may be even more effective at making *The Lord of the Rings* experiential, both because the landscape unfolds for the hearer the same way it does for the reader and because the passages of description are not skipped or rushed through when read aloud.

"Doubtless there is such a thing as the sheer number of pages the reader has had to turn that can add poignancy to the story—one almost feels this is the case as we come to the great close of Malory's epic. But not with Tolkien's book, for we have never been very much involved anyway," wrote Colin Manlove in 1975.[72] If we cut through the doubletalk so characteristic of 1970s criticism—"*doubtless*," "*can* add," "one *almost* feels"—we can understand the critic to be claiming that the sheer size of a book can make a reader care more about its story, although not in the case of Tolkien's work (then why bring it up?) because "we" had little emotional investment in the story. I must admit that I never expected to see a piece of literary criticism assert the sunk-costs fallacy, but even if we set that aside, Manlove's statement probably cracks the top twenty in any list of Dumb Things Said about Tolkien—readers do not get emotionally involved in *The Lord of the Rings*? Really? Nevertheless, there is something potentially useful behind the tangle of Manlove's assertions, and if he could have restrained his urge to sneer for a moment, he might have been able to recognize its significance. It is not so much that *The Lord of the Rings* is very long (even though that is pretty much all Manlove is say-

* Like seemingly all readers of *The Lord of the Rings*, my children loved Treebeard as a character, but because I read his passages very slowly and deliberately—as an Ent would speak—my son became impatient. Indeed, the slow speech of the Ents is something that works flawlessly in the book but does not translate well to other media.

ing about it), but that Manlove unconsciously recognizes the experiential nature of Tolkien's masterpiece: He focuses on the action of turning pages, not the content of what is written on them, and he suggests that there is a poignancy to reaching the end of a long set of repeated actions. Had he followed up this insight, he might have progressed toward an understanding of the appeal of *The Lord of the Rings* to so many readers.

But he did not, and neither did many of the other initial critics of Tolkien. Yet once it is pointed out, the experiential nature of *The Lord of the Rings* seems incredibly obvious. Features of the work's architectonics, particularly its repetitions, produce rhythms similar to those of the lives of readers. The visual focalizing of the narrative is consistent with the landscape description so that readers feel that they are seeing the land as the characters see it, not, generally, with a God's-eye-view. Similarly, consistent informational focalization through the least knowledgeable character has the readers learning about Middle-earth along with the characters, producing a shared experience of learning. The anti-ironic epistemic regime also plays a part in mapping readers onto characters, since there are very few opportunities for the readers to feel superior to the characters by knowing more about their world than they do—indeed, the situation is quite the opposite. That so many people have *The Lord of the Rings* read aloud to them or read it aloud to others adds another layer of experientiality.

That much of *The Lord of the Rings* is optimized for oral delivery is surely a result of Tolkien having written it for—and delivered it orally to—his audience of C.S. Lewis and the other Inklings. The effect of the resulting style on silent readers is not likely to have been one that Tolkien was conscious of or thought to optimize. Likewise the other features we have examined in this chapter are very unlikely to have been chosen by Tolkien in order to make *The Lord of the Rings* experiential. Indeed, I doubt the thought ever crossed his mind. But for whatever reasons, what Tolkien believed made for good writing also made for reading or listening that produces the impression of experientiality. And that is sufficient, because if something feels like an experience, well, it is.

CHAPTER 5

Emotions

The price of a memory is the memory of the sorrow it brings.

—Counting Crows, "Mrs. Potter's Lullaby"

Even as it preserves a memory of lost time, a ruin forces us to confront the permanence of our separation from the past. The same flow of time that made the ruin what it is also sweeps us along, and we can resist this current even less than the worn and polished stone that was there before us and remains after. The beauty and the grandeur of a ruin arises from its both having partially succumbed to time and having persisted despite it, and much of the emotional resonance of ruins is the intertwining of awe with sadness.

The textual ruins that Tolkien created generate complex emotions in their readers that are fundamentally akin to the effects physical ruins have upon those who view them. In the moment of reading Tolkien's work or viewing a ruin, we are temporarily unable to ignore the absolute pastness of the past and the loss that comes from our inexorable movement through time. And yet this grief is somehow transformed by the beauty of the ruin or the ruined text into something greater, so that although the pain and sorrow are not taken away, they become something new, an emotion for which we have no specific word, but which we can recognize in Tolkien's description of "a sadness that was yet blessed and without bitterness."

❦

The Silmarillion was first published in the United States in the Autumn of 1977. Waiting for me under the Christmas tree that year, a gift from Santa Claus mixed in among the various Star Wars toys my brother and I had coveted, was my first copy of the book, the cover illustrated with a version of Tolkien's drawing "The Mountain-Path." I was nine years old, living with my parents and my five-year-old brother in Newtonville, Massachusetts, a suburb of Boston. I first read *The Silmarillion* during the school vacation between Christmas and New Year's Day, and I must have started rereading it relatively soon, because I vividly remember coming home from school at the beginning of the great Blizzard of '78 and opening to "Of the Fifth Battle." *The Silmarillion* has ever afterward been part of my inner life.

It was a hard time for my family. Although we had moved to the Boston area from New York City in the bicentennial summer of 1976 with high hopes, living in Massachusetts had turned out to be very difficult. My father was finishing a fellowship in cardiology at New England Medical Center and worked long hours at the hospital, which was no longer just across the street from where we lived. All of our relatives and friends were three hundred miles away; I found it difficult to adjust to New England mores in school. By Halloween of '77 my parents had begun the process of divorcing, so I knew that any roots I might have started to put down would soon be torn up when we returned to New Jersey.

Things in general were bad in 1978. Even though I was nine, I knew this. The US economy was a shambles and my father's fellowship pay, which we had expected to raise our standard of living, had not kept up with the extremely high inflation. Constant money problems led to frequent arguments. My father took a second job moonlighting at a distant hospital in order for us to afford the rent on the first floor of a modest two-family house in which the landlord and his family lived above us. The energy crisis meant that heating was very expensive. We were all used to living on the ninth floor of a high-rise building in

New York City, where the problem had been too much, not a lack of, heat, and I never did adjust to the ever-present chill in the house. I was always cold and uncomfortable, and my brother was often sick—he had to be hospitalized twice for asthma and pneumonia, and it seemed as if one or the other of us was always wheezing, coughing, and being taken to various doctors—none of whom were my father's friends and just across the street. To try to get warm, I developed the habit of sitting on a thin pillow directly on top of the radiator in the living room, my feet propped on the couch in front of me. More than once I burned my calf on the hot pipes, but sitting on the radiator was the only time I ever felt warm enough. I would rest the back of my head against the cold window glass and read *The Silmarillion* as the thin winter light faded and snow sifted down on the dark green needles and tiny red berries of the yews outside.

Although in retrospect this was the worst year of my childhood, I do not think I was either *alienated* or *depressed*, those buzzwords of the preadolescent psychology of the 1970s that I heard so often as I was dragged from one therapist to another over the next few years. No, I knew how to describe what I was feeling with a three-word sentence: I was *sad*. A very old word, with deep roots, *sad* appears in nearly the same form in the Germanic, Italic, Celtic, and Balto-Slavic branches of the Indo European language tree. The core sense of the word seems to be a combination of tired, full, heavy, and having had enough. That seems right. *Sad* is old fashioned, and less jargony than *alienated*, which can be traced back to the fourteenth century but had a different meaning than it does today, or *depressed*, which, meaning downhearted, only goes back to 1621 and with clinical implications, only to 1905. If sad things happen to them, people will feel sad, weary, and tired, and there is nothing abnormal about it. Sadness cannot be cured by medicine, and there is not much to be done internally. Either we change something, or we wait for the circumstances causing the sadness to pass. When you are a child, mostly you wait for the circumstances to pass. Sometimes they do.

At nine years old I did not know these things explicitly, but I did know them, at least to the extent that I knew—to the frustration of my parents and others—that there was nothing a doctor or therapist or pastor could do to eliminate my sadness, which was not some kind of infection or damage inside me. I also recognized that not *all* of my sadness, particularly the lingering sadness, came from the impending divorce, the absence of grandparents and cousins, the knowledge that we would be moving and once again and I would have to make all new friends. There was a sense of something else: Things were passing, including childhood itself, and there was no slowing down and certainly no going back.

Simply by being a human in time, Tolkien must have, at various moments in his life, felt some of the same things my nine-year-old self did, and aside from the general feeling of loss for past time, he had ample specific reasons for sadness: When he was four years old, his father died; when he was nine, his family had to give up living in the idyllic countryside and move into the city; when he was eleven, his mother died, leaving him and his brother orphans; when he was eighteen his guardian insisted that Tolkien break off all contact with the girl with whom he had fallen in love; in his twenty-fourth year two of his three closest friends were killed in World War I and he lost his health to trench fever. In comparison I was very lucky, both because I had experienced nothing nearly as terrible, and I had the aid of something that Tolkien did not have: *The Silmarillion*, which gave shape to grief and loss through art.

I am not claiming that *The Silmarillion* was or is a consolation, and unlike *The Lord of the Rings*, *The Silmarillion* does not even consistently leaven sadness and tragedy with triumph and joy. There is no equivalent to Frodo waking up on the Field of Cormallen, or the eagle telling the people of Minas Tirith to "Sing and rejoice!," the sprouting of the *mallorn* in the Shire, or the return of Bill the Pony. There are not even any lighthearted hobbit conversations or amusing anecdotes in *The Silmarillion*, which is perhaps why so many initial readers who had loved *The Lord of the Rings* were terribly disappointed.[1] But at nine years old I was not sophisticated enough to be angry at an author for not writing a different book than the one he wrote. To me *The Silmarillion* just was the history of Middle-earth, and so what had happened had happened. I never considered the possibility that Tolkien could have made the stories turn out differently.* And because I read the book this way and was not constantly comparing it unfavorably to *The Lord of the Rings*, *The Silmarillion* was able to do much more than provide comfort through distraction.

For me in 1978, Tolkien's art was most powerful not in the beautiful passages of *The Silmarillion*, but in the sweeping grandeur of the tragedies, and I was not so much taken by what I now know to call "the Great Tales" (Beren and Lúthien, Túrin, Tuor and Gondolin) as I was by the epic sweep of the darkness—and the heroic resistance to it. In the winter of 1978, when the cold had formed a thick crust of ice on top of the mounded snow and the joy and surprise of the great storm had given way to exhaustion, chill, worry, and cabin fever, it was easy to understand the feeling that Morgoth was winning and would always win, as if the bitter cold that settled in over us for the next ten days was coming from the gates of Angband.

I hasten to add that I did not believe in the literal reality of Morgoth or Angband or Beleriand. Even at that early age, I recognized symbolic and literary reality: Tolkien had created a set of stories that—as have the stories of the Bible for generations of people—work to shape a view of reality and to provide a set of symbols and motifs by which I might understand and, perhaps, influence it. Although Tolkien himself toyed with the conceit that Middle-earth was a real history of our world, perhaps located in prehistory, I have never felt that Arda needed that kind of historicity.[2] It has already achieved a higher sort of reality, true at a deeply imaginative level that was for me far more satisfying than a Middle-earth located in pre- or interglacial Europe would have been.†

It was probably not a coincidence that I was reading Chapter 20 of

---

* This sentiment is difficult to explain. I never once thought that Tolkien's tales were "real" in the sense that they had been physically instantiated in some ancient time or distant location; to my mind they were simply the only way things had turned out in the story-world. I never entertained counterfactuals.

† This interpretation puts me squarely opposed to Tolkien's own interpretation of myth versus Gospel: the "myths" in the Gospel were not "lies breathed through silver," but were true; *Bio*, 147.

The Silmarillion the day that the blizzard started. "Of the Fifth Battle: Nirnaeth Arnoediad," was the part of the book I reread the most: Almost fifty years later my original copy of *The Silmarillion* falls open to that chapter, the beginning of nine pages of almost unmitigated disaster poured upon all the heroes of the previous chapters. Fingon the valiant, who in heroically freeing Maedhros had temporarily healed the feud within the house of Finwë, was lost:

> But now in the western battle Fingon and Turgon were assailed by a tide of foes thrice greater than all the force that we left to them. Gothmog, Lord of Balrogs, high-captain of Angband, was come; and he drove a dark wedge between the Elvenhosts, surrounding King Fingon, and thrusting Turgon and Húrin aside towards the Fen of Serech. Then he turned upon Fingon. That was a grim meeting. At last Fingon stood alone with his guard dead around him; and he fought with Gothmog, until another Balrog came behind and cast a thong of fire about him. Then Gothmog hewed him with his black axe, and a white flame sprang up from the helm of Fingon as it was cloven. Thus fell the High King of the Noldor; and they beat him into the dust with their maces, and his banner, blue and silver, they trod into the mire of his blood.[3]

A dozen years later, when I was first translating *Beowulf* and came upon *þæt wæs god cyning* [that was a good king] in Line 11, I had a shock of recognition and a reprise of the feeling I had when first reading this passage in *The Silmarillion*, a combination of stomach-tightening horror and admiration for Fingon's bravery.* These feelings are further developed a page later in the scene—much like the ending of the Old English poem *The Battle of Maldon*—of the last stand of the Men of Dor-lómin at the Pass of Sirion:

* My recognition of another bit of Old English via previous exposure to Tolkien is responsible in part for my career as an Anglo-Saxonist because I recognized the phrase *wes thu hal* in the course catalogue: I took John Miles Foley's Old English course at the University of Missouri–Columbia, and subsequently changed my degree from fiction writing to medieval literature.

> Last of all Húrin stood alone. Then he cast aside his shield and wielded an axe two-handed; and it is sung that the axe smoked in the black blood of the troll guard of Gothmog until it withered, and each time that he slew Húrin cried: "*Aurë entuluva!* Day shall come again!" Seventy times he uttered that cry; but they took him at last alive, by the command of Morgoth . . . [4]

It was this bravery and defiance of Angband and everything that could be mapped onto Angband that held me and made the fall of Fingon and the last stand of Húrin part of my personal mythology. Notice that in this passage, even in the midst of some of the most violent and fast-moving action in *The Silmarillion*, Tolkien extends the narrative depth, noting that the description of Húrin's valor comes from some source within a tradition: "It is sung." The memory of Húrin's deeds is understood as having been preserved for a very long time, and that is part of the hero's triumph. Despite the defeat in this passage, and the other defeats and misfortunes visited upon Húrin and his children in this most remorseless of Tolkien's stories, the very fact that "it is sung" means that Húrin's battlefield prophesy was true: Day *did* come again. That the sad story exists is a sufficient triumph and reason for hope.

As our family life steadily degenerated during the ten days after the blizzard, I retreated to the snow fort I had built. In a corner of the back yard the winds had piled an enormous mound of snow, easily ten feet high, and then swirled a hollow inside it. By digging a tunnel under the highest part of the wall to the bowl-like depression, I created a fortress that no larger person could enter or even see. Inside I made a seat like a throne, hardening the snow with water from a spray-bottle, and in the wall behind it I chipped out the word *Nargothrond* with an old screwdriver.

The snow fort was really more like Gondolin—a city hidden by encircling mountains—than the caves of Nargothrond, but Finrod was my favorite character in *The Silmarillion*. The elf most interested in men and their mortality, he represented a kind of compassionate and self-sacrificing nobility that I have always admired (and rarely found).[5] Even when faced with the foreknowledge of his own death and the destruction of his kingdom, he kept his word: "An oath I too shall swear, and must be free to fulfil it, and go into darkness. Nor shall anything of my realm endure that a son should inherit."[6] Unlike King Turgon, Finrod would never have left Húrin wandering forlorn and unanswered, futilely seeking the hidden entrance to Gondolin.[7] And Finrod's valor was the kind I wanted for myself: not leading warriors into battle, but fighting alone in the dark, bursting his bonds and killing a werewolf with his bare hands to save Beren, sacrificing his life to fulfill his oath.[8]

On the night that I look back at as one of the two worst in my life, my parents had their most violent fight and I ran out of the house, crawled through the tunnel into the fort, pushed the concealing block of ice into place, and sat on the throne, by myself, in the dark, in despair. The moon was very bright, and it turned the ice and shadows of Nargothrond a pale blue. I remember watching the shadows flicker as the wind whipped shreds of clouds across the moon. I was cold, but here the wind did not reach. Finally, hours later, I went back indoors. The shredded clouds and the moonlight on the ice, and my trying to believe that I was someone and somewhere else, did not take away the despair, but somehow the beauty transformed the sorrow and made it more bearable. The grief and loss now had a shape.

> They buried the body of Felagund upon the hill-top of his own isle, and it was clean again; and the green grave of Finrod Finarfin's son, fairest of all the princes of the Elves, remained inviolate, until the land was changed and broken, and foundered under destroying seas.[9]

Good things, beautiful things, are destroyed, but they still triumph through their preservation in memory. The symbolism of a fortress made of ice that would eventually melt to nothing is too obvious (although it wasn't at the time), and its connection to Nargothrond may be somewhat tenuous, but the pattern of disaster followed by beauty and the preservation of memory by means of art occurs throughout *The Silmarillion.* Whether it be of the green grass on Haudh-en-Nirnaeth, the hill Morgoth made of all the bodies of the slain, or of the yellow flowers on the mound that covered Glorfindel's body after he was killed fighting the Balrog, the beauty does not redress the harm that has come before.[10] And yet . . .

I have spent more than thirty years attempting to understand that "and yet . . . ," and not only in the works of Tolkien. The object of much of my scholarly research, the Old English poem *Beowulf*, works similarly: There is not much hope in the poem, no real sense that after his death Beowulf has achieved either eternal life or a permanent victory. The poet suggests that all that will remain is memory, as he has the dying Beowulf say to his kinsman:

Hatað heaoðomære hlæw gewyrcean
beorhtne æfter bæle æt brimes nosan;
se scel to gemyndum minum leodum
heah hlifian on Hronesnæsse,
þæt is sæliðend syððan hatan
Biowulfes biorh, ða ðe brentingas
ofter floda genipu feorran drifað (lines 2802–8)

[Command the famed warriors to build a mound, bright after the pyre, at the edge of the sea; it must tower high on the Whale's Headland as a memorial for my people, so that the seafarers, those who guide their ships far over the darkening of the flood, afterward will call it Beowulf's barrow].

Sailors will note Beowulf's barrow as they pass and they will remember his name and, perhaps, for a while, his story, but Beowulf himself does not seem to expect any reward in the afterlife, and a messenger prophesizes that the hero's death will soon lead to the death of his people.[11] There is not much hope in this depiction, and yet almost 1,300 years after *Beowulf* was composed, we are still remembering the poem's hero.

Although he interpreted *Beowulf* similarly, I am not sure that Tolkien himself felt this way about his own work. He was more hopeful. When Huor has decided to hold the Pass of Sirion with Húrin and the Men of Dor-lómin against hopeless odds to allow Turgon to escape back to Gondolin, he says "Yet if [Gondolin] stands but a little while, then out of your house shall come the hope of Elves and Men. This I say to you, lord, with the eyes of death: though we part here for ever, and I shall not look on your white walls again, from you and from me a new star shall arise."[12] That "new star" is hope, literally "Gil-Estel, the Star of High Hope," the silmaril brought by Elwing to Eärendil suddenly appearing in the heavens.[13] It would make sense for the "new star" to have been a consolation to me, but it was not. I loved the grandeur of the idea, but I did not believe that some star would actually arise from what I saw as the destruction of my family, and I do not think that *The Silmarillion* works that way, even in the story of Eärendil. The advent of Gil-Estel is the sign of a coming "eucatastrophe," a sudden and unexpected positive turn, but there are few of these in *The Silmarillion* and even fewer in real life.[14] Tolkien may have intended the War of Wrath to be one, but the chapter as it stands has a very different emotional effect than the horns of Rohan or the fall of the realm of Sauron because the defeat of Morgoth happens in very swift, almost skeletal, narration. And if the arrival of the host of the Valar in Middle-earth to rescue the elves and defeat the Dark Lord is meant to be a eucatastrophe, that moment of joy is diminished or even eliminated because the price paid is so high. I knew that spring would come in 1978, though I did not expect it to bring any healing or reconciliation, and it did not.

This last point is perhaps enough justification for the exceptionally personal nature of this discussion: Other scholars might argue that the War of Wrath; the destruction of the towers of Thangorodrim by the fall of the greatest of all winged dragons, Ancalagon the Black; the chaining of Morgoth and his expulsion from the world; the reconciliation of the Noldor with the Valar; and the recovery (albeit only temporarily) of the silmarils are an ending made all the more happy by the sorrow and disaster that had come before. I could, perhaps, if I put my mind to it, make an argument that the torments suffered by Húrin and his children and all the other horrors were necessary because they elevate the eventual triumph of the West, but I would never really believe that argument, and not only because my interpretation of *The Silmarillion* will forever be entangled with my own life, in which spring fixed nothing.[15] But even in summary the loss and destruction in *The Silmarillion* is overwhelming. Most of the characters are elves and therefore immortal. They die anyway. Two dozen major characters are all killed by violence or by wasting away. Every beautiful hidden elf-kingdom is sacked and utterly destroyed, the silmarils are lost, and the land of Beleriand is mostly covered by the sea—even the river Sirion simply no longer exists. Tolkien is absolutely relentless.

THE DEATHS OF so many characters probably repels some readers of *The Silmarillion*, but all that death is an essential part of what made the book so important to me, not because I was obsessed with or desired death, but because *The Silmarillion* was the first work of literature I discovered that struggled directly with this central problem of human existence and did so in a way that made sense to me.* I have not made a systematic study, but it is my impression that although children certainly fear death, they do not particularly fear, in the abstract, their *own* deaths.† It is not individual immortality that they would seek (or, more accurately: They tend to assume that they are individually immortal and so have no need for reassurance about their individual fates), but immortality for others and things others have made.‡ Even at the age of nine or younger we may know that such hopes are vain, that death is always inevitable, that there are always things happening that cannot be undone—the deaths of loved ones being the most feared. "Love not too well the work of thy hands and the devices of thy heart," is easy to understand—no matter how strong and imposing the snow fortress is, it will melt away—but almost impossible to follow, as Turgon's tragic refusal to leave Gondolin exemplifies.[16]

* That year I also discovered Ursula K. Le Guin's *The Farthest Shore*, the most insightful and poignant, but also the most unflinching, treatment of death in children's fantasy, but I did not understand this subtler book until years later.

† I want to emphasize "in the abstract" here because children faced with a life-threatening diagnosis certainly do consider, and fear, their own deaths, but fortunately most children are not in such a terrible situation.

‡ In the sense that almost all of us find it impossible to imagine one's consciousness not existing in some way. One of the most beautifully heartbreaking moments in my life occurred when my daughter, then six years old, told me that I did not have to worry about dying: "I used my birthday wish to make sure that you and Momma would never have to die," she said. Discussion with other parents of young children has convinced me that this particular wish is not unusual. Just before she passed away, my grandmother sent me one of my fourth-grade school assignments, which she had saved. We had been asked to write down our wishes. Foremost among mine: "I wish my grandmother could live forever."

As discussed earlier, we perceive time in a curiously doubled sense: inexorably sequential, and as part of repeated patterns, Time's Arrow and Time's Cycle. We fear Time's Arrow because it cannot be slowed or halted and because there is no going back: The moment passes and is lost forever. But while in some ways more comforting, Time's Cycle also has a dark side.[17] Endless repetition leads to determinism, stultification, boredom, weariness: The elves at times envy men the "Gift of Death," the freedom to leave "the circles of the world" for some other fate. Time's Arrow generates entropy but enables change and innovation: "In every age there come forth things that are new and have no foretelling, for they do not proceed from the past."[18] So Time's Arrow and Time's Cycle blend into each other. Each individual life is unique, and yet the pattern of birth, growth, and eventual death is the same, with the fact of death ordained at the moment of birth. This is the tragedy, and the freedom, of being human.

Shippey writes that Tolkien was torn between two competing ideas about time and death: "One was the urge to escape mortality by some way other than Christian consolation . . . the other was the total conviction that the urge was impossible, even forbidden."[19] I agree with the explication of this dynamic, but I do not think that for Tolkien the *langoth* [the longing] that Shippey describes is really about an escape from personal, individual death.[20] Even when Tolkien insists in "On Fairy-Stories" that "the oldest and deepest desire" is the "Great Escape from Death," it seems to me that he is really discussing the fact of Death in the abstract rather than the individual death of the self from which humans wish they could escape.[21] That this is a wish shows that Tolkien knows such escape is impossible—or else a wish would not be necessary. I do know that as a nine-year-old, I would have given my own life to restore my parents' marriage, or to save the life of my brother when he was in the hospital, or to prevent the people that I loved—or even my pets—from having to die.[22] (Childhood wishes need not be proportionate.) Thankfully there was no opportunity to make a vain gesture. It is this sense, not just of loss, but of loss inevitable, that pervades *The Silmarillion*. We can play "what if?" with the plot—what if Melkor had not felt himself slighted? If Finwë had been content with his one mighty son? If Fëanor had been willing to unlock the silmarils? If

Gwindor had not been present at Eithel Sirion to witness the mutilation of his brother? If Túrin had, even once, listened to advice? If Turgon had led an exodus from Gondolin as Ulmo instructed? If Maedhros and Maglor had thrown themselves upon the mercy of the Valar?[23] And the answer is both that certain other things would not have happened and that it would not matter that they did not: The eventual results would be the same. That is the view of history and human nature that Tolkien held.*

This uncompromising, pessimistic view of life that fills *The Silmarillion* is due in part to Tolkien's strong Christian faith. The World, the Flesh, and the Devil are recognized as the great temptations for a reason. It is a danger to the Christian soul to love the World too ardently lest the spirit succumb, and I think there are few twentieth-century men who made as great an effort as Tolkien did to believe deeply and fully that there is an eternal life to be had and we have been told the means by which we can achieve it. But as soon as we enter the world, we are inevitably moving toward death.[24] When we bring children into the world we set them—those we love more than we love ourselves—with us on a path to death and the heartbreak of bereavement. Although Tolkien's religion provided explanations for and proper responses to these inherent tragedies of being human, no person's faith is so powerful that he fails to suffer grief for loss, and for people who lack the great gift of faith, there may be little consolation.

I so strongly resist the idea that *The Silmarillion* is a consolation for the good reason that there is simply no relief in the narrative from the sorrow and loss. Only a few paragraphs after Beren is reunited with Lúthien they are both permanently dead. As soon as the War of Wrath is won Maedhros and Maglor steal and then lose the silmarils. *Akallabeth* means "the downfall." But lack of consolation does not mean that the book contains *only* tragedy, death, and loss. There is bravery, and defiance, and heroism, and self-sacrifice, and love stronger than death. And most of all there is beauty, beauty that is utterly essential to the narrative, for without it, all the loss would be unbearable.

---

* Elvish nature is just a set of particular characteristics of human nature, concentrated and emphasized. The same is true of Dwarvish, Manish, Orcish, and Hobbit-ish nature.

> There they dwelt, and if they wished they could see the light of the Trees, and could tread the golden streets of Valmar and the crystal stairs of Tirion upon Túna, the green hill; but most of all they sailed in their swift ships upon the waters of the Bay of Elvenhome, or walked in the waves upon the shore with their hair gleaming in the light beyond the hill. Many jewels the Noldor gave them, opals and diamonds and pale crystals, which they strewed upon the shores and scattered in the pools; marvelous were the beaches of Elendë in those days. And many pearls they won for themselves from the sea, and their halls were of pearl, and of pearl were the mansions of Olwë at Alqualondë, the Haven of the Swans, lit with many lamps. For that was their city, and the haven of their ships; and those were made in the likeness of swans, with beaks of gold and eyes of gold and jet. The gate of that harbour was an arch of living rock sea-carved; and it lay upon the confines of Eldamar, north of the Calacirya, where the light of the stars was bright and clear.[25]

This beauty has been created in the minds of readers even though it was lost permanently from Arda with the destruction of the Two Trees: No gold and silver light shines through the Calacirya, and so even when their exile is over and they are permitted to return, the Elves come back to a place different from and less beautiful than the one that is lost. Lost too are Gondolin—the white city rising like a flower from the Guarded Plain—and the carved halls of Menegroth, and the green plain of Ard-galen, and the havens at the Mouths of the Sirion, and the silmarils and their light. For the loss to be as powerful as it is in *The Silmarillion*, the beauty that is lost must be very great.

One of Tolkien's achievements is to make this lost beauty and the stories to which it is integral seem completely true, as much a part of a personal cultural history of the reader as the stories of the Bible were to so many in previous generations. This is not to say that I have made a religion of *The Silmarillion*, but rather that *The Silmarillion* entered into the part of my psyche that in other people holds stories of Eden or Canaan or the wanderings of the Israelites.[26] Like the Old Testament, *The Silmarillion* is not a tale of forgiveness and redemption but is instead a story of disobedience and rebellion, failure—and greatness. Tolkien's work provides a heroic, mythological, master-narrative, producing abstracted patterns—rise and fall, building followed by loss, beauty becoming wreckage—that undergird human history. In *The Silmarillion* Tolkien made beauty all the more poignant by showing that such beauty never endures and is therefore even more to be cherished while time is, and after—when we can only grieve for what is lost. This vision seems to me more true than any other.

> At last . . . [Túrin] came with the first ice of winter to the pools of Ivrin, where before he had been healed. But they were now but a frozen mire, and he could drink there no more.
>
> Thus he came hardly by the passes of Dor-lómin, through bitter snows from the north, and found again the land of his childhood. Bare and bleak it was; and Morwen was gone. Her house stood empty, broken and cold; and no living thing drew nigh.[27]

This small scene probably does not stand out from the welter of different sorrows in *The Silmarillion*, especially in the context of Tolkien's most tragic story, that of Túrin. But the particular form of grief Túrin feels echoes well beyond his own tale, as the dominant emotion of *The Lord of the Rings* is the same sorrow that pervades the brief scene at the Pools of Ivrin: the pain that comes when we discover that a beloved place is no longer what it was, that even if it is still physically present, what was once home is home no longer. Technically, this emotion could be labeled *nostalgia*, a word that developed a bad reputation in twentieth-century literature and criticism for being self-indulgent sentimentality.[28] Although I believe that the contemporary critical condemnation and denigration of nostalgia is fundamentally misconceived, trying to rehabilitate the word and restore some of its earlier connotations seems a hopeless endeavor, so I will therefore avoid the use of this contested (and thus confusing) term and instead resurrect *Heimweh* [home pain], the German word that Johannes Hofer translated into Greek in 1688 to coin *nostalgia*, which originally was a medical diagnosis.[29]

Heimweh is precisely Túrin's emotion upon seeing the fouled pools of Ivrin and the abandoned house of his mother. The same pain is at the heart of "I Sit Beside the Fire," the quiet, poignant little poem that Bilbo recites to Frodo in Rivendell just after giving him Sting and the *mithril* coat. Although this passing of another inheritance to Frodo is Bilbo's recognition that his adventures are truly over and so could have been an example of nostalgia in its watered-down, twentieth-century meaning, the poem instead transforms that emotion into a keen and subtle pain very different from any wistful self-indulgence.

I sit beside the fire and think
of all that I have seen,
of meadow-flowers and butterflies
in summers that have been;[30]

The pastoral imagery (meadow-flowers, butterflies) at the end of this first stanza at first appears to be the most clichéd form of nostalgia, and there is even some apparent formal weakness, with a form of the verb *to be* taking the final stressed, rhyming position in the stanza. What seems to be mawkish imagery and diction continues with "yellow leaves and gossamer," "morning mist," and "silver sun." But then there is an abrupt shift in emotional resonance as the initial imagery is undercut by the third stanza:

I sit beside the fire and think
of how the world will be
when winter comes without a spring
that I shall ever see.

At this point the stress put on "been" in the first stanza turns out not to have been poetic weakness but hidden foreshadowing: The summers that have *been* are not returning for the speaker, who now envisions the world with himself absent. This technique is akin to that used by James Joyce in "The Dead," in which the scenes of conviviality and mirth are subtly but constantly undercut by cold drafts, disturbing comments, sudden silences, and awkward moments, culminating in a revelation of insignificance and mortality that force the reader to recompile all the previous subtle touches.[31] Ernest Hemingway uses the same trick in the first third of *Islands in the Stream*, in which the tropical idyll is hedged round with death, fear, and sorrow, held just below the threshold of perception until it all bursts forth and makes the reader see that, in retrospect, it was there all along.[32] Likewise, Tolkien's poem is lighthearted and insignificant until suddenly it isn't. As "I Sit Beside the Fire" continues, the high-significance words, those that rhyme or bear stress, *never seen*, *been*, *were*, invoke the never-returning past and the never-to-be-experienced future—*never know*. The poem is just a glimpse of ultimate mortality: poignant, in a house of immortal elves. A sharp, quick pain, gone almost before it started, a cold breath of air on the back of the neck, the shadow of a big fish on the flour-white sand, a pause when all the talking at the Christmas party stops. And so the contrast is heightened between the lost joy, the sounds of hurrying feet, and happy voices at the door.

The sense of loss Frodo feels when he leaves Bag End—subtly conveyed by the "dark, blank windows" that the hobbit looks at before he walks away[33]—is heimweh. Less than three hours into their journey and only a few miles from his old home, Frodo feels the first discrete pang of grief: "When the light of the last farm was far behind, peeping among the trees, Frodo turned and waved a hand in farewell, 'I wonder if I shall ever look down into that valley again,' he said quietly."[34] After this first cold touch, as each step takes Frodo further from his lost home, the heimweh may flood or ebb but the feeling will never entirely dissipate.

By no means is heimweh the only kind of sorrow to be found in *The Lord of the Rings*: Characters die or appear to have died, beautiful things are destroyed, and hope seems lost. But even in scenes of acute loss and grief, there remains the subtle undercurrent of additional heimweh. For example, in the midst of their intense grief for the loss of Gandalf, when the Fellowship is finally safe in Lórien, touches of heimweh are still present, intermingled with the greater immediate sorrow. Aragorn stands on Cerin Amroth and says: "'Here is the heart of Elvendom on earth. . . . and here my heart dwells ever, unless there be a light beyond the dark roads that we still must tread, you and I. Come with me!' And taking Frodo's hand in his, he left the hill of Cerin Amroth and came there never again as living man."[35] Although in "Many Partings" in *The Return of the King* we see that for Aragorn and Arwen there indeed was a light beyond the dark roads, Appendix A confirms that despite his love for the place, Aragorn never returned to Cerin Amroth. The sense of that loss is generated by the sentence in *The Fellowship of the Ring* and is never entirely erased even in the joyful celebration of the wedding of Aragorn and Arwen.

When Merry, grieving over the death of Théoden, reflects on the king's last words—"when you sit in peace with your pipe, think of me! For never now shall I sit with you in Meduseld"[36]—both the character and the readers feel heimweh. Even in his madness, when Denethor has been so overcome by acute grief that he is in the process of murdering his wounded son and committing suicide, the Steward of Gondor feels heimweh. Trying to forestall Denethor's self-immolation, Gandalf asks him what he would have if his "will could have its way?" and Denethor answers: "I would have things as they were in all the days of my life . . . and in the days of my longfathers before me."[37] Unassuageable pain from the loss of past is the steward's final lament, and readers feel this undercurrent even though grief for the great loss of life in battle and the apparently inevitable death of Faramir and fear for the destruction of the city are more dominant emotions in the moment.

A devastating rush of heimweh for both characters and readers occurs at the end of the long narrative, in "The Scouring of the Shire." When the four hobbits finally reach Hobbiton, the destination they have longed for throughout their immense journey, things have changed:

> It was one of the saddest hours in their lives. The great chimney rose up before them; and as they drew near the old village across the Water, through rows of new mean houses along each side of the road, they saw the new mill in all its frowning and dirty ugliness: a great brick building straddling the stream, which it fouled with a steaming and stinking overflow. All along the Bywater Road every tree had been felled.

> As they crossed the bridge and looked up the Hill they gasped. Even Sam's vision in the Mirror had not prepared him for what they saw. The Old Grange on the west side had been knocked down, and its place taken by rows of tarred sheds. All the chestnuts were gone. The banks and hedgerows were broken. Great wagons were standing in disorder in a field beaten bare of grass. Bagshot Row was a yawning sand and gravel quarry. Bag End up beyond could not be seen for a clutter of large huts.
>
> "They've cut it down!" cried Sam. "They've cut down the Party Tree!" He pointed to where the tree had stood under which Bilbo had made his Farewell Speech. It was lying lopped and dead in the field. As if this was the last straw Sam burst into tears.[38]

A few minutes later Sam—who has been there and so can make an informed comparison—says "This is worse than Mordor! . . . Much worse in a way. It comes home to you, as they say; because it is home, and you remember it before it was ruined."[39]

Ruin, the root of the final, essential word of this emotionally devastating scene occurs eighty-nine times in *The Lord of the Rings*. By far the greatest cluster of forms of *ruin* as both verb and subject complement occurs at the very end of book VI, once in "Many Partings," when Saruman bitterly notes that all his plans are ruined,[40] and then in a cluster in "The Scouring of the Shire," when forms of *ruin* are used to describe what Saruman and the ruffians have done to the hobbits' beloved homeland, damage that seems irreparable. Sharkey and his men have tried to ruin the Shire, not specifically to turn it into *a* ruin but to wreck it so completely that it cannot return to its original form, so that the past incarnation of the Shire is forever inaccessible. The damage makes even perceiving the Shire painful because the land seems to have been permanently changed and broken, what the Mouth of Sauron threatened to do to Frodo through the long, slow torment of years in the Dark Tower.[41] Heimweh is exactly what the hobbits and the reader are feeling when they see the defilement of Bag End. And although Tolkien gives us a happy ending for the Shire thanks to the magical soil in Galadriel's gift to Sam and the glorious summer of 1420, Frodo's pain is not relieved, and he cannot enjoy the Shire. It can be healed, but he never is, and we as readers are not spared the sadness from his loss of his home.

Despite its stark contrast to the joy-filled climax of the victory over Sauron and the golden year of 1420, the melancholy ending of *The Lord of the Rings* is never described as incongruous or surprising. Readers and critics do not question the book concluding with Frodo's inability to find peace and healing in the Shire and his sorrowful parting from Sam, Merry, and Pippin, because the emotion of heimweh has been interwoven throughout the entire narrative both explicitly (in scenes discussed previously), and through the emotional resonances of the physical ruins spread throughout the landscape: the broken foundations on Weathertop, the decayed castles in the Lone-lands, the ancient remains that surround the Fellowship as they travel through the Land of Hollin, lost Eregion, the tumbled stones that speak a paraphrase of the Anglo-Saxon poem *The Ruin* to Legolas.[42]

On the return journey from Gondor, before Celeborn and Galadriel prepare to turn aside from the road to Rivendell and leave the company, they tarry for seven days, lingering:

> still in converse with their friends. Often long after the hobbits were wrapped in sleep they would sit together under the stars, recalling the ages that were gone and all their joys and labours in the world, or holding council, concerning the days to come. If any wanderer had chanced to pass, little would he have seen or heard, and it would have seemed to him only that he saw grey figures, carved in stone, memorials of forgotten things now lost in unpeopled lands.[43]

Tolkien shows the great figures of the Third Age as mute statues that, as "memorials of forgotten things," would make the evidence of the past permanent even as that past itself is unreachable and, eventually, forgotten. The elves are returning to the place that, for them, is supposed to be their home because in Middle-earth, they are now to be homeless. Elrond's prophesy about what would happen if the One

Ring were to be destroyed has come true: "when the One has gone, the Three will fail, and many fair things will fade and be forgotten. That is my belief."[44] Because Elrond's words at the eponymous council are rhetorical and in the subjunctive mood, they probably did not at that time produce the same sense of heimweh in readers as did the scene of Frodo looking back at the lights of Hobbiton. But when those words are read they are another cold breeze on the back of the neck, a hint of the heimweh whose full weight will land on readers fifty chapters later:

> Then Elrond and Galadriel rode on; for the Third Age was over, and the Days of the Rings were passed, and an end was come of the story and song of those times. With them went many Elves of the High Kindred who would no longer stay in Middle-earth.[45]

Elrond has no home in the Blessed Land, and although Galadriel once did, she has been separated from it for millennia, and when she returns it will not be what it once was. After Galadriel, in one of the most metaphysically important scenes in the entire narrative, passes the test of the temptation of the Ring, she appears "shrunken: a slender elf-woman, clad in simple white, whose gentle voice was soft and sad. 'I will diminish, and go into the West, and remain Galadriel.'"[46] Soon after, she sings her lament "*Namarië*" [Farewell], which is filled with concentrated heimweh, both for herself and for the person being addressed, which, according to the notes in *The Road Goes Ever On*, is Frodo:

> *Ai! Láurië lántar lássi súrinèn,*
> *yéni ùnotimè ve rámar áldaròn!*
> *Yéni ve linte yúldar avánier*
> *Mi óromárdi lísse-mìruvóreva*
> *Àndúne . . .*

> ["Ah! like gold fall the leaves in the wind, long years numberless as the wings of trees! The long years have passed like swift draughts of the sweet mead in lofty halls beyond the West . . .]

Si vanwa ná, Rómello vanwa Valimar!
Namárië! Nai hiruvalyë Valimar.
Nai elyë hiruva. Namárië!

[Now lost, lost to those from the East is Valimar! Farewell! Maybe thou shalt find Valimar. Maybe even thou shalt find it. Farewell!][47]

Galadriel laments her home, lost not only to her exile in Middle-earth, but to destruction by evil and the passing of the years. In *The Road Goes Ever On*, Tolkien states that at this point in the narrative, Galadriel did not know if she would be permitted to "go into the West," and so those words to Frodo after she refuses the Ring are wishful. Even if she were to be permitted, she would not be able to see the beauty of the light shining through the Calicirya (line 14), for that light has not existed since Morgoth destroyed the Two Trees.[48]

That destruction, whose victims are depicted in silvery *ithildin* on the West-doors of Moria, is reenacted by the monstrous Watcher in the Water, that with its tentacles uproots the ancient holly trees that have flanked the gates for so many centuries.* "I fear from the sounds that boulders have been piled up, and the trees uprooted and thrown across the gate. I am sorry; for the trees were beautiful, and had stood so long," says Gandalf, and his sorrow for the loss of the trees is particularly poignant because there was no good reason for them to be uprooted.[49] They were not casualties of time or entropy, but of malicious destruction.

Hatred, violence, and most of all organized warfare generate heimweh in Tolkien's works the same way they do in the world. Because the landscape of Middle-earth is so depopulated, we do not see the ancillary dispossession, displacement, destruction, and killing that accompanies the movements of armies in the real world—the general atavism of war is reflected only in the actions of the evil armies. The men of Gondor and Rohan do not need to forage, loot, or clear the battlefield of

* It is not unreasonable to see the Watcher in the Water as a "type" of Ungoliant: a multi-limbed, hideous monstrosity driven by unmotivated hatred who destroys two beautiful trees.

civilian dwellings. And in actuality neither do Saruman's orcs and wild men, who are operating close to their home base, though they nevertheless burn the homes and farms of the people of the Westfold:

> "They bring fire," said Theoden. "And they are burning as they come, rick, cot, and tree. This was a rich vale and had many homesteads. Alas for my folk!"[50]

Saruman seems to have ordered his army to behave this way out of sheer malice, since there is no military necessity.* It possibly made some sense to burn the cots to prevent ambushes by any Rohirrim hiding in them, but by destroying ricks, the orcs and wild men are depriving themselves of a stored harvest that it would be better to loot (although at the very beginning of March, most ricks would likely be depleted). And the burning of trees, particularly if they are orchard trees, is stupidly self-damaging regardless of whether Saruman intends to keep his promise to the Dunlendings to let them occupy the lands of Rohan or is going to betray them and renege. Either way there is no reason to waste time and effort burning ricks and trees: The refugees have already fled to Helm's Deep, and Saruman's time horizon is too short to worry about the Westfold provisioning Rohan six months later at harvest time, espe-

---

* Attacking Théoden at Helm's Deep is a grievous military error—Saruman could have trapped Théoden's army there and waited them out while taking over the rest of undefended Rohan—but could just possibly be justified as a decapitation strike, though such an attempt to kill the leadership only makes sense if Saruman intended to keep the people working the land for his benefit. The assault on the fortress combined with the burning of the Westfold makes no tactical or strategic sense and must therefore have been done purely out of spite. Tolkien—who clearly understood preindustrial warfare—most likely intended this implied criticism, because he obliquely mocks Saruman and his army in the opening sentence of "The Battle of the Pelennor Fields," quoted previously: "But it was no orc-chieftain or brigand that led the assault upon Gondor"; *RK,* V, vi, 114. Compare the attack on Minas Tirith, in which both Denethor and the Lord of the Nazgûl optimize their strategies based on their resources, to the assault on Helm's Deep, in which Saruman's army makes multiple strategic errors. Saruman truly was just a pathetic imitation of the real Dark Lord, and everything he did "was naught, only a little copy, a child's model or a slave's flattery" of the Dark Tower; *TT,* III, viii, 161. Loser. For a military historian's analysis of the strategies used in the wars in Middle-earth, see Bret Devereaux's essays collected at *A Collection of Unmitigated Pedantry* ("Collections: The Siege of Gondor, Part I: Professionals Talk Logistics" and "Collections: The Battle of Helm's Deep, Part I: Bargaining for Goods at Helm's Gate").

cially if everyone who can work the fields is either dead or taking refuge in the caves. But regardless of whether they are destroyed for the purposes of war or for no reason other than the desire to harm, the lost homes and fields of the Westfold are a source of heimweh for all of those who survive the onslaught. On behalf of their pain and grief (as well as his own) Théoden later asks Saruman "What will you say of your torches in Westfold and the children that lie dead there?"[51]

War threatens each person caught up in it with potential grief for the lost home. But as bad as the destruction wrought by Saruman's vicious attack on Rohan—and his later purely spiteful attempt to do the same to the Shire—is, Sauron's victory would be far worse. With the Ring, Sauron would have the power to destroy not just the homes of people, but the very land that is the home of all, transforming all of Middle-earth into the wasteland that lies just outside Mordor:

> Here nothing lived, not even the leprous growths that fed on rottenness. The gasping pools were choked with ash and crawling muds, sickly white and grey, as if the mountains had vomited the filth of their entrails upon the lands about. High mounds of crushed and powdered rock, great cones of earth fire-blasted and poison-stained, stood like an obscene graveyard in endless rows, slowly revealed in the reluctant light.
>
> They had come to the desolation that lay before Mordor: the lasting monument to the dark labour of its slaves that should endure when all their purposes were made void; a land defiled, diseased beyond all healing—unless the Great Sea should enter in and wash it with oblivion.[52]

This wasting and poisoning of the earth itself is the threat that hangs over not just the Free Peoples, but Middle-earth itself, as long as the One Ring exists. Even if Sauron does not possess the Ring, his remaining power is such that he can, over time and through the labor of his servants, "torture and destroy the very hills" and by so defiling the land itself, defeat all other powers, even, eventually, Tom Bombadil, who was otherwise immune to the power of the Ring: "If all else is conquered, Bombadil will fall," Glorfindel says at the Council of Elrond.

"Last as he was First; and then Night will come."[53] Among the terrible results of such a night would be universal heimweh, as every living person would be an exile, forever separated from the lost home.

In a discussion and partial translation of the Anglo-Saxon poem *The Wanderer*, Tolkien notes that the word from which the title is taken, *eardstapa*, in line 6a, is more accurately taken as one who haunts the land alone, an exile.[54] The character in the poem is not traveling aimlessly but simply cannot go where he wants to—back to the warmth and joy of his past:

> *Þinceð him on mode　　þæt he his mondryhten*
> *clyppe ond cysse,　　ond on cneo lecge*
> *honda ond heafod,　　swa he hwilum ær*
> *in geardagum　　giefstolas breac.*
> *Ðonne onwæcneð eft　　winleas guma,*
> *gesihð him biforan　　fealwe wegas,*
> *baþian brimfuglas,　　brædan feþra,*
> *hreosan hrim ond snaw,　　hagle gemenged* (41–48)

> [It seems to him in mind that he clasps and kisses his friend-lord, and on knee lays hand and head, as he at times previously had done, in earlier days, enjoyed the gift-throne. Then the friendless man awakens, sees before him the fallow waves, the sea birds bathing broad feathers, the tossing rime and snow mingled with hail].[55]

The power of these lines inheres in the way the depiction of the warmth and companionship is transformed to the loss of those things, which in the exile's circumstances are only accessible in dreams. The bathing of the birds and winter weather on the sea, beautiful and stark, dramatize the pain of exile, the yearning for what is now lost. A few lines later the poet writes "*sorg bið geniwad*" (50b) [sorrow is renewed]. The key word is the last one: The sorrow has come back; it is not new but a recurrence, another cycle in a pattern of joy followed by grief. We were never told that the protagonist has previously been exiled, only that he now is, and yet the sorrow is renewed because the "*an-haga*" [solitary one, line 1a] *has* experienced exile even before his lord and people were lost to him—the exile that is forced upon all individuals, not just the unlucky or guilty: exile from our own pasts imposed by the force of time, which relentlessly separates us from our original homes, from any and all happiness in our past, from those we have loved.[56] A person need commit no crime to be forced into this sort of exile: It is part of the condition of being human.

Beings incarnate in time, we are always exiles, forever estranged from the home to which we can never return. As such, the ache of heimweh that pervades *The Lord of the Rings* is our common heritage as humans. In a January 1945 letter to his son Christopher, Tolkien wrote

> certainly there was an Eden on this very unhappy earth. We all long for it, and we are constantly glimpsing it: our whole nature at its best and least corrupted, its gentlest and most humane, is still soaked with the senses of "exile." If you come to think of it, your (very just) horror at the stupid murder of the hawk, and your obstinate memory of this "home" of yours in an idyllic hour (when often there is an illusion of the stay of time and decay and a sense of gentle peace) . . . are derived from Eden. As far as we can go back the nobler part of the human mind is filled with the thoughts of *sibb*, peace and goodwill, and with the thought of its *loss*.[57]

In Old English *sibb* means the kind of unity, togetherness, and peace that can be found among close, loving kindred. Innocent children are surrounded by *sibb*, but as we pass through and away from childhood we experience individual heimweh, grief for our lost home, an echo of a sorrow of our race at the expulsion from Eden. No matter how much happiness we may later find, we are never fully free of the heimweh that is intrinsic to our existence.

Perhaps the saddest aspect of *The Lord of the Rings*—worse than the deaths of characters, or the destruction of beautiful things, or the departure of the elves from Middle-earth—is Frodo's suffering even after he has returned home to the Shire.[58]

> On the thirteenth of [March] Farmer Cotton found Frodo lying on his bed. He was clutching a white gem that hung on a chain around his neck and he seemed half in a dream.
>
> "It is gone forever," he said, "and now all is dark and empty."[59]

This was the first anniversary of the destruction of the Ring. Later in the year, Sam went into the study

> and found his master looking very strange. He was very pale and his eyes seemed to see things far away.
>
> "What's the matter, Mr. Frodo?" said Sam.
>
> "I am wounded," he answered, "wounded, and it will never really heal"[60]

This was the two-year anniversary of Frodo's having been stabbed with the Morgul-knife by the Lord of the Nazgûl. It seems unlikely that these two incidents alone would have been sufficient for Frodo to need to depart with the elves, so it must be that in addition to these acute episodes, Frodo is dealing with some kind of chronic pain and grief that has made it impossible for him to enjoy living in the Shire. As he explains on the road to the Havens, "I have been too deeply hurt, Sam. I tried to save the Shire, and it has been saved, but not for me."[61] The injuries of "knife, sting, and tooth, and a long burden," that Frodo had mentioned to Gandalf appear to be among those wounds that the wizard feared "cannot be wholly cured."[62] As a result, Frodo's home is no longer a place where he can rest in peace, *sibb*, comfort, and safety. He is in effect in permanent exile, and one that may be even more painful because he is in the physical location that used to be his home. Frodo can find no relief: His home-pain has not abated and may be even more intense than if he were somewhere far away.

The tragedy of Frodo's inability to enjoy the Shire is representative of the inherent tragedy common to all of us. Many (perhaps most) people are fortunate enough that they only experience on occasion the full intensity of the heimweh that Frodo seems to feel constantly, but all of us, even if we are blessed to be in our current homes, are at times unable to escape awareness of the permanent exile we endure. *The Lord of the Rings* gives shape and form—in story and in characters—to this pain that no one avoids forever. The grief is invoked but also kept within boundaries by the story, the poem, the picture, the stones of the ruin, the memory.

In the last pages of his great work, Tolkien names the transformation he works upon the pervasive heimweh of the narrative. After Frodo and Sam meet the High Elves and Bilbo in the woods of the Shire,

> then Elrond and Galadriel rode on; for the Third Age was over, and the Days of the Rings were passed, and an end was come of the story and song of those times. With them went many Elves of the High Kindred who would no longer stay in Middle-earth; and among them, filled with *a sadness that was yet blessed and without bitterness*, rode Sam, and Frodo, and Bilbo.[63]

We do not have a word in English for sadness blessed and without bitterness, but I think we recognize it immediately from the context in this passage and in light of all that has come before. For Frodo and Sam, and for us, the heimweh has not been taken away—the end of the story is still a scene of parting, still drenched in sorrow—but the pain for the lost home has been transmuted into a sadness that we can accept because we have a sense of its full shape and texture. "The price of a memory is the memory of the sorrow it brings," says the song.[64] Transforming that sorrow into something more, into tears that are not bitter, is the great achievement of Tolkien's art and the reason that Sam's final words, "Well, I'm back," are both heartbreaking and blessed, as we, like him, go on as we must despite all that has passed and all that keeps passing away.[65] And, sometimes, we pick up the book and begin again.

CHAPTER 6
Threads

DESPITE ALL THE fantastic elements of the narratives—magic rings, immortal elves, talking trees, wizards, trolls, wraiths, a Dark Lord—many readers have a sense that Tolkien's works are in some essential way true. This impression is shared by readers with wildly different political ideologies, social and cultural backgrounds, and life experiences. I know personally, or have met and spoken to, or have corresponded with: liberal academics, conservative home-schoolers, hard-core environmentalists, free-market capitalists, New Age spiritualists, "Death Metal" enthusiasts, a traditionalist judge, a left-wing labor activist, Roman Catholics, Russian Orthodox Christians, Evangelical Protestants, Mormons, Jews, a young Muslim couple, a Buddhist, atheists, agnostics, members of Holy Orders, and soldiers in combat zones, all of whom believe that Tolkien's works express fundamental truths.

By *true* I mean something like what Tolkien meant when he said that while *The Lord of the Rings* was not allegorical, it did, perhaps, have "applicability to the thought and experience of readers."[1] Some qualities of Tolkien's works are often perceived by readers as being consistent with their lives and beliefs, but as this cannot be true in any literal sense—no reader believes that there really was a Dark Lord who was destroyed when his magic ring was thrown into a volcano—this truth must be at a more abstract level.

In one sense we explored aspects of the truth or applicability of Tolkien's works when we noted the congruence between the rhythms of *The Lord of the Rings* and some of the rhythms of life: stress and release, illness and recovery. In this chapter and the next, however, we move away from subconscious impressions and emotional responses to examine the ways *The Silmarillion*, *The Hobbit*, and *The Lord of the Rings* engage the intellects of readers. To do this, we must discuss *theme*, which is generally understood to be the central, or underlying, or overarching idea, or message, or meaning of a work. Those mix-and-match metaphors are an indicator that *theme* is a term that different scholars use in different ways. Rather than engaging in definition-mongering (surely the most boring type of mongering), I will merely state that for our purposes a theme is an abstraction derived from the perception of patterns that are shared among a literary work and either other literary works or the physical, social, or cultural world.

Although the composition-history of Tolkien's works does not suggest that he began with themes or moral lessons and then shaped his narratives accordingly, Tolkien's letters show that he carefully considered thematic and moral issues during and especially after the creation and publication of his works. The themes and their interaction also heighten the experiential nature and complex emotional effects of Tolkien's works.

This chapter will discuss how parallel or submerged themes generate dynamics or produce structuring contrasts that create repetitions of motive and behavior, of action and response. We will first trace the workings of a parallel theme in *The Silmarillion* to see how its interaction with the dominant theme of the work helps to produce the impression of truth, and then we will examine the effects of a two-part structuring contrast in *The Hobbit* that makes that work more complex, sophisticated, and illuminating of human behavior. In both cases the interactions among the themes and subthemes operate very much the same way as heterotextuality operates at the sentence level of the narrative: creating the impression of truth not despite the apparent divergences and contradictions, but because of them.

❦

THE DOMINANT THEME of *The Silmarillion* is The Working of Evil in the World. The malice of Morgoth, the original Dark Lord, drives most of the narrative both through direct action and by his lies and manipulations motivating the behavior of other characters. The overwhelming influence of this malign demigod causes *The Silmarillion* to be somewhat unusual in fantasy literature by being generally unconcerned with the famous "Problem of Evil," the theological conundrum of why there is evil in a world created by a beneficent, omniscient, and omnipotent God. In Tolkien's works, this mystery has a reasonably simple explanation: Evil exists because one of the supernatural demigods who govern the world, the Valar (generally parallel to the Ancient Greek pantheon), rebelled against the One, Eru Ilúvatar.* Not content to serve the Creator, Melkor continuously strove against the other Valar, spitefully destroying their creations and injecting chaos and destruction into the world.[2] Melkor hates elves and men, the "Children of Ilúvatar," even more than he hates the other Valar, and the Dark Lord continually seeks to destroy, enslave, or immiserate them.[3] Evil exists throughout the world because Melkor corrupted independent spirits—including his servant Sauron and the balrogs—manipulated many men into serving him, and was able to produce and animate malignant beings like wargs, trolls, and dragons by dissipating his own essence into them.†

The published *Silmarillion* itself is a detailed working out of how elves and men respond to supernatural evil after it has manifested itself in physical form. This history of the First Age of the world centers around the light that radiated from the Two Trees of Valinor in the age before the creation of the sun and moon. Fëanor, the greatest craftsman of the elves, manages to capture some of that light within the silmarils, three great jewels that he made and which Melkor stole after he and

---

* The existence of an actual diabolus in the world does not fully solve the Problem of Evil since there is no explanation of why Eru created Melkor, or why he did not destroy him when he started to do evil things.

† The meaning of Melkor's rebellion, the impossibility of purging the evil that, from him, dissolved into the very fabric of the world, and the hope that one day the Creator would find a way to finally remove all evil, bringing about Arda Healed, are the focus of Tolkien's later philosophical writings, which are collected in *Morgoth's Ring*, the tenth volume of *The History of Middle-earth*. *Morgoth*, 399–401.

Ungoliant, a giant, evil spider-being, killed the Two Trees. The *Quenta Silmarillion* is the story of the heroic effort of the Noldorian elves' doomed attempt to take back the silmarils from this first and greatest Dark Lord (from this point on named Morgoth, literally "Dark/Black Enemy") and the tragedies that befall them and their allies and friends. But there is also another kind of evil depicted in *The Silmarillion* that seems to have nothing to do with the Dark Lord. The *racial hierarchy* of the elves causes misery, tragedy, and evil deeds, but no characters even evaluate it as being morally suspect, much less attribute its existence to Morgoth. Indeed, in contradistinction to every analogous hierarchy in the real world, the elvish racial hierarchy has some basis in fact, as there are observable and consistent differences in abilities between the elves at its different levels.

In "Of the Coming of the Elves" we learn that after their initial war against Melkor, in which they defeated and imprisoned him, the Valar feared for the safety of the elves in Middle-earth "amid the deceits of the starlit dusk" and "they were filled moreover with the love of the beauty of the Elves and desired their fellowship." So they summoned the elves to make a great journey from where they had awakened, far in the east of Middle-earth in a place named Cuiviénen, to the Valar's paradisical homeland, Valinor, "there to be gathered at the knees of the Powers in the light of the Trees forever."[4] At first the elves were unwilling to undertake such a long and dangerous journey, so the Valar brought three representatives, Ingwë, Finwë, and Elwë, to Valinor to see the light of the Two Trees and then act as ambassadors. Upon their return to Cuiviénen, the three become the kings of three large divisions of those elves who agree to embark on the journey. "Then befell the first sundering of the Elves," because "many refused the summons, preferring the starlight and the wide spaces of Middle-earth to the rumour of the Trees."[5]

At the end of the published *Silmarillion*, Christopher Tolkien provides a diagram of "the Sundering of the Elves and some of the names given to their divisions" that shows how the later hierarchy of kindreds is related to the "Great Journey."[6] Elves who at least started on the journey are called the Eldar, while those who refused to go are the Avari, the Unwilling. The Eldar themselves are divided into three kindreds:

the Vanyar, the Noldor, and the Teleri ("those who tarry"). All of the Vanyar and Noldor went to Valinor, but only a portion of the Teleri did: One fraction stopped short of the Misty Mountains, and others, although they did go into Beleriand, the most western part of Middle-earth, decided not to cross the sea to Valinor. These are the Sindar, the Grey Elves. Elwë Thingol (their original ambassador and later the father of Lúthien) was their king. The Vanyar, Noldor, and those Teleri who did travel across the sea called themselves the Calaquendi, "Elves of Light," because they saw the light of the Two Trees, and they called the elves that did not travel to Aman the Moriquendi, "the Elves of Darkness."[7]

For reasons that are not fully explained in *The Silmarillion*, the elves who made the journey are in some existential way superior to those who were unwilling, and those who saw the light of the Two Trees outrank those who did not. Additionally, among the "Elves of Light," the Vanyar outrank the Noldor, who outrank the Teleri. In a 1954 letter to Naomi Mitchison, who had been reading page-proofs of the first two volumes of *The Lord of the Rings*, Tolkien states that those elves who passed over the sea "were the High Elves, who became immensely enhanced in powers and knowledge."[8] These unspecified powers must be what make the Calaquendi superior to the Moriquendi, but there is no explanation for why the Vanyar are superior to the Noldor or the Noldor to the Teleri.[9] Note also that although the Elves of Light are more knowledgeable and powerful than other elves, Tolkien never states or even implies that they are *morally* superior. And yet all the elves act as if the racial hierarchy is real and existential; we never see elves rejecting the hierarchy or trying to overturn it. No elf ever seems to question why Ingwë is the "high lord of all the Elvish race" even though he seems to do nothing but sit "at the feet of the Powers." His people, the Vanyar, the "Fair Elves," even forsake their friends, the Noldor, and the beautiful city of Tirion upon Túna to live on the feet of the holy Mountain and do nothing but sing.[10]

Within each kindred, elvish society is also hierarchical. Perhaps surprisingly, this hierarchy of the elves seems to be nearly completely accepted, and we see few struggles for power, kingship, or inheritance—the *Game of Thrones*–style intrigues that are so prevalent in the later kingdoms of men.[11] Elves accept hereditary hierarchies as being natural and existential.* Or so it would seem. But despite the incredible persistence and stability of the elvish hierarchies, a very large fraction of all the disastrous interactions in *The Silmarillion* are caused by prejudices, hatreds, and resentments among individuals at different levels of it. Shippey was the first to point out that in *The Silmarillion*, as in Old Norse literature, an individual's character "is in a sense fixed, static, even diagrammatic," and that it is highly correlated with heredity and group membership.[12] The three kindreds of the High Elves (Vanyar, Noldor, and Teleri) all have particular characteristics that are reflected in the behavior of their members, even to the point that the personalities of mixed-kindred characters can be understood as arising from their particular blends.[13]

Although Shippey explicates the ranking-system of the elves, to the best of my knowledge, no scholars have noted that the hierarchical natures of the peoples and cultures of Middle-earth are essential motive forces in the narratives of *The Silmarillion*, and, to a lesser extent, *The Hobbit* and The *Lord of the Rings*.[14] For obvious reasons I have been hesitant to use the word *racism* to describe the underlying motivation for these conflicts, both because I worry that some readers would think that I am trivializing the word by using it to refer to the social interactions of imaginary elves, and also because racism is such a volatile topic that the very meaning of the word is ever-shifting. But I could not find another term that was accurate but less entangled in contentious contemporary political and social issues. *Prejudice* and *bigotry*, although reasonable descriptions of some of the behaviors I will discuss, do not fully capture the sociocultural dynamics of the interactions the way that *racism* does because individually unmotivated assumptions of superiority or inferiority are based on the characters' membership in groupings that are defined entirely by heredity and its external markers, but are not based solely on narrower familial lineage. Additionally, the hostility, contempt, or condescension directed at individuals in putatively

* The acceptance of hierarchy seems particularly surprising in light of elvish immortality, since in ideal circumstances there would be absolutely no social or even familial mobility: No son would inherit from a father and no one's office, title, or role would ever open up for a younger contender. Imagine being the elf who has the job of washing the dishes or emptying the chamber pots—forever.

inferior categories are not just examples of simple out-grouping, since they regularly occur ex nihilo rather than being motivated by particular actions of the lower-ranking characters. Furthermore, the boundaries of the hereditary groups are basically impermeable: Characters cannot change the groups into which they are born, and those rare individuals who are the product of marriages across group boundaries create classificational and political problems. This *elvish racism* is, I contend, a powerful dynamic underlying most of the tales in *The Silmarillion* and is at minimum a contributing factor to all of them. Even though the malice of Morgoth, the Oath of Fëanor, and the Curse of Mandos are the primary drivers of the plot, the precipitating events of many individual tragedies arise from elvish racism.

As far as most of the characters and the narrator of *The Silmarillion* are concerned, the racial hierarchy is a fact of nature, a fundamental characteristic of elves that is neither questioned nor explicitly recognized as evil. Although the hierarchy must have existed from at least the start of the great journey of the elves to Valinor, its pernicious influence only becomes apparent after the unique event of a married elf deciding not to continue living and refusing to be reincarnated, and her widower choosing to remarry.[15]

Finwë was the first king of the Noldor, the middle-ranked of the three kindreds of the elves. In the era of bliss caused by the original imprisonment of Melkor, Finwë wedded Míriel, a weaver and embroideress of surpassing skill. Their child, "the eldest of the sons of Finwë, and the most beloved," was formally named Curufinwë, but Míriel gave him the by-name of Fëanor, "Spirit of Fire." In the bearing of this great son, "Míriel was consumed in spirit and body; and after his birth she yearned for release from the labor of living. After she had named their son, she said to Finwë: 'Never again shall I bear child; for strength that would have nourished the life of many has gone forth into Fëanor.' "[16] Míriel, weary, went to sleep in the gardens of Lórien and her spirit departed from her body, so that Finwë "alone in all the Blessed Realm . . . was deprived of joy."[17]

Eventually King Finwë remarries, taking as his second wife Indis of the Vanyar (the highest of the elvish kindreds), and they produce two sons. But "the wedding of his father was not pleasing to Fëanor; and he had no great love for Indis, nor for Fingolfin and Finarfin, her sons." This antipathy for half-siblings is hardly surprising if we (reasonably) assume that jealously and fear of divided love is as common among elves as among humans. Additionally, the tension between the three sons of Finwë is deliberately exacerbated by Melkor, who spreads lies that "Fingolfin and his sons were plotting to usurp the leadership of Finwë and of the elder line of Fëanor." A crisis is reached when Finwë assembles a council of the lords of the Noldor and Fingolfin asks him to restrain Fëanor from speaking as if he were king.

> Fëanor strode into the chamber, and he was fully armed; his high helm upon his head and at his side a mighty sword. "So it is even as I guessed," he said. "My half-brother would be before me with my father, in this as in all other matters. Then turning upon Fingolfin he drew his sword, crying: "Get thee gone, and take they due place!"[18]

Fear of a half-brother's usurping an eldest son's position in a royal house is hardly unique to Tolkienian elves. However, there is an additional aggravating factor in the strained relationship between Fëanor and his half-brothers: Indis, the king's second wife, is of a higher-ranking kindred than Fëanor's mother Míriel was. According to the hierarchy of kindreds, Indis's half-Vanyar sons outrank Fëanor, especially because their mother is close kin of Ingwë High King of all elves.[19]

> In those unhappy things which later came to pass, and in which Fëanor was the leader, many saw the effect of this breach within the house of Finwë, judging that if Finwë had endured his loss and been content with the fathering of his mighty son, the courses of Fëanor would have been otherwise, and great evil might have been prevented; for the sorrow and the strife in the house of Finwë is graven in the memory of the Noldorin Elves. But the children of Indis were great and glorious, and their children also; and if they had not lived the history of the Eldar would have been diminished.[20]

By calling them "the children of Indis," this passage emphasizes that Fingolfin and Finarfin are part of the higher-ranking Vanyar. And although Fëanor and his half-brothers are eventually publicly reconciled, the rapprochement does not last long.* In response to Morgoth's murder of Finwë and theft of the silmarils, Fëanor exhorts the Noldor to return to Middle-earth against the command of the Valar. But Fingolfin is appalled by the dreadful oath that Fëanor and his sons swear, so he and his son Turgon argue against Fëanor, "and fierce words awoke, so that once again wrath came near to the edge of swords."[21]

Having assumed the kingship and convinced his people to follow him, Fëanor intends to lead the host of the Noldor back to Middle-earth but is faced with the impediment of a large sea. The land masses of Valinor and Middle-earth only come close together in the far north, where they are linked by the deadly Helcaraxë [Grinding Ice]. The Noldor therefore need ships if they are going to continue their exodus. Fëanor leads the host to the haven of Alqualondë to seek the aid of the Teleri, the Sea Elves, lowest-ranking of the three kindreds who came to Valinor. But instead of assisting the Noldor, the Teleri try to dissuade them from leaving and urge them to return to seek the pardon of the Valar. When this persuasion fails, however, they deny them the use of their white ships.[22]

It is at this point that the elvish racism smoldering within Fëanor bursts into flame. He berates Olwë, king of the Teleri: "You were glad to receive our aid when you came at last to these shores, fainthearted loiterers, and wellnigh emptyhanded. In huts on the beach would you be dwelling still had not the Noldor carved out your haven and toiled upon your walls." Olwë replies that when the Noldor had originally offered their help, they spoke otherwise, saying that "in the land of Aman we were to dwell forever, as brothers whose houses stand side by side."[23] The elvish racism is evident in the insulting universal negative characterization of the Teleri and in the dishonest transformation of what was

* "Half-brother in blood, full-brother in heart I will be," says Fingolfin. "Thou shalt lead and I will follow. May no new grief divide us." Fëanor seems to accept the reconciliation at the time. *S*, VIII, 75.

seemingly a generous offer of assistance into a debt to be repaid. Fëanor implies both that the Teleri are inferior to the Noldor (fainthearted, dilatory, and poor) and that they owe obedience to their creditors.

After Olwë says that his people will not give their ships away "nor sell them for any league or friendship,"[24] Fëanor decides to seize the ships by force "and a bitter fight was fought upon the ships, and about the lamplit quays and piers of the Haven, and even upon the great arch of its gate . . . many were slain on either side . . . [and] at last the Teleri were overcome, and a great part of their mariners that dwelt in Alqualondë were wickedly slain."[25] Tolkien said that the "first fruit of [the Elves'] fall was, in Paradise, the slaying of Elves by Elves."[26] That kinslaying, not disobedience, is the "original sin" of the elves indicates that *The Silmarillion* is fundamentally "Germanic"; the narrative structure of the work sustaining "itself in cycles of cause and effect from the ethical code of Germanic heroes in Anglo-Saxon, Old High German, and Old Norse fiction."[27] In a traditional Germanic context, it is not possible to make up for the killing of kinsmen: *Wergild* [man-price] cannot be paid within a family, and punishing the initial killer with death or exile simply causes additional familial harm. Seeing the Kinslaying as the fundamental sin from which others derive makes a great deal of sense, especially because, as punishment for the Kinslaying, the Valar impose the Curse of Mandos on the Noldor. Among the many dreadful fates it promises that "to evil end shall all things turn that they begin well; and by treason of kin unto kin, and the fear of treason, shall this come to pass. The Dispossessed they shall be forever."[28] The Curse becomes one of the efficient causes of much of the plot of *The Silmarillion*, and so it is easy to see how the killing of kin could be an inexpiable sin that drives the subsequent narrative.

What has not been noted, however, is that Fëanor and his sons are in some ways less implicated in the killing of their own kinsmen than Fingolfin and Finarfin (the children of Finwë and Indis) and those who followed them because Finarfin was married to the Telerian elf Eärwen of Alqualondë, the daughter of king Olwë. The Teleri, therefore, are his kin by marriage and they are actual blood-kin of his children Finrod, Orodreth, Angrod, Aegnor, and Galadriel. His full brother Fingolfin is slightly less close in kinship by marriage to the Teleri but certainly closer than Fëanor. And although we might be tempted to take *kinslaying* as meaning merely the killing of any elf by any other elf, Tolkien does not use the word to describe the assault by the sons of Fëanor on Doriath, which he merely calls "the second killing of Elf by Elf," and he does not call other individual killings of elves by elves "kinslayings."* Additionally, the Curse of Mandos states that the wrath of the Valar lies on the House of Fëanor and that "the Dispossessed *they* shall be for ever," but the next line of the Curse switches from third- to second-person plural: "Ye have spilled the blood of your kindred unrighteously." I interpret this change in pronouns as indicating that the *wrath* of the Valar "lieth from the West unto the uttermost East," on the House of Fëanor and all who follow them, but that the *guilt* belongs to all the rebelling Noldor, perhaps because although Fëanor is ultimately responsible for the Kinslaying at Alqualondë, he did not personally kill any of his own immediate kin.[29]

The Kinslaying rests upon the foundation of elvish racism that is also the precipitating factor in multiple subsequent disasters not tied directly to this atrocity. For example, in what is possibly the most disturbing tale in *The Silmarillion*, Aredhel Ar-Fieniel the "White Lady of the Noldor," daughter of Fingolfin and sister of King Turgon of Gondolin, leaves that hidden city to visit her friends, the sons of Fëanor. Aredhel, who loved wandering alone in the woodlands, "seeking for new paths and untrodden glades," eventually becomes lost in the dark woods of Nan Elmoth, where "Eöl dwelt, who was named the Dark Elf." One of the Sindar (the Teleri who never left Middle-earth), Eöl "shunned the Noldor, holding them to blame for the return of Morgoth, to trouble the quiet of Beleriand." Seeing Aredhel lost and wandering, "he desired her; and he set his enchantments about her so that she could not find the ways out" of the woods. Eventually she came to his dwelling "and he welcomed her, and led her into his house. And there she remained; for Eöl took her to wife, and it was long ere any of her kin heard of her again."[30]

---

* Including the execution of Eöl by Turgon; the killing of Celegorm, Curufin, and Caranthir at Doriath; the slaughter of the refugees of Gondolin by the surviving sons of Fëanor; and the deaths of Amrod and Amras.

What is most disturbing about this story is the next line: "It is not said that Aredhel was *wholly* unwilling, nor that her life in Nan Elmoth was hateful to her *for many years*."[31] The implication that she was at least partially unwilling and that her life in Nan Elmoth eventually became hateful to her makes Eöl's actions seem little more than abduction, rape, and imprisonment. Aredhel gives birth to a son, whom his father named Maeglin, "which is Sharp Glance, for he perceived that the eyes of his son were more piercing than his own, and his thought could read the secrets of hearts beyond the mist of words." His mother taught Maeglin about his Noldorian kinsmen.

Eöl's relationship with his wife and son is twisted by his resentment of the Noldor. He refuses to allow Aredhel to use their language, and when Maeglin decides that he wants to "look on the Noldor and speak with the sons of Fëanor, his kin, who dwelt not far away," his father says:

> "You are of the house of Eöl, Maeglin, my son . . . and not of the Golodhrim. All this land is the land of the Teleri, and I will not deal nor have my son deal with the slayers of our kin, the invaders and usurpers of our homes. In this you shall obey me, or I will set you in bonds." And Maeglin did not answer, but was cold and silent, and went abroad no more with Eöl, and Eöl mistrusted him.[32]

Eventually Maeglin convinces his mother to flee the forest and travel to Gondolin, but Eöl returns from visiting his friends the dwarves sooner than Maeglin had expected, and he pursues his wife and son beyond Nan Elmoth and into the land of two of the sons of Fëanor, Celegorm and Curufin, where he is waylaid by Curufin's retainers. Curufin, who was "of perilous mood" is scornful of Eöl, stating that if Aredhel and Maeglin had been accompanied by the Dark Elf, "they might have found their welcome less warm than they hoped," but he does tell Eöl the direction in which his wife and son were traveling. And when Eöl says "It is good, Lord Curufin, to find a kinsman thus kindly at need. I will remember it when I return," Curufin expresses the full force of his racism toward the Teleri: "Then Curufin looked darkly upon Eöl. 'Do not flaunt the title of your wife before me,' he said. 'For those who steal the daughters of the Noldor and wed them without gift or leave do not gain kinship with their kin.'" Eöl rides away "filled with hatred of the Noldor," and manages to find his way to the secret pathway to Gondolin, where he is captured by the Guard and brought before the king.[33]

Here, even though Turgon, king of Gondolin, "treated him with honour, and rose up and would take his hand" and addressed him as "kinsman," Eöl's heart "was filled the more with anger and with hate of the Noldor" despite the wonder and beauty of the city. He refuses to acknowledge Turgon's law that no one may leave the hidden kingdom and asserts that Turgon and the Noldor have no right "to seize realms or set bounds, either here or there. This is the land of the Teleri, to which you bring war and all unquiet, dealing ever proudly and unjustly." He then commands Maeglin to "leave the house of his enemies and the slayers of his kin, or be accursed!"

The content of Turgon's reply is almost exactly parallel to what Fëanor says to Olwë when that Telerian king refuses to give the Noldor the white ships: "I will not debate with you, Dark Elf. By the swords of the Noldor alone are your sunless woods defended. Your freedom to wander there wild you owe to my kin; and but for them long since you would have laboured in thraldom in the pits of Angband."[34] Like Fëanor, Turgon implies that Eöl owes gratitude and deference to the Noldor for doing something for which he did not ask and for which initially the Noldor did not claim to seek any reward. In Eöl's eyes, there would be no need for anyone to defend his woods if the Noldor had not returned to Middle-earth and begun the war against Morgoth, but Turgon refuses to "debate" with him and transforms the interaction from an argument into a naked imposition of power: "And here I am King; and whether you will it or will it not, my doom is law."[35]

Eöl's attempted murder of Maeglin, which becomes an actual murder of Aredhel when she jumps in front of the poison-tipped javelin, is not called a kinslaying or even mentioned as one of the killings of elf by elf, and neither is Eöl's subsequent execution by being cast off the precipice of Caragdûl, despite the Dark Elf being obvious kin by blood to Maeglin and by marriage to both Aredhel and Turgon. This textual silence is consistent with the words of Curufin that Eöl's marriage did not "gain" him kinship with Aredhel's kin, and although Eöl had called the sons of Fëanor "slayers of our kin," he is clearly referring to the Kinslaying at Alqualondë. Note also that the only Noldo whom he directly accuses of kinslaying is Turgon, who, being the son of Fingolfin, had closer kinship with the Teleri of Alqualondë than did Fëanor and his sons.

The chapter "Of Maeglin," in *The Silmarillion*, which concludes before Maeglin's betrayal of Gondolin to Morgoth, ends with the unrequited desire of Maeglin for Turgon's daughter Idril. Although Maeglin "grew great among the Gondolindrim, and high in the favour of Turgon," Idril "mistrusted" him from the time of Eöl's execution, which Maeglin had stood and watched silently. In any event, she was his first cousin and "the Eldar wedded not with kin so near, nor ever before had any desired to do so," but Maeglin "loved *the beauty* of Idril Celebrindal and *desired her*," and this desire "robbed him of all joy" in Gondolin.[36] The text does not say that Maeglin *loved* Idril, merely her beauty, which is racially coded: "*for* she was golden as the Vanyar, her mother's kindred."[37] If we read this sentence literally, Maeglin's desire is motivated by Idril's having the physical markers of the superior kindred of the elves. It is not difficult to infer—particularly in light of all that comes after in *The Fall of Gondolin*—that Maeglin's desire for Idril is a sublimation of his father's resentment of the Noldor. Maeglin, who is tall, black-haired, and dark-eyed like his mother and father and resembled one of the Noldor in "face and form," watched Idril and waited, "and his love turned to darkness in his heart. And he sought to have his will in other matters, shirking no toil or burden, if he might therefore have power."[38] Maeglin thus does not desire Idril just because she is the king's daughter (he seeks and gains that kind of power in other ways), but because she represents the higher-ranked race, which he both desires and resents. The dislike of Idril for Maeglin is explained by his desire seeming "to her a thing strange and crooked within him, as indeed the Eldar ever since have deemed it: an evil fruit of the Kinslaying, whereby the shadow of the curse of Mandos fell upon the last hope of the Noldor."[39]

The description of Maeglin's moral deformity as "an evil fruit of the Kinslaying" would appear to militate against my interpretation of the racism generated by the racial hierarchy as being the cause of so many of the tragedies of *The Silmarillion*. But the elves not recognizing the existence of such a dynamic actually supports the thesis. *The Silmarillion* is, after all, written from the perspective of Noldor in general and the Vanyar-descended side of the House of Finwë in particular.* The unnamed compiler of *The Silmarillion* consistently sides with Fingolfin and Finarfin and their children over Fëanor and his sons, and the Kinslaying is always blamed on all the Noldor who returned to Beleriand despite the members of the houses of Finarfin and Fingolfin being more likely than members of the house of Fëanor to have killed actual kin.† The narrator or narrators of *The Silmarillion* credit treason, betrayal, and other disasters to the Oath of Fëanor and the Kinslaying—working, as it does, through the Curse of Mandos. There is never any recognition that the implied racial hierarchy and both the racism and the resentment that this causes is behind nearly all of these interactions—including, as we have seen, the strife in the House of Finwë that is the initial movement toward the "original sin" of the Kinslaying at Alqualondë—because this racial hierarchy legitimizes the superiority of the houses of Fingolfin and Finarfin among the Noldor due to their being half-Vanyar. Elvish racism is not an obvious and visible problem in Tolkien's Middle-earth; it is something more powerful and pernicious: an underlying dynamic, a set of widely held assumptions, neither consciously accessible to the characters nor

---

* On his father's side, Elrond is a descendant of Idril and therefore is of the house of Fingolfin.

† The compiler also portrays Maedhros and, most of all, Maglor, as being more noble, compassionate, and accepting of responsibility than the other sons of Fëanor, which leads me to believe that the text is told from the point of view of Elrond, who, with his brother Elros, was saved from the destruction of the assault by the sons of Fëanor on the exiles at the Mouths of Sirion: "For Maglor took pity on Elrond and Elros, and he cherished them, for love grew between them, as little might be thought"; *S*, XXIV, 247. Maglor is portrayed as hesitating about stealing the remaining two silmarils, arguing against his brother; *S*, XXIV, 252–54. No one can have witnessed this conversation between just the two brothers, and there seems to have been no opportunity for them to have spoken to anyone after the theft, so Maglor's portrayal must have been imagined by the narrator of the tale. Elrond seems the most likely candidate for being the historian who would depict Maglor so sympathetically.

explicitly named in the narrative, which nonetheless shapes the interactions that make up the complex plot of *The Silmarillion*.*

THE CULTURAL MINDSET of elvish racism is not restricted to intra-Elvish relations: Men and dwarves are both inferior to all elves in the existential hierarchy. In the three Great Tales (Beren and Lúthien, the Túrin story, and the Fall of Gondolin) the derision of an elf for a man, based entirely on the presumed inferiority of men, contributes significantly to the eventual tragedy. When Thingol, the king of the Sindar (those Teleri who remained in Beleriand), discovers that his daughter Lúthien has fallen in love with a man, he calls Beren "unhappy mortal" and "baseborn mortal," and "he thought in his heart 'Unhappy Men, children of little lords and brief kings, shall such as these lay hands on [Lúthien] and yet live?'" He then says Beren may only marry Lúthien if he brings Thingol one of the silmarils from Morgoth's iron crown, thus intending to send Beren to his death but keeping to the letter of his promise to his daughter that he would neither slay nor imprison the man.[40]

Although Thingol's possessiveness toward Lúthien would seem merely to be the typical fairy-story reaction of a father to his daughter's suitor, the way Tolkien explains it refers to the idea of the existential hierarchy that produces elvish racism: "for Lúthien he loved above all things, *setting her above all the princes of the Elves*; whereas mortal Men he did not even take into his service."[41] What infuriates Thingol about Beren and Lúthien's love is the inferiority of Beren. Because Lúthien is half Maia (her mother, Melian, belongs to the angelic order of beings that includes Gandalf, Sauron, and Saruman), Thingol ranks her even above the princes of the Noldor, but Beren ranks below even ordinary elves, which is why the Elven-king is so derisive.

Thingol seems to have mellowed after the quest of the silmaril and the disastrous Fifth Battle, Nirnaeth Arnoediad, for he takes a man—Túrin, the son of the great hero Húrin Thalion—into Doriath and

* Parallels to the real world are sufficiently obvious.

honors him as his foster son. Nevertheless, elvish racism precipitates another disaster. Saeros is an elf of the Nandor, one of the Teleri who left the Great Journey while still east of the Misty Mountains and only entered Beleriand much later. The Nandor rank below the Grey Elves in the intra-elvish hierarchy, but they are still above mortal men, and so Saeros "had long begrudged to Túrin the honour he received as Thingol's fosterson." Túrin had just returned from the wild and was "unkempt, and his gear and garments . . . wayworn," so Saeros taunted him, saying "If the Men of Hithlum are so wild and fell, of what sort are the women of that land? Do they run like deer clad only in their hair?"* Túrin threw a drinking vessel into Saeros's face, injuring the elf. The next day, Saeros tried to waylay the man, but Túrin "overcame him, and set him to run naked as a hunted beast through the woods." In a panic, Saeros fell into a chasm and died, and Túrin, afraid that he will be punished by Thingol, leaves Doriath and takes up with a band of outlaws, setting in motion the tragic action of the rest of the tale. Túrin may have reacted so violently in part because the taunt about the women of Hithlum going about mostly naked implies that they are sexually available, and Túrin's mother and sister are, as far as he knows, still in Hithlum. He therefore takes the jibe personally, and it stings even more because of Saeros's unarticulated presumption of racial superiority.

The interaction of the racial hierarchy with sexuality is also evident in "Of Tuor and the Fall of Gondolin." Previously we noted Maeglin's unreciprocated desire for the king's daughter, Idril. A mortal man, Tuor (cousin of Túrin) is sent to Gondolin by the Vala Ulmo to urge King Turgon to abandon the hidden city and go down the river Sirion to the sea so as to avoid the Curse of Mandos. The king, although he believes that Tuor has indeed been sent by Ulmo, in the end refuses to heed the warning but instead walls up the secret entrance to Gondolin and completely

* The particular sexualized insult about the women of Hithlum running naked in the woods becomes instantiated when Túrin's sister Nienor recovers from the blindness and deafness with which Glaurung the dragon had afflicted her (the spell of forgetting remains in effect). Hearing the voices of the orcs that attacked the company of elves that was protecting her, she "fled as in a madness of fear, swifter than a deer, and tore off all her clothing as she ran, until she was naked"; *S*, XXI, 218–19.

withdraws from the external world. Tuor remained in the hidden city, and "then the heart of Idril was turned to him, and his to her, and Maeglin's secret hatred grew greater, for he desired above all things to possess her." After seven years Turgon allows Idril and Tuor to wed. Their son is Eärendil the Halfelven: "of surpassing beauty was Eärendil, for a light was in his face as of the light of heaven, and he had the beauty and the wisdom of the Eldar and the strength and hardihood of Men of old."

Maeglin, seeking for metals beyond the boundary of the encircling mountains, is taken prisoner by orcs and brought before Morgoth. He agrees to betray the city not only from fear of torture but because Morgoth promises him "the possession of Idril Celebrindal, when the city should be taken; and indeed the desire for Idril *and the hatred for Tuor* led Maeglin the easier to his treachery, most famous in all the histories of the Elder days."[42]

Maeglin had been in Gondolin for many years. He knew that Idril did not reciprocate his desire long before Tuor arrived, and Idril and Tuor were not married until seven years after that, but Maeglin nevertheless hates Tuor, even though the man had nothing to do with Idril's not responding to Maeglin's desire, which in any event could never have been instantiated because the Eldar did not practice cousin-marriage. Maeglin's disproportionate response, however, can be explained as the workings of elvish racism. If Maeglin inferred that part of the reason for Idril's rejection of him was his being half Teleri (through his father Eöl, the Dark Elf), then her responding to and eventually marrying someone from even lower in the hierarchy added enormous insult to injury. Idril's marriage to Tuor implies to Maeglin that she ranks him even lower than a mere mortal, and this is to him an unforgiveable insult, although he transfers his anger and perhaps self-loathing into his hatred of Tuor because he still desires to have "the possession" of Idril.* The negative effects of racial hierarchies cascade downstream, since each stratum

* In *The Fall of Gondolin*, the hatred Maeglin (then spelled Meglin) feels is so extreme that he attempts to drag Idril by her hair to the battlements just so he can force her to watch him throw her child into the flames, and when Tuor arrives to rescue his wife and child, Maeglin still attempts to stab Eärendil. He is thwarted both by the child's biting him and by the small coat of mail that Eärendil is wearing beneath his clothes (a motif Tolkien will use with Frodo in *The Lord of the Rings*); *Gondolin*, 81–82.

is usually unable to unseat those that rank above it but can effectively oppress lower tiers, and it is the nature of the resentments created by such hierarchies to flow in both directions: Condescension and entitlement from above generate resentment from below, and the interaction of these emotions eventually leads to distrust and hatred all around.

DWARVES DEFINITELY RANK BELOW the elves in the racial hierarchy, but whether they are below or above men is difficult to determine.[43] In the story of Túrin, we learn of the existence of the "Noegyth Nibin, the Petty-Dwarves" who had long ago been banished from the great dwarf-cities of the East and had come into Beleriand.

> Before the Dwarves of Nogrod and Belegost came west over the mountains the Elves of Beleriand knew not what these other were, and they hunted them, and slew them; but afterwards they let them alone . . . they loved none but themselves, and if they feared and hated the Orcs, they hated the Eldar no less, and the Exiles most of all; for the Noldor, they said, had stolen their lands and their homes.[44]

That the elves of Beleriand *hunted* the Petty-Dwarves certainly implies that they ranked them lower in the racial hierarchy than men (whom the elves never hunted), and the ways that the other outlaws in Túrin's band treat Mîm and his fellow Petty-Dwarves indicates that they believe themselves to be superior to them.[45] In *Unfinished Tales*' "Narn i Hîn Húrin," of which "Of Túrin Turambar" in the published *Silmarillion* is a compressed epitome, it is more obvious that the outlaws, particularly Andróg, look down on Mîm and the other Petty-Dwarves: "For Andróg does not like Dwarves. His people brought few good tales of that race out of the East."[46]

The only other interactions between men and dwarves are not particularly helpful in determining where they sit relative to each other in the racial hierarchy. When Húrin, the father of Túrin, kills Mîm in the ruins of Nargothrond, the reason he gives—"and not unknown is it to me by whom the Dragon-helm of Dor-lómin was betrayed"—is obviously personal. Similarly, Beren's slaying of the Lord of Nogrod, whose army had just plundered the halls of his father-in-law Thingol, is so well-motivated that we can draw no conclusions about the racial hierarchy from it.

But the interactions between Thingol and the dwarves that lead to death of the elven-king and the sacking of Doriath are obviously motivated by elvish racism. From ruined Nargothrond Túrin's father Húrin brought out only one treasure, the Nauglamír, the necklace of the dwarves "most famed of all their works in the Elder Days," and threw it at Thingol's feet as an ironic payment "for thy fair keeping of my children and my wife!" But Melian's power overcomes the lies of Morgoth that had bewitched Húrin, and he finally understands that Thingol had done his best to help and honor Túrin, Nienor, and Morwen. Húrin "spoke no more of what was past, but stooping lifted up the Nauglamír from where it lay before Thingol's chair, and he gave it to him, saying: "Receive now, lord, the Necklace of the Dwarves, as a gift from one who has nothing, and as a memorial of Húrin of Dor-lómin."[47] There is no curse on the necklace, but Thingol has become obsessed by the silmaril that Beren and Lúthien took from Morgoth's crown, and he summons the great craftsmen who are part of a large group of dwarves doing stone- and metalwork in Thingol's halls and asks them to remake the Nauglamír to include the jewel.

> Then the Dwarves looked upon the work of their fathers, and they beheld with wonder the shining jewel of Fëanor; and they were filled with a great lust to possess them, and carry them off to their far homes in the mountains. But they dissembled their mind, and consented to the task.[48]

Eventually "the greatest of the works of Elves and Dwarves were brought together and made one." But the dwarves now withheld the necklace, claiming that since their ancestors made it for Finrod, and Finrod was dead, Húrin had taken it "as a thief out of the darkness of Nargothrond." These words are obviously "a pretext and a fair cloak" for the dwarves' true intent to take the jewels.

To this point the well-established lust for possession that the silmarils trigger in many of those who see them is sufficient explanation for the interaction, and Thingol's being offended by the bogosity of the dwarves' arguments as well as their attempt to steal the silmaril upon which they had no claim at all seems reasonable. But the specifics of the king's angry response displays the elvish racism that must have been lurking below the surface of his previous interactions with the dwarves:

> "How do ye of uncouth race dare to demand aught of me, Elu Thingol, Lord of Beleriand, whose life began by the waters of Cuiviénen years uncounted ere the fathers of the stunted people awoke?" And standing tall and proud among them he bade them with shameful words be gone unrequited out of Doriath.[49]

The racial coding of Thingol's insults is obvious: He condemns the dwarves not for breaking an agreement, attempting to steal something upon which they have no claim, or even for insulting his intelligence with their ridiculous justifications. Instead, he attacks their race in exactly the terms in which the racial hierarchy makes the dwarves' most vulnerable: They are asserted to be inferior to elves in seniority in Middle-earth, in knowledge, and even in physical development ("stunted"; note that the narrator of passage describes Thingol's superior height and bearing: "tall and proud"). These are the characteristics that the narrator or narrators of *The Silmarillion* consistently note about the dwarves: The Sindar who first encounter dwarves, named them "the Naugrim, the Stunted People"; the other, more respectful Elvish name, "Gonnhirrim, Masters of Stone" is only mentioned once in the narrative and is never spoken in dialogue.[50] When the Noldor came back to Middle-earth, the people of Caranthir (one of the sons of Fëanor), met the dwarves "and Caranthir was haughty and scarce concealed his scorn for the unloveliness of the Naugrim, and his people followed their lord."[51] Note that here the narrator does not say that Caranthir and his people *perceived* the dwarves to be unlovely: Their supposed unloveliness is treated as an established fact.

By focusing his invective on racially coded characteristics, Thingol does not merely assert his personal authority as "Lord of Beleriand"; he invokes the permanent Elvish superiority over the dwarves, which provides self-justification for not only his scornful speech, but his abusive behavior: Commanding them to leave "unrequited" indicates that he is not even going to pay them for the labor they spent in remaking the Nauglamír. No wonder the dwarves respond by killing him "in the deep places of Menegroth" and fleeing back to the dwarf city of Nogrod.* There, two of the slayers of Thingol are able to convince their fellow dwarves to seek revenge by sending forth a great host to attack Doriath: "a thing most grievous among the sorrowful deeds of the Elder Days. For there was battle in the Thousand Caves, and many Elves and Dwarves were slain; and it has not been forgotten."[52] In fact, the enmity between elves and dwarves that is seen in the Third Age—the Elven-king's response to Thorin and Company in *The Hobbit* and the initial treatment of Gimli in Lothlórien in *The Fellowship of the Ring*—can be traced to this event, since up to that point in *The Silmarillion* the Dwarves of Nogrod and Belegost were allies, if somewhat inconsistent ones, of the elves in the war against Morgoth.[53] The echoes of Thingol's racialized abuse persisted for thousands of years, in great part because the racial hierarchy that generated them did also.

Although *The Silmarillion* is the focus of this discussion, it is worth noting that racial hierarchies are also present in *The Lord of the Rings*, though their workings are far more subtle in Tolkien's more mature work. With the exception of the Lórien elves' distrust of Gimli at the beginning of the Fellowship's sojourn in Lothlórien, we do not see active race-based discrimination against or mistreatment of putatively inferior races by the few surviving Noldor in Middle-earth, concentrated as they are in Rivendell and Lothlórien.[54] Perhaps we should infer that the elves learned from their experiences in the wars against Morgoth that treating members of other kindreds or races as inferiors is not a successful strategy for building and maintaining a coalition of peoples against a Dark Lord. Be that as it may, in the Third Age elvish racism is not a significant factor in the plot dynamics except, perhaps,

* It may not be an entirely unwarranted inference that Thingol's racialized insults might have helped convince the other dwarves of Nogrod to seek revenge. The dwarf craftsmen who were killed in escaping from Doriath were among the killers of the Elven-king.

in the way that the Elvish racial hierarchy is echoed in the views of the Men of Gondor with regard to the kindreds or races of men.

Faramir tells Frodo that "we reckon Men in our lore, calling them the High, or Men of the West, which were Númenóreans; and the Middle Peoples, Men of the Twilight, such as are the Rohirrim and their kin that dwell still far in the North; and the Wild, the Men of Darkness."[55] In one of the draft versions of this passage Tolkien explicitly matched the three divisions of men to three divisions of elves: "the High Elves, and the Middle Elves . . . their kindred that lingered on the shores, and the Wild Elves . . . of the woods and mountains."[56] "The need for a classification of the Men of Dale found in *The Hobbit* . . . generated this division of Men in Third-Age Middle-earth. Since both of these subdivisions could not be Númenóreans but still were on the good side, Tolkien invented a pedigree for them so that they became descendants of the same 'races' as the Númenoreans," but the ancestors of the Men of the Twilight had stayed in Middle-earth rather than crossing the sea to Númenor.[57]

Regardless of the reasons for its creation, the hierarchical tripartite division of men in the Third Age does not seem to have the same pernicious effects as the elf-focused racial hierarchy of the First Age. The men who serve Sauron or Saruman are said to have been cozened, "deluded," or misled, not in some way born to evil or otherwise intrinsically warped or inferior—although there are two examples of some of them being described in terms that could be seen as racially coded (both within Middle-earth and extratextually).[58] But unlike the Elvish racial hierarchy, which remained unchanged in both structure and significance throughout the First Age, the hierarchy of men is incomplete (hobbits are not included) and appears to be undergoing revision or renegotiation. Race and kindred are far less of a factor in narrative of *The Lord of the Rings* than in *The Silmarillion.*

Given the overwhelming prominence of studies of race and racism in contemporary academia, it is surprising that the significance of the racial hierarchy being the cause of many disasters in *The Silmarillion* has not been widely noted. There are two mutually reinforcing explanations. This neglect may be the result of critical attention with regard to problems of race being almost entirely focused on *The Lord of the Rings.*

This is especially true of work by nonspecialists who are unacquainted with the full range of Tolkien's writings but are instead concerned primarily with the mass-culture phenomenon of the Peter Jackson films. But as noted above, in Tolkien's mature work the interactions around race are both complex and subtle, making it difficult to recognize the pattern that is so obvious in *The Silmarillion*. Second, there is obviously a great deal of critical anxiety around these issues with regard to Tolkien and his works. In order to defend—in most cases—the subjects of their study against a general critical industry that has spent the past two decades generating charges of racism against authors, works, fields of study, and even individual scholars, scholarship has focused on demonstrating that Tolkien held no race-based hatred in his heart because those aspects of his fiction to which the all-purpose pejorative *problematic* has been applied are usually merely relics of the common inherited culture of his time.[59] Those scholars who have attacked rather than defended Tolkien around these issues seem for the most part to accept the argument that Tolkien may not personally have felt race-based hatred, but they assert that oppositions in his fiction between good and evil—with stereotypically "white" characters on the side of the good and some evil characters being described as "black" or "swarthy"—represent and propagate a racist mindset.[60]

For what it is worth, I think both sets of judgments, although at least arguable at a superficial level, are fundamentally misconceived, in that they reduce the analysis of works of literature to the comparison of features against arbitrary checklists of contemporary shibboleths. They are also not particularly interesting, because they are predictable and can be applied to any work from any era or culture.* It is important to note that I make no claim that Tolkien was somehow "ahead of his time" in his entirely negative depiction of Elvish racism. Quite the opposite: I am asserting that the kind of race-based prejudice, hatred, and violence

* Evaluating works of art (literary and otherwise) by ephemeral contemporary mores has a long and undistinguished history, and the judgment of anything even tangentially connected to race in terms of the American politics of the 2020s is just the latest instance of a critical practice that goes back at least as far as the English Civil War, the Protestant Reformation, and the Spanish Inquisition, and probably reached its apogee in the Soviet Union in the 1930s and in China during the Cultural Revolution of the 1970s. These comparisons are not meant as compliments.

that we see depicted entirely negatively in *The Silmarillion* could be, and was, recognized as dehumanizing and destructive of community and social cohesion not only in Tolkien's time, but earlier, and well before its rise to preeminence in Anglo-American academic-political discourse. People knew it was morally wrong to act in these ways long before academics realized that it could be gratifying to tell them so.*

Tolkien never explicitly delineated the underlying social dynamics of the elves as I have characterized them, but in his 1951 letter to Milton Waldman he had noted that

> There was nothing wrong essentially in [the Elves'] lingering against counsel . . . but they wanted to have their cake without eating it. They wanted the peace and bliss and perfect memory of "The West," and yet to remain on the ordinary earth where their *prestige as the highest people*, above wild Elves, dwarves, and Men, was greater than at the bottom of the hierarchy of Valinor.[61]

Thus Tolkien did recognize that the Noldor's position in the hierarchy was important to them and that they very much believed that this hierarchy was both existential and immutable: They *knew* that if they returned to Valinor they would be at a lower rank than they are in Middle-earth.[62]

My personal conclusion is that the existence or creation of hierarchies based on heredity but extending beyond the bounds of relatively close family, hierarchies which generally prohibit entry via marriage or adoption and within which mixed children create affiliation- and classification-problems, produces racism whether or not that is the conscious intent of any of the participants (indeed, even if racism is what they hope to avoid). Identify one group defined by heredity as being superior—particularly morally superior—and racism follows. Inevitably. Obviously this is far too large an argument to even attempt to prove

* It would make us feel better about human nature to think that ignorance is the reason people accept moral evils, but, sadly, the evidence of even very recent history shows that this is not the case.

here (it is likely too large to prove at all), but if I can perceive such a pattern as being obvious in both literary and historical examples, Tolkien surely could as well, and the consistently pernicious effects of the racial hierarchy in *The Silmarillion*—as well as his justly famous rejection in a 1938 letter to his publisher of the "lunatic" German race-laws and "wholly pernicious and unscientific race-doctrine," and his sharp-tongued reply to the German publisher that asked him if he was Aryan[63]—suggest that he might have been somewhat amenable to this conclusion. However, we must accept that there is simply not enough evidence to be confident in it.

Identifying the parallel theme of the poison of the racial hierarchy does allow us to see more easily how the dominant theme of *The Silmarillion*—the Working of Evil in the World—is subsumed within what Tolkien saw as the overarching theme of all his works: Death and Immortality. In a 1958 letter to Rhona Beare, Tolkien wrote: "In the Elvish legends there is a record of a strange case of an Elf (Míriel mother of Fëanor) that tried to die, which had disastrous results, leading to the 'Fall' of the High-elves."[64] I did not pay sufficient attention to this comment whenever I initially read it, so it was a very happy surprise to rediscover this letter. Suddenly one of the sentences from my lecture-notes no longer seemed so extreme: "Conflict among the Noldor: Finwë remarries and child from first marriage won't accept children of blonde trophy-wife, but trophy-wife and her children are higher-class than husband and first-born." As we have discussed previously, the animus between the son of Míriel and the sons of Indis is not directly responsible for the Kinslaying, but it is one of the dramatic initial events in a chain of causation that leads to that disaster, so Tolkien's assertion that Míriel's death led to the Fall of the High-elves makes my hyperbolic summary seem a little closer to the truth (it is comforting to think that I might not have been teaching an entirely wrong interpretation for two decades). However, although Míriel's death is the ultimate antecedent of the Fall of the High-elves, the closer efficient cause is not her death, or death itself, but instead the deep contradictions within the Elvish social structure. These fatal flaws are not created by her death; they are merely exposed by it.

That the evils caused by the racial hierarchy do not arise from Morgoth but nevertheless are the causes of misery and tragedy is one of the qualities of Tolkien's work that makes it appear true.[65] We have an intuitive sense that although great evils in the world are instantiated in the forms of leaders, or institutions, or governments, there are also other kinds of evil, perhaps less overwhelming in their size and power, but far more widespread. Among them is the evil that arises from a sense of unearned superiority and a set of privileges founded on arbitrary, race-based placement into a hierarchy. That everything bad cannot be blamed on the devil (or equivalent) but arises from ordinary human social behavior, that *both* kinds of evil exist in the world, and that both must be fought, albeit in different ways, is one of the thematic features of Tolkien's works that feels particularly true to readers with any number of different ideological commitments.

THE DOMINANT THEME of *The Hobbit* is not the same as that of *The Silmarillion*, so we have no reason to expect that any parallel themes would be the same, either. Rather than The Working of Evil in the World, the main theme of *The Hobbit* is The Development of a Small or Ordinary Person into a Hero, or "the journey into maturity."[66] Bilbo grows from a somewhat timid, self-satisfied, and even mildly pompous little man who has never been outside of his own country (and seems proud of, or at least comfortable in, his insularity), and who is initially quite hapless in navigating the wider world; to the "real leader in their adventure" who "had begun to have plans and ideas of his own"; to the heroic individual whom the Elven-king calls "Bilbo the Magnificent" when he names him "Elf-friend," and to whom King Dain says "this treasure is as much yours as it is mine."[67] The Elvish racial hierarchy, therefore, does not play nearly as large a role in *The Hobbit* as it does in *The Silmarillion*. Although the imprisonment of the dwarves by the Mirkwood elves is obviously rooted in traditional racial distrust, it is also true that Thorin and Company had trespassed on the Elven-king's lands and, more importantly, they refused to divulge the reason they were passing through them. These reasons are sufficient to explain this aspect of the narrative in *The Hobbit* without invoking the influence of the racial hierarchy.

Instead, parallel to the overarching theme of individual heroic development in *The Hobbit* runs a dialectical engagement between what can be called the *epic* and the *bourgeois* worlds, which exist in a hierarchical but contested relationship that generates some of the tension that both structures and drives the narrative of *The Hobbit*.* Although he does not use exactly the same terminology, Shippey also identifies an opposition between the epic and the bourgeois worlds as a structuring principle of *The Hobbit*. In his "The Bourgeois Burglar" chapter in *The Road to Middle-earth*, Shippey calls attention to the "anachronistic" qualities of the mediating figure of Bilbo, who

> represents and often voices modern opinions, modern incapacities. He has no impulses toward revenge or self-conscious heroism, cannot "hoot twice like a barn-own and once like a screech owl" as the dwarves suggest, knows almost nothing about Wilderland, and cannot even skin a rabbit, being used to having his meat "delivered by the butcher all ready to cook."[68]

---

* I am adopting Shippey's terminology of *bourgeois* for what Bilbo's world represents and choosing *epic* from among several possible terms for the contrasting world of heroes, kings, dragons, and magic from whence the dwarves come. Despite a valiant effort (if wasting enormous quantities of time retyping the same few paragraphs over and over can be considered "valiant"), I have been unable to communicate the ideas in this part of the argument without using this word. I resisted the use of *bourgeois* for a variety of reasons, not the least of which is my inability to type it correctly even two times in a row. It is my experience that the word *bourgeois* causes some substantial portion of readers (for those under age fifty-five it is close to 100 percent) to skip ahead to the first paragraph that does not contain it, so horribly was it overused in bad twentieth-century criticism. Additionally, despite the term originating as a semi-neutral description of "middle-class" people who both work and own property but do not rely entirely on unearned income and are not members of the aristocracy, a glance at any list of supposed synonyms for *bourgeois*—such as one might make when desperately seeking an alternative word—reveals all of them to be needlessly pejorative (*close-minded*? *conformist*? *provincial*? *commonplace*?) except for *middle-class,* but this term is not quite expansive enough and means different things in Britain and America. Also, adding many instances of *middle-class* to a book that already includes 163 appearances of *Middle-earth* seems both a recipe for error and an imposition on the patience of readers—perhaps almost as bad an imposition as long digressive footnotes.

Furthermore, Bilbo "takes pride in being 'prosy,' pooh-poohs anything out of the ordinary and is almost aggressively middle middle-class in being more respectable than the Tooks, though rather 'well-to-do' than 'rich.'"[69] Shippey explains that "the early moves of *The Hobbit* depend very much on [a] tension between ancient and modern reactions," as both the humor and the drama comes from Bilbo attempting to act and communicate according to the somewhat unfamiliar conventions of the epic world of the dwarves, who are awkwardly trying to act and communicate according to their understanding of the somewhat alien conventions of the hobbit's bourgeois world.[70]

The dialectical relationship between the epic and bourgeois worlds in *The Hobbit* is, at the beginning, resolved mostly in favor of the former. As Shippey notes, Bilbo appears quite ridiculous in his early interactions with the dwarves, who only seem moderately obnoxious in their demands for food and drink and are not even particularly awkward in their use of commercial language in their contract for Bilbo's services.[71] In contrast, the superiority of the epic world in the imaginations of the bourgeois is illustrated by Bilbo's initial charmed response to the dwarves' song and his desire to travel to new lands "and wear a sword instead of a walking-stick."[72] Although the bourgeois worldview abruptly reasserts itself in Bilbo's terror at the idea of a dragon descending on Hobbiton, Bilbo's anger at Glóin's description of him as being "more like a grocer than a burglar," demonstrates both the entanglement of the two worlds and the cultural dominance of the epic, even in the imagination of a denizen of the fully bourgeois enclave of the Shire.[73] Being more like a shopkeeper than a criminal could not possibly be an insult in Bilbo's home culture, but it most certainly is one in the world of heroes and dragons—and the hobbit knows it.

Shippey argues that "Lake-town, at the centre of the book, functions as another primarily hostile image of modernity, against which Thorin and the dwarves seem both splendid and realistic."[74] The Master of Lake-town is portrayed as unimaginative and venal, "giving his mind to trade and tolls, cargoes and gold, to which habit he owed his position."[75] He never is convinced by Thorin's claims or plans, but goes along with the populace, whose enthusiasm for the return of the "King

Under the Mountain" demonstrates the superiority of the epic world in people's imaginations, as does their embrace of Bard and the rejection of the Master after the destruction of the town by Smaug: "Up the Bowman, and down with Moneybags!"[76]

Perhaps the most dramatic illustration of the assumed and generally accepted superiority of the epic world can be seen in Bilbo's conversation with Smaug, in which the dragon demonstrates that while having nothing but contempt for bourgeois culture, he in some ways knows more about Bilbo's world than the hobbit does. At the beginning of the exchange Smaug attempts to make Bilbo distrust the dwarves, and he scoffs at characteristics of bourgeois cooperation:

> "I supposed you got a fair price for that cup last night?" he went on. "Come now, did you? Nothing at all! Well, that's just like them. And I suppose that they are skulking outside, and your job is to do all the dangerous work and get what you can when I'm not looking—for them? And you will get a fair share? Don't you believe it. If you get off alive you will be lucky."[77]

Smaug sneers at the *fair* in "fair price" and "fair share" not only because he is playing on an in-world stereotype about dwarves (their hard bargaining) and wants to convince Bilbo that his companions will betray him, but also because—as we soon see—in the epic world that the dragon dominates, the very idea of prices, contracts, bargains, and division of labor is ridiculous and even pathetic.

> "I don't know if it has occurred to you that, even if you could steal the gold bit by bit—a matter of a hundred years or so—you could not get it very far? Not much use on the mountain side? Not much use in the forest? Bless me! Had you never thought of the catch? A fourteenth share, I suppose, or something like it, those were the terms, eh? But what about delivery? What about cartage? What about armed guards and tolls?" And Smaug laughed aloud. He had a wicked and wily heart, and he knew his guesses were not far out.[78]

Smaug knows the logistical problems created by the difficulty of transporting treasure and the proper commercial terminology—his use of *cartage* is particularly telling, as this word in contemporary English is *only* employed in commercial technical contexts. In a few sentences the dragon shows that he has greater and more sophisticated knowledge of Bilbo's world than the hobbit does: He is at home in a discussion of the bourgeois solutions to the problems of how to move valuable things around without them being stolen. But not only does Smaug demonstrate greater mastery of language about these aspects of the bourgeois world than its own representative, he then displays his mastery of a separate discourse, that of the epic world. When Bilbo suggests that he and the dwarves have come for revenge, Smaug's language shifts to a wholly different register, one marked by poetic characteristics, including meter, near-rhyme, and alliteration:

> *"Revenge!" he snorted, . . . "Revenge!*
> *The King under the Mountain is* ***dead*** *and where are his kin that* ***dare seek*** *revenge?*
> *Girion Lord of Dale is* ***dead,*** *and I have eaten his people like a wolf among sheep*
> *and where are his sons' sons that* ***dare approach*** *me?*
> *I kill where I* wish *and none* ***dare*** **resist**. [iamb / anapest|iamb / anapest]
> *I laid low the warriors of old, and their like is not in the world today.*
> *Then I was but young and tender, now I am strong, strong, strong,*
> *Thief in the shadows . . .*
> *My armour is like tenfold shields, my teeth are swords,*
> *my claws spears, the shock of my tail a thunderbolt,*
> *my wings a hurricane, and my* breath death!"[79]

Smaug asserts that he is superior to all challengers within the epic world (the King Under the Mountain, Girion, Lord of Dale and his sons and their sons, the warriors of old), and by having terrorized Bilbo and the dwarves and eaten many of their ponies he has already shown that he is utterly physically superior to anything in the bourgeois world as well, which very much lacks the warriors of old and is indeed at this moment represented only by a lone hobbit. Smaug does not just *represent* the epic world, he is fully *of* the epic world, and his superiority and domination is its traditional superiority and domination over the bourgeois world.

The world of the readers of *The Hobbit* is bourgeois: The epic is entirely legendary and its superiority exists only in the imagination. But in the world of *The Hobbit* the epic still functions—it just stays outside the borders of the Shire.[80] Like the young hobbits Gandalf has supposedly lured into going on adventures, Bilbo could at any time have entered into the epic world, but he had no interest in doing so until hearing the dwarves' song.[81] Then, the narrator tells us, the "Tookish" side of Bilbo's nature (inherited from his mother) "woke up" and overcame the bourgeois caution and respectability of the "Baggins" side. Tolkien conceptualizes Bilbo's character development as a conflict between these two sides of his nature, but as regards theme, my terms of *epic* and *bourgeois* are a more useful opposition: Bilbo's Took side is often aligned with the epic world, but it is not itself epic in the way that the Baggins side is utterly bourgeois.

Although the way he solves it is unique, this dialectical conflict between epic and bourgeois is not original to Tolkien. In Mark Twain's *A Connecticut Yankee in King Arthur's Court*, the epic "medieval" world is hopelessly inferior to the modern, bourgeois world, and thus its inhabitants are subject to constant manipulation by the protagonist of the story, "the Boss."[82] In contrast, William Morris, H. Rider Haggard, and their inspiration, Walter Scott, depict a medieval world that is not only morally superior to the modern, commercial, bourgeois world, but also more beautiful, exciting, and meaningful. Tolkien, however, does not in *The Hobbit* make either the epic or the bourgeois world unequivocally superior.

Bilbo's awkwardness in the epic world is a regular source of both humor and tension in the first half of the narrative.[83] Bilbo's various heroic achievements after finding the Ring—single-handedly killing the giant spider, saving the dwarves from the other spiders, arranging the escape from the Elven-king's dungeons—would appear to indicate both that Bilbo has earned admission to the epic world and that this world is superior. After all, Bilbo's success is due to his luck, intelligence, and newly found personal courage (and to the equalizing power of the magic Ring), not to anything particularly bourgeois, and those same qualities are the reasons for the hobbit's successes in the dragon-focused portion of the story.[84] It is only after the quest has been achieved—the dragon defeated, the treasure recovered—that Bilbo's bourgeois nature comes into play.

In my J.R.R. Tolkien classes there are always a few students who have never read *The Hobbit* (or seen the Peter Jackson movies). In their weekly responses these students often question why, in what is ostensibly a children' book, Tolkien chose to prolong the narrative beyond the death of the dragon and add a lot of complicated conflict. Although I do not agree with some of the assumptions about children's literature (and children) that underpin this response, I also understand why the students feel this way. The tone of the narrative suddenly becomes very different once the ravens inform the dwarves that an army of Lake-men and elves is approaching the Mountain. The conflict is no longer between a monster and good people but is instead between two sets of basically good people, and—most disturbing to many readers—it is not obvious that any of the participants are fully in the right.

The conflict is reasonably straightforward: With Lake-town destroyed and its people homeless, Bard, slayer of the dragon and leader of the Lake-men, and his ally the Elven-king proceed to the Lonely Mountain to seize Smaug's treasure, presumably to use it to rebuild the ruined town. That Thorin and Company are alive and have fortified the gate makes taking the treasure somewhat more complicated. Some sort of negotiation seems necessary.

On the one side, the Lake-men helped the dwarves when they were destitute, implying that they perhaps deserve some remuneration. More significantly, Bilbo's stealing the cup from Smaug had "aroused the dragon from his slumber," leading to the destruction of Lake-town, and Bard as the slayer of the dragon would traditionally have been due a substantial reward. Finally, Smaug had comingled into his hoard treasures looted from Dale, the old ruined town whose lordship Bard inherits. Taken together, these arguments suggest that the dwarves should give some portion of the treasure to Bard and the Lake-men, and indeed, Bilbo initially thinks that Thorin will acknowledge the reasonableness of the claims.

But from the point of view of Thorin and the dwarves, the Lake-men and elves are in the wrong. "To the treasure of my people, no man has a claim because Smaug who stole it from us also robbed him of life or home," Thorin asserts. "The treasure was not his that his evil deeds should be amended with a share of it."[85] The problem with this complex statement is that although each part of it seems reasonable, the pieces do not fit together into a coherent argument. The second statement does make a kind of sense: Since the treasure had first belonged to the dwarves and was only stolen by Smaug, the restitution for the dragon's evil actions should not come from taking the treasure from the dwarves a second time. Thorin's first statement, however, although it has the shape of a logical proposition, is not one, and furthermore it ignores a relevant and essential claim by Bard. Why Smaug's having killed many of the dwarves of Erebor and made others homeless puts their treasure beyond claim is never explained: The conclusion does not follow from the premise, and Smaug also killed the people of Dale. But Thorin ignores this fact and that of the hoard also containing the riches of the town. Instead, he shifts the argument from logic to rhetoric, asserting that by arriving at the gates of the Mountain with an army, the Lake-men and elves are threatening the dwarves rather than in good faith requesting assistance for Lake-town (a fair point). He then uses this asserted threat as a justification for refusing to bargain and concludes his rejection of Bard's claims with "it is in my mind to ask what share of their inheritance you would have paid to our kindred, had you found the hoard unguarded and us slain?"[86] Bard accepts this as a "just question," which means that he implicitly agrees that the Lake-men and elves would have been unlikely to give any treasure to Thorin's kin if Smaug had killed the dwarves before attacking Lake-town, but the dragon slayer does not back down or admit any fault. Indeed, he presses his claims most aggressively, insisting upon one twelfth of the hoard as both his reward for slaying the dragon and to restore the treasure stolen from Dale. The herald says that Bard will from these funds help to restore Lake-town, but he advises Thorin to spend additional treasure on the rebuilding so as to earn goodwill from his neighbors.[87]

Both the complex dueling rhetoric of this exchange and the refusal of either side even to suggest a negotiation or compromise are entirely of the epic world. The lack of mutually shared values or agreed-upon rules of logical argument, the intensity of feeling, the refusal to compromise, and the insistence upon historical claims all make any settlement impossible: Thorin is willing "to sit on a heap of gold and starve" rather than compromise, and Bard and the Elven-king are no less intransigent.[88] The Lake-men and elves declare the Mountain besieged, and the dwarves refuse to treat with them, counting on their kinsmen arriving from the Iron Hills to break the siege and free them from having to pay any of the treasure to Bard and the Elven-king.

The epic world's utter inability to compromise even if the resulting open warfare would make both sides worse off causes Bilbo to return to his bourgeois roots despite having operated within the cultural expectations of the epic for multiple chapters. Compromises and mutually beneficial exchanges are, after all, at the very heart of bourgeois culture. Sitting on a heap of gold until you starve might be admirable in an epic system that values transcendent (if futile) gestures and does not recoil from the spiteful destruction of life or property if doing so harms an enemy, but in the bourgeois world, wasting resources is unacceptable when there are potential trades and exchanges that can make both sides better off than they otherwise would have been.

Bilbo therefore reconsiders his contract with Thorin and Company and sees the possibility of an exchange to facilitate a settlement of the conflict. Thorin and Company owe Bilbo one fourteenth of the profits of the expedition. Bard seeks one twelfth of the treasure. Bilbo wants the conflict to be over so that he can go home. If, therefore, Thorin transfers one fourteenth of the treasure to Bard, the dwarves will be no worse off than they would have been after paying Bilbo. If Bard accepts this share of the treasure, although he would be getting less than his requested one twelfth, he will still be massively better off than he is now, with no treasure, and perhaps ever, if he or large numbers of his men are killed in a battle against the dwarves of the Iron Hills. Bilbo will be better off, even though he would not have his share of the treasure, because he would be free to go home, and without the "war and murder all along the way" that Smaug predicted if the hobbit tried to transport the gold and silver across Wilderland.[89]

The transfer of Bilbo's share to Bard in exchange for ending the siege is *Pareto efficient*: No one is worse off, and at least some are better off than they would be in the absence of the trade.[90] To a bourgeois mind, such a trade is an obvious good, and there is no rational reason for not making it. But within the epic mindset, accepting the compromise would be a humiliating and shameful capitulation. Bilbo knows Thorin well enough that he does not even raise the possibility. Instead, he acts on his own initiative, using a bargaining chip that he had acquired via the performance of his role in the epic world: burglar. While clambering over the piled treasure, Bilbo had found the Arkenstone of Thrain, the great gem that Thorin coveted above all other treasures in the mountain.* Acting as a burglar, though not without doubts about the morality of this behavior, he had taken the jewel and hidden it away.[91] At first it seems as if this semi-theft might be a result of the greed that the narrator asserts is often triggered by dragon-brooded treasure, but Bilbo's decision to give the Arkenstone to Bard and the Elven-king as an aid to bargaining with Thorin demonstrates that he has not succumbed to the irrational covetousness of the "dragon-sickness." He only feels a small pang of desire upon handing over the stone and is more concerned (and quite reasonably so) about what his friends will think.

Even though Bard, using the leverage given to him by Bilbo, essentially forces the trade, the whole exchange is nevertheless Pareto efficient: Thorin gets the stone that he values "above a river of gold"—which we can assume is at least as much as one fourteenth of the treasure—and he loses only the gold and silver that he was contractually obliged to pay Bilbo anyway.[92] But Thorin, being entirely of the epic world, does not see things this way. He is understandably furious at Bilbo's apparent betrayal of his companions, and although he agrees to the exchange, he hopes the arrival of his kinsmen from the Iron Hills will allow him to avoid payment.

The arrival of the goblins and the subsequent Battle of Five Armies temporarily intervenes, but that unexpected disaster does not invalidate the bargain, which is eventually fulfilled after Thorin's death.

* The name of the Arkenstone comes from the a-verse of line 1208 of *Beowulf*: *eorclanstanas*. The b-verse of this line was the source for "over the cup of the waves" in Tolkien's Earendel poem.

For years, therefore, I have wondered about Bilbo's apparent self-condemnation when he thinks to himself that he "made a great mess of that business with the stone."[93] Although there was a battle despite all his efforts, that battle was going to happen regardless of what Bilbo did with the Arkenstone, since the goblins and wargs were intent on seizing the Mountain and the treasure. It is possible that Bilbo feels at that moment, before Thorin's death, that the exchange he attempted to facilitate would not be made—although just a few pages later it is, and as a result, peace and prosperity come to the Mountain, the Forest, and the Lake—because Bilbo's next words to himself, "but I suppose you could hardly be blamed for" the seeming failure of his plan indicates that he understands more about the epic world, in which "efforts to buy peace and quiet" are fundamentally impossible.*

In contrast to much of the rest of *The Hobbit*, in which Bilbo struggles to keep up with the epic world's feats of strength and endurance, bravery, and heroism, in the Arkenstone subplot Tolkien illustrates some of the greatest weaknesses of the epic and concomitant strengths of the bourgeois world. The epic mindset simply does not allow compromise or settlement when it comes to points of honor or pride—exactly those issues that are most likely to provoke conflict. Thorin will "sit on a heap of gold and starve" to demonstrate that the suffering that dwarves endured from the dragon obviates all other claims to the treasure—even though a substantial portion of it was stolen from other victims. Bard and the Elven-king are unwilling to withdraw their armies for

* It is just barely possible that Bilbo had interpreted Thorin's agreement to purchase the Arkenstone with Bilbo's share of the treasure as a prevarication. Since I was ten years old I have been confused by Thorin's statement that he will pay "one fourteenth of the gold and silver, setting aside the gems" (*H*, XVII, 278). There is nothing in the contract about excluding the gems, but no one objects to this unreasonable and unilateral declaration by Thorin. I now wonder if the reason Tolkien included it was to suggest that Thorin never intended to honor the agreement (although then he would never get the Arkenstone), and this was why Bilbo thought he had "made a great mess" by trying to force a compromise. I have not seen an explanation for "setting aside the gems" in a single piece of Tolkien scholarship, and no lawyer with whom I have discussed the situation has been able to explain it. It is not unusual for a few students to object to the idea of "buying" peace, but if peace is a valuable thing (and it is), why would not buying it be preferrable to imposing it by force? The issue is not whether the peace is bought, but if having bought peace just provides more incentive for additional non-peace; "Once you pay the Danegeld, you never get rid of the Dane" in the words of Rudyard Kipling. But if you can buy lasting peace with money rather than blood, it is a purchase worth making.

the purpose of negotiation, Bard himself seems willing to go to war over gold, and Thorin is willing to cut off his nose to spite his face with regard to his near neighbors, whose goodwill he will need in order to have a prosperous kingdom.

The inability of the epic world to resolve conflicts like these without violence is hardly limited to Tolkien's fiction; indeed, it is far more prominent in many of the early medieval texts he studied professionally. The legal system of the Icelandic sagas, for example, is an effort to create mechanisms of conflict-resolution that apply even to murder, but, as William Ian Miller argues in his magisterial *Why Is Your Axe Bloody?* the "Balanced Exchange Model" of blood-feud that underpins the saga-era legal system in Iceland not only *does not* work, as is most evident in *Njal's Saga*, it *cannot* work.[94] The use of silver coins (or, for that matter, cows or lengths of homespun cloth) as compensation for a killing almost always fails to satisfy one of the parties or their relatives, and so tit-for-tat or steadily escalating feuds can not only endure for decades but eventually grow to become, in effect, civil war.[95] The failure to compromise is not the result of an inferior legal system or a primitive economy but is caused by the underlying epic mindset that any kind of yielding or compromise is shameful.

In contrast, the bourgeois world does an excellent job of settling conflicts, even transforming many of them into mutually beneficial exchanges. In the epic world, gold, silver, and treasure are marks of status, power, and relationships; in the bourgeois world, they are just money, and the single most important quality of money is that it is fungible; all pieces of money are mutually interchangeable, so it does not matter which particular silver penny is used to balance accounts and to make both parties in a trade happy. This is why Bilbo is able to settle the messy problem of his possessions having been in the process of being auctioned off by Messrs. Grubb, Grubb, and Burrowes when he returns home: Although, "the legal bother . . . lasted for years," in contrast to lawsuits in the Icelandic sagas, no one kills or even threatens anyone else, and even people "who had got specially good bargains at the sale" end up being satisfied because "in the end to save time Bilbo had to buy back quite a lot of his own furniture."[96] In the bourgeois mindset, a sufficient amount of money can solve almost any problem, and the arbitrage between the value of gold and silver in the wider world and in the Shire is extremely favorable to Bilbo, so everything is settled except for the missing silver spoons. Related, the "feud" with the Sackville-Bagginses is settled when Lobelia leaves the remains of her fortune to Frodo to compensate poor hobbits for their suffering during the Ruffians' occupation that had been enabled by Lotho.[97]

Since at least the Victorian era, it has been a commonplace cultural critique to lament the power of money in the bourgeois world,* but this criticism comes from within the context of an already existing bourgeois culture in which a broken contract is punished by the loss of some money rather than by hitting someone with an axe. For all its obvious flaws, the bourgeois system usually works so smoothly that we rarely consider its value except when that system breaks down (for example, the violence associated with the trade in illegal drugs being a direct result of there being no other way of enforcing contracts in the underworld), and we have little cultural memory of a time when the theft of some cheese could lead directly—and legally—to multiple killings.† But that is the reality of the epic world, which is one reason why the nuts and bolts of money and finance are so often absent from its depiction. Bilbo's attempt to resolve the conflict over Smaug's treasure might have been premature—or it might have eventually worked—but it was not wrong. Shippey connects to the epic world the "scrupulosity" of Dáin honoring Thorin's agreement, even though Thorin is dead, the situation has changed, and Dáin had nothing to do with the negotiations, and suggests that this quality, along with the "dignity" of Thorin's death scene and the loyalty of Fili and Kili dying by the side of their uncle, "present a challenge to modern values." But in fact Dáin keeping Thorin's agreement is consistent with the contract Thorin and Company made with Bilbo (and thus equally bourgeois), in that the responsibilities of the signing parties could be passed along to their heirs: "funeral expenses to be defrayed by us or our representatives."[98] Nevertheless, Shippey is certainly correct in his underlying

* Probably because writers and artists, in general, have so much less money than people who engage in commercial occupations.

† This is only a slight oversimplification of a chain of events that happens in *Njal's Saga*.

premise that the epic world is simply better at many behaviors—honor, dignity, self-sacrifice, endurance, and memory among them—than the bourgeois world.[99] Nothing in *The Hobbit* ever denigrates the positive qualities of the epic world, and in fact characters are shown to be wanting in terms of their own epic standards: Bilbo calls out Thorin's failure to keep his promises in epic fashion—"Is this all the service of you and your family that I was promised, Thorin?"—and Gandalf delivers the most stinging insult in the entire book when he says, "You are not making a very splendid figure as King Under the Mountain."[100]

Tolkien puts the epic and the bourgeois in dialogue, but unlike his predecessors (and most of his successors) he does not artificially resolve the issue by placing his thumb on the scale and asserting the overall superiority of one or the other. There is actually a kind of synthesis out of the two conflicting theses, but it is a subtle one that allows both thesis and antithesis to persist in mostly their own forms. In Middle-earth both the bourgeois world, in the person of Bilbo, and the epic world, in the persons of Thorin and Company (and perhaps also the Elven-king and Dáin) learn from each other and incorporate some aspects of the other world into their own worldviews—and even their behavior. Bilbo, very much in the literary tradition of ordinary or even weak characters suddenly pushed into unfamiliar epic circumstances, learns some of the virtues of bravery, stamina, determination, and toughness, but he does so without losing his footing in the bourgeois world and thus can evaluate himself in both new and old terms: "'I feel magnificent,' he thought" when he put on the *mithril* coat. "'But I expect that I look rather absurd. How they would laugh on the Hill at home! Still I wish there was a looking-glass handy!'"[101] Bilbo also comes to understand those who live in the epic world in a way that he did not before his adventure began: "You don't know Thorin Oakenshield as well as I do now. I assure you, he is quite ready to sit on a heap of gold and starve, as long as you sit here."[102]

Some of the dwarves' learning from the bourgeois world must have occurred even before the action of *The Hobbit* begins.[103] They know how to write an effective contract that procures for them the services they want from Bilbo. That contract also eventually allows the treasure to be divided without rancor or bloodshed, which in epic contexts is a substantial achievement.* More significantly, the dwarves, at least in part, were able to adjust to the bourgeois world's money-based method for resolving the conflict over the treasure. Although both the military victory and the death of Thorin surely helped them to set aside their epic refusal to compromise, they did in the end exchange a share of the treasure for peace and good relations with their neighbors. Even Thorin himself learned something about the value of bourgeois culture from its representation by Bilbo. His last words are "if more of us valued food and cheer and song above hoarded gold, it would be a merrier world."† Note that although these words show that Thorin has learned to respect some of Bilbo's values, the dwarf remains fully in the epic world. He does not reject hoarded gold or say that people should not value it, only that the world would be a "merrier" place if a larger fraction of the people in it had Bilbo's values. He thus validates the hobbit's culture without disparaging his own.‡

The mutual learning and the beneficial adjustment of worldviews that has come about as the result of Bilbo's adventure is perfectly encapsulated by the final exchange between Bilbo and Balin:

> Then the dwarves bowed low before their Gate, but words stuck in their throat. "Good-bye and good luck, wherever you fare!" said Balin at last. "If ever you visit us again, when our halls are made fair once more, then the feast shall indeed be splendid!"

"If ever you are passing my way," said Bilbo, "don't wait to knock! Tea is at four; but any of you are welcome at any time!"

---

* From the first few lines of the *Iliad* to the present day, the single best way of fracturing a functioning group of warriors is to get them quarrelling over the spoils.

† Is this another example of Thorin not replying to what was actually stated or asked?

‡ The qualities of hobbits that Thorin celebrates may be more pronounced in Bilbo, but they are not absent from the epic mindset, where the feast can indeed be splendid. It would make no sense for the dwarves to leave the epic world or recognize the bourgeois world as being superior. The point, after all, is not to convince the characters to change worlds or to show that one is superior to the other, but to demonstrate that each world is valuable in its own right and that they can learn from each other.

As Shippey first noted, "both speakers are *saying exactly the same thing*."[104] I will only add that this time each finally understands the other. Bilbo understands the true warmth and affection concealed by the formal language of the invitation, and the dwarves understand that the hobbit is offering them sincere respect and high honor with his light and informal words. The synthesis at the end of the dialectic is a continuing, mutually comprehensible dialogue.

PARALLEL THEMATIC ELEMENTS both reinforce and elaborate the dominant themes of *The Silmarillion* and *The Hobbit*. Recognizing that the Elvish racial hierarchy is a source of evil that is independent of the malice of Morgoth allows us to see that despite its highly mythological and legendary nature, *The Silmarillion* possesses some of the characteristic complexity and sophistication of the dominant literary form of Tolkien's lifetime, the novel. Although no one would mistake *The Silmarillion* for a novel per se, it does possess some of the *разноречие*, ["varied speech-ness," usually translated as "heteroglossia"] that Mikhail Bakhtin saw as being the novel's most important quality.[105] Although most scholars tend to see heteroglossia as inhering primarily in variations of style or ideological perspective, Tolkien's works show that it can also exist at the thematic level.

The interplay between the epic and bourgeois worlds that helps shape the narrative of *The Hobbit* is a form of heteroglossia as well as being a significant factor in the book's being more than a simple children's story.* The dialogic, parallel theme enables the complex moral, ethical, and rhetorical interactions surrounding the Arkenstone because readers have already seen the differences between the value systems and cultural conventions of the epic and bourgeois worlds and can therefore understand the motives and responses of the characters

* I hasten to add that I long ago learned from my dear colleague, the late Beverly Lyon Clark, that the "great" children's books—those that continue to be read more than a decade after their publication dates, are *universally* "more than a simple children's story," almost as if critics assume that having "greatness" removes the story from the "children's" category.

involved. Not merely a satire of one or the other of the two cultural worlds, *The Hobbit* is a sophisticated mediation that allows readers to see the strengths and weaknesses of both. In other words, *The Hobbit* exhibits thematic heteroglossia because a reader can easily interpret the narrative as demonstrating sympathy for or criticism of either the epic world or the bourgeois world (or both).

There appears to be a single major parallel theme in *The Silmarillion*, a dialogic pair of parallel themes in *The Hobbit*, and, as we will discuss in detail in the next chapter, a multiplicity of parallel themes in *The Lord of the Rings*. This thematic heteroglossia in Tolkien's mature works is a key factor in producing the sense of truth felt by readers of wildly divergent ideological commitments. The interplay of themes implies that the work represents not the unitary and totalizing vision of a single, God-like author, but multiple viewpoints representing various interests, biases, and predilections, leaving readers free to find the truths in the story that most resonate for them.

CHAPTER 7

Tapestry

The Lord of the Rings is more complex, subtle, and sophisticated thematically than its antecedents *The Silmarillion* and *The Hobbit.* Tolkien's earlier works include one or two substantial parallel themes whose operation is reasonably transparent; his mature masterpiece weaves together multiple thematic threads, most of which seem unresolved, and many whose connections to the work's larger, overarching themes are not immediately obvious. The resulting thematic tapestry, in which unresolved or seemingly conflicting themes contribute to a larger pattern without themselves being entirely subsumed by it, is in part responsible for the impression of depth and richness that *The Lord of the Rings* makes on readers. The interweaving of themes and subthemes also contributes to the apparent chameleon-like ability of the work to be perceived by readers as supportive of their own strongly held ideologies, despite these being mutually contradictory. This sense of truth is not created by Tolkien's being vague or lukewarm in his commitments, or failing to engage with difficult moral and ethical problems, but by the thematic heteroglossia enabling readers to hear multiple voices and understand conflicting points of view.

For example, in *The Silmarillion*, Yavanna, the Vala of plant fertility, is concerned about what the axes of the dwarves (the children of her husband Aulë, the Vala of smithcraft) will do to her forests. She is relieved to learn that Eru will create the Ents to protect the trees, and with some glee informs her husband that the dwarves should be cautious about what they fell. " 'Nonetheless they shall have need of wood,' said Aulë, and he went on with his smith-work."[1] Similarly, although Tolkien obviously hates the wanton destruction of trees, when those of the Old Forest menace the border of the Shire, the hobbits in retaliation cut down and burn a great number of them, and there is no authorial comment that what they did was wrong. Yet in the posthumously published "The New Shadow," Tolkien's abortive attempt at a sequel to *The Lord of the Rings*, a wise character says "To trees, all men are orcs."[2] Tolkien does not provide an author-imposed resolution.

A source of thematic heteroglossia is Tolkien's habit of solving narrative problems—ranging from temporary failures of inspiration to seemingly intractable plotting issues—by further elaboration and invention rather than by removing plot- or character-elements that had become contradictory or obsolete in the revised form of the narrative.* The question of why Gandalf was late for his meeting with Frodo in the Shire eventually spawned the entire Saruman subplot; the problem of the identity of "Trotter," the helpful "wild hobbit" Frodo and company meet in Bree led first to the character of Aragorn and then to his being the heir of Isildur and thus the rightful king-in-exile of the Númenórean kingdoms of Arnor and Gondor; a vague idea that there would be a giant named Treebeard who would capture Frodo produced the Ents; an enigmatic object thrown out of the window of the tower of Orthanc became the explanation for Saruman's betrayal and Denethor's despair.[3] And even after the main body of his great work had passed through editing and typesetting, Tolkien continued

* Tolkien seems to have felt that he could not simply delete and replace even minor features of the story (such as the two main antagonists both having names that begin with *S*) if these had been the result of gradual evolution through revision. For my view on how this "treatment of his imagined world as a real place with the concomitant limits upon authorial invention" helps produce the "powerful and compelling illusion that there is a truth to the story and its world that exists beyond the mind of its creator," see my introductory essay to William Cloud Hicklin's edition of "The Chronology of *The Lord of the Rings*," Supplement to *Tolkien Studies* 19 (2022): 9–14 at 13.

to add new material in the appendices, creating histories for the places and peoples that added layers of complexity to the already ramified main narrative.[4]

It is no wonder, then, that scholars have never been able to agree on the one theme to rule them all in *The Lord of the Rings*. A glance at the books on my library shelves supports this assertion. Tolkien's masterpiece is about or is best explained in terms of Christian faith, environmental awareness, world-building, power, good and evil, forgiveness, war, politics (of *many* persuasions), wisdom, mythology, Western civilization, the problem of evil, free will, duty, spirituality, heroism, rewriting or recovering the Middle Ages, music, history, light, time, England, healing, loss, death, and immortality.[5] I hasten to note that these are taken from books that I have read and kept because I found them insightful or explanatory: There are probably even more putatively central themes in books that never occupied or have not remained on my shelves. The cliché of the blind men and the elephant comes to mind, but if Christian faith is the trunk, environmentalism the foot, the problem of evil the tail, and heroism the ears, what is the elephant?* The short answer should probably be what Tolkien himself claimed to be the "real" or "dominant" or main theme of his works: Death and Immortality; we will turn to this theme at the conclusion of this volume.[6] But the many scholars who have identified some other thematic elements as being particularly significant in *The Lord of the Rings* are not wrong. The elephant does have a great many parts, primarily because Tolkien weaves together the tapestry of his overarching theme out of multiple subthemes, which still remain visible as part of the larger pattern (this metaphor is certainly a more helpful intuition-pump than that of the elephant).

In the discussion that follows we will start with a small and seemingly minor thread, the extended comparison between the cultures of Gondor and Rohan, and trace its development as it is intertwined with progressively larger and more abstract subthemes, until we reach some of the largest and most significant thematic problems in *The Lord of*

---

* Please give me credit for restricting "the blind hobbits and the oliphaunt," to an apophatic footnote.

the Rings, including the ways the Ring works and the moral effects of imposing one's will upon others. The complexity and sophistication of these intertwined themes is one of the reasons that people from vastly different ideologies can all believe that Tolkien's work is consistent with their beliefs.

ALTHOUGH THE RACIAL HIERARCHY does not play as large a role in *The Lord of the Rings* as it does in *The Silmarillion*, its effects are not entirely absent, either. The superiority of the elves has not been challenged, much less overturned, but there are simply many fewer elves in Middle-earth, and those that are still there, for the most part, occupy spaces into which men do not go, so the influence of the hierarchy is less frequently visible. Indeed, we only see it working in one or two instances: in Lothlórien, when the Silvan Elves are hesitant to let a dwarf move freely and so require that he be blindfolded, and possibly when Boromir, ranting to Frodo just before he attempts to seize the Ring, contrasts "elves and half-elves and wizards" with "true-hearted Men."[7] Compared to the many tragic examples in *The Silmarillion*, these are trivial, but the racial hierarchy has not entirely disappeared; it has merely been shifted from the relationships among elves or between elves and everyone else to the intragroup relationships of men, described by Faramir as occupying three ranks: High, Middle, and Wild.[8]

The Númenóreans occupy their elite rank in the hierarchy of men both because of the gifts given to their ancestors as a reward for their service in First-Age wars against Morgoth, and because they learned from the more culturally advanced elves, adopting the elvish language, acquiring elvish knowledge, and imitating elvish craftsmanship and technology.[9] Elendil's people who escaped the Downfall of Númenor were members of "the Faithful," who especially treasured the knowledge and culture of the elves, so the culture of the Númenórean realms in exile was much more elvish than that of any other men: "the old wisdom and beauty brought out of the West remained long in the realm of the sons of Elendil the Fair, and they linger [in Gondor] still."[10] As a result, the Men of Minas Tirith are like the elves in their skills of creating and building, their desire and respect for learning, their sophistication of thought, their love of beauty—and their strong desire to hold on to these things by living as long as possible.

Faramir is meant to represent the ideal Man of Gondor: valorous in battle, strong in leadership, unflinchingly brave and hardy in the face of toil, but also humble, thoughtful, and kind; deeply learned in history; cosmopolitan and curious about other cultures. Faramir does not love martial prowess for its own sake; he loves what that valor defends: the "City of the people of Númenór," which he loves for "her memory, her ancientry, her beauty, and her present wisdom," rather than her military might.[11]

But despite the impression of the hobbits, particularly Sam, that the elves and everything they do are entirely beneficent and righteous, Tolkien's own conception of his Elder Children of Ilúvatar, as is evident from his depictions of them in *The Silmarillion*, *Unfinished Tales*, and the appendices of *The Lord of the Rings*, is far more complex. In a 1954 letter to Naomi Mitchison he wrote:

> The Elves are not wholly good or in the right. Not so much because they had flirted with Sauron; as because with or without his assistance they were "embalmers." They wanted to have their cake and eat it: to live in the mortal historical Middle-earth because they had become fond of it (and perhaps because they had there the advantage of superior caste), and so tried to stop its change and history, stop its growth, keep it as a pleasaunce, even largely a desert, where they could be "artists"—and they were overburdened with sadness and nostalgic regret.[12]

The similarities of Gondorian and Elvish culture are indicated by the first three qualities of Minas Tirith that Faramir names, memory, ancientry, and beauty, all of which are consistent with what Tolkien says are the deepest concerns of the elves. In a draft of a 1956 letter to Michael Straight he wrote that

> the Elvish weakness . . . is naturally to regret the past, and to become unwilling to face change: as if a man were to hate a very long book still going on, and wished to settle down in a favorite chapter. Hence they fell in a measure to Sauron's deceits: they desired some "power" over things as they are (which is quite distinct from art) to make their particular will to preservation effective: to arrest change, and keep things always fresh and fair.[13]

The Noldor who remained in Middle-earth after the defeat of Morgoth were particularly susceptible to this weakness: "Those who lingered were those who were enamoured of Middle-earth and yet desired the unchanging beauty of the Lands of the Valar. Hence the making of the Rings; for the Three Rings were precisely endowed with the power of preservation, not of birth."[14] In the absence of the Three Rings (and their being controlled by Sauron's One Ring), these flaws or weaknesses in elvish culture would likely be relatively harmless. Elves might feel intense sorrow at the passage of time, they might put great efforts into different kinds of preservation, and, after such efforts failed or waned over time, their long lives might become more and more infused with sorrow and regret until eventually they would "fade" from Middle-earth. In all this they would be fulfilling the role Eru created them to perform, so no injury would come to others—or themselves—from their actions.[15]

The elves may always have had a tendency for metaphorically "embalming" the past in a hopeless attempt to preserve it, and a belief that the past was and would always be less sullied, more beautiful, and more full of joy than the present is certainly not a recipe for ongoing happiness. But the elves do not die. Their bodies may be destroyed by violence, and elves can pass away from grief, but their spirits are never destroyed and, because they are bound forever to the circles of the world, elves can be reincarnated. Their sorrows at the losses and griefs caused by the unstopping flow of time are mitigated somewhat by this immortality. They may, and do, grow weary of the world, and indeed many come to desire some sort of respite that they cannot find, but they can always try again. They never run out of time.[16]

This is not the case for men. The nostalgia, or heimweh, that inevitably arises *within* elvish culture may not necessarily be more painful for men than it is for elves (although there is no way for either race to know), but the responses of men to these emotions—to react with horror when things lose their first blush of youth and beauty, to try to hold on to what is passing away, and even to try to resurrect what is lost—are not so benign. What the elves have as part of their nature and which they may wish to escape, men desperately long for because they are unable to possess it. As Faramir explains, in their realms in Middle-earth after the Downfall of Númenór the Men of Gondor

> hungered after endless life unchanging. Kings made tombs more splendid than the houses of the living, and counted old names in the rolls of their descent dearer than the names of sons. Childless lords sat in aged halls musing on heraldry; in secret chambers withered men compounded strong elixirs, or in high cold towers asked questions of the stars. And the last king of the line of Anárion had no heir.[17]

Although it was the specific weakness Sauron exploited in teaching the Elven-smiths of Eregion how to make the Rings so that they could be enslaved to his One Ring, the tendency to embalm the past in elvish culture was not actively destructive. But when the elvish need to preserve is blended with men's fear of inevitable death, the results are a perverse misapplication of cultural energy into actions that are selfish and useless, triggering a slow decline to cultural sterility.[18] The embalming tendency of immortal elves is metaphorical, but when men succumb to this temptation, they devote their energies to the creation of elaborate stone mansions for preserved corpses, wasteful relics that serve no purpose except to be, ironically, a grisly reminder of the futility of trying to escape man's inevitable mortality.[19] The tombs are carefully tended and preserved while many houses in Minas Tirith stand empty and the voices of children were few even before the War of the Ring.[20]

Sauron beguiled the elves by giving them, through the technology of the Three Rings, a means of avoiding the painful choice of either leaving Middle-earth or accepting inevitable change and decay.* To men he offered a seeming escape from death, an ability to persist in the world beyond their normal span of years, and this was clearly appealing to at least the nine powerful men of Númenórean race who accepted Rings that enabled them to avoid death, though at the cost of being enslaved to Sauron as undead wraiths.[21] Sauron's title or epithet in *The Hobbit*, the Necromancer, also implies that his power is associated with death, or, as Tolkien suggested in the 1951 letter to Milton Waldman: perhaps that he seduces or tempts men with claims of being able to overcome death, or to raise or communicate with the dead.[22] In their reaction to their deep fear of death, we see how the Númenórean's otherwise elvish characteristics are transformed by occurring in mortal men, producing a culture with unique strengths and great weaknesses. Númenóreans and their descendants will undertake massive, long-term projects, building things that no other culture in Middle-earth can create, but they regret (and even come to resent) that they do not have enough time to enjoy the fruits of their labors. One of the significant themes that Tolkien develops throughout *The Lord of the Rings* is a comparison of the ways different cultures (Gondor, Rohan, elves, dwarves, men, hobbits) deal with fundamental issues of hope, despair, loss, grief, and mortality.

Although not as prominent a narrative force in *The Lord of the Rings* as it is in *The Silmarillion*, at the very least the racial hierarchy can be seen to influence the thinking of the men of Gondor, who are the highest in the hierarchy that Faramir describes because as a reward for fighting against Morgoth the Valar granted them greater height as well as "wisdom and power and life more enduring" than those groups of men who were not allied to the elves in the First Age,[23] and they benefited from the instruction by their friends, the Noldor. (Also, they determined the ranking.) But after the destruction of Númenor, the gifts were slowly taken away, and over the years men of Númenórean

* I use this word intentionally because although to mortals the power of the Three Rings seems to be magic, to Sauron it is merely technology, since he understands the process for creating this power well enough to teach variations of it to others.

descent became more like the "lesser" men, with whom they intermarried.[24] "This mingling did not at first hasten the waning of the Dúnedain, as had been feared; but the waning still proceeded, little by little, as it had before. For no doubt it was due above all to Middle-earth itself, and to the slow withdrawing of the gifts of the Númenóreans after the downfall of the Land of the Star."[25] But despite the convergence of the Númenóreans and the "middle" men, there are still important cultural differences in the Third Age of Middle-earth. It is therefore useful to compare two obviously parallel scenes in *The Return of the King* in which a hobbit swears an oath of fealty to a lord of men: Pippin to Denethor in Gondor and Merry to Théoden in Rohan.

"Stung by the scorn and suspicion" in Denethor's voice in their initial conversation about the death of Boromir, Pippin is suddenly moved to offer his service to the Steward of Gondor:

> "Little service, no doubt, will so great a lord of Men think to find in a hobbit, a halfling of the northern Shire; yet such as it is, I will offer it, in payment of my debt." Twitching aside his grey cloak, Pippin drew forth his small sword and laid it at Denethor's feet.
>
> A pale smile, like a gleam of cold sun on a winter's evening, passed over the old man's face; but he bent his head and held out his hand, laying the shards of the horn aside. "Give me the weapon!" he said.
>
> Pippin lifted it and presented the hilt to him.
>
> . . .
>
> "I accept your service. For you are not daunted by words; and you have courteous speech, strange though the sound of it may be to us in the South. And we shall have need of all folk of courtesy, be they great or small, in the days ahead. Swear to me now!"
>
> "Take the hilt," said Gandalf, "and speak after the Lord, if you are resolved in this."
>
> . . .
>
> The old man laid the sword along his lap, and Pippin put his hand to the hilt, and said slowly after Denethor:

> "Here do I swear fealty and service to Gondor, and to the Lord and Steward of the realm, to speak and to be silent, to do and to let be, to come and to go, in need or in plenty, in peace or in war, in living or dying, from this hour henceforth, until my lord release me, or death take me, or the world end. So say I, Peregrin son of Paladin of the Shire of the Halflings."
>
> "And this do I hear, Denethor son of Ecthelion, Lord of Gondor, Steward of the High King, and I will not forget it, nor fail to reward that which is given: fealty with love, valour with honour, oath-breaking with vengeance." Then Pippin received back his sword and put it in its sheath.[26]

"Filled suddenly with love" for Théoden after being invited to ride beside the king of Rohan on the way from Isengard to Dunharrow, Merry offers his service:

> "May I lay the sword of Meriadoc of the Shire on your lap, Théoden King?" [Merry] cried. "Receive my service, if you will!"
>
> "Gladly will I take it," said the king; and laying his long old hands upon the brown hair of the hobbit, he blessed him. "Rise now, Meriadoc, esquire of Rohan of the household of Meduseld!" he said. "Take your sword and bear it unto good fortune!"
>
> "As a father you shall be to me," said Merry.
>
> "For a little while," said Théoden.[27]

In contiguous chapters, and separated by barely twenty pages, these two scenes are a more-developed example of the phenomenon represented by the final exchange between Bilbo and Balin at the end of *The Hobbit*: Two different cultures are depicted as using very different words to express exactly the same idea.[28] In *The Hobbit*, the exchange is the culmination of the dialogic engagement of the epic and the bourgeois worlds; in *The Return of the King*, it is part of an extended comparison of Gondor and Rohan, two cultures fully within the epic world. One impetus for this cultural dialogue is, as Shippey notes, that Tolkien wanted to celebrate the Germanic heroic virtues of the Rohirrim, "not the first children of Tolkien's imagination but the ones he regarded with most affection," and to celebrate the virtues of the Rohirrim, they need to be compared to a different culture.[29] Also, Tolkien was using the relationship of Gondor and Rohan to investigate "an observably recurring pattern of human historical change" in which a "lesser" culture contacts, allies with, and begins to integrate into a "higher" established culture.[30] The loose model for this kind of interaction was the "power dynamics between Rome and the *gentes* of the Migration period," although, as usual, Tolkien did not limit himself to "reflect[ing] real history."[31]

The two oath-taking scenes highlight fundamental differences between the two cultures, differences that are related to other major themes of *The Lord of the Rings*, including power and domination, individual freedom, and the influence of history. The oath to Denethor is a patterned, formal statement, characterized by paired antitheses (speak or be silent, come or go) and stylized cause-and-effect pairings (fealty generating love, valor generating honor). The rhetoric of the oath implies that the world is predictable and consistent so that all possible actions and circumstances are accounted for by the oath's elaborate structure; for example, there are only three possible ways for the oath to be terminated. Such a verbal artifact is the product of a long-established culture with deep traditions, and the oath's verbatim repetition subsumes the individual agreement between Pippin and Denethor beneath all the other agreements in the past that used the same words. A young man, who happens to be Pippin, is swearing fealty to the Steward of Gondor, who happens to be Denethor, son of Ecthelion. The parties' agreement to establish a defined relationship is formalized, universal, and impersonal.

In contrast, Merry's oath is informal, individual, and personal. Meriadoc Brandybuck is swearing an oath to Théoden, son of Thengel, who happens to be the King of Rohan. The hobbit offers his service, and the king accepts. Théoden then blesses Merry—assuming that the laying on of hands is a blessing—grants him the rank of esquire, accepts him as a member of his household, and wishes him good fortune. The verbal performance is much less complex than Pippin's oath to Denethor, but there is no doubt that the same sort of relationship has been created. By saying "As a father you shall be to me," Merry is agreeing to follow Théoden's commands and serve him loyally. A shared understanding of what it means to be a member of a household and an esquire, to treat a lord like a father, and to treat an esquire like a son is sufficient to establish the same mutual obligations that are spelled out in formulaic detail in Pippin's oath. The difference in oaths is a synecdoche for a comparison of the cultures of Gondor and Rohan.

The major differences between the men of Gondor and their friends and allies in Rohan, those "Men of the Twilight," are cultural (the descendants of the Númenóreans have longer lifespans, but that seems irrelevant to their interactions with Rohan), and perhaps this is the reason that the racial hierarchy does not seem to create the injustice, strife, and resentment that is elsewhere its primary product.* Indeed, of the Rohirrim, Faramir says, "we love them: tall men and fair women, valiant both alike, golden-haired, bright-eyed, and strong; they remind us of the youth of Men, as they were in the Elder Days." However, he does interpret his own culture as superior in some domains: "Yet now, if the Rohirrim are grown in some ways more like to us, *enhanced in arts and gentleness*, we too have become more like to them . . . for as the Rohirrim do, we now love war and valour as things good in themselves, both as a sport and an end; and though we still hold that a warrior should have more skills and knowledge than only the craft of weapons and slaying, we esteem a warrior, nonetheless, above men of other crafts."[32]

For their part, the Rohirrim do not seem to desire to be what the Men of Gondor are or to have what they have. When Éomer describes Boromir as "more like to the swift sons of Eorl than to the grave Men of Gondor he seemed to me, and likely to prove a great captain of his people when his time came," the context that he has just learned that Boromir is dead indicates that the Third Marshal of the Mark intends

---

* Although Aragorn has a far greater lifespan than ordinary men, we have no evidence that the Men of Minas Tirith are on the whole much more long-lived than the Rohirrim, and indeed, the Rohirrim appear to be more vigorous, even in old age, although judging vigor in old age from Théoden and Gamling in Rohan and Denethor in Gondor would be to draw a sweeping a conclusion from too few examples.

this description as the highest praise.[33] Éomer feels no sense of existential inferiority to the Men of Gondor if the nicest thing he can say about the dead son of the steward is that he could easily have been a Man of Rohan.

As is reflected by the two oaths, the culture of Gondor is more sophisticated than that of Rohan. The more complex social organization of Minas Tirith enables the people of the city to create more elaborate fortifications, dwellings, and artifacts; to have greater specialization of labor; and to pursue longer-term projects. Thus the Men of Gondor build in stone, while the Golden Hall of Meduseld is made of wood, and even if its gilded roof is not thatched, the roofs of the other dwellings in Edoras are—which is why Saruman's "thatched barn" insult stings.[34] The descendants of the Númenóreans have more advanced technology and are literate, while Aragorn says that the Men of Rohan do not write books, though they do sing many songs.[35] There appear to be far fewer hierarchical levels in Rohan than there are in Minas Tirith, and characters show far less deference to those who outrank them.*

I am fond of pointing out to my students that one of the more remarkable characteristics of the Rohirrim is that, based on their interactions with the members of the Fellowship, no one in Rohan ever seems to follow orders. And yet, despite the culture of Rohan being ruled by a military aristocracy, there are no repercussions for insubordination. When Aragorn, Legolas, and Gimli meet Éomer, the Third Marshal of the Mark admits to them—with no signs of shame and few of worry—that "indeed in this riding north I went without the king's leave, for in my absence his house is left with little guard." After Aragorn has refused to come with the Riders, Éomer states that he is "not free to do all as I would. It is against our law to let strangers wander at will in our land, until the king himself shall give them leave, and more strict is the command in these days of peril," and then he proceeds to give horses to the three companions and allow them to travel through

* We see Minas Tirith only during a time of war and in imminent danger of siege: Women, children, the aged, and those otherwise unable to fight have for the most part been evacuated, so perhaps we do not have a completely accurate picture of the society in ordinary times.

Rohan.[36] We later learn that Éomer was arrested and imprisoned when he returned to Meduseld, though from Théoden's phrasing—"he rebelled against my commands and threatened death to Gríma in my hall"—and from Éomer's own brief recounting it seems as if it was the threat to kill Gríma Wormtongue that was the dispositive action, not all the other disobediences.[37]

Failure to follow instructions among the Rohirrim is not limited to Éomer. The door-warden Hama similarly ignores orders, allowing Gandalf to retain his staff despite Wormtongue's explicit command, and setting Éomer free and giving him his sword back without instructions to do so.[38] Perhaps most egregious of all, Éowyn, who has agreed to be the interim ruler of Rohan, simply walks away from her responsibilities, dresses herself as a young male rider, and heads off to Minas Tirith. She also, while disguised as Dernhelm [Secret Helm], invites Merry to ride with her despite the king having specifically commanded the hobbit—when Éowyn was present!—to remain in Dunharrow.[39] This particular disobedience is not even limited to Merry and Éowyn: "There seemed to be an understanding between Dernhelm and Elfhelm, the Marshal who commanded the troop in which they are riding. He and all his men ignored Merry and pretended not to hear if he spoke."[40]

We can conclude that the culture of Rohan values individual initiative and personal judgment. People disobey orders if they think those orders are misguided, and they accept responsibility if their judgments turn out to be incorrect. Hama's "trembling" suggests that he violated some norm or procedure by returning Éomer's sword and allowing him to bring it into the presence of the king before any pardon of Éomer has been granted: "Such joy was in my heart that maybe I have erred. Yet, since he was free again, and he a Marshal of the Mark, I brought him his sword as he bade me."[41] He explains his reasoning to the king and accepts responsibility for his decision, and no one seems particularly surprised that Théoden only punishes him with a mildly disparaging comment that since Hama "proved untrustworthy as a doorward, let him become an errand-runner."[42] The failure to follow orders is not interpreted as rebellion or even insubordination because in the culture of Rohan, loyalty is defined primarily in terms of a shared cultural understanding that each party is, to the best of his ability, attempting to do what is in the best interests of the other. Merry says "as a father you shall be to me," and neither he nor Théoden ask for or produce a list of specific acts that would be expected in such a relationship. Good will and shared understanding are assumed.

In contrast to the Rohirrim, the Men of Gondor follow orders even if the particular commands make no immediate sense to them or even seem unreasonable. Denethor commands Faramir to engage the enemy at the river, and Faramir obeys even though he has already expressed his misgivings, reminding his father that "the retreat of those we put out far afield will be perilous" if enemies cross the river in force, as Faramir knows they will. But despite his judgment that it is a tactical error to try to defend the river crossings, Faramir leads his men to battle there: "in truth Faramir did not go by his own choosing. But the Lord of the City was master of his Council, and he was in no mood that day to bow to others."[43]

This difference between Rohan and Gondor is at its most stark when Denethor, concluding that the war is lost and believing that Faramir's wound and subsequent sickness are fatal, commands his servants to carry his still-living son to the tombs and then to bring "wood quick to burn, and lay it all about us, and beneath, and pour oil upon it. And when I bid you thrust in a torch."[44] Not one of the Men of Gondor present speaks out against these frankly insane orders; instead, they attempt to carry out Denethor's wishes. Even when the horrified Pippin, dismissed by Denethor, informs Beregond that the steward has commanded his servants to burn himself and Faramir alive, the guardsman says that he cannot leave his post guarding the gate of the now-vacant citadel, even though the fighting is far below in the lower circles of the city—because "the Lord does not permit those who wear the black and silver to leave their post for any cause, save at his own command"—and indeed, later we learn that the penalty for leaving one's post is death.[45]

Fortunately, Beregond does eventually follow his conscience rather than his orders and so manages to delay Denethor's servants long enough that Gandalf, summoned by Pippin, arrives in time to save the unconscious Faramir.[46] However, such is the rigidity of the rule-bound hierarchy of Minas Tirith that despite his actions being both existentially justified and obviously heroic, Beregond must be brought in judgment before King Elessar. Aragorn's merciful and reasonable ruling—that Beregond must leave the Guard and go forth from Minas Tirith because he will be the captain of the White Company, the Guard of Prince Faramir in Ithilien—is particularly illuminating. Tolkien could easily have not mentioned Beregond's actions in Minas Tirith, and readers would hardly have noticed or objected for exactly the same reasons that Aragorn gives for pardoning him for the killing of the porter at the gate to the tombs: Beregond's valor in battle and love of Faramir.[47] But instead, Tolkien ties up this particular loose end of the plot by reinforcing the rule-based, hierarchical culture of Gondor. Aragorn describes the crime, notes the traditional punishment, and in fact exiles Beregond from the city, thus maintaining the law even as he tempers justice with mercy and properly rewards the guardsman for his heroism and loyalty to Faramir.* Contrast the way the dying Théoden handles Merry's confession that he "broke [the king's] command" by excusing all disobedience with three brief sentences, one of which is an aphorism: "Grieve not! It is forgiven. Great heart will not be denied."[48]

DESPITE THEIRS BEING a culture that has had to fight to survive for almost their entire history and which therefore organizes society along military lines and preferentially celebrates the feats of warriors, the Rohirrim seem far less troubled by the fear of death than the Númenóreans are. In the battle of Helm's Deep, when confronted with the likelihood of his death once the Hornburg is fully besieged by Saruman's forces, Théoden neither despairs nor seeks a means of escape, but instead expresses defiance:

> "I will not end here, taken like an old badger in a trap. . . . When dawn comes I will bid men sound Helm's horn, and I will ride forth. Will you ride with me then, son of Arathorn? Maybe

* The narrative does not tell us if the family of the porter thought Aragorn's ruling was just.

> we shall cleave a road, or make such an end as will be worth a song—if any be left to sing of us hereafter."[49]

Later, in the Battle of the Pelennor Fields, when Théoden has received his death wound, he expresses not regret, but pride: "I go now to my fathers. And even in their mighty company I shall not now be ashamed. I felled the black serpent."[50] He then speaks a few half-lines of alliterative verse, connecting himself with the cultural traditions of his people: "*A grim morn, and a glad day, and a golden sunset.*" His last words to Éomer are "Hail, King of the Mark! . . . Ride now to victory! Bid Éowyn farewell!" Éomer then responds with alliterative verses that, as they seem to be traditional rather than composed specifically for Théoden, we should interpret as epitomizing his culture's response to death in battle:

> *Mourn not overmuch! Mighty was the fallen,*
> *meet was his ending. When his mound is raised,*
> *women then shall weep. War now calls us!*[51]

Contrast these reactions with Denethor's refusal to speak, his gray and deathlike face as he hovers around Faramir's unconscious body, his complete abandonment of his role as leader of Minas Tirith in the city's moment of greatest crisis, his tears, and eventually his deranged decision to immolate himself and his son.[52] In particular, compare the Steward's reaction with Éomer's response to the shock of discovering Éowyn's body on the battlefield. The apparent death of his sister, who he thought was back in Dunharrow leading the people who remained in Rohan, is no less horrifying, and quite a bit more unexpected, than Faramir's wounding and sickness or whatever Denethor saw in the palantír (the Stone of Seeing) the night after his son was brought back to Minas Tirith. But when the "fey mood" took Éomer after he saw Éowyn, instead of giving up, or either turning his "cold fury" inward at himself or lashing out at those near him who need his leadership, the new king of Rohan spurred his horse back to the head of the host of Riders. Once there, he blew a horn "and cried aloud for the onset. Over the field rang his clear voice calling: 'Death! Ride, ride to ruin and the world's ending!' " as he led his men into battle to do as much damage to their enemies as they could.[53]

Even when Éomer finds his forces vastly outnumbered by the seemingly inexhaustible hosts of Mordor, he does not surrender, quit the battle, or blame others for the situation: "Stern now was Éomer's mood, and his mind clear again. . . . He thought to make a great shield-wall at the last, and stand, and fight there on foot till all fell, and do deeds of song on the fields of Pelennor, though no man should be left in the West to remember the last King of the Mark." Again he recites lines of alliterative poetry, though these staves seem as if they are composed extemporaneously for the specific situation rather than being the more traditional phrases he spoke at Théoden's death: "To hope's end I rode and to heart's breaking," the b-verse of which appears to refer to the discovery of Éowyn's death. But the final line, instead of indicating despair, surrender, or recriminations, returns to the Rohirric virtue of defiance: "Now for wrath, now for ruin, and a red nightfall!"[54]

Éomer might not have felt any despair until he saw his sister apparently dead on the battlefield, but Éowyn herself certainly seemed to have lost the will to live when Aragorn refused to allow her to come with him on the Paths of the Dead. Although Faramir later asserts to Éowyn that the love she felt for Aragorn was more like what a young soldier might feel for a great captain, Aragorn himself recognizes that the woman of Rohan was at that moment very much in love with him: "few griefs amid the ill chances of this world have more bitterness and shame for a man's heart than to behold the love of a lady so fair and brave that cannot be returned."[55] Éomer also believes that Éowyn fell in love with Aragorn, noting that he did not think his sister was "touched by any frost, until she first looked on you."[56]

The scene at Dunharrow when Éowyn begs Aragorn either to abandon his plan of travelling on the Paths of the Dead or to allow her to accompany him is poignant even if many contemporary readers do not recognize the intensity of emotion indicated by Éowyn's use of the familiar pronoun *thee* in a desperate attempt to get Aragorn to recognize her love for him and thus perhaps return it. That even this self-abasement by the proud, untamed, "wild shieldmaiden of the north" does not move Aragorn to respond with anything more than great courtesy seems to break Éowyn's spirit in the same way that whatever he sees in the palantír shatters Denethor's, and both characters choose suicide. As the Riders move out of Harrowdale, Merry makes eye-contact with what he thinks is a young man near the end of the line: "he caught the glint of clear grey eyes; and then he shivered, for it came suddenly to him that it was the face of one without hope *who goes in search of death*."[57] The final relative clause is extremely important for understanding Éowyn's character. She is not merely accepting all the risks of battle or even going into battle and not caring what happens to her: She is explicitly trying to find her own death. But even though both she and Denethor respond to seemingly hopeless situations by deciding to end their own lives, Éowyn's attempted self-destruction takes a radically different form than that of the Steward of Gondor. She does not command anyone else to assist her; she does not distract others from their immediate duties in the war; she does not think to take the life of any of her people; and she does not even fall on her own sword or otherwise attempt to kill herself directly. Instead, she seeks death by riding into battle against the enemies of Rohan, attempting to do something that aids her people even as she hopes to perish in the attempt.*

That Éowyn is still trapped in suicidal despair even after the Rohirrim reach Minas Tirith and the battle begins is indicated by her language in her combat with the Lord of the Nazgûl—the changing of the wind, the inspiration of Théoden's call to battle, and the great ride onto the Pelennor Fields have not brought her out of her depression. Nothing Éowyn says relates to her former goals of seeking glory in

---

* Her bringing Merry to the battle seems to be an oblique parallel to Denethor having Faramir brought with him to the tombs, but it is not clear to me what the significance of this would be. However, if Éowyn were to find the death in battle that she seeks, what would become of Merry? If Éowyn were to die, her having aided the hobbit would most likely result in his being stranded on foot on a calvary battlefield. Does this imply an ethical failing on her part? I think that Tolkien simply needed a way to get Merry to Minas Tirith, so some of these details are merely plot machinery, but there certainly could be a thematic interpretation that I am missing.

deeds of arms and to "vie with the great Riders."[58] Her language is instead focused solely on the protection of the body of Théoden. She even makes her threat to the Black Rider conditional: "I will smite you *if* you touch him."[59]

Just as Éomer neither abandons his leadership responsibilities nor harms himself, Éowyn's self-destructive impulses are transformed into engagement with an enemy. Éomer may have cried "Death take us all!" but he seeks to visit that death upon the hosts of Mordor, not upon himself and his men. Éowyn likewise is undaunted by the Witch King, and her desire for—and therefore lack of fear of—death seems to strengthen her ability to resist the supernatural terror he generates. Perhaps the Black Rider has an ability to sense this, which might explain his threatening her not with death, but with having her "flesh [. . .] be devoured, and [her] shriveled mind [. . .] left naked to the Lidless Eye." But regardless of what Éowyn feels as she raises her shield "against the horror of her enemy's eyes," the Lord of the Nazgûl is unable to intimidate her and, in the single most heroic individual action-sequence in *The Lord of the Rings*, she decapitates the Witch King's flying steed and then, after Merry has distracted him by piercing his knee from behind with the barrow-blade, destroys the Black Rider by stabbing him in his invisible face, defeating her enemy in what she surely must have thought was her last moment of life.[60]

Both Théoden and Éomer think of doing deeds worthy of song even though both raise the possibility—even the probability—that there will be no continuing culture in which the song would be sung. Their desires, and Éowyn's in her fight against the Nazgûl Lord, are not for fame itself but to be *worthy of fame*. Such a culturally consistent desire implies an existential order in which the memorialization of fame is far less important than its having being earned. The Rohirrim do not act as if they believe that there is a supernatural entity who is watching and judging them, but they do behave as if there exists a universal and unchanging standard of conduct to which all good people aspire and against which all people are judged. This belief would certainly be called naïve in the post–World War I era (and today), but perhaps that is the point: Lacking the introspection and philosophizing of the

Númenóreans, the Rohirrim have not reasoned themselves out of their culture's very effective system for promoting valued behavior.* In this, Rohan's culture is superior to the culture of Gondor that otherwise surpasses them in so many other ways.

No reasonable reader would believe that Théoden, Éowyn, and Éomer are merely representations of abstract ideas. Their emotional responses and heroic actions are completely consistent with their individual characters and are fully motivated by the specifics of the plot. Nevertheless, Tolkien does use these richly drawn characters, along with Denethor, Boromir, and Faramir, to develop one of his thematic threads. The isomorphism of the two oath-taking scenes is too obviously an invitation to compare not just individual characters, but the cultures of Gondor and Rohan. Tolkien dramatizes the influence of cultural tendencies, strengths, and weaknesses in various moments of crisis for the purposes of developing subthemes relating to what people's responses in extreme situations show us about human culture and human nature.

Denethor's self-immolation further entwines the comparison of Gondor and Rohan with the larger themes of power, domination, freedom, and obedience as well as with Tolkien's overarching theme of Death and Immortality. Before the forces of Mordor can reach Minas Tirith, they must cross the Great River. But while Anduin seems like a natural defensive barrier, the front is too large for the army of Minas Tirith to defend against a numerically superior foe. Nevertheless, as a demonstration of his power, a test of obedience, and, possibly, a punishment for Faramir not having taken the Ring from Frodo and returned with it to Minas Tirith, Denethor orders his son to go into what they both know is a dangerous and almost certainly futile battle.[61] When

---

* Rather than having been demoralized by the existential crisis of meaning in an absurd world, they have either ignored the problem or just crashed right through it to the other side. Shippey notes the example of one old Viking, Víga-Glúm [Killer Glum], who is able to state precisely what he believes in: his axe. Also his money-bag. And his barn packed full of grain. I would pay good money to watch Víga-Glúm and Jean Paul Sartre discuss the absurdity of existence, although I imagine that the conversation would be a short one. Shippey, *Road*, 80–81; John McKinnell, trans. *Víga-Glúms Saga: With the Tales of Ögmund Bash and Thorvald Chatterbox* (Edinburgh: Cannongate, 1987), 83.

Faramir is brought back wounded by a dart, the shock of seeing his son lying unconscious, seemingly "with poison in his veins," coupled with the guilt he feels for having sent him "unthanked, unblessed, out into needless peril" appears to break Denethor's spirit.[62] He sits silently through the reports of his son's heroism, orders a sickbed for Faramir to be made up in the high chamber from which he has been directing the defense of Minas Tirith, and then goes up

> into the secret room under the summit of the Tower; and many who looked up thither at that time saw a pale light that gleamed and flickered from the narrow windows for a while, then flashed and went out. And when Denethor descended again he went to Faramir and sat beside him without speaking, but the face of the Lord was grey, more deathlike than his son's.[63]

Denethor, as we learn soon enough, was using the palantír of Minas Tirith, presumably to gather information about Sauron's forces as they continued to stream toward the city. We cannot be certain what specifically Denethor saw that "overthrew his mind" (as Gandalf says), but it is either the full magnitude of the armed might of Mordor or, as I have argued elsewhere, the sight of Frodo in captivity in the topmost room of the Tower of Cirith Ungol.* The latter might come closer to justifying the steward's mental breakdown than the former—the approach of the Corsairs of Umbar should not have been that much of a surprise if Denethor had previously used the palantír to survey Sauron's war preparations—but for the purposes of this argument it does not matter what specifically Denethor sees, only that his vision leads him to conclude that Sauron now has the Ring. Denethor's situation is thus at least as hopeless as Théoden's in the Hornburg or Éomer's on the

---

* Denethor cannot have seen Frodo's *mithril* coat, Elven-cloak, and Sam's sword, because according to the timelines in Appendix B, the orc Shagrat did not reach the Dark Tower with the bundle of plunder until March 17, and Denethor's death occurs on March 15, and he had looked into the palantír either late in the night of March 13 or early in the morning of March 14, when Frodo was being questioned by the orcs in the top of the tower of Cirith Ungol. *RK*, V, iv, 132. See Drout, "Editor's Introduction," to Hicklin, "The Chronology of *The Lord of the Rings*," 9–14; *RK*, Appendix B, 374–75.

Pelennor Fields. It is also objectively worse than Éowyn's after being rejected by Aragorn.* But Denethor's response is very different from that of the three Rohirric characters. Although, despite his age, he is still able, as he told Pippin, to wield a sword and has in fact been sleeping in his mail for years in order not to become soft, he does not rush to the gate to boost the morale of the defenders of the city or prepare to lead a heroic counterstrike against the besieging foes; instead, he decides to have his servants burn him and his son alive on a makeshift funeral pyre in the great mausoleum in which the embalmed bodies of the Stewards of Gondor are preserved,[64] an act that seems unlikely to contribute substantially to the defense of the city in its hour of greatest need. Fortunately, the steward's having released Pippin from his service allows the hobbit to summon Gandalf to prevent the cremation of Denethor's still-living son.

Gandalf physically removes the unconscious Faramir from the pyre and then tries to talk the steward out of his destructive madness, reminding Denethor of his duty "to go out to the battle of your City, where maybe death awaits you. This you know in your heart."[65] Gandalf's words almost seem to work, but when the wizard says "We are needed. There is much that you can do," Denethor's sorrow over Faramir's peril is transformed into fury. He lifts up the palantír that had been hidden in a pillow-case and rages at Gandalf, asserting that the power of Sauron is so great that resisting it is not just futile but "Vanity! For a little space you may triumph on the field, for a day. But against that Power that now arises there is no victory."[66]

Then Denethor reveals another reason for his hopelessness and fury. We can conclude that he has seen or been shown Aragorn in the palantír and, putting together bits of information from his conversations with Pippin, he has determined that Gandalf intends to "with the left hand . . . use me for a little while as a shield against Mordor, and with the right bring up this Ranger of the North to supplant

---

* It is not possible to determine whose emotional pain is greater, although we might conclude that Denethor is, at least currently, in slightly better circumstances than was Théoden, in that the King of Rohan's only son was already dead when Théoden was surrounded by hostile forces in the fortress at Helm's Deep, while Faramir still lives.

me."* But Denethor has no intention of ever turning Gondor over to a new ruler. Even if Aragom's claim to be the lineal descendant of Isildur were true, Denethor would refuse to serve as the "dotard chamberlain of an upstart."[67]

The steward's hyperbolic denunciation of Aragorn, and his mixing of abusive false characterizations (upstart, long bereft of dignity) with trivially true ones (long bereft of lordship) is a sign of intense rationalization. His violent rejection of the mere intimation that anyone could have a strong legal claim to be Ruler of Gondor or might be better at leading Minas Tirith—ironic, given that Denethor has now abandoned his leadership role in the moment of greatest crisis—shows how threatening even the idea is to him, especially because neither Gandalf nor anyone else has ever even broached the subject. The rationalization hints at the reasons behind Denethor's mental breakdown, which become somewhat clearer after Gandalf, like an experienced hostage-negotiator, asks the steward to describe the ideal outcome if all constraints were removed: "if your will could have its way?"

> "I would have things as they were in all the days of my life," answered Denethor, "and in the days of my longfathers before me: to be the Lord of this City in peace, and leave my chair to a son after me, who would be his own master and no wizard's pupil. But if doom denies this to me, then I will have *naught*: neither life diminished, nor love halved, nor honour abated."[68]

Denethor starts off reasonably, in that there is certainly nothing wrong with a man, seeing his city on fire and likely to be destroyed, his sons dead or dying, and a vicious enemy relentlessly advancing, expressing

---

* Denethor's father Ecthelion had been served by a great captain, who was in fact Aragorn under the assumed name Thorongil. Denethor is said to have viewed Thorongil as a rival, which may be why the man had left Gondor for parts unknown after a great victory against the Corsairs of Umbar. We are not told if Denethor recognized Aragorn as Thorongil when he saw the "Ranger of the North" in the palantír, although it is certainly possible; *RK*, VI, Appendix A; I, iv, 335–36.

a desire to return to an idealized past before the disastrous present. But the steward's delusions begin to surface with the next sentence. His son Faramir is not a "wizard's pupil": He had allowed Frodo to keep the Ring and continue his quest not because the hobbit invoked Gandalf or because the wizard had preinstructed Faramir in some way, but because Faramir's Númenórean insight (which he shares with his father) told him that Frodo's quest was righteous and the hobbit could be trusted. Additionally, as a man of Minas Tirith, he held himself to the standard of honor that a casually made assertion was as binding as a formal oath.[69] Faramir had already refused the temptation of the Ring, decided to help Frodo, and asked the hobbit where he intended to go before Frodo acknowledged Gandalf's having defined his quest: "I must find the Mountain of Fire and cast the thing into the gulf of Doom. Gandalf said so."[70] Furthermore, both Frodo and Faramir thought Gandalf was dead when Faramir's decision was made, so Denethor's conclusion that his son is somehow under the wizard's control or that his love for his father is "halved" is utterly wrong. Faramir's decision arose from self-knowledge and prudence based on what he knows of the Ring, "which [was] enough" to convince him that he did not want to see, touch, or learn more about it "lest peril perchance waylay me and I fall lower in the test than Frodo son of Drogo."* Being a "wizard's pupil" had absolutely nothing to do with Faramir's not seizing for his father the "mighty gift" of the Ring that Denethor delusionally asserts Boromir would have brought him.[71]

Denethor's reasoning is nearly as faulty in the third item in his list of rejections. As Gandalf points out, a steward who, as the culmination of centuries of service by his predecessors, preserves the kingdom and turns it over in good order to the returning king would have fulfilled his office and for this should and would be honored above all other previous stewards. His *honor* would not be abated at all, just his *power*, and that is what Denethor cannot abide. He has confused his

* *TT*, IV, v, 290. Some of what Faramir knew about the powers of the Ring undoubtedly came from Gandalf, though the most secret knowledge that Faramir has—that Isildur "took somewhat from the hand of the Unnamed"—comes from Faramir's own deductions rather than being something Gandalf said. He has concluded that what Isildur took was "a fell weapon, perchance, devised by the Dark Lord." *TT*, IV, v, 279–80.

power to rule with the purpose of his office, the good of his people, and even his individual life, which is why he speaks the single most selfish and terrifying sentence uttered by any character in Tolkien's works: "If doom denies this to me, then I will have *naught*," and commands his servants to burn him, his posterity, and his ancestry, just as he earlier told the messengers who informed him that the first circle of the city was burning and defenders were abandoning the walls to "Go back to your bonfire! . . . Go back and burn!"[72] Denethor's words reveal that he has inverted the proper moral order of things. Instead of understanding that the only purpose of his having individual power is to serve his people (thus being worthy of his ancestors and providing for his and their posterity), he sees his own possession of that power as the primary good. Minas Tirith not being ruled by Denethor is in his mind equivalent to Minas Tirith being destroyed, and so he chooses to reduce its present, future, and past stewards to smoke and ashes.

Gandalf had told Pippin that in Denethor "by some chance the blood of Westernesse runs nearly true." From this statement I infer that, in addition to it being a function of his individual character, the steward's destructive response to his seemingly hopeless circumstances represents a flaw in the Númenórean psyche.[73] The contrast with the words and deeds of Théoden, Éomer, and Éowyn in situations that are similarly hopeless supports this conclusion. The specific, self-focused features of Denethor's madness illustrate how the tendency toward introspection and self-awareness that makes Faramir and Aragorn so appealing, and which enables the Númenóreans to achieve so much intellectually and culturally, has a dark side. Too much introspection, or the mindset that generates it, can be a sign of or can begin to cause too much concern for the self, which can lead to neglect of one's duties to others. Selfishness in its various forms does seem to be a particular trap for Númenóreans, most visibly, perhaps in Ar-Pharazôn's attempt to conquer the undying lands in order to forestall his own death and in Isildur's insistence on keeping the One Ring, but there are many other examples in the appendices to *The Lord of the Rings*, in the "Akallabêth" in *The Silmarillion*, and in *Unfinished Tales*. The very temperament and long-term outlook that allows Númenóreans to accomplish great works over many years produces a sense of being *entitled* to enjoy the fruits of that labor and a concomitant resentment for anything or anyone that interferes with that enjoyment. The Rohirrim may not build monuments that last millennia or write books of lore that preserve the wisdom of the ages, but they do not cling greedily to their own lives, and in extremity they seek to sacrifice themselves so as to help their fellows by destroying their enemies, not "slaying themselves in pride and despair, murdering their kin to ease their own deaths," like the "heathen kings, under the domination of the Dark Power."[74]

Selfishness and the greed and desire for power that goes along with it may be a cultural weakness of Númenóreans, but one of the reasons that Tolkien's works ring so true to people of so many different philosophical, religious, and ideological persuasions is that no single tendency is ever determinative. Denethor's fall is not an inevitable result of his ancestry or culture but instead arises from his individual character as this is displayed in a series of choices. Even at the bitter end, Denethor still had the ability to take Gandalf's advice, walk away from his pyre, and fight for his city. Maybe if Gandalf had said not "Come! . . . *We* are needed," but "Let us go! *You* are needed!" Denethor might have redeemed himself. But, perhaps because the wizard's employment of the plural pronoun *we* implies that Gandalf is equal to the steward and his using the imperative "Come!" suggests the authority to command him, Denethor responds with the spiteful defiance that ends in his death and the destruction of the House of the Stewards.

That Denethor's response to his admittedly terrible circumstances was not an inevitable result of his heritage is demonstrated by the way his son Boromir reacted to a similarly bleak situation—indeed, one in which his own death was far more imminent, and for which he bore substantially more responsibility than Denethor does for the collapsing defenses of Minas Tirith. Until the Fellowship left Lothlórien, Boromir had seemed to accept that Elrond and Gandalf were correct in their assertion that the Ring could not be used for good purposes. But once the Fellowship takes to the Great River, he seems to become increasingly obsessed with the desire to use the Ring as a weapon against Sauron's forces.[75] Eventually, when Frodo makes it clear to him that he will not agree to come to Minas Tirith, Boromir gives in to this temptation and tries to seize the Ring. This "madness" as Boromir describes it, soon passes, but not before Frodo has used the Ring to become invisible and escape. The terrified hobbit never sees Boromir regain control of himself and bitterly regret his actions.[76]

Boromir's spirit seems broken when he returns to the camp, where his report of Frodo using the Ring triggers the panicked search that scatters the Fellowship. But even though in a state of despair—"he put his head in his hands, and sat as if bowed with grief"—Boromir responds to the surprise assault of the orcs not by giving up, lashing out at those on his own side, or cursing Frodo, but by making his heroic last stand in which, despite it being a battle of one against one hundred, he single-handedly kills so many orcs that the rest panic.[77] Perhaps fearing that the horn calls of the Man of Minas Tirith have summoned other equally valiant warriors, even after they have killed Boromir with a rain of arrows, the orcs quickly flee with their two hobbit captives, not pausing to seek additional members of the Fellowship or to observe Frodo's and Sam's tracks near the riverbank.[78]

In retrospect, we can infer that had Boromir not fought with such superhuman determination, the large company of orcs would have no reason to rush away from Parth Galen. They therefore would have encountered and almost certainly killed Aragorn, Legolas, and Gimli, who—doughty as they are—could hardly have prevailed against eighty to a hundred orcs that, according to Éomer, were "swift and well-armed."[79] There was also every chance that had they not been panicked by the ferocity of Boromir's last stand, the orcs would have tracked Frodo and Sam to the river and reached the same conclusion as Aragorn that the two hobbits had crossed to the East bank. Frodo and Sam had enough trouble simply navigating the Emyn Muil; it is difficult to imagine them escaping pursuit by tracker orcs or a hunting Nazgûl.[80] The quest would have ended with the capture of all the hobbits by the servants of Sauron, resulting in the enslavement of Middle-earth.

But none of this happens. Boromir's extreme heroism in a hopeless situation results in the Three Hunters surviving, meeting Éomer, encountering Gandalf in Fangorn, and helping him to inspire Théoden to throw off the weakness caused by Wormtongue and thus to ride out of Edoras to meet Saruman at the tactically advantageous fortress of Helm's Deep. Further rehearsal of the plot is unnecessary, the point already being made that Boromir's sacrifice of his own life sets in motion the chain of events that are absolutely essential to the eventual success of both the military response to Sauron and the Ring-quest. By responding to a hopeless situation not with despair and self-destruction as his father does, but with the same kind of heroism that Théoden, Éomer, and Éowyn later demonstrate, Boromir saves Middle-earth.* His self-aware confession—"I tried to take the Ring from Frodo . . . I am sorry. I have paid"—the penance of suffering that he has endured, and the absolution Aragorn grants him—"You have conquered. Few have gained such a victory. Be at peace!"—allows the Man of Gondor to die with a clear conscience.† Indeed, he seems to have been beatified through his self-sacrifice: When Faramir sees him in the funeral boat, Boromir appears to be peacefully asleep and a mysterious light seems to be coming from the clear water that covers him; Faramir feels a sense of grief and pity.[81]

One factor contributing to Boromir's redeeming himself while Denethor chooses suicide and the murder of kin may be found in Éomer's description of the elder son of the steward as being "more like the swift Sons of Eorl rather than the grave Men of Gondor," and in Gandalf's assertion that the blood of Númenor ran more true in Denethor and Faramir than in Boromir.[82] Both evaluations suggest that Boromir's personality is more like a Rider of Rohan than a Númenórean Man of Minas Tirith, and this is perhaps why he is able to break out of the trap

---

* Although I recognize that this interpretation cuts against the grain of seemingly all previous critical discussions, I take some comfort in knowing that the writers for Lord of the Rings Online must have come to a similar conclusion, as their depiction of Minas Tirith during the wedding of Aragorn and Arwen includes memorial statues of both Boromir and Denethor, the former for his heroism, the latter for his foresight in sufficiently preparing the city to withstand the siege long enough for the Rohirrim to arrive.

† *TT*, III, i, 15–16. Aragorn is not merely referring to killing orcs when he says "Few have gained such a victory." He understands that Boromir overcame the temptation to despair after having been mastered by the Ring and thus has triumphed, which is why, I think, he promises (or prophesies?): "Minas Tirith shall not fall!"

of mistaking one's own power or renown for the reason for having that power or renown: serving something greater than oneself. When he tries to convince Frodo to come to Minas Tirith, Boromir starts by talking about saving his city, but under the influence of the Ring, he is soon relating a power-fantasy about his own heroic and commanding actions.[83] However, after this madness passes, and after Aragorn has given him the task of finding and protecting Merry and Pippin, the last moments of Boromir's life are devoted to self-sacrificing service to others. Boromir, in Gandalf's words, "died well," a judgment authenticated by Faramir's vision of his brother's saintly final repose in the Elven-boat.[84]

The historico-anthropological themes Tolkien develops for Middle-earth directly in the comparison of Gondor and Rohan are also implicitly entangled with his (and our) understanding of our own history and culture, in that they have parallels in the interactions between the culture of the Roman Empire and that of the Germanic tribes who became its allies.[85] But because Tolkien does not restrict himself to mirroring—and therefore of necessity allegorizing—these historical antecedents, the comparison of Gondor and Rohan becomes a thematic investigation of the somewhat abstract qualities of different human cultures and the ways these are reflected in individual characters. Denethor, Boromir, Faramir, Théoden, Éomer, and Éowyn are each unique characters, but they possess distinct but related constellations of personality traits that are drawn from their cultures. The result is a rich and sophisticated depiction of the interplay of culture and individuality that rings as true in our own world as it does in Middle-earth.

From what Gandalf says to Pippin, Beregond, and Denethor's servants after the steward's death, it was Denethor's use of the palantír that caused his suicidal and homicidal madness. The hopelessness that is generated by Sauron's manipulation of what Denethor sees is also augmented by the loss of Boromir, the apparently fatal wounding of Faramir (and Denethor's guilt about the circumstances of the injury), and the knowledge that even if Minas Tirith against all odds survives, the steward will likely be replaced by the returning king. Surely Denethor's despair is well motivated. Nevertheless, I believe an additional factor contributes to the Steward of Gondor's spitefully destructive madness. Some of Denethor's delusions are similar not only to those of his elder son, but, perhaps surprisingly, they are fundamentally akin to those experienced by Sam and Gollum, implying that their ultimate source is something these characters all have in common: desire for (or, in Sam's case proximity to) the Ring.

It seems very likely that Denethor knows at least as much as his younger son has been able to figure out about Isildur's actions after the defeat of Sauron. Gandalf's report at the Council of Elrond of the steward's words implies that Denethor had studied his city's lore and explored its records, so even if he never saw the specific scroll in which Isildur describes the fiery writing on the Ring, he, like Faramir, could have pieced together enough information from other records and general lore to have an understanding of what Isildur did after the defeat of Sauron.[86] Denethor would then have drawn the same conclusion as Faramir: that Isildur had taken something from the hand of the Dark Lord.[87] Since even Boromir knew of "the Great Ring of him that we do not name," Denethor could have gone further than Faramir and concluded that the "heirloom of power and peril," the "fell weapon, perchance, devised by the Dark Lord" was in fact that Ring. After the steward questions Pippin, and once Faramir has reported on his meeting with Frodo and Sam, all the pieces fall into place: Even if Denethor does not know that the heirloom was specifically a ring, he knows that it was in the possession of the hobbit who had traveled with Boromir and been met by Faramir in Ithilien, and he is able to infer that Gandalf's plan was for hobbits to bring the Ring into Mordor—whether he has deduced that the purpose is to destroy it or something else, we cannot tell from the evidence given.

At this time, Denethor begins to construct the delusions that will contribute to his fall. He tells Faramir that if his brother had met the hobbits in Ithilien, Boromir "would have remembered his father's need, and would not have squandered what fortune gave. He would have brought me a mighty gift."[88] I call this fantasy a delusion because Denethor is conveniently forgetting that Boromir had traveled alongside the Ringbearer for two full months without taking anything to bring to his father as a "gift," so to assume that he would have seized the Ring and returned with it to Minas Tirith and then surrendered it to Denethor, if by chance he had encountered Frodo and Sam in Ithilien is, to say the least, a stretch. But Denethor, as is evident from his phrasing in his argument with Gandalf, has already transitioned—as people caught up in power-fantasies do—from the supposedly remote possibility of something happening to an exploration of what he will do once it has occurred.* Denethor asserts that the Ring should have been "kept, hidden, hidden dark and deep," in such a place that Sauron could not get to it unless he had utterly triumphed over Minas Tirith, and therefore Denethor and those around him were dead.[89] Unfortunately for our analytical purposes, Tolkien has Gandalf suddenly drag a red herring across the trail by insisting that the defeat of Gondor would not be the defeat of all free people, unless, he implies, that defeat resulted in Sauron regaining the One Ring. This is undoubtedly morally correct and most likely literally true, but Gandalf's rhetoric is utterly ineffective on the self-focused steward and probably serves only to further increase his anger and self-justification as he imagines people living carefree lives behind the shield of Minas Tirith, ungrateful for the sacrifices of the Men of Gondor.†

What is most troubling about Denethor's words in this conversation—

---

* This dangerous step along the path of delusion is all too common in contemporary discourse, political and otherwise. A construction like "if the charges are true, then the penalty should be . . ." focuses discussion on an imagined situation in which the questionable premise is true, which causes that premise to become more and more accepted as the hypothetical discussion goes on and further elaborate structures are built upon the assumption. The investment of mental energy in these imagined scenarios makes it far more difficult to determine objectively if the initial premise *is* true, since if that is not the case, all the cognitive effort discussing the likely results will have been wasted.

† Despite Gandalf's quasi-theological authorization, the wizard's rhetoric is at times ineffective. His "he that breaks a thing to find out what it is has left the path of wisdom" comment to Saruman neither convinces Saruman nor wins the argument (and Gandalf knows it), and Gandalf himself indicates that he regards his entire rhetorical battle with Saruman in Orthanc's high chamber as futile; *FR*, II, ii, 272–73. This has not stopped the line from being quoted many times as a rejection of literary scholarship about Tolkien's works. Gandalf's invocation of all the people who have sheltered behind Gondor is hardly likely to persuade Denethor; and his effort to convince Saruman to give up his evil plots and help the West likewise falls flat. For the belief that the people shielded by the military valor of Gondor are unknowing and ungrateful, see Boromir's exchange with Aragorn at the Council of Elrond; *FR*, II, ii, 258–62.

and what must surely have been noticed by Gandalf—is that in the midst of averring that he would not use the Ring, Denethor describes the conditions in which he *would* use it: "at the uttermost end of need."[90] But given the current situation of Minas Tirith, these conditions are not particularly unlikely. This is also the slipperiest of slippery slope arguments, as the distinction between the "uttermost end of need" and simple "need" is purely a matter of degree. Without realizing it, Denethor has told Gandalf precisely what the wizard had surmised before the conversation began: that had the Ring come to Minas Tirith, Denethor would have attempted to use it. Despite his denial, and his eventual exasperated dismissal of counterfactuals—"If I had! If you had! . . . Such words and ifs are vain."—we can see that even before the full-on crisis triggered by Faramir's wounding, Denethor has already constructed a delusional fantasy in which, despite claiming to believe that "to use this thing is perilous," he would save his city and defeat Sauron with the power of the Ring.

The key feature of Denethor's delusion, and what connects it to Boromir's description of his own fantasy in his rant to Frodo, is its first-person focus, the idea of the Ring being used by a single person who individually achieves glory. Denethor says that if Boromir had encountered the Ringbearer in Ithilien, his elder son "would have remembered *his father's need*, and would not have squandered what fortune gave. He would have brought *me* a mighty gift," And a paragraph later he laments "Would that this thing had come to *me*."[91] Boromir says, "The Ring would give *me* power of Command! How *I* would drive the hosts of Mordor, and all men would flock to *my* banner!" and a bit later, as his desire for the Ring gains a greater hold over him: "It is not yours save by unhappy chance. It might have been *mine*. It should be *mine*. Give it to *me*!"[92]

Boromir has never touched the Ring, and Denethor has never been within fifty miles of it, so it is possible that the similar egocentric qualities of their power-fantasies are more a result of their family relationship or their Númenórean cultural background.[93] But the fantasy perceived by Sam in Mordor has similar features, which strongly implies that the Ring is the shared cause of the delusions. When Sam takes the Ring from Frodo after Shelob's assault, his delusional vision is also one of *individual* power: "Wild fantasies arose in his mind; and he saw Samwise the Strong, Hero of the Age, striding with a flaming sword across the darkened land, and armies flocking to *his call*" and then "at *his command* the vale of Gorgoroth became a garden of flowers and trees and put forth fruit."[94] Note also the similarity in language between Boromir's "all men would *flock* to my banner!" and Sam's vision of "armies *flocking* to his call."

Even Gollum's somewhat pathetic fantasy of what he would do if he were to get the Ring from Frodo has similar contours: "Perhaps we grows very strong, stronger than Wraiths. Lord Sméagol. Gollum the Great? *The* Gollum. Eat fish every day, three times a day, fresh from the sea. Most Precious Gollum."[95] Note that Gollum imagines himself being individually powerful and, presumably, ruling the others who give him his lofty titles and bring him his fish.

Their shared Númenórean culture seems likely to be a contributing factor to Denethor and Boromir both being taken in by the delusional fantasies generated by the Ring. Sam, with his far less exalted hobbit-background, is not as easily cozened. Too much of the introspection that seems a fundamental quality of the Númenórean character has the potential to lead to the egocentrism that makes the two Men of Gondor particularly susceptible to the way the Ring initially tempts people. Note that the first-person-focused language of Boromir's and Denethor's fantasies is also found in Bilbo's angry words to Gandalf when the hobbit temporarily decides not to leave the Ring for Frodo as he had planned: "It is *my* own. *I* found it. It came to *me*. . . . It is *mine*, I tell you. *My own. My* precious. Yes, *my* precious."[96] And Bilbo's words are in turn similar in their focus on the self and its desires to what Sméagol says to Déagol when the Ring is first pulled from the river:

> "Give us that, Déagol, my love," said Sméagol, over his friend's shoulder.
>
> "Why?" said Déagol.
>
> "Because it's *my* birthday, my love, and *I* wants it," said Sméagol.

> . . . and he caught Déagol by the throat and strangled him, because the gold looked so bright and beautiful. Then he put the ring on his finger.[97]

Gandalf reports about his own observations of Gollum:

> The murder of Déagol haunted Gollum, and he had made up a defense, repeating it to his "precious" self over and over again, as he gnawed bones in the dark, until he almost believed it. It was *his* birthday. Déagol ought to have given the ring to *him*. It had obviously turned up just so as to be a present. It was *his* birthday present, and so on, and on.[98]

Finally, Frodo's words in the Sammath Naur (discussed in more detail shortly) are likewise egocentric: "*I* have come. . . . But *I* do not choose now to do what *I* came to do. *I* will not do this deed. The Ring is *mine*!"[99]

The similarities among each of the fantasies and the egocentric nature of the language in which they are reported allows us to see how the Ring works initially to seduce or addict its possessors. The Ring seems to offer people their heart's desires, but in an I-focused form in which the person commands but never seems to cooperate with others and never shares any victory or glory with them or in any way serves them. For example, the Ring does not create in Sam a fantasy of what he really most desires: Frodo's return from death, the quest completed, and both of them home in the Shire. Instead Sam sees a vision he finds ridiculous because it is not even one of his real desires. He does not want "a garden swollen to a realm . . . the hands of others to command."[100] This narrated statement is completely consistent with Sam's character: In his forestry work repairing the Shire after the depredations of Sharkey's men Sam never organizes a conservation corps of helpful hobbits; he does all the traveling and planting on his own.[101]

As one of its first moves* in its capture of an owner, in the delusions it

* The very first move the Ring makes is simply to appear to be so beautiful as to be immensely desirable, but this is only relevant for Isildur, Sméagol, and perhaps Déagol.

promotes, the Ring amplifies the selfish and egocentric aspects of a person's nature, transforming even desires for altruistic or shared goals into individual benefits and framing the achievement of all ends as exercises of command over others. The Ring's conferral of invisibility further isolates the user from other people both in practical terms—Bilbo can disappear and not have to talk to the Sackville-Bagginses—and for the purposes of evading the correctional or disciplinary power of the social group, as when Gollum uses it to spy on and abuse his relatives before his grandmother turns him out of her hole.[102] This effect of the Ring is essentially what Plato dramatizes in his story of the Ring of Gyges: When one's actions are not observed by the social group, behavioral norms cannot be enforced, resulting in abusive and eventually criminal conduct.[103] The result is for the owner of the Ring to become self-focused and disconnected from others. We see this alienation most dramatically in Gollum, expelled from his family and eventually hiding alone in a cave for 478 years; but Bilbo, by his eleventy-first birthday, seems to have no close friends except Frodo; and Frodo himself, after Bilbo's departure, seems to spend a great deal of his time walking alone (although he does still interact with his friends Merry, Pippin, Sam, and Fredegar Bolger).

The isolation the Ring encourages is enhanced by its power to make its owner desire it and to think about it frequently. We have already noted how both Isildur and Sméagol immediately desire the Ring for its beauty (Isildur says that the Ring is "of all the works of Sauron the only fair").[104] Denethor and Boromir, who have not touched the Ring, use egocentric first-person language in their descriptions of their fantasies. The characters who have had long-term possession of the Ring—Gollum, Bilbo, and Frodo—are still first-person focused in their discourse related to the Ring, but, particularly in moments of tension, they use first-person possessive pronouns as much as or more than they use *I* and *me*. The Ring initially generates a strong desire for ownership, so much so that Bilbo lies about the exact details of how he came to possess it in order to solidify his claim to it despite none of the dwarves—or anyone else he ever speaks to—disputing his ownership.[105] That this lie seems both unnecessary and disturbingly similar to the lies Gollum constructed to justify his murder of Déagol implies that we are seeing the workings of the Ring rather than the individual psychologies of the possessors.

The combination of social isolation, self-focus, and the intense desire for ownership eventually results in Gollum lurking alone in the dark on his little island deep below the Misty Mountains with only the occasional meal of raw fish or goblin to interrupt his contemplation of his Precious.[106] Gollum's world has been reduced to himself and the Ring, so much so that he has come to use the words "My Precious" to describe both. Horrible as this result is, it cannot be what the Ring was created to do. Sauron did not put the best part of his native strength into the Ring for the purpose of transforming some future owner into an emaciated near-corpse squatting in a damp cave, muttering to himself and infrequently strangling baby goblins for over 450 years.[107] Indeed, Sauron certainly never intended and probably never even contemplated the possibility that anyone other than he would possess the One Ring. The effects of long-term ownership that we see in Gollum and, albeit to a lesser extent, in Bilbo and Frodo must therefore be side-effects of the Ring's primary powers.

Exactly what those powers are has been a subject of some debate, but close readings of several important scenes in Books IV and VI can help us understand how the Ring works both when it is used for the purpose for which it was created and in the very different circumstances of being carried by someone with no innate desire to dominate or command. In the first chapter in Book IV of *The Two Towers*, Frodo and Sam have finally found their way through the Emyn Muil, the maze of rocky hills that separates Rohan from the Dead Marshes, when they spot Gollum, who had followed them down the Great River from Lórien. Overpowering the creature after he tries to climb down a sheer cliff-face, the hobbits are suddenly faced with a dilemma. They cannot simply set Gollum free either to summon enemies or to attack them in their sleep, but when Sam ties a rope to his ankle, Gollum begins writhing and screaming, insisting that the Elven-rope burns, bites, and freezes him.[108] Frodo realizes that if he wants to preserve his and Sam's lives and continue the quest, the hobbits may have to kill Gollum. As Frodo considers the impossible situation, it seems to him that he heard, quite plainly but far off, voices out of the past:

What a pity Bilbo did not stab the vile creature when he had a chance!

Pity? It was Pity that stayed his hand. Pity, and Mercy: not to strike without need.

[. . .] I do not feel any pity for Gollum. [. . .] He deserves death.

Deserves death! I daresay he does. Many that live deserve death. And some that die deserve life. Can you give that to them? Then be not too eager to deal out death [in judgment] in the name of justice, fearing for your own safety. [For] Even the wise cannot see all ends.

"Very well," he answered aloud, lowering his sword. "But still I am afraid. And yet, as you see, I will not touch the creature. For now that I see him, I do pity him."[109]

This is one of only two times in the entire *The Lord of the Rings* that Tolkien uses italics to indicate words that a character has only thought without saying aloud or has heard only in his mind. Elsewhere, italics indicate reported speech or written text, so it is tempting to view these particular italics as a quotation of Frodo's conversation with Gandalf in Bag End in "The Shadow of the Past" (similar to the italicization of Bilbo's farewell speech).[110] However, what Frodo hears in the Emyn Muil cannot be merely a quotation of the earlier conversation because the words are not exactly what Gandalf said. There is some elision of Frodo's own remarks (which I have marked with brackets and ellipses), and there is also material *added* to Gandalf's part of the conversation (which I have underlined). Christopher Tolkien has determined that while writing the later passage, his father went back and revised the earlier one, but nevertheless the two passages "remain different in detail of wording, perhaps not intentionally at all points."[111] I always hesitate to contradict Christopher Tolkien, who is second only to his father as an analyst of his works, but I believe that the differences between the initial conversation and Frodo's memory or vision* of it are significant.

* Obviously Frodo does not *see* anything, but English does not have a word for the audio equivalent of a vision, and "auditory hallucination" seems both unwieldy and likely to be at least subtly incorrect.

The deletions, which we might expect in the memory of a conversation, eliminate some of the give-and-take of the exchange and therefore emphasize Gandalf's exhortations by removing much of Frodo's resistance to them. The additional lines, however, work rhetorically to call into question Frodo's possible motives for killing Gollum. In the Bag End conversation, Gandalf urged against "deal[ing] out death in judgment," that is, executing Gollum as a punishment for his crimes. The implication of *judgment* is that there has either been some sort of proceeding or that it is obvious that, as Gandalf has agreed, Gollum "deserves" death as punishment. The later version, in contrast, eliminates the idea that killing Gollum would be done for the purposes of justice, thus ruling out any pretense of higher morality, by insisting that such a killing would be purely a response to fear for one's own safety—the implications may be that this is both cowardly and selfish. Intention is often impossible to prove, and Christopher Tolkien implies that the differences between the two versions are not particularly important, but it seems to me that if Frodo is attempting to balance his and Sam's life and the fate of Middle-earth against Gollum's life and the hobbits' reluctance to carry out a cold-blooded killing, Tolkien has in fact put his thumb rather firmly on the scale.[112] If this was an accident, it was an extremely happy one, but I believe it is actually part of Tolkien's deliberate design, with the use of italics being a marker of this intentionality. The only other place in which the use of italics without quotation marks indicates voices that a character is hearing is the scene in which Frodo sits on the high seat of Amon Hen while wearing the Ring, and the Eye of Sauron looks toward him:

> He heard himself crying out: *Never, never!* Or was it: *Verily I come, I come to you*? He could not tell. Then as a flash from some other point of power there came to his mind another thought: *Take it off! Take it off! Fool, take it off! Take off the Ring!*[113]

The identification of the three voices is a minor critical conundrum, although for our purposes it is sufficient to note that the use of the word "Fool!" would by itself mark the third voice as Gandalf's, and indeed the wizard, returned to Middle-earth as Gandalf the White, tells Aragorn, Legolas, and Gimli that the Ring was very nearly "revealed to the

Enemy, but it escaped. I had some part in that: for I sat in a high place, and I strove with the Dark Tower; and the Shadow passed."[114] Since Tolkien used italics to indicate some kind of quasi-telepathic communication from Gandalf to Frodo in that scene, it seems likely that the relevant voice Frodo hears in the Emyn Muil is also that of the wizard, especially since the differences in wording from the original conversation implies that the voices are not solely a product of Frodo's memory.[115]

Gollum's hysterical reaction to the Elven-rope rules out the possibility of physically restraining him unless the hobbits can bring themselves to impose a relentless torment (and even so, his screaming would likely attract enemies); the words Frodo hears rule out the possibility of the hobbits justifying his killing as anything other than a selfish expedient; setting Gollum free dooms Frodo and Sam and, as far as the hobbits can tell, all of Middle-earth.* Frodo is thus forced to find another way.

My students invariably interpret the subsequent "Taming of Sméagol," Gollum's transformation from a creature hoping to kill the hobbits into Good Sméagol the Helpful Guide as the result of Gollum's gratitude for Frodo sparing his life, coupled with the shock of being treated with kindness and respect. One student wrote "Frodo is probably the first person who has spoken kindly to Gollum since he killed his best friend Déagol. Why wouldn't Gollum want to help him?"[116] This is an insightful interpretation, especially if we recall Gandalf's intuition that when he encountered Bilbo, Gollum might have found it "actually pleasant . . . to hear a kindly voice again"; the narrator's report in *The Hobbit* that Gollum had "been less lonely and sneaking and nasty" before he "lost all his friends and was driven away"; and Bilbo's sudden flash of pity for Gollum's loneliness during the creature's "endless unmarked days without light or hope of betterment, hard stone, cold fish, sneaking and whispering."[117] But gratitude for Frodo's kindness cannot be the whole explanation, if for no other reason than that although Gollum agrees to come with the hobbits and help them, he attempts to escape the moment he thinks they have fallen asleep. It is only after offering to swear "on the Precious" and

* Remember that at this point the hobbits fear that Gollum is in some way working for Sauron.

the subsequent interaction with Frodo that Gollum's dramatic change of personality occurs.

The scene itself certainly implies the exercise of some kind of power in a formalized manner. Drawing himself up, Frodo recites from the Ring inscription, "One Ring to Rule them all and in the Darkness bind them," thus invoking the Ring's power of binding, and then asks Gollum to confirm that he is committing his promise to the Ring. Gollum grovels at Frodo's feet, "whispering hoarsely: a shudder ran through him, as if the words shook his very bones with fear." Frodo refuses Gollum's repeated entreaties to swear "on the Precious," but he does confirm that he holds the Ring: "you know where it is. Yes, you know, Sméagol. It is before you."

> For a moment it appeared to Sam that his master had grown and Gollum had shrunk: a tall stern shadow, a mighty lord who hid his brightness in grey cloud, and at his feet a little whining dog. Yet the two were in some way akin and not alien: they could reach one another's minds. Gollum raised himself and began pawing at Frodo, fawning at his knees.
>
> "Down! down!" said Frodo. "Now speak your promise!"[118]

Because Frodo does not put on the Ring, this famous and much-quoted passage is usually interpreted as Frodo extracting the oath from Gollum through the implied *threat* of the Ring's power rather than by actually using it. Hillman, the most insightful reader of this scene, argues that the question of whether or not Frodo is actually using the power of the Ring "may not matter" because manipulating Gollum is morally equivalent.[119] This is certainly a reasonable interpretation, especially when coupled with the idea that Frodo's kindness was such an unexpected shock that it led Gollum to *want* to serve and please "nice Master," but the fear, groveling, and fawning is too abject and the transformation too complete to be explained solely by these factors.

In addition, the vision that Snaga the orc has of Sam in the tower of Cirith Ungol is surprisingly similar to what Sam sees in the Emyn Muil when Gollum swears by the Precious:

> for what [the orc] saw was not a small frightened hobbit trying to hold a steady sword: it saw a great silent shape, cloaked in a grey shadow, looming against the wavering light behind; in one hand it held a sword, the very light of which was a bitter pain, the other was clutched at its breast, but held concealed some nameless menace of power and doom.[120]

And on the slopes of Mount Doom Sam has another vision of Frodo and Gollum that shares features with both the orc's vision and what Sam saw previously:

> Then suddenly, as before under the eaves of the Emyn Muil, Sam saw these two rivals with other vision. A crouching shape, scarcely more than the shadow of a living thing, a creature now wholly ruined and defeated, yet filled with a hideous lust and rage; and before it stood stern, untouchable now by pity, a figure robed in white, but at its breast it held a wheel of fire. Out of the fire there spoke a commanding voice.[121]

The similarity of all three visions despite their differing locations, circumstances, and viewers strongly implies that rather than being just individual perceptions, they are produced by the Ring, and from this we can infer that the Ring imposes upon the person being dominated a vision of the Ring-wielder as emitting light but also cloaked or robed in shadow, towering over a smaller being, and giving the impression of being stern, commanding, and possessed of additional hidden power. If Gollum sees what Sam or the orc saw, it is no wonder he is cowed by Frodo, reduced to a whimpering, abject, less-than-human creature.

Further evidence that Frodo uses the Ring to dominate Gollum can be seen in the change in the hobbit's demeanor that occurs almost immediately. In contrast to his energetic, even at times frenetic, leadership in the Emyn Muil, in the Dead Marshes and subsequently Frodo becomes passive and slow; from this point on, with the exception of a few moments at the Black Gate, Sam essentially takes over the leadership of the quest. Additionally, immediately after the first sighting of the flying Ringwraith, "Frodo seemed to be weary, weary to the point of exhaustion. He said nothing, indeed he hardly spoke at all; and he did not complain, but he walked like one who carries a load, the weight of which is ever increasing." This is not just Sam's perception:

> with every step towards the gates of Mordor Frodo felt the Ring on its chain about his neck grow more burdensome. He was now beginning to feel it as an actual weight dragging him earthwards. But far more he was troubled by the Eye: so he called it to himself. It was that more than the drag of the Ring that made him cower and stoop as he walked. The Eye: that horrible growing sense of a hostile will that strove with great power to pierce all shadows of cloud, and earth, and flesh, and to see you: to pin you under its deadly gaze, naked, immovable.[122]

It is certainly possible that the sudden increase in the weight of the Ring and the pressure of the Eye are merely a function of Frodo's and the Ring's proximity to Mordor, especially because the burden grows greater the closer Frodo gets to Barad-dûr. However, neither the weight of the Ring nor the pressure of the Eye, except when it was actively searching for Frodo on Amon Hen, is mentioned until after Frodo makes Gollum swear to serve "the Master of the Precious."

I have to this point relied only on the published text of *The Lord of the Rings* to make the argument for Frodo having employed the power of the Ring, and for about fifteen years this was all I used to try to convince my students. But in 2022, upon rereading *The Treason of Isengard*, I discovered (or rediscovered, although I do not remember seeing it before) that Tolkien himself thought similarly, or at least he did in August 1939. In a plot sketch that Christopher Tolkien titles "The Story Foreseen from Moria," Tolkien summarized a version of the breaking of the Fellowship:

> Frodo hears following feet. And flies. But Sam comes up too to his surprise. The two are too much for Gollum. Gollum is

> daunted by Frodo—who has power over him as Ringbearer. (But use of Ring proves bad since it re-established power of Ring over Frodo after his cure. At end he cannot willingly part with it.)[123]

I recognize that this was a preliminary sketch of a scene that Tolkien would not write for a number of years, and that he certainly could have changed his mind about whether or not Frodo actually used the powers of the Ring or simply manipulated Gollum psychologically. But the combination of Tolkien's having written "use of Ring" and all the evidence presented above makes what I believe is a compelling case for Frodo's having dominated Gollum by employing the supernatural power of the Ring.[124]

That power is almost surely not limited to creating visual illusions in the minds of people whom the Ring is tempting or trying to dominate. Galadriel tells Frodo that the Ring has allowed him to read more of her thoughts than most people can, and he is able to see her Elven-ring, which is just a bright light to Sam.[125] But the Ring also seems to give the power to dominate directly and to command other wills. Galadriel's words to Frodo after he offers her the Ring imply that with its power she could force others to love her:

> In place of the Dark Lord you will set up a Queen. And I shall not be dark, but beautiful and terrible as the Morning and the Night! Fair as the Sea and the Sun and the Snow upon the Mountain. Dreadful as the Storm and the Lightning. Stronger than the foundations of the earth. All shall love me and despair![126]

The final word in this exceptionally powerful declamation is both the most enigmatic and the most important, because it not only demonstrates Galadriel's admirable self-awareness and wisdom but also sheds light on the effects of the Ring on those at whom its power of domination is directed. It is easy to understand that people forced to feel fear or hatred—or even just to obey the power of Command that Boromir believed the Ring would give him—would experience a feeling of despair upon having their freedom taken from them. Tolkien's deep insight is that even if something as positive as the feeling of love were to be imposed upon people by the power of the Ring, those experiencing the feeling would despair rather than rejoice. The moral theme that Tolkien develops through this entwinement of the subthemes of individuality, free choice, and domination, with questions of love, happiness, and autonomy, is the belief that violations of individual freedom are fundamentally negative regardless of the specific form of the domination or the reason it is imposed.[127] The forced feeling of love that "all" would feel for Galadriel would lead to the same feeling—despair—that Denethor experiences when he believes that all that he has ever loved or valued is about to be forcibly taken away. In both cases the despair comes from the lack of free action, from being imposed upon by an outside force. Forcing love is as intrinsically evil as forcing hate or fear: *The great moral wrong is the domination itself*, not what flavor it is.

One of the more remarkable features of *The Lord of the Rings* is that even though almost all the societies it depicts are ruled by hereditary monarchs and are hierarchical and socially stratified, Tolkien consistently celebrates individual freedom as one of the preeminent values across the positive cultures of Middle-earth. The opponents of the Dark Lord are called the Free Peoples, and the various efforts of Sauron, Saruman, and even Lotho to restrict freedom through domination are robustly condemned both by implication and in statements by characters who appear to be speaking authoritatively.* No single statement does as much to highlight how important individual freedom is to Tolkien as Galadriel's self-aware "all would love me and despair," in which one of the most positively portrayed characters in the entire work insists that all coercion—even that which would create beauty and seeming love for an otherworldly queen—is morally wrong.

---

* One of the reasons that a small but noisy subset of critics so dislikes Tolkien is that he depicts a world in which human freedom is a transcendent value but does not link this freedom to "revolution" of any ideological stripe. Given the wider sociopolitical discourse throughout his entire adult life, this has to be a deliberate choice by Tolkien to reject the facile (and consistently wrong) assumption that freedom can only come from the subversion, upheaval, and reinvention of a social order on ideological grounds.

Tolkien's commitment to the transcendent value of individual freedom is even more remarkable when we note how completely it runs against the grain of all the major political philosophies favored by Tolkien's own intellectual class in the interwar era and even during World War II. It was a foregone conclusion among mainstream European intellectuals and political leaders that society would be reorganized along collective lines: The only real debate was over whether the collective would be ruled at the national or international level and whether the government would own everything or just command the businesses that owned most everything. Only a few lonely, old-fashioned, and primarily religious thinkers disagreed. This intellectual context makes Tolkien's consistency that much more surprising—although, given C.S. Lewis's famous statement that "No-one ever influenced Tolkien; you might as well try to influence a Bandersnatch," perhaps we should not be completely surprised—and the ways different individuals and cultures negotiate questions of individual freedom is one of the thematic threads binding together the tapestry of *The Lord of the Rings*.[128]

Having developed some understanding of how the Ring can be used to dominate other wills, and why this elimination of individual freedom is understood as being morally wrong, we can now attempt to figure out how and why the Ring harms its owners—even those who merely use it for occasional invisibility. We begin with the inference that Sauron never intended the Ring to be used by anyone other than himself, and the assumption that the kind of damage the Ring does to Bilbo, Frodo, and, most of all, Gollum was not experienced by Sauron when he possessed it. The psychological injuries the Ring inflicts on its users would therefore be side-effects of its primary power to dominate other wills. My working hypothesis is that at least some portion of the harm that its owners suffer results from the Ring's powers of domination being applied to the bearers themselves. Although it might initially seem that self-domination would be either positive (exerting complete control over oneself seems to be potentially a good thing) or paradoxical and thus meaningless, careful examination of the effects of the Ring on its bearers suggests otherwise.

Gergely Nagy, in the single most insightful essay on this topic, shows that the power of the Ring can be best understood through the ways it changes and constrains the language of Gollum, the individual who, after Sauron, possessed it the longest.[129] Gollum's distinctive language is characterized by the prominence of meaningless bodily sounds (the gulping *gollum* noise), sibilance (characteristic of whispering, particularly in subvocal monologues that do not require distinct articulation), the substitution of plural pronouns (*we*, *us*, *our*) for singulars, and, most of all, the use of the word *precious*. This word "acts as a central signifier in Gollum's language . . . 'precious' is the addressee of Gollum's language: it is both himself and something else which at least superficially seems to be the Ring."[130] This feature of Gollum's idiolect, "broadens into a whole independent discourse in which Gollum speaks without ever being heard or heeded." The "desire generated by the Ring" enters into "the subject's own symbolic system . . . and subverts it from within."

We know that almost immediately upon being seen, the Ring can generate a powerful desire for its possession. The rapid onset and intensity of this desire is a strong indicator that it is a supernatural effect of the Ring rather than just an idiosyncratically strong response to its appearance.* The Ring also grants the ability to impose one's will upon others, but when there is no external object at which this power is directed, rather than somehow amplifying or reinforcing its owner's strength, the power produces a positive feedback loop: The command is to value the Ring itself, thus increasing the desire for its possession. This desire can be understood as a sense of emptiness that is only filled by the Ring.[131] But this emptiness is never completely filled, even when the Ring is possessed, since the Ring's power of command continues to operate on the owner, further increasing the desire for the Ring. This positive feedback explains Bilbo's feeling that the Ring had been growing on his mind: "Sometimes I have felt it was like an eye looking at me. And I am always wanting to put it on and disappear, don't you know; or

---

* However fair or flawless a small bit of gold might be, a desire so strong that it leads Gollum without hesitation to strangle his best friend or Isildur to reject immediately the admonitions of Elrond and Círdan seems unlikely to be solely an effect of its physical beauty.

wondering if it is safe, and pulling it out to make sure. I tried locking it up, but I found I couldn't rest without it in my pocket."[132]

As noted, the fantasies and delusions produced by the Ring are self-focused visions in which the possessor of the Ring commands others to do things rather than working in concert with them. Combining these several effects of the Ring together with the Ring's ability to dominate wills produces a dynamic in which the egocentric individual, alone, is driven to desire the Ring more and more, until the Ring and the individual have together excluded everything else (note the loneliness implied by the situation in which Gollum speaks but no one ever listens). The only thing that matters to the possessor is that he possesses the Ring, and yet possession is not enough.

The ultimate result of such a dynamic is Gollum's using the same expression to refer to himself and the Ring, one that invokes both the fact of possession (*my*) and the thing possessed (*precious*), but also can refer reflexively to the entity who is possessing (*My Precious*). Naming the person, the thing, and the combination of person and thing with a single phrase serves to erase the independent identity of the possessor except when he possesses the thing possessed: *My Precious*. If those last two sentences seem circular, repetitive, tangled, and confusing, that is because this is what the Ring does to the bearer's language. The epithet *My Precious* is "a signifier which signifies, as it were, both sides of desire."[133] We can thus understand why, when Gollum suddenly has to use pronouns—because for the first time in over four centuries there is someone else to talk to—he employs plurals: *My Precious* is a single signifier, one name for both the body of Gollum and the physical Ring, and in Gollum's psyche these have become inseparable. The self becomes *that which has* My Precious and the self *is* My Precious. It is not so much that the Ring has replaced the self as that it has made itself so essential to the self that the self no longer exists independently but only as part of an endless cycle of circular reference.

Eventually the original natural, singular, undamaged subject that coexists with a physical body and is represented grammatically by the first-person singular pronoun *I* will have been replaced by the unnatural and forced pairing of the Ring and the self: *we*, *us*, *My Precious*. The dual subject that calls itself *My Precious* replaced the unitary subject Sméagol, who as a result was lost, but then when Gollum lost the Ring, that paired subject was broken, and the dyadic self remains incomplete without the object that is lost.[134] The subject—Gollum after the loss of the Ring—is defined at its very core by the thing it lacks and thus will constantly feel an emptiness that desperately needs to be filled. This is why Shippey's analogizing the effects of the Ring on its bearer to "addiction" is so apposite.[135] The addict's self becomes bound to the addicting substance or action in the same way that Sméagol became bound to the Ring: isolated, self-focused to the exclusion of all others, eventually becoming a dyad of the self and the thing to which it is addicted, and thus defined by the presence or absence of the thing.* It is no wonder that so many addicts respond so strongly to Gandalf's statement that Gollum both hated the Ring and loved it, "as he hated and loved himself."[136]

Toward the beginning of their encounter in the Emyn Muil, after Frodo has pressed him about having gone to Mordor, Gollum responds with what seems like a traumatic memory of torture by Sauron and then says:

> "Poor, poor Sméagol, he went away long ago. They took his Precious, and he's lost now."
>
> "Perhaps we'll find him again, if you come with us," said Frodo.
>
> "No, no, never! He's lost his Precious," said Gollum.[137]

The pronouns in this exchange are both confusing and important. Gollum talks about himself in the third person, and he implies that there are two other entities that are in some way related to him: Sméagol,

* Nonaddicts fundamentally misunderstand the central problem. It is not that the addict merely lacks sufficient access to the substance, or that the substance causes substantial physical harm (as bad as those things can be), but that the addict's fundamental self-conception feels incomplete without the substance but is also immiserated by being dependent upon the substance. The problem is the *unnatural* dependence, so feeding that dependence does nothing to end the addict's suffering.

who "went away" after "they" (unspecified) took his Precious (unspecified; it would seem to be the Ring, but then who are "they"?).* Frodo, attempting to reach the "little corner of [Gollum's] mind that was still his own" that Gandalf had asserted still existed, uses the first-person-plural to attempt to create a connection: "Perhaps *we'll* [Gollum and Frodo together] find him [Sméagol] again," but then shifts to the singular, "if *you* [Gollum] come" and then returns to a plural that must indicate the two hobbits "with *us*." [Frodo and Sam]. It seems unlikely that the first "we" also refers to Frodo and Sam, so I have parsed its antecedent as Frodo and Gollum (although technically the antecedent could be Frodo and the Ring, that seems an interpretation too dark even for me). I parse the full sentence as: Perhaps Frodo and Gollum together can find Sméagol if Gollum will come with Frodo and Sam on their journey. But Gollum insists that Sméagol cannot be found because Sméagol lost his Precious. The referent of the final word in this sentence is utterly ambiguous. It could mean the Ring itself, or it could mean the pairing of Gollum and the Ring that makes up *My Precious*, or it could mean just Gollum's self. The import of the sentence does seem to be that Gollum does not believe he can ever find his lost earlier unitary self unless he regains the Ring. If this is the case, then it further illustrates the insidious workings of the Ring on the psyche of the bearer, whom it deceives into believing that the original unitary self (Sméagol) will forever remain inaccessible (lost) to the remaining half of the broken dyad (Gollum) unless the missing half (the Ring) is reacquired, even though we know this is a lie, as it was the Ring that caused the very emptiness that it is seen as filling.

Sauron created the Ring with the ultimate goal of so dominating others that they lose their selves and become fully the slaves of the Dark Lord. The power of the Ring thus eventually abjects the bearer, stripping away everything else. The Witch King or Lord of the Nazgûl has two titles but no name; The Lieutenant of the Tower of Barad-dûr, who

* The antecedent of "they" is ambiguous. Could "they" be the tides of the world? Bilbo and Frodo? Does "his Precious" refer only to the Ring, or also to his self, with "they" then meaning Sauron and the Ring? There does not appear to be an obvious answer.

is also called The Mouth of Sauron, has forgotten his.[138] Gollum, in contrast, has too many names: He refers to both his physical body and his psychological self as *Gollum*, *Sméagol*, and *My Precious*, depending on the situation. What he lacks is the first-person singular pronoun: Gollum, except on a few occasions, seems incapable of using the word *I*, instead talking about himself in the plural, in the third person, or avoiding pronouns entirely and using "My Precious."

Hillman's discussion of Gollum's rare uses of *I* is characteristically nuanced and thorough. He notes that after Frodo imposes the power of the Ring on him a second time as a punishment for saying "Give it to Sméagol,"[139] Gollum never again uses the first-person singular pronoun. In this exchange, for which, as Hillman points out, Frodo has far less justification than the initial extraction of the promise in the Emyn Muil, Frodo threatens Gollum not for having done anything, but merely for articulating the thought that he might recover the Ring from Frodo.* That is, Frodo has used the Ring's power to see into other minds ("One Ring to find them"), and he threatens Gollum by openly articulating the power the Ring gives him: "If, I wearing [the Ring] were to command you, you would obey, even if it were to leap from a precipice or to cast yourself into the fire. And such would be my command."[140] If the use of *I* was a sign that Gollum, as a response to Frodo's kindness, had started to recover or heal from the damage done to him by the

* To the best of my knowledge Hillman is the only scholar who has recognized the abusive nature of Frodo's treatment of Gollum in "The Black Gate Is Closed," *Pity, Power, and Tolkien's Ring*, 142–49. The many times I had read this scene before reading Hillman, I was so aligned with Frodo (and Sam; the narrator tells us that Sam strongly approves of Frodo's harsh tone) that I never realized that the whole interaction is triggered by Gollum's understandable panic when it seems like Frodo is about to walk straight to the Black Gate. Terrified of what would happen if Frodo did this, Gollum starts blurting out words in a desperate attempt to stop the hobbit from a disastrous course of action. Gollum first warns Frodo that Sauron is sure to get the Ring and will "eat us all" if he does. He then urges Frodo to keep the Ring for himself (and thus away from Sauron) and be kind to Sméagol, or to escape and "go to nice places." Only then does he say the fateful words "and give it back to little Sméagol" that so anger Frodo (*TT*, iii, 245–46). Frodo's threatening response is disproportionately harsh, and it cannot be explained away as a heat-of-the-moment reaction: There is additional discussion between Gollum and Frodo, and Frodo takes time to consider his options before he first announces his plan and then punishes Gollum for articulating the desire that they both know has been in his mind since Gollum first sensed that Frodo had the Ring.

Ring, then Frodo's harsh threat outside the Black Gate undoes all that good and undermines any trust built up during the passage of the Dead Marshes. Hillman interprets this exchange as an example of Gandalf's and others assertions that the Ring turns everything to evil.[141] I agree, and would only add a small observation and a deduction. The observation is that the unnecessarily harsh threat occurs just when Frodo is doing what the voice of Gandalf implicitly criticizes him for doing: justifying immoral conduct because he is "fearing for [his] own safety." Gollum is no immediate threat, but Frodo has been brought face-to-face with the undeniable hopelessness of the quest, so his frustration and fear overwhelm the kindness with which he has tried to engage Gollum, and the result is abuse. And it seems likely that Frodo does more than verbally intimidate Gollum here, because after Frodo's threat Gollum stops even the halting and inconsistent use of *I* that he had started to develop. After collapsing in a gibbering heap, followed by a long time in which he is only able to crawl around begging for kindness, Gollum suggests that they enter Mordor through the secret way that we later learn is the pass of Cirith Ungol. In hindsight, Gollum's abandonment or loss of the first-person singular happens at the same time he decides to betray the hobbits to Shelob as a way of avoiding directly breaking his promise, and both seem to be responses to having been terrified and humiliated by Frodo's use of the power of the Ring.

A character's inability to use the singular first-person pronoun is, to the best of my knowledge, Tolkien's own invention and therefore seems particularly significant.[142] Indeed, it may be the last piece in the puzzle of how and why the Ring does what it does. The loss of *I* is the final stage of abjection of a person dominated by the Ring, either externally, as Gollum is by Frodo, or internally, as Gollum was by his long possession of the Ring. A pronoun without an antecedent is a placeholder; it fulfills a grammatical function, indicating relationship. An antecedent that seems to be precluded from being referred to by a certain pronoun, however, is strange indeed. It is hard to understand why Gollum is so reluctant or unable to use *I*, since even though he primarily uses plural pronouns, he does frequently refer to himself with singular nouns: *Sméagol* and *Precious*.

My tentative explanation is that Gollum does not use *I* because this pronoun no longer refers to himself, but to something else that he does not wish to or cannot invoke. The normal antecedent of *I* is the Cartesian *cogito*, the thing that thinks, the mind employing the pronoun.[143] But the Ring inserts itself into the bearer's psyche by transforming that original unitary *cogito* into a plural, self-referential entity: The thing that thinks and the Ring it is always thinking about, always together. Plural pronouns replace singulars, and the new name, *My Precious*, is an interchangeable token that refers to the plural subject and to either of its parts. The original unitary subject, which exists as the organizing function for the bearer's memories, finally becomes inaccessible. Gollum says Sméagol is lost; on the slopes of Mount Doom Frodo tells Sam that although he can remember that certain things happened, "I cannot see them. No taste of food, no feel of water, no sound of wind, no memory of tree or grass or flower, no image of moon or star are left to me. I am naked in the dark, Sam."[144]

At this point the loss or removal of the Ring leaves the subject broken, characterized by a great emptiness that can only be filled by the Ring. The plural subject is torn apart, but the singular subject cannot return because it feels half of itself to be missing; what had been a set of repeating circular equations (Precious [self] = Precious [Ring] = Precious [self] = Precious [Ring]) is now a single broken equation, Precious [self] = Nothing. *I* = Nothing. This is Denethor's "Naught"; the "Nada" that Hemingway's character in "A Clean Well-Lighted Place" prays to because he has lost everything else; the Nothing that C.S. Lewis describes in *The Screwtape Letters* as being "strong enough to steal away a man's best years not in sweet sins but in a dreary flickering of the mind over it knows not what and knows not why"; the empty space in the addict that the addiction always fails to fill.[145] But "I am Nothing" is logically self-contradictory and therefore unstable. Something fills the empty space of Nothing, and in Middle-earth, that is Sauron, spirit of malice, bottomless desire to dominate other wills, of whom Gollum says, "He'll eat us all, if he gets it, eat all the world."[146] Once the subject has been reduced to I = Nothing, the power of the Ring inserts Sauron into the equation and the singular first-person pronoun becomes a reference not to the self, but to that ultimate other who seeks to subsume all other selves. The Ring's final victory is when I = 👁. Sauron's is when this applies to everyone.

Gollum has met Sauron. He has been close enough to see that there are only four fingers on one of the Black Hands. He was tortured either by Sauron or at his behest, and he has borne Sauron's Ring for centuries.[147] And yet Sauron is never able to dominate Gollum completely and transform him into the willing slave that so many others become.[148] Although Tolkien does not explain why—unless the Warden of the Houses of Healing, despite his pomposity about herb-lore, is more right than he knows when he says that hobbits are just "very tough in the fibre"—he does suggest multiple times that hobbits are at some deep level spiritually tougher, more indomitable, and less easily tempted than the other races of Middle-earth.[149] In the same way that people of the culture of Rohan are less prone to fall into despair than those of the culture of Gondor, the Shire-folk are less able to be completely dominated—because they have less desire to dominate—than men. It is this intrinsic hobbitish quality that allows Gollum to resist Sauron's commands and instead pursue the Ring solely for his own purposes and thus, albeit unintentionally, cause Sauron's downfall. That Gollum does not use *I* despite enduring nearly half a millennium of the Ring's influence, followed by Sauron attempting to mentally enslave him, may indicate that Gollum's core of indomitability is due to his hatred and resentment of the Dark Lord: He gives up *I* entirely rather than using it to mean Sauron.

Gollum had recovered some use of *I* as a consequence of Frodo's kindness and perhaps also because Frodo's use of the Ring to dominate him counterbalanced the "Shadow of Fear" with which Sauron had tried to control him.[150] He stops using the first-person singular after Frodo has hurt him such that he no longer trusts his "nice Master." The recovery of Sméagol, which would be advanced by Gollum being able to use *I* to refer to his own body *and* to the Sméagol self who has been lost is halted because Gollum no longer sees Frodo as a potential counter to Sauron but instead views him as being qualitatively similar to the Dark Lord, someone who humiliated and hurt

Gollum. Even with the Ring, Frodo cannot fully dominate Gollum any more than Sauron can, and Gollum's response to the attempt is to decide to betray Frodo (as he has betrayed Sauron) and convince himself that he is still following the letter of his promise to serve The Master of the Precious.

Understanding how the Ring's power works, and thus the significance of Gollum's uses of the first-person singular pronoun, allows us to recognize how the tragic climax of *The Lord of the Rings*—Gollum's near-repentance being interrupted by Sam's harsh words—resonates with the scene of Frodo's threatening Gollum. Frodo's harsh and angry castigation and threats in "The Black Gate Is Closed" are what primes Gollum to react to Sam's belligerent distrust the way he does. As noted above in Chapter 4, because Frodo and Sam are unconscious, Tolkien needs a character through whom he can focalize the narrative of the scene on the Stairs of Cirith Ungol, but he cannot use Gollum for that purpose without giving away that Gollum has decided to betray Frodo's trust and lead the hobbits into the trap of Shelob's lair, knowledge that would undercut the emotional effect of the entire scene and introduce an unwelcome element of irony to the next chapter. Tolkien therefore is forced to shift the point of view to a not-physically-present, but non-omniscient narrator (i.e., one who does not have post-facto knowledge of what Gollum will soon do) in order to describe Gollum's external behavior but only speculate about his internal states. As noted previously, the conceit that *The Lord of the Rings* is a translation primarily of Frodo's and Sam's written version of their story breaks down at this point—although so briefly that it does not significantly disturb the experiential quality of the narrative—just as it does when Sam narrates what Frodo sees after the ship leaves the Grey Havens. Hillman's clever solution is to interpret the scene on the Stairs of Cirith Ungol as being the result of Frodo synthesizing what Sam told him (that the latter awoke to find Gollum pawing at Frodo) with what he infers Gollum might actually have done, which is based on what Frodo—who understands what the Ring does to its possessor—imagines Gollum to have felt.[151] The result is the tragic vision of the old, withered hobbit far from friends and home.[152]

Hillman's solution is far more elegant than my deduction that there are a few brief instances in which Tolkien, due to the constraints of the narrative, simply abandons the conceit that *The Lord of the Rings* is written by Frodo and Sam. If Hillman is correct, then Frodo, in the process of writing *The Downfall of the Lord of the Rings and the Return of the King*, never realized that his treatment of Gollum in front of the Black Gate was abusive, or that it contributed to Gollum's failure to achieve redemption, and so he constructed a scene in which Sam's distrustful reaction is to blame for the missed opportunity for Gollum to repent. However, based on the totality of the evidence, Sam is correct in distrusting Gollum, who *has* decided to lead the hobbits to their deaths. The only counterweight to his evaluation is a scene *that he did not witness*. If Frodo is responsible for the scene, he has treated Sam very unfairly, and I am not sure that I believe that this is what Tolkien has done.

However, if Hillman is correct, then we here observe additional pernicious effects of the Ring at work. Frodo is guilty of abusing Gollum, and from the moment of this abuse, Gollum retreats from the recovery of Sméagol—as evidenced by the abandonment of the first-person singular pronoun. But Frodo in his narrative shows no self-awareness of his treatment of Gollum being inappropriate or counterproductive, and he then imagines that the two characters most affected by the Ring—himself and Gollum—come near to a rapprochement only to be thwarted by the distrustful reaction of Sam, thus implying that *Sam* is to blame for what happens subsequently. Earlier Sam had asked Gollum (who was, fittingly, absent) if he wanted to be the hero or the villain. Gollum never answered, but in Frodo's imagination the Ring does: The villains are everyone *except* the bearer of the Ring.

Frodo's use of the Ring in the Emyn Muil to dominate Gollum is justified and is by far the lesser evil of the alternatives of killing Gollum or risking the failure of the quest. As noted previously, Tolkien takes significant pains to overdetermine the conclusion of Frodo's internal debate, carefully constructing the situation so as to preclude some good and kindly middle path or clever third way that Frodo can use to escape the double-bind. The circumstances are such that the hobbits would have to kill Gollum in cold blood, because physical control of him is impossible due to his reaction to the Elven-rope, and Tolkien revises Gandalf's earlier argument against killing Gollum into an even more morally and rhetorically effective form.* The combined effect is to make the reader absolutely certain that Frodo, despite his having been warned against doing this by all of his wise counsellors and by his own intuition, must use the Ring to dominate Gollum. *He has no other option.* But then, almost immediately after he makes this essentially forced choice, Frodo begins to suffer from both the Ring's terrible perceived weight and the sense that he is now more visible to the searching Eye of Sauron. In only a few days his personality changes to being far more passive, introverted, and depressed, and he never—even when the journey is over—recovers the vigor, leadership ability, or decisiveness that once characterized him and contributed to Bilbo and Gandalf both thinking that he was the "best hobbit in the Shire."[153] All this for making the *right* choice.

To my knowledge it has not previously been noted that when the Fellowship arrives in Lothlórien without Gandalf, Galadriel is faced with a dilemma similar to Frodo's in the Emyn Muil. She and Celeborn were already familiar with Aragorn, and Legolas is an Elf and a distant kinsman, but the four hobbits, Gimli, and Boromir are unknown quantities, and if one of them were to be treacherous, disloyal, or even weak, the quest would fail. The Elven-ring she wears allows Galadriel to perceive the thoughts of others, and it, like the One Ring, seems to have the power to project a fantasy or delusional vision. The failure of the quest would bring about her own and her people's enslavement and destruction by Sauron, so she seems to be quite justified in using her ring to try to determine if "all the Company is true." She therefore creates visions of temptation for the members of the Fellowship and then observes their thoughts to see if they might succumb.[154] Sam articulates his sense of violation—"I felt like as if I hadn't got noth-

* It is hard to believe that Frodo and Sam could ever have killed Gollum in cold blood even without Frodo's being reminded of the moral issues by the voices. Indeed, as we later discover, Sam cannot bring himself to kill Gollum in far more adrenaline-hyped circumstances.

ing on"—and explains that his vision was of being able to fly "back home to the Shire to a nice little hole with—with a bit of garden of my own."[155] The other companions felt something similar and conclude that each "felt that he was offered a choice between a shadow full of fear that lay ahead, and something that he greatly desired: clear before his mind it lay, and to get it he had only to turn aside from the road and leave the Quest and the war against Sauron to others."* Gimli adds that he felt as if "my choice would remain secret and known only to myself," which I think is meant to communicate the idea that in their visions, the members of the Fellowship were free of social pressure—they could turn aside without shame or guilt. Boromir's response is the most telling:

> Maybe it was only a test, and she thought to read our thoughts for her own good purpose; but almost I should have said that she was tempting us, offering what she pretended to have the power to give. It need not be said that I refused to listen. The Men of Minas Tirith are true to their word.†

Again, it is difficult to blame Galadriel for her testing. Her fate, that of her people, and that of Middle-earth itself hangs in the balance. How

---

* *FR*, II, vii, 373. Although the narrator says that each companion felt that he had been offered a choice, Aragorn, Legolas, and Frodo—the characters already known to or trusted by Galadriel—do not speak.

† *FR*, II, vii, 373. I have often wondered if this final sentence can be construed as an indication that Elrond's decision not to have the Fellowship swear an oath was, in the case of Boromir, a mistake. It is not (as I had misremembered for years despite multiple readings of *The Lord of the Rings*) Boromir, but Gimli who says "But sworn word may strengthen quaking heart" to be rebuked by Elrond with "Or break it"; *FR*, II, iii, 294. But perhaps if Boromir had sworn an oath to protect Frodo he would have been better able to resist the temptation of the Ring due to his self-image as a Man of Minas Tirith, always true to his word. I raise this issue in order to point out that Tolkien does not depict the Wise as being infallible, and indeed even the wisest characters make what are in retrospect poor decisions. I wonder what Gandalf thought when he saw the balrog and realized that he had deliberately excluded Glorfindel, Balrog-slayer from the Nine Walkers. (That is, if the Glorfindel the hobbits meet is actually the same Glorfindel who heroically died killing a balrog in the battle in Gondolin—the answer: probably not, but perhaps—see *Peoples*, 377–82).

could she, having the power to do so, *not* test the hearts of the Fellowship if that testing could prevent a catastrophe? And yet her temptation of Boromir is partly responsible for his fall and thus for the quest almost ending in the very disaster she sought to prevent.

I do not think this interpretation is overreaching on my part. When talking to Faramir, Sam blurts out "that in Lórien [Boromir] first saw clearly what I guessed sooner: what he wanted. From the moment he first saw it he wanted the Enemy's Ring!"[156] There is no reason to suspect that any other event in Lórien would have caused Boromir to realize that he did indeed desire the One Ring, so the blame must accrue to Galadriel's temptation. Further support for this interpretation comes from Faramir's words when he is recounting his vision of Boromir lying dead in the Elven-boat: "*What did she say to you, the Lady that dies not? What did she see? What woke in your heart then?*"[157] Note that Faramir asks these rhetorical questions several hours *before* Sam tells him that his brother wanted Sauron's Ring, and Faramir knows nothing at all about Galadriel's producing visions of temptation, yet his questions fit perfectly with the scene: Galadriel may not have offered her temptation in words, but it was the functional equivalent of speaking to Boromir, and she did look into his thoughts, and something did indeed wake in his heart.[158] As a result, Middle-earth came very close either to Boromir becoming a Dark Lord or, in his arrogance as a new Ring lord, being defeated by Sauron, who would then have recovered the One Ring. In hindsight, Galadriel's temptation of Boromir was unwise, because she managed to awaken but not see the desire in his heart—perhaps because it only grew strong after days of close proximity to the Ring—or, if she did see the desire, did not take it seriously enough.[159] But given the circumstances, what other choice did she have?

From these examples and many others we can conclude that a very important subtheme of *The Lord of the Rings* is the idea that morally incorrect actions always exact a price: even if they are forced moves, even if they are performed with the best intentions, even if the world may be destroyed if they are not taken. That the key illustrations of this theme are actions taken by Frodo and Galadriel, two of the most admirable characters in the entire work, shows that Tolkien means for the theme to be without exceptions. Regardless of how much he loves a character—and material written after the publication of *The Lord of the Rings* demonstrates that the more he thought about Galadriel, the more he loved her—Tolkien refuses to give special dispensation.[160] Immoral actions invariably cause harm, and dominating other minds, forcing people to do things against their wills, are always immoral actions. Tolkien is the anti-Machiavelli: No matter how much the ends seem to justify the means, no matter how much notional good might be expected to result from an evil action, the price of those actions will be paid. There is always a trade-off rather than a have-your-cake-and-eat-it-too situation, like that which the elves attempted to create through the power of their Three Rings.

Frodo's fate is the most heartbreaking example of these unavoidable costs. He, and the readers, have experienced the eucatastrophe of Sauron's defeat and then the soul-lifting events of the Field of Cormallen: the song of the minstrel, Sam's tears of pure happiness, and the eagle, in the words of the most joyous psalms, exhorting the people of Minas Tirith to "Sing and Rejoice!" But the story continues, and we see Frodo when he is sick and in pain, sad and worried. Then the Shire, despite being saved from Sauron, is despoiled and in danger. Finally, even in the blissful year of 1420, Frodo is still suffering from wounds of knife, sting, and tooth, and most of all, from the loss of the Ring, which is gone forever.[161]

Frodo only stays in the Shire until the autumn of 1421, and in the time leading up to that, he has not only been ill but has seemingly isolated himself from most other hobbits and given up any involvement in social affairs. Although Frodo tries to disguise this suffering, especially so as not to cast any shadows on Sam's marrying and becoming a father, Sam knows that there is something wrong, although he does not realize how bad it is. Frodo even lets Sam think that he is eventually going to Rivendell when he asks him to be his companion on the first part of a journey in late September. It is only when they encounter the High Elves on their way to the Grey Havens that Sam realizes that Frodo will be leaving Middle-earth.

> "But," said Sam, and tears started in his eyes, "I thought you were going to enjoy the Shire, too, for years and years, after all you have done."
>
> "So I thought too, once. But I have been too deeply hurt, Sam. I tried to save the Shire, and it has been saved, but not for me. It must often be so, Sam, when things are in danger: someone has to give them up, lose them, so that others may keep them. But you are my heir: all that I had and might have had I leave to you."[162]

Frodo says "I tried to save the Shire." We expect a sentence that begins with "I tried" to be completed by another verb in the first-person such as *succeeded* (or *failed*). But instead Frodo puts the accomplishment in the passive voice, refusing to attribute even part of it to himself: "And it has been saved." Some critics interpret this speech as Frodo recognizing that the Shire was saved by Providence, but it seems to me less a quasi-religious recognition than a marker of his permanent depression and loss. Like many depressed people, Frodo seems to believe that he does not deserve happiness. He does not give himself credit for saving the Shire because he knows that he was not able to complete the quest on his own.

This is a terrible echo of the grandiose savior-delusions that the Ring used to tempt Boromir, Denethor, and even Sam. We have never been told what fantasy the Ring dangled before Frodo, though we do know that he tried to command the Black Riders at the Ford of Bruinen, and that when he was just outside of Minas Morgul and had to restrain his own hand from touching the Ring, he thought to himself that he did not have the power to face the Witch King "—not yet."[163] And we know that when he claimed the Ring for his own in the Sammath Naur he was not attempting to surrender to Sauron. Was he deluded into believing that with the power of the Ring at its strongest, in the ancient forges in the heart of Sauron's realm, he could have commanded the Ringwraiths to turn against their master? Or that he could defeat or destroy Sauron? What shame does Frodo feel for having been cozened or overpowered by the Ring? Is he wracked with guilt because he never had a chance to reconsider and take it off before Gollum took the choice away from him? In a letter, Tolkien said that Frodo probably believed that the only way to achieve the quest was to throw himself along with the Ring into the Crack of Doom, sacrificing his life to save Middle-earth.[164] If Frodo believes that he does not deserve happiness in the Shire because in the end he was not able to break the Ring's hold over himself through sheer force of will, he would not be the first addict to feel this way. If we reread his words to Sam in this light, we see that he had meant to save the Shire by sacrificing his own life on Mount Doom, but not having been able to follow through, he feels as if he must give up the things he had been willing to sacrifice: "all that I had and might have had." The Ring's domination of its bearers' wills replaces their futures with its unfillable emptiness.

In the tragedy of Frodo's inability to enjoy the Shire, many thematic threads are intertwined: The ways death and despair are handled by different cultures, their interconnection with individual psychologies and circumstances, the selfishness and disfigurement of the soul that the Ring produces, the evil effects of domination on both the abuser and the victim, and the loss of self that comes with either exercising or experiencing such power. Finally, and perhaps most of all, in Frodo's suffering we see the workings of one of Tolkien's great themes: the idea that everything has a cost that someone must pay, and that there are no shortcuts, there is no perfected world or utopia achievable by some simple if-only. Middle-earth may be saved from Sauron, but it is lost to the elves. The Ents have no offspring. As Théoden intuits, "much that was fair and wonderful shall pass for ever out of Middle-earth."[165] And however beautiful and peaceful the reign of King Elessar turns out to be, Frodo will not see or enjoy it.

I suspect that a great deal of the disproportionate reaction against Tolkien's works among politically active critics is an unconscious response to this particular theme. The political programs supported by most twentieth- and twenty-first-century critics are fundamentally arguments about which people get to force which other people to do which particular things, so a recognition that dominating other wills is inherently morally wrong threatens writers' and critics' sense of being "on the right side of history." That no anti-Tolkienian critics (to my knowledge) seem to have engaged Tolkien on this specific thematic point is a telling sign that Tolkien's moral argument is extremely strong and convincing, for if it were not, we would expect many direct refutations.*

Throughout the writing of this book I have been disciplining myself not to quote and refute some of the stupider things critics have ever written about Tolkien or *The Lord of the Rings*, mostly because Shippey has already done a better job of this in both *The Road to Middle-earth* and *Author of the Century*, but also because continually referring to the most unfortunately idiotic or self-contradictory statements by critics like Catharine Stimpson, Nick Otty, and Edmund "Bunny" Wilson gives those bad ideas a prominence they do not deserve. But I just cannot resist the urge to quote Edwin Muir's spectacularly wrong take on *The Lord of the Rings* that he published in *The Observer* in 1955. Muir does not fit either of the two most common profiles of critics who seem to lose the ability to think coherently when confronted by Tolkien's works: He is neither a self-righteous mediocrity attempting to curry favor with a critical establishment nor a gatekeeper panicked by a sudden realization that something outside is far more valuable than everything within the fortress he guards. Nevertheless, Muir's major evaluation of *The Lord of the Rings* contains two sentences that together are contenders for the stupidest thing ever written about Tolkien's works: "The good boys, having fought a deadly battle, emerge at the end of it well, triumphant and happy, as boys would naturally expect to do. There are only one or two minor casualties."[166]

The first time I read this passage as part of Shippey's very diplo-

---

* The simplest argument would be that there is no practical way to organize a complex society that does not rely upon coercion in one way or another. Because Tolkien is working in the fantasy genre, he is able to have everyone *want* to obey Aragorn's commands, so that the reader never sees represented the domination and force that are unavoidable in a large polity made up of people with differing values, interests, and worldviews; therefore Tolkien's worldview is impractical. Except that this is not a refutation, since Tolkien's thesis is not *No one must ever force anyone to do anything* but rather *Forcing people to do things disfigures both your own soul and theirs, and there will always be a price to pay for doing it.* The most "utopian" place in Middle-earth, the Shire, is shown to have plenty of problems of its own, including insularity, forgetfulness of history, and the inability of the hobbits to defend their land against outside aggression without the clandestine efforts of the Rangers or, later, the power of King Elessar.

matic refutation in *The Road to Middle-earth*,[167] I thought that perhaps Muir had just been lazy and not actually finished the book, but upon reading the rest of his review, that cannot be the explanation (he at least mentions "The Scouring of the Shire"). Instead, he seems simply not to have understood things Tolkien states with utter clarity. How else could someone presumably literate in English come to the conclusion that "Lórien . . . returns to its ageless felicity," when Galadriel explicitly states that if the Ring is destroyed, Lórien will fade and no longer be magical, and she and her people will depart into the West or dwindle?[168] I cannot bring myself to believe that Muir was really that dense. It must be, instead, that there is something about Tolkien's work that triggers a critical blindness or a perverse reflex to claim the opposite of the truth even though this can so easily be checked.

I think I can identify one of the major factors. The standard, clichéd twentieth-century rejection of any works of literature that depict humanity and its works as being substantially good and beautiful and thus worthy of preservation is to call them "fairy-tales," with the implication that such are just simple, happy stories that only children would believe. Muir's dishonest characterization of *The Lord of the Rings* as "A Boy's World" is just another way of doing this. Muir's surface-level excuse for this criticism is that there is not a lot of sex in Tolkien's works, but what he is really getting at is *The Lord of the Rings*' absolute and unwavering insistence both that real evil exists and that there is much worth saving in the world, and that the former assertion does not negate the latter, which need not be hedged or qualified, but naturally arises from people's true perceptions. There is nothing childish in the cultural comparisons between Gondor and Rohan or in the complexity of what the Ring does to people, or in the overpowering sense of heimweh that runs throughout *The Lord of the Rings*. What is perhaps child*like*, in the best possible sense, is the belief that there really is good and evil in the world rather than just one side and another side, and that the good is deserving of personal sacrifice if that is required to preserve it. Tolkien's readers all believe this. In fact, almost all people who are not practicing intellectuals believe this about our own world.*

* The most recent experience that reinforces my belief that, regardless of what relativism

To reject this view of life by dismissing it with the equivalent of "that's just a fairy-tale," is easy, which is why Muir and others assert that *The Lord of the Rings* has a simplistic, wish-fulfilling happy ending despite the protagonist's suffering so badly he leaves behind his home and everyone he loves, the loss of the magical and transcendent places of Lothlórien and Rivendell, and the overwhelming emotion of heimweh that pervades the story. Blanket dismissal is a sign that engagement on the merits is too difficult. Tolkien has so effectively developed his thematic tapestry that he makes a compelling case that even if real, active evil—not just misunderstanding or competition for resources—exists, there is *still* so much beauty and goodness in the world that it deserves to be saved, and that the way to accomplish this is not in adopting evil's own methods and dominating others, but through integrity, self-sacrifice, and humility: the voluntary actions of free individuals.

The characteristics that make Tolkien's works experiential and the emotional effects that align them with sorrows that every human being feels combine with thematic interweaving to produce a sense in many readers that *The Lord of the Rings*, despite being fantasy, is nevertheless deeply true. The victory over darkness comes only with a terrible cost that is not distributed evenly. The temporary triumph does not lead to boundless rewards for the heroes or to an earthly paradise. The defeat of the supernatural evil does not remove all evil from that world. Although some beauty is preserved, much perishes and the author provides no tidy resolutions to conflicting themes and moral problems. These characteristics make the story a better representation of our human experience in this fallen world than "and they lived happily ever after" could ever be.

---

they profess publicly, nearly everyone actually believes they can distinguish good from evil in very stark terms was hearing two colleagues (not at Wheaton) who had made their careers as orthodox, everything-is-relative, power-creates-truth postmodernists, in some kind of performative escalation of agreement, yelling louder and louder that a certain candidate for president absolutely could not be allowed to win an election because he is "Evil! EE-vil!" The raw emotion in their voices convinced me that they were not cynically trying to manipulate an audience but believed what they were saying despite this contradicting the central theses of their lives' work. The irony was lost on them even when I helpfully pointed out the apparent contradiction. "This is serious!" replied one, demonstrating, sadly, that their academic work was not.

CONCLUSION

Fathers and Sons

ALMOST EXACTLY fifty years ago my father read me *The Hobbit* and *The Lord of the Rings* for the first time. This great gift, for which I am forever grateful, continued for the next two to three years as we reread the books even after I was able read them on my own. But there was no more bedtime reading after my parents divorced, and visits with my father were usually filled with more active pursuits. He did take me to the Ralph Bakshi *The Lord of the Rings* movie even though it was not showing in our part of New Jersey, and he helped with the various staffs, bows, and swords I made out of tree branches or scraps of wood. When the Bakshi film came to cable television, after watching it multiple times I had the idea of making a tape recording so that I could listen whenever I wanted (this was a year or two before the advent of affordable VCRs), and my father indulged me, tiptoeing around the apartment and even turning off the ringer on the phone and muffling his pager so that I could make a good recording with my cassette recorder sitting on the floor in front of the TV.

But Tolkien was not really a day-to-day part of my father's and my relationship; in the second half of high school and most of college I was focused on other things. So I was not expecting my father to reach back to our early bedtime readings when, in a time of crisis, he needed a metaphor to help me understand something important. Step

9 of most twelve-step programs is to make amends to the people one has hurt. I never thought my father was an alcoholic, so I was shocked and horrified when he called to tell me so and to say that he needed to apologize. I vividly remember standing in my apartment in Columbia, Missouri, my eyes flicking from the bare trees out the window to the fish obliviously swimming around in the aquarium while my hands trembled uncontrollably.

Because I did not think he had ever done anything to hurt me, and because the call was so upsetting, I tried to argue my father out of apologizing for anything at all. I even tried to convince him that there was no way that he could possibly be an alcoholic (denial, I have learned, can run just as deeply in family members as it does in people struggling with substance abuse). I kept interrupting, trying to reject the very premise of the conversation, and then he said: "It was like Frodo on Mount Doom. I could not take off the Ring. I just couldn't do it." And I understood, not because I knew anything about substance-abuse or recovery, but because the effects of the Ring on Frodo are the most profound and powerful representation of addiction that has ever been written.* My father's invocation of the story we had shared so many times and which we both felt so deeply enabled him to communicate some of what he needed to tell me. The words "Frodo at the Crack of Doom" made me listen, made me stop denying, stop trying to argue everything away. And for this reason neither that call and the twelve-step program it was a part of, nor the addiction that led to them, caused any break in my father's and my relationship. He continued his recovery and had twenty-five more years of his life's calling: healing the sick.

I have a vivid memory from when I was probably eight years old, very ill, shivering with fever and struggling to breathe. My father came home from the hospital, sat on the edge of my bed, listened to my chest with his stethoscope, held his hand on my forehead, and then without

* Despite there being absolutely no evidence that Tolkien or anyone close to him had a substance-abuse problem. The first scholar to note the addiction parallel was Shippey; *Road*, 139–40.

saying anything, picked up *The Fellowship of the Ring* from the nightstand and began to read:

> Frodo began to listen. At first the beauty of the melodies and of the interwoven words in elven-tongues, even though he understood them little, held him in a spell, as soon as he began to attend to them. Almost it seemed that the words took shape, and visions of far lands and bright things that he had never yet imagined opened out before him; and the firelit hall became like a golden mist above seas of foam that sighed upon the margins of the world. Then the enchantment became more and more dreamlike, until he felt that an endless river of swelling gold and silver was flowing over him, too multitudinous for its pattern to be comprehended; it became part of the throbbing air about him, and it drenched and drowned him. Swiftly he sank under its shining weight into a deep realm of sleep.[1]

Tolkien's words in my father's voice melted away the fear and discomfort, I was no longer so cold, and I saw that shimmering mist rise and felt myself swept along in the river of gold and silver as I drifted in and out of sleep and dreamed of music and water and light and warmth and peace.

Tolkien wrote that the theme of *Beowulf* is "within time, the monsters would win."[2] He was not wrong, and that theme is not limited to the poem. Within time the monsters always win, and so in early 2020, just before the pandemic, my father passed away from a series of complications from heart surgery. Until the week before he died he was telling me that he was fine, that there was nothing to worry about, that he would be getting back to work soon. But, while my son and I were visiting, he slipped into a final sleep, surrounded and lifted up, I hope and pray, on that same mist, which carried him into the river of gold and silver that I saw and felt so many years before.

❦

MY SON MITCHELL died from a fentanyl overdose in June of 2022. He was eighteen years old.

I read Mitchell *The Hobbit* when he was five, and I read it again, and *The Lord of the Rings*, and *The Silmarillion* to him when he was seven. He made me sing many of the poems, and I had to do voices for most of the characters. He got impatient with the Ents because they talked too slow: "Not Treebeard *again*!" he would say and roll over and pretend to sleep. When he was still small enough that we were playing baseball with a tennis ball, whenever the neighbor's oak tree got in the way of a home run he would say, sarcastically, "Thanks, Treebeard!" Mitchell came with me to various conferences and conventions. When he was only two years old, a vendor gave him several miniature orcs, which he would mix into the games he played with his cars and plastic animals. He kept, until it stopped working, the "Phial of Galadriel" someone had made out of a saltshaker and some LEDs, and he had a Ranger cloak that a woman from a Tolkien cosplay group sewed for him to go with his replica sword.

When we first started playing The Lord of the Rings Online, Mitchell was too young to really understand the user interface, but he knew that he liked the Fishing "hobby," and one time, when I left him alone at the computer too long, he sold all of his sister's characters' possessions and filled every storage spot with nightcrawlers so he could catch more fish. When he was a little older, he made his own character, which he named MitchellinMan, and he insisted on being a Lore-master (even though that was one of the most complicated classes) because he wanted to have a bear as an animal helper. He named it MommaBear. He liked having the bear defeat wolves and goblins.

One Saturday morning Mitchell and his sister were crawling around the house, snarling at each other. I asked them what they were playing:

"Baby Warg, Momma Warg," my daughter said. "Come on, Baby! Let's go back to the den."

"OK, Momma," said Mitchell.

"If you two are wargs," I asked, "what are your names? Bone-gnawer and Flesh-biter?"

Mitchell looked up at me: "She's Patches," he said. "I'm Cookie."

Then they both crawled off growling. I did wonder, after I was done laughing, if there was maybe a little too much Tolkien in our lives.

When he was fifteen, Mitchell took paperback copies of *The Fellowship of the Ring*, *The Two Towers*, and *The Return of the King* home from my office. Even though I had many nicer editions at home, he kept those three beaten-up volumes next to his bed. He must have brought those copies with him when he moved into his own place, because after he passed away and we cleaned out his apartment, they, and a new copy of *The Hobbit*, were among the things that came back home. The new copy of *The Hobbit* makes me wonder if he reread it and the other books in his last few months. I hope so.

In the first terrible days after Mitchell's passing I could do nothing but pace, frantically treading water in the great black wave of grief and anguish that had swept over us. "No taste of food, no feel of water, no sound of wind, no memory of tree or grass or flower, no image of moon or star" were left to me, either. All the good memories of eighteen years were locked behind a wall of overwhelming pain. I understood why Tolkien has Frodo say "I am naked in the dark,"[3] because that was exactly how it felt.

I wish I could write what I thought I would be writing when I reached this point in the book: that Tolkien's works were a consolation, that they took away my grief and sorrow. That would tie up the argument in a neat bow. I would be able to claim that the power of Tolkien's works to remediate grief and loss—which is enabled, or at least amplified, by their experiential nature and seeming truth—makes them psychologically and socially valuable, and that therefore their difference from other works of literature is actually superiority.

That all may be so, but I cannot use my own experience to support the claim. My grief over the death of my son has not healed, and absolutely nothing can ever fill the emptiness of his loss: He "is gone forever . . . and now all is dark and empty."[4] I wish I could say that reading *The Lord of the Rings* for the fiftieth time brought me to acceptance, even enlightenment, but I have experienced neither. Every time the house is too quiet I rediscover what the *Beowulf*-poet knew a thousand years ago: that upon the loss of a son, *an æfter anum* | *þuhte him eall to rum* [solitary on account of one, it seems to him that there is all too much room].[5] There is no real consolation, just things that can temporarily blunt the pain, distract from the loss, allow us to take another step, and then another, and to go on, and these have to be enough, because they are all we have.

Tolkien ends his essay "On Fairy-Stories" with a passage from "The Black Bull of Norroway" from Andrew Lang's *The Blue Fairy Book*. A washerwoman's daughter has endured a series of awful tasks, including climbing out of a valley of glass using iron shoes nailed to her feet. After much suffering, she is given three chances to wake a sleeping knight, her true love, with her singing, but each evening a witch gives the knight a sleeping potion. Down to her last chance, the girl laments:

> *"Seven long years I served for thee,*
> *The glassy hill I clamb for thee,*
> *The bluidy shirt I wrang for thee;*
> *And wilt thou not wauken and turn to me?"*
> He heard and turned to her.[6]

That last is the moment of eucatastrophe, when, even though logic and pattern-recognition and experience all combine to tell us that there will certainly be no happy ending—there is one. But in *our* story, on the very worst day, when the tears of his mother, father, and sister all fell upon his face, Mitchell did not waken and turn to us. He did not smile his enormous smile and laugh his deep laugh and ask us why we were crying. We were not in that kind of story. We do not live in that kind of world.

But we can imagine that world, one in which we get "a piercing glimpse of joy, and heart's desire, that for a moment passes outside the frame, rends indeed the very web of story, and lets a gleam through."[7] We can imagine that world because Tolkien created it for us, that world in which the horns of Rohan come at cockcrow, in which a standard unfurled on a ship with black sails shows a white tree and seven stars, in which Gandalf cries: "The realm of Sauron is ended!" and it is.[8] That this same Middle-earth is filled with heimweh and with so many other griefs and sorrows only helps us to believe that perhaps the sudden turn to the good, the eucatastrophe, may also happen in our own fallen existence, that we may catch a glimpse of the joy beyond the walls of the world because it is real.

All our towers become ruins; theirs, and ours, is the fate of everything caught in the stream of time. "Men, each man and all men, and all their works shall die."[9] In a moment of great despair, Sam sings "Beyond all towers strong and high" and, beyond hope, a voice answers him.[10] There is more in the world than the works of man, more than the sum of our ambitions.[11] The ruin cannot bring back the tower, nor redeem its fall, but it shows us that beauty can arise from loss. The toppled statue garlanded with flowers catches the light of the setting sun and we know: "They cannot conquer forever."[12]

I wrote that Tolkien's works were not a true consolation for me because they did not assuage the pain of the loss of a child, but that is an impossible standard. No literature or art or music, no work of human hands or mind can bring back my son, and nothing less could close the wound his death made. What art *can* do is to give shape and form to grief and loss, which does not take away the pain but does, in some strange way, make it able to be borne. In Tolkien's works we find beauty rising out of catastrophe: A light springs from the shadows, a single star gleams high above the cloud-wrack, and we see a path toward a place not free of sorrow, but in which tears are blessed without bitterness because beyond the circles of the world there is more than memory. We find hope.

ACKNOWLEDGMENTS

This book is the product of several decades of research and teaching, so the number of people to whom I owe thanks is enormous. I have spoken about Tolkien for hundreds of hours with students, alumni, colleagues, friends, acquaintances, audience members, tour participants, and even strangers on airplanes. Each of those conversations added something to my understanding of the man and his works, but limits of time and space force me to thank most of these people en masse and only mention here those who directly helped me with some identifiable aspect of this particular book.

The Tower and the Ruin would still be in the state of being "80 percent finished for eight years" if my editor, Daniel Gerstle, had not reached out and suggested that I send him a proposal for a book on Tolkien. I am grateful for his support and guidance, and especially for his patience. Thanks also to Zeba Arora for her help and patience, and to Rebecca Rider for her superb copyediting.

Roger, Christine, and Fez Silk have encouraged and generously supported my research and teaching for over a decade, enabling me to do work that otherwise would have been impossible. Many hours of conversation about Tolkien with Fez are reflected throughout this book.

My colleagues at Wheaton College have for twenty-seven years not just tolerated my obsessions but have contributed their insights, knowledge, guidance, and encouragement. I'm proud to be a member of the best English department at a small liberal arts college and want to especially thank Beverly Lyon Clark†, Sam Coale, Shawn Christian, Sue Standing, Winter Jade Werner, and Wesley Jacques. Outside the department, Joel Relihan, Betsey Dexter Dyer, Evie Staudinger, and my research partners Mark LeBlanc and Michael J. Kahn contributed immensely to the development of many of the arguments in this book. I am also grateful to Wheaton College for the Fall 2023 sabbatical leave that allowed me to write the bulk of the first draft, and for the Mars, Hood, Gebbie, and Clemence summer fellowships that supported so many faculty-student research partnerships over the years.

The generosity and kindness of Christopher Tolkien† enabled me to get my start in the world of Tolkien scholarship, and I am grateful to him and to Cathleen Blackburn for their patience with a junior scholar learning how to navigate academia and fandom.

Since co-founding the journal *Tolkien Studies* in 2001, I have had the privilege of reading and editing two decades of much of the very best scholarship on Tolkien, all of which has influenced this book. I cannot thank enough my co-editors, Douglas A. Anderson, Verlyn Flieger, David Bratman, and Yvette Kisor, who have taught me far more than they can know, as has Tom Shippey, who has also been a friend and mentor for almost my whole career. Other colleagues in academia have also generously supported and encouraged my work, and I want to thank especially Robert Bjork, Richard Gallant, Patrick Conner, Geoffrey Russom, Patrizia Lendinara, Helen Damico†, and most of all, my teachers, Peggy Knapp, John Miles Foley†, and my *Doktorvater* Allen J. Frantzen, who taught me how to be a scholar.

I think of Mary Dockray-Miller, Susan Rosser, Stephen Harris, Gergely Nagy, and Marcel Bülles primarily as friends, but they are also colleagues who have encouraged, challenged, corrected, and improved my research. I am grateful for Peizhen Wu's research collaboration, though I value her kindness and friendship even more. For almost twenty years John Alexander has been my producer, editor, tour manager, and most of all, friend. I am grateful to him and to all those who accompanied me on "Imagining Middle-earth" in 2022 and all the other participants on Scholarly Sojourns I have had the privilege to "lead" over the years, especially Kimberly Kobayashi, Jo Mooney, Noelle Carter, and the Gunn family.

Since I was first introduced to him as "The Tolkien Professor" (ahem), Corey Olsen has been unfailingly generous, encouraging, and insightful. I want to thank him for all his support through Signum University, and I am particularly grateful to Amy Troolin and my "Creator's Circle": Liza Gold-Nyden, Tom Hillman, David Maddock, Takako Tasai, and Matthew DeForrest, all of whom read this book in serial draft and gave invaluable advice and even more precious encouragement throughout the entire process. Chris Pierson of The Lord of the Rings Online has been a collaborator and friend for almost two decades, and I can never repay him for the kingly gift of Mitchell's Pond. I am also honored to be a shirttail cousin in the ALEP family; special thanks to Mr. Baggins, the Grey Wizard, Eowyn Shieldmaiden, Frodan G., and Alassea Envinyatore (and so many others) for all your kindness and generosity.

Except for my family, the most important contributors to my work over nearly thirty years have been my students at Wheaton College. Special thanks to Laura Comoletti, Hilary Wynne, Kate Malone Hesser, John Walsh, Amy Tucker West, Christopher Scotti, Laura Kalafarski, Melissa Higgins Maleri, Lorien Lawrence, Melissa Patricio, Stephanie Olsen, Rachel Scavera, Courtney LaBrie, Leah Smith, Namiko Hitotsubashi, Simone Hartwell-Ishikawa Quinn, Suzanne Lima Pickford, Elie Chauvet, Emily Bowman, Phoebe Boyd, Benny Berger, Mei Ling MacDougall, Kathryn Paar, Kieran Paar, Adrienne Green, Rebecca Epstein, Jillian Valerio, Rowan Lowell, Lauren and Jason Rea, Tara McGoldrick, Elizabeth Peterson, Jonathan Gerkin, Wenzhu Shi, Julia Huang, Helen Meng, Olivia Bullock, Marissa Gamache, Hannah Abraham, Caiden Kumar, Emily Bues, Tyler Thoms, David Sharp, and Lillianna Brenneis.

There are not words to express my gratitude to Christianne Noll, Bill Goldbloom Bloch, Deyonne Bryant, and Paula Smith-MacDonald. Without their carrying me through the darkest time there would be no book, and perhaps not much of anything else, either.

But none of this would have been possible or worth doing without the love and encouragement of Raquel, Rhys, and Mitchell† (and Lancelot and Percival). My deepest wish is that we are not bound to the circles of the world and beyond them is more than memory.

CONVENTIONS

Because there are so many editions of *The Hobbit* and *The Lord of the Rings*, citations will be by book and chapter as well as by page number (referenced to the editions listed on the following pages). Thus a citation from *The Fellowship of the Ring*, Book II, Chapter iv, page 318 is written: *FR*, II, iv, 318. References to the appendices of *The Lord of the Rings* are abbreviated by appendix, section, and subsection, so Subsection iii of Section I of Appendix A is written (*RK*, Appendix A, I, iii, 321). The Silmarillion indicates the body of stories and poems developed over many years by Tolkien; *The Silmarillion* indicates the volume first published in 1977.

ABBREVIATIONS

WORKS BY TOLKIEN

ATB — *The Adventures of Tom Bombadil.* Eds. Christina Scull and Wayne G. Hammond. 50th anniversary ed. London: HarperCollins, 2014.

B&C — *Beowulf and the Critics.* Ed. Michael D.C. Drout. Rev. 2nd ed. Tempe, AZ: Arizona Medieval and Renaissance Texts and Studies, 2011.

B&L — *Beren and Lúthien.* Ed. Christopher Tolkien. Boston: Houghton Mifflin Harcourt, 2017.

Beowulf T&C — *Beowulf: A Translation and Commentary Together with Sellic Spell.* Ed. Christopher Tolkien. Boston: Houghton Mifflin, 2014.

Children — *The Children of Húrin* Ed. Christopher Tolkien. Boston: Houghton Mifflin, 2007.

FR — *The Fellowship of the Ring.* (First published: London: Allen and Unwin; Boston: Houghton Mifflin, 1954.) 2nd ed., rev. impression. Boston: Houghton Mifflin, 1987.

Gondolin — *The Fall of Gondolin.* Ed. Christopher Tolkien. Boston: Houghton Mifflin Harcourt, 2018.

H — *The Hobbit.* (First published: London: Allen and Unwin, 1937.) Boston: Houghton Mifflin, 1966.

KL4 — *Klaeber's Beowulf,* Eds. R. D. Fulk, Robert E. Bjork, and John D. Niles. 4th ed. Toronto: University of Toronto Press, 2008.

Kullervo — *The Story of Kullervo.* Ed. Verlyn Flieger. Boston: Houghton Mifflin Harcourt, 2016.

Lays — *The Lays of Beleriand.* Ed. Christopher Tolkien. Boston: Houghton Mifflin, 1985.

Letters — *The Letters of J.R.R. Tolkien.* Revised and Expanded Edition. Ed. Humphrey Carpenter, with the assistance of Christopher Tolkien. London: HarperCollins, 2023.

Lost Road	*The Lost Road and Other Writings*. Ed. Christopher Tolkien. Boston: Houghton Mifflin, 1987.
Lost Tales I	*The Book of Lost Tales, Part One*. Ed. Christopher Tolkien. Boston: Houghton Mifflin, 1984.
Lost Tales II	*The Book of Lost Tales, Part Two*. Ed. Christopher Tolkien. Boston: Houghton Mifflin, 1984.
MC	*The Monsters and the Critics and Other Essays*. London: Allen & Unwin, 1983.
Morgoth	*Morgoth's Ring*. Ed. Christopher Tolkien. Boston: Houghton Mifflin, 1993.
OFS	*Tolkien On Fairy-Stories*. (Essay first published 1947.) Extended edition, ed. Verlyn Flieger and Douglas A. Anderson. London: HarperCollins, 2008.
Peoples	*The Peoples of Middle-earth*. Ed. Christopher Tolkien. Boston: Houghton Mifflin, 1996.
RK	*The Return of the King*. (First published: London: Allen and Unwin, 1955.) 2nd ed., rev. impression. Boston: Houghton Mifflin, 1987.
S	*The Silmarillion*. Ed. Christopher Tolkien. Boston: Houghton Mifflin, 1977.
Sauron	*Sauron Defeated*. Ed. Christopher Tolkien. Boston: Houghton Mifflin, 1992.
Shadow	*The Return of the Shadow*. Ed. Christopher Tolkien. Boston: Houghton Mifflin, 1988.
T&L	*Tree and Leaf*. London: Unwin Books, 1964.
TT	*The Two Towers*. (First published: London: Allen and Unwin, 1954.) 2nd ed., rev. impression. Boston: Houghton Mifflin, 1987.
Treason	*The Treason of Isengard*. Ed. Christopher Tolkien. Boston: Houghton Mifflin, 1989.
UT	*Unfinished Tales of Númenor and Middle-earth*. Ed. Christopher Tolkien. Boston: Houghton Mifflin, 1980.
WJ	*The War of the Jewels*. Ed. Christopher Tolkien. Boston: Houghton Mifflin, 1994.
WR	*The War of the Ring*. Ed. Christopher Tolkien. Boston: Houghton Mifflin, 1990.

REFERENCE WORKS

Artist Wayne G. Hammond and Christina Scull. *J.R.R. Tolkien: Artist and Illustrator.* London: HarperCollins; Boston: Houghton Mifflin, 1995.

Author Tom Shippey. *J.R.R. Tolkien: Author of the Century.* New York: William Morrow, 2002.

Bio Humphrey Carpenter. *J.R.R. Tolkien: A Biography.* London: Allen and Unwin, 1977. As *Tolkien: A Biography.* Boston: Houghton Mifflin, 1977.

Chronology Christina Scull and Wayne G. Hammond. *The J.R.R. Tolkien Companion and Guide*, vol. 1, *Chronology.* New York: Houghton Mifflin Harcourt, 2006.

Guide Christina Scull and Wayne G. Hammond. *The J.R.R. Tolkien Companion and Guide*, vol. 2, *Reader's Guide.* New York: Houghton Mifflin Harcourt, 2006.

Road Tom Shippey. *The Road to Middle-earth.* London: Allen and Unwin; New York: Houghton Mifflin, 1982.

NOTES

Introduction: Son and Father

1. *H*, I, 10.
2. *Shadow*, 42; *UT*, 266–67; *Shadow*, 28, 37; John D. Rateliff, *The History of the Hobbit, Part I: Mr. Baggins*, 2 vols. (Boston: Houghton Mifflin, 2007), 374.
3. The first is an error in stress, common in words from foreign languages with unknown stress patterns, the other two the result of a process called *monophthongization*, in which the two vowel sounds of a diphthong like /au/ or /eo/ become a single sound.
4. Initially Tom Shippey, Verlyn Flieger, and Jane Chance.
5. As Tolkien said of *Beowulf* in his famous "*Beowulf*: The Monsters and the Critics," lecture; *MC*, 9.
6. John Keats, *Lamia, Isabella, The Eve of St. Agnes and Other Poems* (London: Taylor and Hessey, 1820), 41; *FR*, II, ii, 272.
7. See *Road*, 96–97, 101–3.
8. Richard P. Feynman, *The Pleasure of Finding Things Out: The Best Short Works of Richard P. Feynman* (New York: Basic Books, 2005).
9. Paul Kocher, *Master of Middle-earth: The Achievement of J.R.R. Tolkien* (London: Thames and Hudson, 1972), 1–18.
10. Christina Scull, "Opening Address." *Mallorn: The Journal of the Tolkien Society* 33 (1995): 10; Chris Pierson, Standing Stone Games, personal communication with author.
11. "The Rohirrim, the Anglo-Saxons, and the Problem of Appendix F: Ambiguity and Reference in Tolkien's Books and Jackson's Films," in *Picturing Tolkien: Essays on the Peter Jackson Lord of the Rings Trilogy*, ed. Janice M. Bogstad and Philip E. Kaveny (Jefferson, NC: McFarland, 2011), 248–63.
12. *TT*, III, viii, 164.
13. *FR*, I, vii, 142.
14. Tom Shippey, "Light-Elves, Dark-Elves, and Others: Tolkien's Elvish Problem," *Tolkien Studies* 1 (2004): 1–15.
15. *Letters*, #211, 399, although he forgot to remove (or chose to leave in) the reins that Frodo uses to check the horse to a walk at the Ford of Bruinen; *FR*, I, xii, 225.
16. See Douglas C. Kane, *Arda Reconstructed: The Creation of the Published Silmarillion* (Bethlehem, PA: Lehigh University Press, 2011).
17. *MC*, 7–8.
18. For an explication, see *Road*, 46–48.
19. *MC*, 23.
20. KL4, line 955a; *Völsunga Saga*, Chapter 12; Wilhelm Ranisch, ed., *Die Völsungasaga* (Berlin: Mayer and Müller, 1891), 20; *FR*, II, iii, 297.
21. *RK*, VI, ix 311.

CHAPTER 1. ORIGINS

1. Tolkien relates the story in his 1955 letter to W. H. Auden, which is the source of a large portion of the most famous autobiographical details of Tolkien's writing. This letter should be read with an understanding of its audience, purpose, and rhetorical effect, not merely accepted uncritically; *Letters*, #163, 309–16. Tolkien tells substantially the same story in his 1968 BBC interview; see Stewart D. Lee, " 'Tolkien in Oxford' (BBC, 1968): A Reconstruction," *Tolkien Studies* 15 (2018): 115–76.
2. John D. Rateliff, *The History of the Hobbit, Part 1: Mr. Baggins*, 2 vols. (Boston: Houghton Mifflin, 2007), xi–xxvi.
3. *Bio*, 92. I will follow the *Tolkien Studies* convention of using "the Silmarillion" to indicate the frequently revised and never completed accumulation of stories and poems set in the same imagined world (Arda, of which Middle-earth is just a part) and *The Silmarillion* to indicate the volume edited by Christopher Tolkien and published in 1977.

   "Vast backcloths" comes from Tolkien's famous 1951 letter to Milton Waldman; *Letters*, #131, 203.

   "Goblin Feet," Tolkien's first published poem, was written in April 1915 and published later that year in *Oxford Poetry*; Scull and Hammond, *Chronology*, 340. Tolkien told Humphrey Carpenter that he wrote it for his wife, Edith, who liked "spring and flowers and trees, and little elfin people"; *Bio*, 75. Later he claimed to loathe the tiny goblins and fairies cliché; *Lost Tales I*, 32; *Lost Tales II*, 267–69. The poem is also reprinted with invaluable commentary in John Garth, *Tolkien and the Great War: The Threshold of Middle-earth* (Boston: Houghton Mifflin, 2003), 44–47. *Bio*, 70–71.
4. Similarly, interpretations, insights, and investigations all have their own nested origins and origins of origins. One of this chapter's is John Garth's groundbreaking article " 'The Road from Adaptation to Invention': How Tolkien Came to the Brink of Middle-earth in 1914," *Tolkien Studies* 11 (2014): 1–44. None of my discussion of the evolution of Tolkien's earliest writings would have been possible if Garth had not comprehensively identified and traced the influence of Tolkien's most important early sources from his initial literary works through to his legendarium. In what follows, I will be tracing a particular section of that complex web, but it was Garth who identified all the initial connections.
5. Tom Shippey argues that Tolkien was likely to have read through *The Denham Tracts* when he was a professor at Leeds; Tom Shippey, "The Ancestors of the Hobbits: Strange Creatures in English Folklore," *Lembas-extra* (2011): 97–106. John Rateliff, however, thinks it unlikely that Tolkien had seen the word *hobbit* in written form before he coined it. *The History of The Hobbit, Part Two: Return to Bag End*, 2 vols. (Boston: Houghton Mifflin, 2007), 841–49 at 849. When Google's Ngram Viewer was first made available to the public, *Tolkien Studies* was deluged with articles claiming to have found the origins of *hobbit* in a variety of unlikely sources, including a word, *hobbet*, which was a measure of grain. The most plausible of these potential origins was the great six-volume *English Dialect Dictionary* of Joseph Wright, who was one of Tolkien's tutors at Oxford, but Wright prints *hob*, not *hobbit*, and says it is a type of supernatural creature like a hobgoblin. Although Tolkien definitely would have used this dictionary, it seems unlikely that he read every single word or that he was inspired to invent *hobbit* by the entry on *hob*.
6. Carpenter's not being sufficiently well-informed about Anglo-Saxon poetry and J.R.R. and Christopher Tolkien's having followed one particular out-of-date convention (which was never widely adopted) has sown considerable confusion in both pop-

ular writing and (sadly) scholarship about the source of Tolkien's inspiration. The title Carpenter used, *Crist*, is the Old English spelling of *Christ*, which is the conventional name of the first three poems (although until the 1920s they were was often taken to be a single poem) in the Exeter Book manuscript of Old English poetry. For a short while the affected spelling *Crist* was used for the three poems in question, but as the conventional titles of all the other poems in the manuscript are in Modern English, it makes little sense to title only this poem in Old English, and no one has—except in writing about Tolkien's work—since the 1930s.

Additionally, it is now understood that what Albert S. Cook claimed was a single "poem in three parts" on Christ is actually three separate poems copied one after the other into the manuscript: The opening lines of each poem are written in all capital letters, and the subjects and styles are quite distinctively different. The subject of *Christ I* is the Advent, *Christ II* the Ascension, and *Christ III* the Last Judgment. The poet Cynewulf included his runic signature in *Christ II*, but the poem in which Tolkien found the word *Earendel* is *Christ I* (ll, 104–8).

Therefore, the standard formulation, taken primarily from Carpenter, that Tolkien was inspired by the poem *Crist* written by Cynewulf is almost guaranteed to produce confusion: Cynewulf did not write the poem that inspired Tolkien; there is no poem called *Crist* in the Anglo-Saxon Poetic Records; and scholarship about the poem that did influence Tolkien is indexed under *Christ I* (or, less commonly, *Christ A*). For the sake of clarity, scholars writing about Tolkien should call the poem *Christ I* and not attribute it to Cynewulf.

Because every manuscript is unique, a given manuscript is cited by its *shelfmark*, which indicates where it is physically located. The shelfmark for the Exeter Book is "Exeter, Cathedral Library, Dean and Chapter 3501."

7. George Philip Krapp and Elliott Van Kirk Dobbie, *The Exeter Book*, vol. 3 of The Anglo-Saxon Poetic Records (New York: Columbia University Press, 1936), 6.
8. Unless otherwise noted, all translations from Old English, Old Norse, and Latin are my own.
9. Garth, "Road from Adaptation to Invention," 1–2.
10. Shelley uses the same visual arrangement as Tolkien's Earendel poem in "The Cloud."
11. Although Garth's subtle reading finds loose connections between Tolkien's astronomical mariner and the story of the nymph pursued by the river-god in Shelley's poem, these are at best minor and tangential. Garth, "Road from Adaptation to Invention,"16–18.
12. Garth discovered that in Tolkien's notebook (Oxford, Bodleian Library, MS Tolkien A21/9 fol. 4r), the half-line is written *ofer yþa ful*, substituting <þ> for <ð> (Garth, "Road from Adaptation to Invention," 38n27). The two Old English graphemes <þ> [*thorn*] and <ð> [*eth*] are phonetically identical (they both indicate the sounds Modern English represents with the digraph <th>), so the substitution probably indicates that Tolkien was not directly copying his edition of *Beowulf*, but writing from memory—although I can attest that it is very easy for a scholar reasonably fluent in the language to substitute a *thorn* for an *eth*—and vice versa—even when copying Old English directly from an edition or manuscript.
13. Tolkien discusses how *Éala Éarendel engla beorhtost* inspired him, and his identification of Earendel as Venus, in a draft 1967 letter to a "Mr. Rang"; *Letters*, #297, 542–43.
14. The Blickling Homilies (shelfmark Princeton, Scheide Library, MS 71) are a collection of Old English sermons from the tenth century, generally considered to be written somewhat earlier than the other great anonymous Anglo-Saxon homily-collection, the Vercelli Book. In the Épinal-Erfurt glossary, a list of Latin words and

their Anglo-Saxon equivalents dating from the very end of the seventh or the beginning of the eighth century, *earendel* is equated to *jubar* [brightest, the light of dawn].

15. See Benjamin W. Fortson IV, *Indo-European Language and Culture*, 2nd ed. (Oxford: Wiley-Blackwell, 2010), 367.
16. Eventually that light would come from the silmaril that Earendel was carrying, but in 1914 that story had not yet been envisioned.
17. *FR*, II, i, 246–49; *RK*, Appendix A, I, i, 314; *S*, XXIV, 246–55.
18. This phrase is from a letter of April 30, 1970, that Tolkien wrote to Tom Shippey (*Road*, xviii).
19. *Letters*, #163, 313.
20. Jane Chance, *Tolkien's Art: "A Mythology for England"* (London: Macmillan, 1979).
21. "May you say the things I have tried to say long after I am not there to say them," *Bio*, 89.
22. See Michael D.C. Drout and Hilary Wynne, "Tom Shippey's *J.R.R. Tolkien: Author of the Century* and a Look Back at Tolkien Criticism since 1982," *Envoi* 9, no. 2 (2000): 101–67 at 111–13; Anders Stenström, "A Mythology? For England?" in *Proceedings of the J.R.R. Tolkien Centenary Conference*, eds. Patricia Reynolds and Glen GoodKnight (Milton Keynes, UK: Tolkien Society, 1996), 310–14; Verlyn Flieger, *Splintered Light: Logos and Language in Tolkien's World* (Kent, OH: The Kent State University Press, 2002); Dimitra Fimi: *Tolkien, Race, and Cultural History: From Fairies to Hobbits* (New York: Palgrave Macmillan, 2009), 53–56.
23. Allen and Unwin, Tolkien's eventual publisher, had decided that they could not publish *The Silmarillion*; *Letters*, #131, 201–33. Fimi, *Tolkien, Race, and Cultural History*, 129–30.

    C.S. Lewis's statement—"Tollers, there is too little of what we really like in stories. I am afraid we shall have to try and write some ourselves"—should not be interpreted, as it sometimes is, as indicating that, at that moment, Tolkien decided it was time to create a mythology; *Bio*, 170.
24. *Bio*, 89, Carpenter's emphasis. The quote about the *Kalevala* does not appear in Tolkien's published *Letters*; Carpenter had access to more material than was eventually published.
25. *Letters*, #1 and #4, 3–5.
26. *Letters*, #5, 5–7.
27. *Letters*, #163, 312–13.
28. *Letters*, #131, 202–4. See Flieger, *Splintered Light*, for a penetrating analysis of Tolkien's rhetoric in this letter, and note her explanation of his apparent self-deprecation; xiv–xv.
29. The best and most influential book on Tolkien, Tom Shippey's *Road*, does take as its starting point an understanding of a connection between the objects of Tolkien's academic study and his literary works. In some ways much of what follows is just a gloss on Shippey (whose book I have wished I had written since I read it for the first time in 1996), but my emphasis is somewhat different.
30. *Letters*, #163, 312–13.
31. *Letters*, #163, 313.
32. Tolkien was sent to Furness Auxiliary Hospital in Harrogate, Yorkshire, around February 27, 1917. He had started writing *Gondolin* at the "end of 1916–first half of 1917" and was still writing it in Spring 1917, when he was in Roos, Holderness, so it is entirely possible that he was working on the story while in hospital at Harrogate; *Chronology*, 97, 99.
33. H. Rider Haggard, *Eric Brighteyes* (London: Longman, 1891).
34. *Laxdæla Saga* is probably the biggest influence, but Haggard borrows plots points,

scenes, and characters from the rest of the "big five" sagas: *Egil's Saga*, *Njal's Saga*, *Eyrbyggja Saga*, and *Grettis Saga*.

35. Haggard, *Eric Brighteyes*, xix.
36. "The novel is written in the distinctive style of contemporary Victorian saga translations," Heather O'Donoghue, *Old Norse-Icelandic Literature: A Short Introduction* (Oxford: Blackwell, 2004), 164–65.
37. One exception in *Eric Brighteyes* may be the narration of the prophetic dream of Asmund the Priest at the very beginning of the novel, assuming that a dream is the equivalent of inner thoughts. Elsewhere in the novel readers learn of dreams because characters retell them to other characters.
38. *Egil's Saga*, trans. Bernard Scudder (New York: Penguin, 1997), 122–24.
39. *Njal's Saga*, trans. Robert Cook (New York: Penguin Books, 1997), 106–7, 160.
40. Haggard, *Eric Brighteyes*, 80–81.
41. Chrystalla Thoma, "The Function of the Historical Present Tense: Evidence from Modern Greek," *Journal of Pragmatics* 43 (2011): 2373–91.
42. Paul Kiparsky, "Tense and Mood in Indo-European Syntax," *Foundations of Language* 4, no. 1 (1968): 30–57. This article continued an unbroken tradition of every article that I have read by Kiparsky illuminating multiple features of language, not just the one I was searching for information about. See also Nessa Wolfson, "The Conversational Historical Present Alternation," *Language* 55, no.1 (1979): 168–82.
43. Monika Flundernik, "The Historical Present Tense Yet Again: Switching and Narrative Dynamics in Oral and Quasi-Oral Storytelling," *Text* 11 (1991): 365–98.
44. I believe that Atwood's use of historical present in her novel is intended to reflect the protagonist's knowledge of Latin histories—and therefore her education and reading—before the imposition of the oppressive totalitarian system. Margaret Atwood, *The Handmaid's Tale* (Boston: Houghton Mifflin, 1985); John Updike, *Rabbit, Run* (New York: Alfred A. Knopf, 1960).
45. The evaluation of the lack of consensus is Ludger Zeevaert's; the hypothesized explanation is my own. Ludger Zeevaert, "The Historical Present Tense in the Earliest Textual Transmission of *Njál's Saga*: An example of Synchronic Linguistic Variation in Fourteenth-Century Icelandic *Njáls Saga* Manuscripts," in *New Studies in the Manuscript Tradition of Njáls Saga: The historia mutila of Njála*, eds. Emily Lethbridge and Svanhildur Óskarsdóttir (Kalamazoo, MI: Medieval Institute Publications, 2018), 149–78.
46. Zeevaert, "Historical Present Tense," 166.
47. Haggard, *Eric Brighteyes*, 11.
48. See Christina Scull and Wayne Hammond's entry on Haggard in the revised and expanded edition of their *Reader's Guide*, Vol. III (London: HarperCollins, 2017), 355–58. In the drafts of "*Beowulf:* The Monsters and the Critics," Tolkien asserts that Haggard's novel is "as good (if rather longer) and as heroic" as most traditional hero-tales; *B&C*, 90. Oronzo Cilli, *Tolkien's Library: An Annotated Checklist* (Edinburgh: Luna Press Publishing 2019), items 907–914, 111–112. Jamie Williamson, in his excellent guide to the evolution of modern fantasy states that "Tolkien read all the Haggard that he could get his hands on, and (along with Morris) Haggard was the only modern writer he would concede as an influence"; Jamie Williamson, *The Evolution of Modern Fantasy: From Antiquarianism to the Ballantine Adult Fantasy Series* (New York: Palgrave Macmillan, 2015), 205n36. See also Dale Nelson, "Literary Influences: Nineteenth and Twentieth Centuries" in *J.R.R. Tolkien Encyclopedia: Scholarship and Critical Assessment*, ed. Michael D.C. Drout (New York: Routledge, 2007, 366–78 at 369.
49. *Guide*, 1054.

50. Page-number references are for *Gondolin*: 52, 69, 72 (one initial sentence), 80 (one initial sentence), 86 (full paragraph), 86 (one medial sentence), 88–89 (most of a paragraph), 90 (most of a long paragraph), 90 (most of a paragraph), 94 (one medial sentence in a long paragraph), 95 (two medial sentences in a long paragraph), 97 (two initial sentences in along paragraph), 98 (complete short paragraph), 98 (two initial sentences in along paragraph), 99 (two terminal sentences in a long paragraph), 103 (one clause of past-tense sentence in past-tense paragraph).
51. *Gondolin*, 52–53.
52. *Gondolin*, 86.
53. Tolkien said that his enthusiasm for Finnish nearly caused him to fail his important Honour Moderations examinations; *Letters*, #163, 313.
54. *Letters*, #163, 312.
55. See *Chronology*, 29, for Tolkien's checking out from the library Finnish grammars and material related to the *Kalevala* on November 25, 1911.
56. *Letters*, #1, 3. For more discussion of how this initial form is also related to the Icelandic sagas, and how it developed into an important characteristic of the structure of *The Lord of the Rings*, see Carl Phelpstead, "'With Chunks of Poetry in Between': *The Lord of the Rings* and Saga Poetics," *Tolkien Studies* 5 (2008): 23–38.
57. J.R.R. Tolkien "'The Story of Kullervo' and Essays on *Kalevala*," ed. Verlyn Flieger. *Tolkien Studies* 7 (2010): 211–78. J.R.R. Tolkien, *The Story of Kullervo*, ed. Verlyn Flieger (Boston: William Morrow, 2015).
58. Karelia includes both southeastern Finland and the area of western Russia upon which it borders. Portions of Russian Karelia were part of Finland until they were seized by Russia after the Winter War and World War II. They were "ethnically cleansed" of Finns, and the territory has not been returned.

    In classifying the *Kalevala* as "medieval," I am following a long scholarly tradition and going against the grain of some more recent criticism. Some scholars, particularly from what I describe to my students as "the era of overzealous 'debunking'" in the 1970s, asserted that the published *Kalevala* is a nineteenth-century text authored by Lönnrot and therefore tells us nothing about the Middle Ages. This is a good example of throwing out the baby with the bathwater: Although there is certainly a great deal of nineteenth-century influence on the structure and theme of the final work, and we should not assume that anything like the *Kalevala* as a whole ever existed, comparison of the published *Kalevala* with the material in the archive of Lönnrot's collections has convinced more recent scholars that the stories themselves—and the charms and songs that appear within some of them—came from Lönnrot's traditional informants, not from the collector himself; Lauri Honko, "*The Kalevala* and the World's Epics: An Introduction," in *Religion, Myth and Folklore in the World's Epics*, ed. Lauri Honko (Berlin: de Gruyter, 1990), 1–28. Lauri Harvilahti, "The Production of Finnish Epic Poetry: Fixed Wholes or Creative Compositions," *Oral Tradition* 7, no. 1 (1992): 87–101.
59. *Runos* are equivalent to *cantos* or chapters.
60. The stress system of English makes finding alliterating words that can be squeezed into the eight syllables of a trochaic tetrameter line an almost impossible challenge, in contrast to Finnish, in which all words are accented on the first syllable, ensuring that the first two syllables in a word will form a trochee. Finnish is also much more heavily and consistently inflected than English, allowing for greater compression: The small, unstressed words that English requires for indicating grammatical relations are handled by unstressed inflectional endings in Finnish. Tolkien was later to become a master of alliterative poetry in both Old and Modern English, but even he must have found it too difficult to force English into a form that had evolved in Finn-

ish. Tolkien's alliterative poems use the Old English stress-based system, which does not depend on a fixed count of syllables. All major poetic translations of the *Kalevala* into English use trochaic tetrameter, and none employs alliteration. It was only after writing this section that I discovered Iwona Piechnik's valuable essay, which I strongly recommend, that compares the *Kalavala* with both Kirby's and Tolkien's translations. Iwona Piechnik, "Finnic Tetrameter in J.R.R. Tolkien's *The Story of Kullervo* in Comparison to W. F. Kirby's English Translation of the *Kalevala*," *Studia Linguistica Universitatis Iagellonicae Cracoviensis* 138, no. 4 (2021): 201–20.

61. There is no reason to consider these close correspondences as some kind of plagiarism: Tolkien never tried to publish this work, and starting with another author's work and then modifying it until it is no longer recognizable stylistically is a form of adaptation, not plagiarism. We only know that Tolkien worked this way because he left off work on *The Story of Kullervo* before he had completed the process of transformation.
62. I do not think an alternative interpretation of the evidence—that Tolkien found himself unable to compose a full-length poem in trochaic tetrameter—is warranted. Tolkien's poetic passages do not seem particularly labored, nor does he regularly depart from the metrical pattern, so I think we can safely conclude that he had developed some facility in this kind of poetic composition.
63. *There was a dwelling of Kings ere the world was waxen old;*
    Dukes were the door-wards there, and the roofs were thatched with gold:
    Earls were the wrights that wrought it, and silver nailed its doors.

    Tolkien called this "not in itself a good meter"; *B&C*, 116n2.
64. Archibald Strong took this approach to translating *Beowulf* for his 1925 *Beowulf, Translated into Modern English Rhyming Verse*, which, Tolkien wrote, was "on the whole the best English translation of *Beowulf* that I know, though it is more a transformation than a close representation of the original, since, in spite of the reasons urged by the translator, I remain of the opinion that he selected of all those available the one metre most foreign in mood and style to the original (the metre used by Morris in *Sigurd*); *B&C* 116n2a. As bizarre as it now seems to us to translate one poetic form into an entirely different—and not particularly good—poetic form, we can infer that even as late as 1925, a poem needed to be presented in translation as another poem (a prose translation was a mere "trot" for the purposes of aiding student translation), and poems were required to have at least some formal characteristics, as the era of free verse had not yet arrived.
65. See *Chronology*, 51.
66. As Phelpstead explains, "'With Chunks of Poetry in Between,'" 23–38.
67. *H*, I, 24.
68. *H*, IV, 71–72; *H*, VI, 116–17.
69. *H*, VIII, 170–71; *H*, XIX, 313.
70. J.R.R. Tolkien, *The Annotated Hobbit*, ed. Douglas A. Anderson, rev. ed. (Boston: Houghton Mifflin, 2002), 92n8.
71. Gergely Nagy, "'The Great Chain of Reading: (Inter)Textual Relations and the Technique of Mythopoesis in the Túrin Story," in *Tolkien the Medievalist*, ed. Jane Chance (New York: Routledge, 2002), 239–58. This is one of the most insightful articles ever written about Tolkien's works.
72. *B&C*, 341–437.
73. *Letters*, #163, 313.
74. First, I do not see how that could be done any better than in John Garth's investigation. Second, although this kind of reconstruction is obviously valuable for numerous reasons, it does not particularly help identify the ineffable quality of medieval works

that Tolkien sought to reproduce—and succeeded in creating—in his own writing. Third, as Jamie Williamson argues, in fundamental ways such "retrojection" can occlude the actual literary history; *The Evolution of Modern Fantasy*, 12–23. Retrojection would lead us to conclude erroneously that *because* Tolkien saw a map in *The Marvelous Land of Snergs*, he therefore decided to include a map in *The Hobbit*. The actual process by which Tolkien came to use the map is almost certainly very different. E. A. Wyke-Smith, *The Marvelous Land of Snergs* (Baltimore, MD: Old Earth Books, 1996).

75. *FR*, Prologue, 11.
76. See Douglas A. Anderson, "R.W. Chambers and *The Hobbit*," *Tolkien Studies* 3 (2006): 137–47.
77. *Chronology*, 20, 293; *Artist*, 15; William Shakespeare, "That Time of Year (Sonnet 73)."

Chapter 2. Frames

1. *Chronology*, 96–97. By far the best synthetic evaluation of *The Book of Lost Tales* is the entry in *Guide*, 120–37.
2. See Allen J. Frantzen, *Troilus and Criseyde: The Poem and the Frame* (New York: Twayne, 1993).
3. Larry D. Benson, ed. *The Riverside Chaucer*, 3rd ed. (Boston: Houghton Mifflin, 1988), 3–4.
4. It seems that at some points in Tolkien's composition of the stories, Eriol and Ælfwine were two different characters, but at other times they were just two names for the same character. Thus, as Christopher Tolkien notes, it is not incorrect to "treat the two names as indicative of different narrative projections—'the Eriol story' and 'the Ælfwine story' "; *Lost Tales I*, 300–301. For the purposes of my argument, however, it is not necessary to disambiguate this exceptionally tangled matter. For further discussion see Verlyn Flieger, *A Question of Time: J.R.R. Tolkien's Road to Faërie* (Kent, OH: Kent State University Press, 1997), 64–67; Verlyn Flieger, "The Footsteps of Ælfwine," in *Tolkien's Legendarium: Essays on the History of Middle-earth*, eds. Verlyn Flieger and Carl F. Hostetter (Westport, CT: Greenwood, 2000), 186–91 and 195–97.
5. *Lost Tales I*, 17–18. "Of all houses this seems to me the most lovely" is echoed in Éowyn's description of the Houses of Healing as "of all dwellings the most blessed," written more than thirty years later; *RK*, VI, v, 243. That Tolkien wrote the original passage either while in or just after having been released from the hospital (either at Birmingham or Harrogate) may have some biographical relevance.
6. *Lost Tales I*, 22.
7. *Lost Tales II*, 287; words in square brackets are Christopher Tolkien's; emphasis in original.
8. The spelling "Angelcynn" (*Lost Tales II*, 300) in Anglo-Saxon means "kin of the Angles," not "kin of the angels."
9. Flieger, "Footsteps," 185–90.
10. As Tom Shippey notes, *Ottar* would definitely be Old Norse, *Ohthere* would definitely be Old English, but *Ottor* could be either; Tom Shippey, "Tolkien and Iceland: The Philology of Envy," lecture delivered at the Sigurður Nordal Institute, September 2002. An Ohthere appears in *Beowulf* (lines 2380, 2394, 2612, 2928, 2932), where he is the son of Ongentheow, the king of Sweden, and the father of the Swedish princes Eadgils and Eanmund who play a part in the fall of Beowulf's cousin Heardred. Chambers notes that the name Ottar in the *Ynglinga tal* "is certainly the

Ohthere of *Beowulf*"; R. W. Chambers, *Beowulf: An Introduction to the Study of the Poem with a Discussion of the Stories of Offa and Finn*, 3rd ed. (Cambridge, UK: Cambridge University Press, 1963), 343.

11. Janet Bately, "The Nature of Old English Prose," in *The Cambridge Companion to Old English Literature*, eds. Malcolm Godden and Michael Lapidge (Cambridge, UK: Cambridge University Press, 1991), 72. For an edition of the Old English *Orosius*, see Janet Bately, ed., *The Old English Orosius*, vol. 6, 2nd ser. (London: Early English Text Society, 1980). Every Anglo-Saxonist knows of "The Voyages of Ohthere and Wulfstan" because it is regularly used in introductory teaching. Tolkien would have had additional reasons to be familiar with the text: The Voyages include the Old English word for *walrus* [*horshwæl*], a word that Tolkien defined for the *OED*. See Peter M. Gilliver, "At the Wordface: J.R.R. Tolkien's Work on the *Oxford English Dictionary*," in *Proceedings of the J.R.R. Tolkien Centenary Conference*, eds. Patricia Reynolds and Glen H. GoodKnight (Moorestown, NJ: Mythopoeic Press, 1995), 173–86 at 182.
12. *Lost Tales I*, 21–25; *Lost Tales II*, 290–91.
13. *Ecclesiastical History*, Bk I, ch. xv; Bede, *The Ecclesiastical History of the English People*, ed. and trans. Bertram Colgrave and R.A.B. Mynors (Oxford: Clarendon, 1969), 48–53. For a discussion of the ways that stories of the Anglo-Saxon migration may be more mythical than historical, see Nicholas Howe, *Migration and Mythmaking in Anglo-Saxon England* (New Haven, CT: Yale University Press, 1989), and Allen J. Frantzen, *Desire for Origins: New Language, Old English, and Teaching the Tradition* (New Brunswick, NJ: Rutgers University Press, 1990). Tom Shippey discusses the parallels between Hengest and Horsa and the leaders of the hobbit migration, Marcho and Blanco (both names can also be translated as "horse"). He notes that Tolkien's explanation that the hobbits came from the "Angle" between the Hoarwell and Loudwater rivers is an obvious parallel to the "angle" between Flensburg fjord and the river Schlei, where the Angles are supposed to have originated; *Road*, 92–93.
14. *Lost Tales I*, 24. Bede notes that Hengest and Horsa were the sons of Wictgils, the son of Witta, the son of Wecta, the son of Woden; Tolkien does not use these names (i.e., he does not make Wictgils = Ælfwine), but he does link his mythological construction to Woden by connecting this name (the Old English form of Oðínn / Odin) to Manweg (Manwë) of the Valar; *Lost Tales II*, 290.
15. *Lost Tales II*, 290.
16. Tolkien notes that both Hengest and Horsa seem to be connected to place names in England, including Hinksey (Ferry), which may be derived from "Hengestes + ig" (Hengest's island); *Author*, 57.
17. R. W. Chambers thought that fighting on frozen lakes between the Cwenas and the Northmen was analogous to the fighting between the Geats and Swedes in *Beowulf*. Chambers, *Beowulf*, 403.
18. J.R.R. Tolkien, *Finn and Hengest: The Fragment and the Episode*, ed. Alan Bliss (Boston: Houghton Mifflin, 1983), 66–69.
19. *B&C*, 54, 197; Tolkien, *Finn and Hengest*, 12–16.
20. *Lost Tales II*, 300–301
21. *Lost Tales II*, 301.
22. Or, "may this also pass away." G. P. Krapp and E. van K. Dobbie, *The Exeter Book: The Anglo-Saxon Poetic Records in Modern English Verse*, vol. 3 (New York: Columbia University Press, 1936), 178–79. At an earlier stage of Tolkien's composition, Deor was the name of Ælfwine's father, which possibly complicates, but does not obviate, the reading I am developing; *Lost Tales II*, 313.
23. Christopher Tolkien notes that "when lecturing on *Beowulf* at Oxford [J.R.R. Tol-

kien] sometimes gave the unknown poet a name, calling him Heorrenda"; *Lost Tales II*, 323. This comment is substantiated by some of Tolkien's unpublished *Beowulf* commentaries and associated materials. See for example, Oxford, Bodleian Library, MS Tolkien A28 C, fol. 6v., in which Tolkien suggests calling the *Beowulf*-poet Heorrenda rather than X.

24. The text breaks off after "know." *Lost Tales II*, 290–91.
25. In various conference presentations and panel discussions Verlyn Flieger and I have both noted Tolkien's tendency to get bogged down in ever-more-elaborate frame narratives and asserted that *The Hobbit* and *The Lord of the Rings* were only completed because Tolkien did not start either of them with a developed frame narrative.
26. Christopher Tolkien explains that *The Lord of the Rings* had reached "the end of what would become *The Two Towers* and a few pages had been written of 'Minas Tirith' and 'The Muster of Rohan' when his father began a time-travel story, which he worked on during a year-and-a-half period in which *The Lord of the Rings* "had been at a halt"; *Lost Road*, 145–48.
27. *Sauron*, 155.
28. Colin Duriez, "The Inklings," in *J.R.R. Tolkien Encyclopedia: Scholarship and Critical Assessment*, ed. M.D.C. Drout (New York: Routledge, 2007), 295–96.
29. Jason Fisher, "*Sauron Defeated*," in Drout, *J.R.R. Tolkien Encyclopedia*, 592–93.
30. Verlyn Flieger, "Do the Atlantis Story and Abandon Eriol-Saga," *Tolkien Studies* 1 (2004): 43–68.
31. In hindsight, then, it might have been possible, had *The Notion Club Papers* been completed, to return to the initial dialogues and determine which characters were correct in their theorizing and in what ways, thus giving us some additional insight into Tolkien's views of the relationship between past and present, mind and body. Such a project is far outside the scope of this book, but it would be a valuable contribution to Tolkien studies and might be facilitated by the *Anduin* electronic archive resources at Marquette University.
32. The work includes several compositions in Old English by Tolkien, including *King Sheave*, Tolkien's expansion of some of the putative legendary material in the opening verses of *Beowulf.*
33. *Sauron*, 146–47.
34. "It may well be that he was deeply torn between the burgeoning of Adunaic (later Adûnaic) and Anadûnê and the oppression of the abandoned *Lord of the Rings*"; *Sauron*, 147.
35. *Sauron*, 152.
36. Jorge Luis Borges, "Tlön, Uqbar, Orbis Tertius," in *Collected Fictions*, trans. Andrew Hurley (New York: Viking, 1998), 68–81. Vladimir Nabokov, *Pale Fire* (1962; New York: Vintage, 1989).
37. See Tom Shippey, "Learning to Read Science Fiction," in *Hard Reading: Learning from Science Fiction* (Liverpool: Liverpool University Press, 2016), 6–23.
38. *H*, I, 10.
39. *H*, II, 41; *H*, III, 56. *H*, V, 79.
40. *H*, I, 10.
41. *H*, IV, 71.
42. *H*, VIII, 170–71.
43. In a letter to W. H. Auden, Tolkien wrote that *The Hobbit* "was unhappily really meant, as far as I was conscious, as a 'children's story,' and as I had not learned sense then, and my children were not quite old enough to correct me, it has some of the silliness of manner caught unthinkingly from the kind of stuff I had served to me"; *Letters*, #163, 311–12.

44. In William Goldman's book that frame is of a father trying to share with his son a book that his own father had shared with him; in the film version it is a grandfather wanting to read a beloved book to his grandson.
45. See *Bio*, 227–28; John Rateliff, *The History of The Hobbit, Part Two: Return to Bag End*, 2 vols. (Boston: Houghton Mifflin, 2007), 765–812.
46. This legend is the origin of the "Golfimball" game played at Mythcons (meetings of the Mythopoeic Society) A doll's head painted to look like a goblin is hit off a batting tee with a stick or other bat-like implement. Prizes are awarded for distance and accuracy, the latter determined by how close the head lands to a stuffed toy rabbit.
47. Rateliff, *Return to Bag End*, 812.
48. The Ballantine paperback with the Remington illustration does not include the runes on the cover.
49. As first noted by Douglas A. Anderson in J.R.R. Tolkien, *The Annotated Hobbit*, rev. ed. (Boston: Houghton Mifflin, 2002), 378.
50. Contemporary with the time it was written (the mid to late 1930s). But nearly a century after its composition there is little in *The Hobbit*'s prose style or cultural references to distance even a young twenty-first-century audience.
51. *FR*, Note on Shire Records, 23
52. *RK*, VI, ix, 307.
53. All of this is laid out very clearly and thoroughly discussed by Christopher Tolkien in the introduction to *Lost Tales I*, 5–7.
54. *RK*, Appendix A, III, 362; *RK*, Appendix B, 378; *RK*, Appendix D, 386; *RK*, Appendix F, II, 411–16. *FR*, Prologue, Note on the Shire Records, 23–25.
55. *RK*, VI, vi, 265.
56. *RK*, Appendix F, ii, 411.
57. Jeremy Painter, "'A Honeycomb Gathered from Different Flowers': Tolkien-the-Compiler's Middle-earth 'Sources' in *The Lord of the Rings*," *Tolkien Studies* 13 (2016): 125–47. See also Dennis Wilson Wise, "Book of the Lost Narrator: Rereading the 1977 *Silmarillion* as a Unified Text," *Tolkien Studies* 13 (2016): 101–24.
58. *Peoples*, 12–18.
59. *Peoples*, 24 and 19.
60. *FR*, I, i, 37–39.
61. *Shadow*, 23–24.
62. *ATB*, 7–9.
63. Verlyn Flieger, *Interrupted Music: The Making of Tolkien's Mythology* (Kent, OH: Kent State University Press, 2005), 79.

CHAPTER 3. TEXTS

1. It is possible that not all of the "several others" Frodo sees sitting with Elrond are named; *FR*, II, ii, 252.
2. *Road*, 117–22.
3. *Author*, 68–82 at 69.
4. *FR*, II, ii, 260, 262.
5. *Author*, 77.
6. *FR*, II, ii, 254.
7. *FR*, II, ii, 255. See also Peter Grybauskas, *A Sense of Tales Untold: Exploring the Edges of Tolkien's Literary Canvas* (Kent, OH: Kent State University Press, 2021).
8. Tolkien used the phrase to describe the effect of *Beowulf*, the whole of which "must have succeeded admirably in creating in the minds of the poet's contemporaries the illusion of surveying a past, pagan but noble and fraught with a deep significance—a

past that itself had depth and reached backward into a dark antiquity of sorrow. This impression of depth is an effect and a justification of the use of episodes and allusions to old tales, mostly darker, more pagan, and desperate than the foreground"; *MC*, 27. See also *Road*, 228–29.

9. *MC*, 72.
10. *Letters*, #247, 469.
11. For the foundations of this analysis, see Christopher Tolkien's Foreword to *Lost Tales I*, 1–7; *Road*, 223–26; *Author*, 261–63.
12. Walter Ong, "The Writer's Audience Is Always a Fiction," *PMLA* 90, no. 1 (1975): 9–21.
13. *FR*, I, i, 34; *FR*, I, i, 45–46; *FR*, I, iii, 81.
14. Many of the ideas and much of the specific data in the argument that follows were developed in two previous coauthored papers: Michael D.C. Drout, Namiko Hitotsubashi, and Rachel Scavera, "Tolkien's Creation of the Impression of Depth," *Tolkien Studies* 11 (2014), 167–210; and Peizhen Wu and Michael D.C. Drout, "'The Course of Actual Composition': Analysis of Some Aspects of the Revision History of *The Lord of the Rings* Using "Lexomic" Digital Methods," *Tolkien Studies* 21 (2025).
15. *Lost Tales I*, 3.
16. *Lost Tales I*, 13; *Bio*, 185–87; *Shadow*, 3, 11–13.
17. *Road*, 229; *Letters*, #131, 202–4.
18. See Diana Pavlac Glyer, *The Company They Keep: C. S. Lewis and J. R. R. Tolkien as Writers in Community* (Kent, OH: The Kent State University Press, 2007), and also *Road*, 223–35, 244–53.
19. *Lost Tales II*, 69–116; *WJ*, 3–4.
20. As Christopher Tolkien says in the Foreword to *The Silmarillion*, "it became long ago a fixed tradition . . . but it was far indeed from being a fixed text"; *S*, Foreword, 7. See also *Author*, 228–29.
21. The others are the Beren and Lúthien story and the Fall of Gondolin. See *Letters*, #163, 312–14. See Drout, et al. "Tolkien's Creation of the Impression of Depth" for a detailed discussion.
22. No analogous archive has been published from later fantasy works inspired by Tolkien, including, among others, series by Terry Brooks, Stephen R. Donaldson, and David Eddings. It is a commonplace that fantasy authors invent and compile significant background material, but Tolkien's was *textualized* in a way that the others' seem not to have been.
23. Among these, the *Necronomicon*, the *Book of Eibon*, the Pnakotic Manuscripts, and the City of R'lyeh. For the adaptable nature of the Lovecraftian mythos, see David E. Schultz, "Who Needs the Cthulhu Mythos?," in *A Century Less a Dream: Selected Criticism on H. P. Lovecraft*, ed. Scott Conners (Holikong, PA: Wildside Press, 1987). Compare also Robert W. Chambers's references to the imaginary *The King in Yellow* or Frank Herbert's many epigraphs in *Dune* that are said to be taken from pseudotexts like the *Orange Catholic Bible*, the *Azhar Book*, *The Manual of Muad'Dib* and the *Tleilaxu Godbuk*, none of which ever existed.
24. With the exception of the Beren and Lúthien story that Aragorn narrates at Weathertop; *FR*, I, xi, 203–6.
25. *FR*, II, iii, 287; viii, 390.
26. *FR*, I, xi, 193.
27. *FR*, II, iv, 325.
28. *TT*, IV, x, 337–38.
29. *RK*, VI, vi, 256.
30. Line 1424 of "The Merchant's Tale" and line 3394 of "The Nun's Priest's Tale,"

in *The Riverside Chaucer*, ed. Larry D. Benson (Oxford: Oxford University Press, 1988), 156, 260; line 2446 of J.R.R. Tolkien and E. V. Gordon, eds., *Sir Gawain and the Green Knight*, (Oxford: Clarendon, 1949), 115–16.

31. For discussion, see John Miles Foley, *The Singer of Tales in Performance* (Bloomington: University of Indiana Press, 1995), 53–54. For a provocative thought experiment that models the process in a more abstract manner, see Daniel C. Dennett, *Darwin's Dangerous Idea: Evolution and the Meanings of Life* (New York: Simon and Schuster, 1995), 419–22.
32. KL4, 193–99.
33. For discussion of this point and the demonstration that a meme cannot contain metadata about itself, see Michael D.C. Drout, *Tradition and Influence in Anglo-Saxon Literature: An Evolutionary, Cognitivist Approach* (New York: Palgrave MacMillan, 2013), 88, 103–7.
34. What I am calling "broken references" Nagy calls "contentless allusions," contrasting them with "genuine" allusions; Gergely Nagy, "'The Great Chain of Reading: (Inter)Textual Relations and the Technique of Mythopoesis in the Túrin Story," in *Tolkien the Medievalist*, ed. Jane Chance (New York: Routledge, 2002), 242. I believe my nomenclature eliminates a potential misunderstanding, in that broken referents still contain *some* content, which can be inferred from local context (for example, that the named elf-friends did heroic things that helped the elves). Calling them "contentless," therefore, potentially invites unproductive arguments. For discussion of the influence of such broken references on Tolkien's imagination, see Shippey on *woodwose* and other cruces of absence; *Road*, 65.
35. *Road*, 228–29.
36. *FR*, II, ii, 284.
37. Tolkien creates the cognitive situation of a *non*-participant in a tradition—the exact opposite of what Foley's scholarship in *The Singer of Tales in Performance* tries to reconstruct. In fact, the local context in this particular case is somewhat misleading, since Túrin is a much more ambiguous character than a reader can infer. Tolkien's other reference to Túrin, in the *Adventures of Tom Bombadil*, is opaque enough to be misleading; *ATB*, 8. Tolkien's statement that "The Hoard" "seems to contain echoes of the Númenorean tale of Túrin and Mim the dwarf" even led Robert Foster to conclude erroneously—but reasonably, given the available evidence—that "Túrin seems to have killed a dragon in his youth and later to have become a king. He was perhaps slain in old age by an invading army"; Robert Foster, *A Guide to Middle-earth* (New York: Ballantine Books, 1971), 259.
38. Malory did use French sources, but, as Eugène Vinaver demonstrated, he often deliberately misleads his readers when he authorizes elements of his narrative with the phrase: "As the French booke seyeth"; Sir Thomas Malory, *The Works of Sir Thomas Malory*, 3rd ed., ed. Eugene Vinaver, rev. P. J. C. Field, 3 vols. (Oxford: Oxford University Press, 1990), 1260; Bonnie Wheeler, "'As the French Book Seyeth': Malory's *Morte Darthur* and Acts of Reading," *Cahiers de recherches médiévales* 14 (2007): 116–25. Thanks to Gergely Nagy for pointing out this parallel with Malory.
39. Nagy calls imaginary books like these "pseudo-texts"; "Great Chain," 240–41. All pseudo-texts are pseudo-references, but not all pseudo-references are pseudo-texts. It is important to differentiate between the actual published story "The King in Yellow" and the imaginary book of the same name that the story discusses. The former is not a pseudo-text.
40. See Roland Barthes, "The Reality Effect," in *The Rustle of Language*, trans. Richard Howard (New York: Hill and Wang, 1986), 141–48. Tolkien's pseudo-references

were the direct inspiration for many subsequent fantasy writers, including Ursula K. Le Guin in her original Earthsea trilogy, in which the referenced stories of Elfarran, Morred, and the Firelord (among others) were only written decades after the original three books were published. See the introduction to Ursula K. Le Guin, *Tales from Earthsea* (New York: Harcourt Brace, 2001).

41. People in the audience of the "original" story of *Beowulf* would not have noticed losses in cultural continuity since the poem would have arisen out of their immediate (and thus broadly continuous) culture. However, if Tolkien is correct, and *Beowulf* as we have it was "already antiquarian, in a good sense," and "its maker was telling of things already old and weighted with regret" when the poem was made into its current form, then there could have been broken or at least attenuated references in the materials used by the poet; *MC*, 33.
42. *Letters*, #163, 316; #174, 331; #180, 336. In the draft of letter #180 to a "Mr. Thompson" of January 14, 1956, Tolkien adds "the names and adventures of the other 2 wizards" to Queen Berúthiel's cats, but even these two deliberately broken referents acquired back stories, as noted by Christopher Tolkien in *UT*, 401–2n7.
43. In a letter of December 15, 1937, Stanley Unwin suggested that Tolkien should use the Silmarillion material for exactly this purpose: "*The Silmarillion* . . . in fact is a mine to be explored in writing further books like *The Hobbit* rather than a book in itself. I think this was partly your view, was it not?" (quoted in *Bio*, 184).
44. *M&C*, 17.
45. See *Bio*, 184–87, 207–12. As David Bratman pointed out, the situation may be somewhat more complicated. A decade later, Tolkien was attempting to get Collins to publish both *The Silmarillion* (even though it was not in publishable form) and *The Lord of the Rings*, perhaps because he now worried that the many references he had built into the latter text would be incomprehensible to a reader who did not have access to *The Silmarillion*; David Bratman, "A Corrigenda to *The Lord of the Rings*," *The Tolkien Collector* 6 (March 1994): 17–27. If this is the case (and without additional information, such as may be contained in Tolkien's diaries, we cannot be sure about his state of mind at the time), then the impression of depth of the published text is even more of a happy accident.
46. These references would be broken for any imagined audience for the published work, but the reading experience for the Inklings and Tolkien's son Christopher, who had some familiarity with the older stories, would be qualitatively different.
47. That enough information was to be found in *The Lord of the Rings* and its appendices to figure out almost all of Tolkien's references enabled the creation of works like Foster's *A Guide to Middle-earth*. However, for some references, the available information was so limited that very little of the meaning of the reference could be reconstructed. For example, in the pre-*Silmarillion* version of the *Guide*, Húrin is described merely as "elf-friend and hero"; Foster, *Guide to Middle-earth*, 124.
48. *Pace* Derrida and orthodox deconstructionists, there *is* something outside the text: The significance of the name "Háma" or of "the cats of Queen Berúthiel" can only be found *outside Beowulf* or *The Lord of the Rings*. That such relations are textual, however, could be used—if one were so inclined—to rewrite Derrida's dictum as "there is nothing outside the text<u>s</u>."
49. John Miles Foley, *Immanent Art: From Structure to Meaning in Traditional Oral Epic* (Bloomington: Indiana University Press, 1991), 6–7.
50. Foley, *Immanent Art*, 6–8; John Miles Foley, *Traditional Oral Epic: The Odyssey, Beowulf, and the Serbo-Croatian Return Song* (Berkeley: University of California Press, 1990), 389–90.
51. For more discussion, see Michael D.C. Drout, *How Tradition Works: A Meme-Based*

Cultural Poetics of the Anglo-Saxon Tenth Century (Tempe, AZ: ACMRS Press, 2006), 22–35, 236–38; Drout, *Tradition and Influence*, 103–10. For an explanation of how the conserved form might not be identical to its surface-structure representation, see Drout, *Tradition and Influence*, 34–45, 112–14.

52. For a discussion, see Drout, *Tradition and Influence*, 86–94, 102–7.
53. The adjective can either fill the fourth colon or, when paired with *megas*, the entire second hemistich. See Foley, *Traditional Oral Epic*, 146; Foley, *Immanent Art*, 146–47.
54. For tradition dependence, see Foley, *Traditional Oral Epic*, 9–10.
55. For a discussion of linguistic marking, see Britt Mize, *Traditional Subjectivities: The Old English Poetics of Mentality* (Toronto: University of Toronto Press, 2013), 102–5.
56. See Drout, *Tradition and Influence*, 126–27. See also, Mize, *Traditional Subjectivities*, 97–102.
57. For parataxis and anaphora as characteristic of oral traditional poetics, see Foley, *Immanent Art*, 9–10, and Michael D.C. Drout "A Meme-Based Approach to Oral Traditional Theory," *Oral Tradition* 21, no. 2 (2006): 283–86.
58. *TT*, IV, v, 287; *FR*, II, ii, 259; *FR*, I, vi, 130; *FR*, I, vii, 134–37; As is the often-used "Theoden king"; *TT*, III, ii, 35 and throughout *TT* and *RK*.
59. *FR*, I, xi, 197–98; *TT*, III, xi, 200.
60. *FR*, II, ii, 280.
61. See Douglas A. Anderson's "Note on the Text" in the standard edition of *The Fellowship of the Ring*; see also Amy Sturgis, "*Lord of the Rings, The*," in *J.R.R. Tolkien Encyclopedia: Scholarship and Critical Assessment*, ed. Michael D.C. Drout (New York, Routledge, 2007), 385–86; and *Chronology*, xviii–xliv.
62. See *TT*, III, ii, 42, and *TT*, III, xi, 202; *Chronology*, 191.
63. *Letters*, #211, 399; *FR*, I, xii, 221.
64. *FR*, I, xii, 223, 225.
65. *FR*, I, vii, 142; *TT*, III, v, 102.
66. Some have speculated that Bombadil is not technically a "living thing" but a spirit of some sort. In Shippey's view, Tom is a *lusus naturae*, a unique individual belonging to no category or class, and a *genius loci*, a spirit of the particular countryside; *Road*, 107–8. Gene Hargrove, on the other hand, reads the same evidence differently to suggests that Tom and Goldberry are the Valar Aulë and Yavanna in "mortal" form; Gene Hargrove, "Who Is Tom Bombadil?" *Mythlore* 13, no. 1 (1986): 20–24. However, as Caiden Kumar has pointed out (personal communication), the wording "When the Elves passed westward, Tom was here already, before the seas were bent. He knew the dark under the stars when it was fearless—before the Dark Lord came from Outside" (*FR*, I, vii, 142) and the relevant passage in *The Silmarillion* (*S*, I, 37) indicate that Bombadil has been in existence since the Spring of Arda, before the great lamps were destroyed, while the first Ent would not have appeared until sometime after the fathers of the Dwarves had been created by Aulë, which happened after the destruction of the lamps; *S*, 36–37, 45–46.
67. "I could, I suppose, answer: 'a trick cyclist can ride a bicycle with handle-bars!' "; *Letters*, #211, 399.
68. See Wayne G. Hammond and Christina Scull, *The Lord of the Rings*, 50th Anniversary ed. (New York: Houghton Mifflin, 2004), 107; *Chronology*, 118; John Rateliff, *The History of The Hobbit, Part Two: Return to Bag End*, 2 vols. (Boston: Houghton Mifflin, 2007), 12–14; and Bratman, "Corrigenda," 18–19.
69. See Judith Klinger, "Hidden Paths of Time: March 13 and the Riddles of Shelob's Lair," in *Tolkien and Modernity 2*, eds. Thomas Honegger and Frank Weinrich (Zollikofen, Switzerland: Walking Tree Publishers, 2006), 143–209. *TT*, III, i, 18; *FR*, II, ii, 254; *RK*, V, x, 165–67. Again, these seeming inconsistencies can be finessed.

70. *FR*, I, v, 117; *Chronology*, 118.
71. Through extremely tortuous special pleading it is possible to resolve the problem by imagining that the illustrator of the Red Book back-translated Gandalf's interpretation of the writing in the text and made the illustration fit (i.e., Gandalf substituted "Moria" for "Khazad-dûm" just as he substituted "Hollin" for "Eregion" in his speech, and the illustrator made the drawing based solely on Gandalf's description). For more discussion, see *Chronology*, 281–82.
72. A list of putative inconsistencies (which is perhaps too extensive) can be found at "Possible Inconsistencies in the Legendarium," Tolkien Gateway, accessed September 10, 2023, https://Tolkiengateway.net/wiki/Possible_inconsistencies_in_the_legendarium. At the time Tolkien wrote the passage, the character who is Finrod in the published *Silmarillion* was named Inglor and his father was Finrod (instead of Finarfin). Finrod would have no "house," since he had no wife or son; *S*, XV 130. For the interchanges between the names Finrod, Inglor, and Finarfin, see *Lost Tales I*, 44; *Shadow*, 72, 188n9.
73. *TT*, III, ii, 45; *TT*, III, v,102, 108. In *The Treason of Isengard*, Christopher Tolkien discusses the problem, noting that although his father wrote "Vision of Gandalf's thought" in the margin next to the mention of the old man, in a time-scheme written around the time of "Helm's Deep" and "The Road to Isengard," he had noted that "Aragorn and his companions spend night on the battle-field, and see 'old man' (Saruman)"; *Treason*, 427–28. Tolkien was attempting to resolve the apparent contradiction, but in the end he still failed to do so. The ambiguity is resolved in favor of Saruman in the synoptic chronology; William Cloud Hicklin, "The Chronology of *The Lord of the Rings*," *Tolkien Studies* 19 Supplement (2022): 58.
74. *FR*, II, x, 417.
75. *TT*, IV, x, 339; *RK*, V, vi, 117. In his essay in *Meditations on Middle-earth*, Terry Pratchett speculated that the Lord of the Nazgûl was not completely destroyed and, since the Third Age ends quite soon after the main action of *The Lord of the Rings*, the Witch King would return in the Fourth Age. This interpretation would be more convincing if Tolkien had capitalized "age" in the passage. I once had the same idea, and in a (fortunately) abortive novel of 1989, tried to tell the Witch-king's story from his point of view. In a 1963 letter to Mrs. Eileen Elgar, Tolkien wrote that "The Witch-king had been reduced to impotence"; *Letters*, #246, 466. Hypothetically, he could have recovered his power over many years, as Sauron did, but the Witch-king was not a Maia like Sauron but merely the spirit of a man.
76. *TT*, III, iv, 78–81; *TT*, III, x, 191; *RK*, VI, vi, 259–60; *Letters*, #144, 269.
77. *Shadow*, 401.
78. *FR*, I, x, 177.
79. Compare *Shadow*, 153, 342–43.
80. *FR*, II, iii, 299.
81. *Shadow*, 422.
82. *Shadow*, 434n20.
83. *Treason*, 167.
84. Although readers may also have a sense that the characters in the story have an existence independent of the author. Stephen King noted that part of his inspiration for writing *Doctor Sleep* was a question at an autograph session: "Hey, any idea what happened to the kid from *The Shining*?" He adds, "This was a question I'd often asked myself about that old book"; Stephen King, *Doctor Sleep* (New York: Scribner, 2013), 423.
85. *MC*, 72.
86. Gergely Nagy, "'Ye Old Authour': Tolkien's Anatomy of Tradition in *The Silmaril-*

lion" (PhD diss., University of Szeged, 2012), 1–17. For additional discussion of the Red Book frame inside *The Lord of the Rings*, see Kristin Thompson, "*The Hobbit* as part of The Red Book of Westmarch," *Mythlore* 56, 15.2 (1988), 11–16. For analysis of the significance of imagined book frames in Tolkien's corpus, see Verlyn Flieger, "Tolkien and the Idea of the Book," in *Green Suns and Faërie: Essays on J.R.R. Tolkien* (Kent, OH: Kent State University Press, 2012), 41–53; and Flieger, *Interrupted Music*, 55–84.

87. Nagy, "Great Chain," 240.
88. *FR*, I, ix, 197–98.
89. *FR*, I, ix, 204–6.
90. *UT*, 146; *WJ*, 311–12. See Nagy, "Great Chain," 242–46, for more discussion.
91. Nagy, "Great Chain," 243.
92. Stylistic heterogeneity *among* Tolkien's texts has long been remarked on by many critics, who have noted (some have also lamented) the differences between *The Hobbit*, *The Lord of the Rings*, and *The Silmarillion*. David Bratman's taxonomy of style in The History of Middle-earth volumes, published in his essay in *Tolkien's Legendarium*, is useful and can be extended beyond Tolkien's posthumously published works; David Bratman, "The Literary Value of The History of Middle-earth" in *Tolkien's Legendarium: Essays on the History of Middle-earth*, eds. Verlyn Flieger and Carl. F. Hostetter (Westport, CT: Greenwood Press, 2000), 69–91 at 72–73.
93. In "The Adapted Text: The Lost Poetry of Beleriand," Nagy is building upon Bratman's three-part classification scheme into Annalistic, Antique, and Appendical styles; see Bratman, "Literary Value," 71–75.
94. Nagy, "Adapted Text," 21. The latter description is Christopher Tolkien's, in the Foreword to *The Silmarillion*, of his father's conception of that book; *S*, 8.
95. Nagy, "Adapted Text," 22.
96. These are collected in *The Lays of Beleriand*. For an exhaustive list and discussion, see Reno E. Lauro, "Poems by Tolkien: The History of Middle-earth," in *J.R.R. Tolkien Encyclopedia*, 517–20.
97. Nagy, "Adapted Text," 29.
98. Nagy, "Adapted Text," 29; *S*, XXI, 204, 219; Nagy's example 15; *S*, XXI, 212.
99. Nagy's example 15; *S*, 212.
100. *FR*, I, v, 131–32; vi, 135–40; *Road*, 107.
101. Nagy, "Adapted Text," 25; see also Christopher Tolkien's discussion of the evolution of his father's work in *Shadow*, 430–31.
102. Nagy, "Adapted Text," 25.
103. Nagy, "Adapted Text," 25.
104. For discussion of these processes and their relative speeds, see Drout, *Tradition and Influence*, 185–86; Drout, *How Tradition Works*, 51–53.
105. See Drout, *Tradition and Influence*, 102–10.
106. For a discussion, see Michael D.C. Drout and Elie Chauvet, "Tracking the Moving Ratio of *þ* to *ð* in Anglo-Saxon Texts: A New Method, and Evidence for a Lost Old English Version of the 'Song of the Three Youths,'" *Anglia* 133, no. 2 (2015): 278–319.
107. Nagy, "Adapted Text," 30; *S*, XXI, 208. I have not underlined the <s> in "silence" because I believe that Tolkien is following the Anglo-Saxon alliterative tradition in which the /st/ consonant-cluster is the alliterative unit.
108. *Lays*, 47. The textual history of this passage is complex, and it is somewhat difficult to interpret some of Christopher Tolkien's explanation in the Appendix to *The Children of Húrin*. In the *Narn* published in *Unfinished Tales*, the death of Beleg and other material is omitted, with the reader being directed to pages 204–15 of the published

Silmarillion; *UT*, 104. In *The Children of Húrin*, Christopher Tolkien integrates this material, word for word, into the main text of the *Narn*, noting that "where there was nothing to be added to the *Silmarillion* version (as in the tale of the death of Beleg, derived from the *Annals of Beleriand*) that version is simply repeated"; *Children*, 288–89. Kane interprets this statement as indicating that Christopher Tolkien himself wrote the passage in *The Silmarillion*, since all the annalistic treatments of Beleg's death are minimal and contain none of the poetic description just quoted; Douglas C. Kane, *Arda Reconstructed: The Creation of the Published Silmarillion* (Bethlehem, PA: Lehigh University Press, 2011), 202. If this line of reasoning is correct, then the lines quoted here were derived by Christopher Tolkien himself from the poem printed in *The Lays of Beleriand*. However, it seems somewhat unlikely that Christopher would transmute "stone-faced he stood, standing frozen" into "stood stone still and silent," when his practice elsewhere had been to substitute exact quotations or simple paraphrases rather than invent poetic language of his own. More likely is that this particular phrasing, which, as Nagy notes, has its ultimate source in the "Sketch of the Mythology" and the *Quenta Noldorwina*, was part of one of the "many tentative or exploratory outlines and notes . . . and even short stretches of connected narrative on the scale of the *Narn*" that Christopher Tolkien mentions in the appendix to the *Narn* in *UT*, 150. Furthermore, even if Christopher is indeed responsible for the exact phrasing in *The Silmarillion*, having derived it from the verse Túrin, the point still stands and is perhaps even reinforced: The poetic features of a poetic line have the power to influence later prose treatments of the same material.

109. See Foley, *Immanent Art*, 39–60; Michael D.C. Drout, "Variation within Limits: An Evolutionary Approach to the Structure and Dynamics of the Multiform," *Oral Tradition* 26, no. 2 (2011): 447–50; Lauri Honko, *Textualizing the Siri Epic* (Helsinki: Academia Scientarium Fennica, 1998), 100–14.
110. Albeit possibly unintentionally. But see Shippey on the effects of writing and rewriting; *Road*, 316–17.
111. This section of the argument is based on research Peizhen Wu and I collaborated on in the summer of 2018 and thereafter. I am grateful to Gretchen Young and Wheaton's Center for Global Education for facilitating Peizhen's and my summer research, and I would also like to thank the members of Wheaton College's 2018 Lexomics Research Group, particularly Mark LeBlanc, Elizabeth Peterson, Abigail Cahill, Marissa Gamache, Nina Treese, Ginger Ciaburri, and Yenny Bautista.
112. Coined by Betsey Dexter Dyer, the term *lexomics*, modeled on *genomics*, refers to computer-assisted analytical approaches that are focused on words rather than genes. Lexomic methods build upon previous work in bioinformatics and the computational stylometry of John Burrows and David Hoover.

    Lexomics research has been supported by the generosity of Wheaton College; the Teagle Foundation; the Mars, Hood, and Clemence families; the Mellon Foundation; Central Children's Charities; the Youth Initiative Fund; and the National Endowment for the Humanities, who sponsored the research in three grants: NEH HD-50300-08, "Pattern Recognition Through Computational Stylistics: Old English and Beyond," 2008–2009; NEH PR-50112011, "Lexomic Tools and Methods for Textual Analysis: Providing Deep Access to Digitized Texts," 2011–13; and NEH HD-228732-15, National Endowment for the Humanities, Digital Humanities Start-up grant: "Easing Entry and Improving Access to Computer-Assisted Text Analysis for the Humanities," 2015–17. Any views, findings, conclusions, or recommendations expressed in this text do not necessarily reflect those of the National Endowment for the Humanities.

The Lexomics software is available for free use via Wheaton College's "Lexos Software" page. The code can be downloaded from GitHub.

113. G. K. Zipf, *Human Behavior and the Principle of Least Effort* (Reading, MA: Addison-Wesley, 1949).
114. For more information about hierarchical agglomerative clustering, see Michael D.C. Drout, Michael J. Kahn, Mark D. LeBlanc, and Christina Nelson, "Of Dendrogrammatology: Lexomic Methods for Analyzing the Relationships Among Old English Poems," *Journal of English and Germanic Philology* 110, no. 3 (July 2011): 301–36. For rolling window analysis, see Drout and Chauvet, "Tracking the Moving Ratio of *þ* to *ð*," 278–319. For a combined approach, see Michael D.C. Drout and Leah Smith, "A Pebble Smoothed by Tradition: Lines 607–661 of *Beowulf* as a Formulaic Set-Piece," *Oral Tradition* 32, no. 1 (2018): 191–228.
115. I do not include the Prologue, Foreword, or appendices in the analyses in this discussion. As might be expected, these sections of the work are massively different from the narrative chapters in both overall vocabulary distribution and the frequencies of individual words, so their inclusion in the figures merely increased visual clutter.
116. See Sarah Downey, Michael D.C. Drout, Veronica Kerekes and Douglas Raffle, "Lexomic Analysis of Medieval Latin Texts," *Journal of Medieval Latin* 24 (2014): 233–48.
117. *FR*, I, x, 175–87. The anomalous nature of the vocabulary distribution of Chapter 10 was first noted by Namiko Hitotsubashi in 2012.
118. "The Departure of Boromir," Ch. 23, and "Helm's Deep," Ch. 29 (*TT*, III, I and vii). "The Battle of the Pellenor Fields," Ch. 49 (*RK*, V, vi); "The Black Gate Opens," Ch. 53 (*RK*, V, x); "The Field of Cormallen," Ch. 57 (*RK*, VI, iv); "The Steward and the King," Ch. 58 (*RK*, VI, v); and "The Grey Havens," Ch. 62 (*RK*, VI, ix).
119. *FR*, II, v.
120. See the Foreword to the second edition of *The Lord of the Rings* (London: Allen and Unwin, 1966) and Christopher Tolkien's comments in *Shadow*, 460–61.
121. *WR*, 121.
122. As we might expect of an author with a distinctive style, Tolkien's "natural" vocabulary distribution differs slightly from that of large English corpora: Tolkien uses *and* somewhat more frequently and *is* and *was* somewhat less frequently than the language as a whole.
123. *Shadow*, 415.
124. *Shadow*, 4.
125. For example, Chapters 6 and 7, "The Old Forest" and "In the House of Tom Bombadil" (*FR*, I, vi and vii) were each only substantially revised twice; *Shadow*, 112, 120.
126. Invented by Elie Chauvet and myself in 2013–14, *rolling window analysis* begins by calculating the relative frequencies of features of interest in a given "window" of text (for example, words 1–1000). The window is then shifted one unit to the right (words 2–1001), and the process is repeated until the window reaches the end of the text. A plot of the paired values of location and frequency produces a visual representation of the prevalence of the features of interest at every point in the text.
127. See Downey et al., "Lexomic Analysis of Medieval Latin Texts," 225–74; Mary Dockray-Miller and Michael D.C. Drout with Sarah Kinkade and Jillian Valerio, "The Author and the Authors of the 'Vita Ædwardi Regis': Women's Literary Culture and Digital Humanities," *Interfaces: A Journal of Medieval European Literatures* 8 (2021): 160–213; and Drout et al. "Of Dendrogrammatology." I hypothesize that the frequencies of coordinating conjunctions are often proxies for stylistic character-

istics such as sentence length, degree of detail, and, most of all, the balance between parataxis and hypotaxis. Coordinating conjunction frequency, therefore, may be more closely correlated with authorial style than the frequencies of definite articles or other function words.

128. *Shadow*, 112, 118, 127, 362; *Treason*, 411; *WR*, 134–36.
129. *FR*, I, v. As Christopher Tolkien notes "in this chapter the original narrative was far from what finally went into print"; *Shadow*, 88. Among the many changes is the deletion of a long discussion among the hobbits of how anyone could possibly live in a house with stairs, and a scene in which Frodo, invisible, picks up Farmer Maggot's mug and, to the discomfiture of the old hobbit, drains it; *Shadow*, 96–97. Like "Strider," "A Conspiracy Unmasked" was originally part of the preceding chapter, "A Short Cut to Mushrooms."
130. *TT*, IV, i.
131. "'A few pages for a lot of sweat,' my father said in his letter of 5 April 1944, in which he told me of his turning again to the adventures of Sam and Frodo; and 45 years later one can feel it, reading these pages in which he struggled (in increasingly impossible handwriting) to discover just how Sam and Frodo did in the end get down out of the twisted hills into the horrible lands below"; *WR*, 86.
132. Flieger, *Interrupted Music*, 79.

CHAPTER 4. PATTERNS

1. Luke Shelton, "Ofer Zivony's Experience—Tolkien Experience (216)," Tolkien Experience Project, April 4, 2023, https://luke-shelton.com/2023/04/04/ofer-zivonys-experience-Tolkien-experience-216/.
2. Wolfgang Iser, *The Implied Reader: Patterns of Communication in Prose Fiction from Bunyan to Beckett* (Baltimore: Johns Hopkins University Press, 1974); H. R. Jauss, *Toward an Aesthetic of Reception*, trans. Timothy Bahti (Minneapolis: University of Minnesota Press, 1982).
3. "Horizon of expectations" is a term from Jauss's "reader response" criticism. This is not meant to imply that all reader response criticism is wrong, just that it describes only what the particular critics writing it experience, or what they imagine other readers experience, which may or may not align with what actual readers experience, and there is no way to know in the abstract.
4. A good synthesis and critique of various approaches up until around 1980 can be found in Gérard Genette's *Narrative Discourse: An Essay in Method*, trans. Jane E. Lewin (Ithaca: Cornell University Press, 1983).
5. I refer interested readers to Stephen Jay Gould's discussion of linear and cyclical time (in history and lived experience as well as in literature) in *Time's Arrow, Time's Cycle*. Gould's synthesis of the fundamental characteristics of both linear and cyclical time is apposite: Within linear time, "history is an irreversible sequence of unrepeatable events. Each moment occupies its own distinct position in a temporal series, and all movements, considered in proper sequence, tell a story of linked events moving in a direction." In contrast, within cyclical time, "events have no meaning as distinct episodes with causal impact upon a contingent history. Fundamental states are immanent in time, always present and never changing. Apparent motions are parts of repeating cycles, and differences of the past will be realities of the future. Time has no meaning." Stephen Jay Gould, *Time's Arrow, Time's Cycle: Myth and Metaphor in the Discovery of Geological Time* (Cambridge, MA: Harvard University Press, 1987), 10–11.
6. Richard C. West, "The Interlace Structure of *The Lord of the Rings*" in *A Tolkien*

Compass, ed. Jared Lobdell (New York: Ballantine Books, 1975), 85–102 at 83–84. Although I quote from this revised 1975 version, an earlier form of the essay was published in *Orcrist*: "The Interlace and Professor Tolkien: Medieval Narrative Technique in *The Lord of the Rings*," *Orcrist* 1 (1966–67): 26–49.

7. West, "Interlaced Structure," 94–95.
8. Despite citing John Leyerle's "The Interlace Structure of *Beowulf*," *University of Toronto Quarterly* 37, no. 1 (October 1967).
9. *MC*, 29–30. But as R. D. Fulk notes, Tolkien's "explanation of the poem's larger structure, though frequently disputed, has never been bettered, and the methodology inherent in this practice of basing claims about the macrostructural level on patterns everyone discerns in the microstructure remains a model for emulation"; R. W. Fulk, "Preface," in *Interpretations of Beowulf: A Critical Anthology* (Bloomington, IN: Indiana University Press, 1991), xi.
10. Leyerle, "Interlace Structure of *Beowulf*," 150–52.
11. Shippey is here quoting Colin Manlove, and elsewhere he notes comments by Mark Roberts that are likewise amazingly 180-degrees wrong: *The Lord of the Rings* does not "issue from an understanding of reality that is not to be denied, it is not moulded by some controlling vision of things which is at the same time its raison d'être." Shippey is not cherry-picking idiotic comments, either: The rest of the review is nearly as bad; *Road*, 135–36; Colin Manlove, *Modern Fantasy: Five Studies* (Cambridge, UK: Cambridge University Press, 1978), 173–84. *Author*, 156–56. Mark Roberts, "Adventures in English," *Essays in Criticism* 6, no. 4 (1956): 450–59.
12. *Road*, 124.
13. *Road*, 114–120.
14. *Author*, 107.
15. *Author*, 107–11. Frodo and Sam's conversation on the Stairs of Cirith Ungol about their being part of a great story (*TT*, IV, viii, 320–25) seems to violate the principle that the characters cannot see the story pattern, but note that although the two hobbits do seem to be able to perceive their positions meta-fictionally in terms of a very large and abstract pattern, they cannot see how their particular actions are fitting the less abstract pattern of the details of the War of the Ring (i.e., they know they are inside a story, but they do not know precisely what their part in it is).
16. *Author*, 107.
17. Entering into the Old Forest, Moria, Shelob's Lair, the Paths of the Dead, the Sammath Naur; walking thorough the Old Forest, Lothlórien, Fangorn, the Huorns' wood around Helm's Deep.
18. *FR*, I, iii; *FR*, I, v; *FR*, I, vii; *FR*, I, ix; *FR*, II, i; *FR*, II, vii; *TT*, IV, v.
19. *FR*, I, viii; *FR*, II, v; *TT*, IV, ix.
20. *FR*, I, iii; *TT*, IV, ii and iii.
21. *Author*, 50–51. Shippey's matched scenes of threat are the Old Forest, Barrow-downs, and Weathertop in Book I, and Caradhras, Moria, and the orcs in Lórien in Book II.
22. *FR*, I, i, 42.
23. *FR*, II, i, 244.
24. *TT*, IV, i, 225.
25. *TT*, III, i, 16; *FR*, II, x, 415.
26. *RK*, V, i, 30.
27. *Road*, 104.
28. And perhaps the elves' outdoor "hall" in the Woody End. *FR*, I, iii, 91.
29. *OFS*, 75.
30. *FR*, I, iii, 88.

31. *FR*, I, vi, 130.
32. *FR*, I, xii, 209–10.
33. *FR*, I, xii, 211.
34. *FR*, I, xii, 212.
35. *FR*, I, xii, 214–15.
36. In "On Fairy-Stories," Tolkien writes that in a high fever "the mind develops a distressing fecundity and facility in figure-making, seeing forms sinister or grotesque in all objects about it." *OFS*, 82.
37. *FR*, I, xii, 215.
38. *FR*, I, xii, 222–23.
39. Hippocrates, "Crises" in *Volume I, Ancient Medicine*, trans. William Henry Samuel Jones, Loeb Classical Library no. 147 (Cambridge, MA: Harvard University Press, 1923).
40. *FR*, I, xii, 227.
41. *FR*, I, i, 237.
42. *FR*, II, i, 237.
43. *RK*, VI, i, 186–7.
44. I would like to thank my former student Emily Bues for the insight that much of what happens to Frodo—his normal clothing being taken away from him, lack of control over his eating, drinking, and sleeping—is parallel to the experiences of people with severe illness being hospitalized, particularly in the case of emergency hospitalizations.
45. *RK*, VI, i, 188.
46. Le Guin, "Rhythmic Pattern," 106.
47. Le Guin, "Rhythmic Pattern," 105.
48. See Chiara Bertoglio, *Musical Scores and the Eternal Present: Theology, Time, and Tolkien* (Eugene, OR: Pickwick Publications, 2021).
49. Le Guin, "Rhythmic Patterns," 106.
50. A caveat: *Good* writers of fantasy and science fiction do not provide such disquisitions. Unfortunately, bad or inexperienced writers often do produce the dreaded "Chapter 2: A Treatise of Tedium" in which they unload all their world-building information in onc giant lump.
51. *FR*, I, v, 108.
52. *Letters*, #131, 203.
53. *Road*, 228.
54. *FR*, I, ii, 57.
55. We later learn from "Concerning Gandalf, Saruman and the Shire," in "The Hunt for the Ring," in *Unfinished Tales* that, in the past, Saruman had even been sneaking around the Shire; *UT*, 348–52.
56. *FR*, I, ii, 57. Three pages earlier the omniscient narrator mentions the expulsion of the evil power from Mirkwood by the White Council.
57. *FR*, I, ii, 61.
58. *FR*, I, iii, 93.
59. *RK*, V, vi, 114.
60. *RK*, V, vi, 114–15
61. *RK*, V, vi, 124.
62. *RK*, V, vi, 118–23.
63. *RK*, V, vi, 124.
64. *FR*, I, iii, 90–91.
65. *TT*, III, vii, 133–37, 139–40; *TT*, III, viii, 152–53.
66. *RK*, V, viii, 321.

67. Verlyn Flieger, *Interrupted Music: The Making of Tolkien's Mythology* (Kent, OH: Kent State University Press, 200), 72–73.
68. For discussion of the metafictional, postmodern, or frame-breaking qualities of the stairs of Cirith Ungol scene, see Verlyn Flieger, "A Post-Modern Medievalist," in *Green Suns and Faërie: Essays of J.R.R. Tolkien* (Kent, OH: Kent State University Press, 2012), 251–61 at 258–260; "Tolkien and the Idea of the Book," in *The Lord of the Rings 1954–2004: Scholarship in Honor of Richard E. Blackwelder*, eds. Wayne G. Hammond and Christina Scull (Milwaukee: Marquette University Press, 2006), 283–99 at 292.
69. *RK*, V, viii, 323–24.
70. René van Rossenberg, "Tolkien's Exceptional Visit to Holland: A Reconstruction," *Mythlore* 21, no. 2, Article 45 (1996).
71. This would be a good topic for future (non-amateur) sociological and historical research.
72. Manlove, *Modern Fantasy*, 206.

Chapter 5. Emotions

1. This disappointment is perhaps one of the sources of the negative impression of *The Silmarillion* held by so many readers. For a discussion of other features that may contribute to this impression, see *Author*, 261–63.
2. Kocher's is perhaps the most detailed elaboration of this idea. His analysis is remarkable because it was written before the publication of the "Númeórean" materials in *The Lost Road* and Tolkien's working out of medieval histories in *The Book of Lost Tales, Part II*, both of which shed more light on Tolkien's attempt to link up his secondary world with the primary world. Paul Kocher, *Master of Middle-earth: The Achievement of J.R.R. Tolkien* (London: Thames and Hudson, 1973), 3–16.
3. *S*, XX, 193–94.
4. *S*, XX, 195.
5. As confirmed by the eventual publication of the "Athrabeth Finrod Ah Andreth." But there must have been enough information about Finrod in the development of the character in *The Silmarillion* that I was not surprised that Tolkien put his most important meditations upon mortality in the form of a dialogue that included the King of Nargothrond.
6. *S*, XV, 130.
7. *S*, XXII, 228.
8. *S*, XIX, 174.
9. *S*, XIX, 175–76.
10. *S*, XX, 197; *S*, XXIII, 243.
11. The dragon fight "is the end of Beowulf, and with him dies the hope of his people" *MC*, 143.
12. *S*, XX, 194.
13. *S*, XXIV, 250.
14. Tolkien discusses *eucatastrophe* in *OFS*, 153. For discussions of *eucatastrophe* see Brian Rosebury, *Tolkien: A Critical Assessment* (New York: St. Martin's Press, 1992), 95, and Christopher Garbowski, "Eucatastrophe and the 'Gift of Ilúvatar in Middle-earth," *Mallorn* 35 (1997): 25–31.
15. Tolkien in *Beowulf and the Critics*: "It has been said that there is mirth and music and gentle talk in *Beowulf*, but 'the light is but a foil to the dark.' This should perhaps have been reversed. The dark is a foil to the light. The dark is the background, and the light is encircled by it. But not of course because mirth and music

were 'vain' and the light too fleeting for esteem. They were valued passionately." *B&C*, 115.

16. *S*, XV, 125.
17. See Verlyn Flieger, *A Question of Time: J.R.R. Tolkien's Road to Faërie* (Kent, OH: Kent State University Press, 1997) for the most thorough discussion, and see also Verlyn Flieger, *Splintered Light: Logos and Language in Tolkien's World* (Kent, OH: The Kent State University Press, 2002).
18. *S*, Ainulindalë, 18.
19. *Road*, 327.
20. Thus here I (with more than a little trepidation) disagree with Le Guin, who, in *The Farthest Shore* speaks of "the traitor, the self; the self that cries *I want to live; let the world burn so long as I can live.*" Ursula K. Le Guin, *The Farthest Shore* (New York: Atheneum, 1972), 135.
21. *OFS*, 153. Compare Tolkien's letter of January 30, 1945, to his son Christopher (discussed in more detail later), in which he writes that the "memory of this 'home of yours in an idyllic hour (when often there is an illusion of the stay of time and decay and a sense and gentle peace . . . [is] derived from Eden.'" Later in this same letter Tolkien discusses "the heart-wracking sense of the vanished past"; *Letters*, #96, 156–61.
22. Compare T. H. White's *The Once and Future King*, when the youthful Arthur says, "If I were to be a knight . . . I should pray to God to let me encounter all the evil in the world in my own person, so that if I conquered there would be none left, and if I were defeated, I would be the one to suffer for it." Merlin replies, "you would be conquered, and you would suffer for it"; T. H. White, *The Once and Future King* (1958; New York: G. P. Putnam, 1987), 181.
23. There is much discussion in the scholarship as to whether or not the Music of the Ainur in the Ainulindalë should be interpreted as saying that elves do not have free will. Like all very abstract philosophical speculation, this argument is fascinating or tedious depending upon the reader's tastes, but for our purposes, is not relevant. It is impossible for readers to accept emotionally the assertion that any sentient being represented in literature (i.e., any character) lacks free will, so imagining that everything the Elves do and say is predetermined is purely an abstract philosophical exercise: Readers project free will onto characters that are rabbits or moles or robots or computer-simulations, and even onto inanimate objects. Richard Adams, *Watership Down* (New York: Avon Books, 1972); William Horwood, *Duncton Wood* (New York: McGraw-Hill, 1980); Greg Egan, *Diaspora* (Seattle: Eos, 1999).
24. Note the focus on being incarnated in Tolkien's unfinished time-travel novel, *The Notion Club Papers*, printed in *Sauron*, 170–71.
25. *S*, V, 61.
26. Some of the first reviews of *The Silmarillion* said that it read like the King James Bible and meant that as an insult. Here also the critics were on to something but could not stop sneering long enough to recognize its significance. Emblematic is the review by L. J. Davis in *The New Republic*, which manages to be both shallow and condescending. It is almost disorienting to read a critic's complaints about Tolkien's style written in prose so relentlessly 1970s that you can just about smell the orange shag carpeting—this has to be an elaborate joke, right? Alas, there is no punchline except in the sense that the author seems to expect his argument to be taken seriously; L. J. Davis, review of *The Silmarillion* by J.R.R. Tolkien, *The New Republic*, October 1, 1977.
27. *S*, XXI, 215.
28. The epitome of which might be the harsh critique of nostalgia by Tennessee Wil-

liams in *The Glass Menagerie*. The consensus view of nostalgia in contemporary literary-theoretical analysis is summed up by Renée Trilling as: "nostalgia, which paradoxically affirms the past (and very often a fictional past at that) by reconstituting the story of its passing, is primarily concerned with the present." Renée Trilling, *The Aesthetics of Nostalgia: Historical Representation in Old English Verse* (Toronto: University Press of Toronto, 2009), 4. Trilling is here synthesizing arguments by, among others, Slavoj Žižek and J. M. Fritzman, that a nostalgic view of the past is really about the political circumstances of the present. Slavoj Žižek, *The Sublime Object of Ideology* (London: Verso, 1989); J. M. Fritzman, "The Future of Nostalgia and the Time of the Sublime," *Clio* 23, no. 2 (Winter 1994): 167–89. However, the projection of present desires does not explain the specific feeling of grief for the lost home, and in fact it transforms the emotion into merely some kind of wish for a utopia, usually political (i.e., a sublimated desire for greater personal status or power), that is utterly different from the actual experience. Though undoubtedly an important emotion in the kind of people who write this kind of criticism, desire for political utopia seems quite disconnected from Tolkien's works and alien to Tolkien himself.

29. *Nostalgia* was coined by Johannes Hofer, *Dissertatio Medica de Nostalgia, oder Heimwehe* (Basel: Jacobus Bertschius, 1688). Alex Davis notes that the title page of this edition misdates it to 1678. There is an accessible Modern English translation by Carolyn Kiser Anspach, "Medical Dissertation on Nostalgia by Johannes Hofer, 1688," *Bulletin of the Institute of the History of Medicine* 2, no. 6 (August 1934): 376–91. For discussion, see Alex Davis, "Coming Home Again: Johannes Hofer, Edmund Spenser, and Premodern Nostalgia," *Parergon* 33, no. 2 (January 2016): 17–38.
30. *FR*, II, iii, 290–92.
31. James Joyce, "The Dead," in *Dubliners* (London: Grant Richards, 1914), 175–224.
32. Although published in 1970, the material in *Islands in the Stream* was written in 1950 and 1951. Carlos Baker, *Hemingway: The Writer as Artist*, 4th ed. (Princeton: Princeton University Press, 1972), 384; Ernest Hemingway, *Islands in the Stream* (New York: Charles Scribner's Sons, 1970).
33. *FR*, I, iii, 79.
34. *FR*, I, iii, 80.
35. *FR*, II, vi, 366–67.
36. *RK*, V, vi, 118.
37. RK, V, vii, 130.
38. *RK*, VI, viii, 296–97.
39. *RK*, VI, viii, 297.
40. *RK*, VI, vi, 261. "Ruined" in this sentence is technically a participle but is used as a subject complement (the traditional predicate adjective).
41. *RK*, V, x, 166.
42. *FR*, II, iii, 297; Shippey was the first to note the parallel with *The Ruin*; *Road*, 32–33.
43. *RK*, VI, vi, 263. My italics.
44. *FR*, II, ii, 282.
45. *RK*, VI, ix, 309.
46. *FR*, II, vii, 381.
47. *FR*, II, viii, 394.
48. "The last lines of the chant express a wish (or hope) that though she could not go, Frodo might perhaps be allowed to do so"; J.R.R. Tolkien, *The Road Goes Ever On* (New York: HarperCollins, 2002), 60.
49. *FR*, II, iv, 323.
50. *TT*, III, vii, 135.
51. *TT*, III, x, 185.

52. *TT,* IV, ii, 239.
53. *FR*, II, ii, 279.
54. Oxford, Bodleian Library, Tolkien 30/1 f. 118; see Stewart D. Lee and Elizabeth Solopova, *The Keys of Middle-earth: Discovering Medieval Literature Through the Fiction of J.R.R. Tolkien* (London: Palgrave Macmillan, 2005), 214.
55. Quotations from the *Wanderer* are taken from George Philip Krapp and Elliot Van Kirk Dobbie, eds., *The Exeter Book* (New York: Columbia University Press, 1936). Translations are my own.
56. Elsewhere the word is used to translate Latin *solitarius*, so we understand the denotation, but literal translation of the two elements of the compound would be "one/alone" and "hedged/enclosed," perhaps implying an understanding that when a man is exiled, he is in some way trapped or enclosed despite his apparent freedom to go anywhere except the place from which he was exiled.
57. Letters, #96, 156–61.
58. I am only classifying Frodo's actual bouts of illness as suffering, not his pacifism or his seeming paralysis in response to the devastation of the Shire—merely "looking shocked and sad," as Merry puts it—although this behavior certainly could be a reaction to traumatic stress; *RK*, VI, viii, 277–300, Merry's comment is at 285.
59. *RK*, VI, ix, 304.
60. *RK*, VI, ix, 305.
61. *RK*, VI, ix, 309.
62. *RK*, VI, vii, 268.
63. *RK*, VI, ix, 309, my emphasis.
64. Counting Crows, "Mrs. Potter's Lullaby," *This Desert Life* (Geffen Records, 1999).
65. *RK*,VI, ix, 311.

CHAPTER 6. THREADS

1. *FR*, Foreword.
2. *S*, Ainulindalë, 16.
3. *Morgoth*, 394–96.
4. *S*, III, 50–52.
5. *S*, III, 52.
6. *S*, 309.
7. *S*, III, 53.
8. *Letters*, #144, 265.
9. Perhaps hinted at by Gandalf's description of Glorfindel to Frodo as one of "those who have dwelt in the Blessed Realm" who lives "at once in both worlds, and against both the Seen and the Unseen they have great power," . . . "one of the mighty of the Firstborn. He is an Elf-lord of a house of princes"; *FR*, II, i, 235.
10. *S*, III, 52–53, 61–62.
11. The dispute between Fëanor and Fingolfin is shown to be based on lies spread by Melkor, and although the House of Fëanor becomes "the dispossessed" because after the death of Fëanor the kingship of the Noldor in Middle-earth passes to Fingolfin and thence from him to his sons Fingon, Turgon, and Fingon's son Gil-galad, we only once see the sons of Fëanor—and only two of them—scheming to acquire kingship. *S*, XIX, 173.
12. *Road*, 248–59.
13. Dimitra Fimi draws upon Shippey's observations, but instead of focusing on the medieval literary sources, Fimi looks for influences from the "racial anthropology" of the nineteenth and twentieth centuries and various theories of race during Tol-

kien's lifetime. Concerned—like many other scholars—to try to determine how Tolkien's work may run afoul of contemporary attitudes toward race and (also like so many others) keen to defend him from shallow, anachronistic, and incoherent charges of racism, Fimi focuses primarily on the ways in which Tolkien has produced "a fantasy world that reproduces some of the concepts and prejudices of the 'primary' world, while at this same time questioning, challenging, and transforming others." Dimitra Fimi, *Tolkien, Race, and Cultural History: From Fairies to Hobbits* (New York: Palgrave, 2009), 131–59 at 159.

14. Shippey explicates the ranking of the kindreds of the elves (*Road*, 248–49) and Fimi titles the chapter in which she discusses this quality of *The Silmarillion* "A Hierarchical World" (Fimi, *Tolkien, Race, and Cultural History*, 131–59).
15. As part of their fundamental natures, Tolkien's elves do not divorce or remarry. See J.R.R. Tolkien, *The Nature of Middle-earth*, ed. Carl F. Hostetter (Boston: Houghton Mifflin Harcourt, 2021), 154, and "Laws and Customs Among the Eldar," in *Morgoth*, 209–14.
16. *S*, VI, 63.
17. *S*, VI, 64.
18. *S*, VII, 70.
19. *S*, VI, 65.
20. *S*, VI, 65.
21. *S*, IX, 82–85.
22. *S*, IX, 85–86.
23. *S*, IX, 86.
24. *S*, IX, 86.
25. *S*, IX, 87. Fëanor and his sons took the white ships and rowed them along the shore while the great host of the Noldor marched north to where the sea between Aman and Middle-earth was narrower. It is here that the Curse of Mandos was put upon the Noldor. Immediately Finarfin and many of his people (but not his sons, or his daughter Galadriel) turned back, eventually receiving the pardon of the Valar and remaining in Aman. However Fëanor and his sons, in one of the first acts of the treachery predicted (or caused) by the Curse, departed suddenly in the ships, leaving behind those Noldor led by Fingolfin, who could only reach Middle-earth by crossing the terrible Grinding Ice. Many of them, including the wife of Turgon, perished on that journey; *S*, IX, 88–90.
26. *Letters*, #131, 208.
27. Richard Z. Gallant, *Germanic Heroes, Courage, and Fate: Northern Narratives of Tolkien's Legendarium* (Geneva: Walking Tree Press, 2024), 23–38.
28. *S*, IX, 88.
29. *S*, XVII, 138; XXII, 236; XXIV, 246–47.
30. *S*, XVI, 131–33.
31. My emphasis; *S*, XVI, 131–33.
32. *S*, XVI, 134. "Golodhrim" is a reference to the Noldor in general, not the people of Gondolin (who are the Gondolindrim).
33. *S*, XVI, 135–37.
34. *S*, XVI, 137.
35. *S*, XVI, 137.
36. My emphases; *S*, XVI, 138–39.
37. My emphasis. This is the first time readers learn that Elenwë, Turgon's wife, who perished in crossing the Grinding Ice in order to reach Middle-earth, was one of the Vanyar. *S*, XVI, 138; S, IX, 90.
38. *S*, XVI, 134.

39. *S*, XVI, 139.
40. *S*, XIX, 166–67.
41. My emphasis; *S*, XIX, 166.
42. *S*, XXIII, 242, my emphasis.
43. That the interactions between elves and dwarves are racialized has not gone unnoticed by scholars: see Renée Vink, "'Jewish' Dwarves: Tolkien and Anti-Semitic Stereotyping," *Tolkien Studies* 10 (2013): 123–145.
44. *S*, XXI, 203–4.
45. Although that could be merely because they had captured Mîm and forced him to lead them to Amon Rhûd as his ransom. *S*, XXI, 203–6.
46. *UT*, 96–97.
47. *S*, XXII, 231–32.
48. *S*, XXII, 232.
49. *S*, XXII, 232–33.
50. *S*, X, 91–92. The language of the dwarves was to the elves "cumbersome and unlovely" and "few ever of the Eldar have achieved mastery of it," though the dwarves themselves "were swift to learn" Elvish: It is a common pattern that the lower ranks of the hierarchy learn the natural language of the higher members, but not vice versa.
51. *S*, X, 113.
52. *S*, XXII, 232–34.
53. *H*, IX, 183–5; *FR*, II, vi, 358, 361, 364; *S*, XX, 189, 193; *S*, X, 91–92.
54. Gildor "of the House of Finrod," whom Frodo, Sam, and Pippin meet in the Shire, is the only Noldo who is not directly tied to either place; we never learn if he and his wandering companions were Elves of Rivendell (although based on his elliptical comment about Bilbo, Gildor seems to have been to the House of Elrond, where he saw Bilbo, in the not-too-distant past); *FR*, I, iii, 92. The affiliation to the House of Finrod is confusing, because Finrod had no children (see his comments to his sister Galadriel (*S*, XV, 130), but is explained by Finrod having been Finarfin's original name (the Finrod character was named Inglor): Tolkien did not make the change in cognomens until after *The Lord of the Rings* was published; see *Shadow*, 72, 188n9. Haldir and the other Elves who insist on blindfolding Gimli are not Noldor, although their queen is.
55. *TT*, IV, v, 287. Note that Fimi (*Tolkien, Race, and Cultural History*), almost certainly because she was using a one-volume version of *The Lord of the Rings*, accidentally cites the passages as appearing in *The Return of the King*.
56. Fimi, *Tolkien, Race, and Cultural History*, 149; *WR*, 157.
57. Fimi *Tolkien, Race, and Cultural History*, 149. In contrast, Richard Gallant interprets this classification of men as being driven by the needs of the exiled Númenóreans in Gondor and Arnor to differentiate among those groups of men that were friendly to the Númenórean imperium and those that fought against it, and also to create a political origin-myth that would justify "(to the comfort of Númenórean pride) the surrender of so large a part of the Kingdom [of Gondor] to Eorl," the leader of the Rohirrim. Gallant, *Germanic Heroes, Courage, and Fate*, 135–40; *Peoples*, 312.
58. *TT*, VII, 142; Erkenbrand tells the men of Dunland that they have been "deluded by Saruman," *TT*, VIII, 150. Sam wonders "what lies or threats had led [the dead Southron soldier] on the long march from his home, and if he would not really rather have stayed there in peace"; *TT*, IV, 269.

    Gollum says that a hundred leagues south of Osgiliath, the sun "is very hot there, and there are seldom any clouds, and the men are fierce and have dark faces." *TT*, IV, iii, 24. Soon after, he describes the men going into Mordor: "Dark faces . . . They are fierce. They have black eyes, and long black hair, and gold rings in their ears . . . and some have red paint on their cheeks, and red cloaks; and their flags are red, and the tips of their spears . . . Not nice; very cruel wicked Men they look. Almost as bad as Orcs, and much bigger"; *TT,* iv, iii, 254. However, as Straubhaar emphasizes, these descriptions are given by the character Gollum, not a narrator or character obviously speaking on Tolkien's behalf; Sandra Ballif Straubhaar, "Myth, Late Roman History, and Multiculturalism in Tolkien's Middle-earth," in *Tolkien and the Invention of Myth,* ed. Jane Chance (Lexington: University Press of Kentucky, 2004), 101–17 at 113–14.

The Southrons are described by the narrator as "swarthy,"; *TT,* IV, iv, 260. In the Battle of the Pellenor Fields there were "out of Far Harad black men like half-trolls with white eyes and red tongues"; *RK,* V, vi, 121. These men seem more monstrous than human, an obvious contrast to the Southron soldier, who has brown skin, black braided hair, and no troll-like or nonhuman characteristics, and whose humanity is emphasized (he is described as the victim of a battle of "Men against Men," not men against half-trolls or other monsters); *TT,* IV, iv, 269.

59. Fimi's sophisticated historical and literary-historical discussion is closer to the mark, but it is surprising that she puts so much effort into trying to tease out the minimal material in *The Lord of the Rings* when, as we have seen, these dynamics are far more visible in *The Silmarillion* and written decades before race and racism became the predominant issues they are today. The most sophisticated and nuanced treatment of race in *The Lord of the Rings* is in Straubhaar's "Myth, Late Roman History, and Multiculturalism," 101–17.
60. See Straubhaar, "Myth, Late Roman History, and Multiculturalism"; Fimi, *Tolkien, Race, and Cultural History;* Gallant, *Germanic Heroes, Courage, and Fate.*
61. My emphasis. *Letters,* #131, 211–12.
62. Fellow academics may recognize a parallel to the Noldor's reaction in the phenomenon of colleagues at schools in the middle of the current (arbitrary) academic pecking-order being much fiercer defenders of the hierarchy than those at the very top. Whenever I have proposed that hypothetically pernicious aspects of "privilege" in academia could be addressed be weighing applications for grants, awards, and fellowships by teaching-load and faculty salary, it is the colleagues at the mid-ranked schools who respond most angrily. They are happy to address notional privilege by race, gender, and sexuality, but appear completely resistant to the idea of addressing reasonably objective and measurable factors contributing to privilege, perhaps because they fear that their position in the hierarchy is more tenuous than those at the very top.
63. *Letters,* #29 and #30, 47–48.
64. *Letters,* #212, 407.
65. In some late, unpublished philosophical writings Tolkien does suggest that the Shadow of Morgoth had marred the very fabric of the world so that no elves or men are "wholly free" of its influence (*Morgoth,* 241). We could therefore infer that Elvish racism is an effect of Morgoth fundamentally corrupting the world.
66. William H. Green, *The Hobbit: A Journey into Maturity* (New York: Twayne, 1995).
67. As is evident in the near-disaster of the engagement with the trolls, *H,* II, 42-52; *H,* XII, 233; *H,* XVIII, 304, 306. "Mr. Baggins . . . is at the start of *The Hobbit* full of nonsense, like modern English society as perceived by Tolkien . . . [but] by the end . . . Bilbo as burglar has progressed so far as to rub shoulders with heroes, even to be (just) considerable as one himself." *Road,* 72.
68. *Road,* 71.
69. *Road,* 72.

70. *Road*, 73–74.
71. *H*, I, 16–19; II, 38. The contract itself is precise and reasonable; the humor arises from there *being* a contract to organize an epic adventure quest.
72. *H*, I, 24.
73. *H*, I, 26.
74. *Author*, 42.
75. *H*, X, 210.
76. *H*, X, 209–13; *H*, XIV, 263–64.
77. *H*, XII, 236.
78. *H*, XII, 237.
79. *H*, XII, 238. I have lineated the prose paragraph so as to make the rhetorical and poetic patterning more easily visible.
80. *H*, I, 13–14; II, 37. Bilbo's homeland is not called "the Shire" in *The Hobbit*, but it is convenient to use the name despite it not having been invented until *The Lord of the Rings*.
81. *H*, I, 14.
82. Tom Shippey, *Hard Reading: Learning from Science Fiction* (Liverpool: Liverpool University Press, 2016), 77–80.
83. His unsuccessful burglary of the trolls almost results in the deaths of the entire party; *H*, II, 43–50. His constantly needing to be carried by Dori slows down the dwarves' flight from the goblins; *H*, IV, 76–78. And see *Author*, 21–29.
84. *Road*, 150–51; 76–86. *Author*, 27–28.
85. *H*, XV, 275.
86. *H*, XV, 275–77.
87. *H*, XV, 277–78.
88. *H*, XVI, 283–83.
89. *H*, XVIII, 304; *H*, XII, 237.
90. John D. Black, N. Hashimzade, and Gareth Myles, eds. *A Dictionary of Economics*, 5th ed. (Oxford: Oxford University Press, 2017), 459.
91. Bilbo's thought of "Now I am a burglar indeed!" at first might indicate that he has accepted his role in the epic world, in this version of which being a "burglar" or "expert treasure-hunter" (*H*, I, 27) is not shameful if the thief is not caught. But his subsequent justification of the theft to himself—"They did say I could pick and choose my own share" (*H*, XIII, 248–49) indicates in two ways that his bourgeois values are still dominant: first, by believing that what he is doing is wrong, and second by attempting to justify it in terms of a verbal contract.
92. *H*, XVI, 284.
93. *H*, XVIII, 301.
94. William Ian Miller, *Why Is Your Axe Bloody?* (Oxford: Oxford University Press, 2014), 75–87.
95. Miller, *Why Is Your Axe Bloody?*, 190–93.
96. *H*, XIX, 314.
97. *RK*, VI, ix, 301.
98. *Author*, 48; *H*, II, 38.
99. For example, in *The Lord of the Rings*, Faramir takes a casual and possibly hyperbolic statement as a binding oath; *TT*, IV, v, 280. A similar "rash promise" would be far less believable in the bourgeois world, where an unfulfilled contract is settled through whatever the noncompletion clause says rather than being a permanent stain on a person's honor that must be avoided even at the cost of life and limb.
100. *H*, XVII, 288. Thorin certainly seems to feel the sting, as he immediately stops threatening and insulting Bilbo and squabbling about the treasure and extricates

himself from the whole interaction as quickly as possible. He knows that both Bilbo and Gandalf are right. The narrator gives the excuse of the "bewilderment of treasure" for Thorin's less-than-epic behavior.

101. *H*, XIII, 252; and see *Author*, 42–43.
102. *H*, XVI, 282–83.
103. The dwarves, particularly the Dwarves of Erebor in exile, understand the bourgeois world better than any other epic subgroup, since they rely on trade. See *RK*, Appendix A, III, 357.
104. *Author*, 39–45 at 44–45. Emphasis in original.
105. M. M. Bakhtin, *The Dialogic Imagination: Four Essays*, ed. Michael Holquist, trans. Caryl Emerson and Michael Holquist (Austin: University of Texas Press, 1981).

CHAPTER 7. TAPESTRY

1. *S*, II, 46.
2. *Peoples*, 413. For discussion see Verlyn Flieger, "Taking the Part of Trees: Eco-Conflict in Middle-earth," in *Green Suns and Faërie: Essays on J.R.R. Tolkien* (Kent, OH: Kent State University Press, 2012), 262–74, and Stentor Danielson, "'To Trees All Men Are Orcs': The Environmental Ethic of J.R.R. Tolkien's 'The New Shadow,'" *Tolkien Studies* 18 (2021): 179–94.
3. *Treason*, 70–73; *Treason*, 6–8; *Treason*, 6, 9, 71–72, 411–19. *S*, II, 45–46; *WR*, 65–67; *Letters*, #163, 316.
4. *Peoples*, vii–xi, and see Christopher Tolkien's introductory paragraphs to each section and Notes.
5. Hilary Wynne and I surveyed all the Tolkien criticism published between 1982 and 2000 and were able to group it into five broad categories (though the fifth is a bit of a catch-all). The efflorescence of scholarship since then can be tracked via the annual (and utterly invaluable) "Year's Work in Tolkien Studies," that has appeared in each volume of *Tolkien Studies* since 2005. "The Year's Work" has regularly needed to add new categories or to subdivide existing ones in response to various currents in the scholarship. Michael D.C. Drout and Hilary Wynne, "Tom Shippey's *J.R.R. Tolkien: Author of the Century* and a Look Back at Tolkien Criticism Since 1982," *Envoi* 9, no. 2 (2000): 101–34.
6. *Letters*, #186, 353; #208, 385–86; #211, 404–5.
7. *FR*, II, vi, 361–62; *FR*, II, x, 414.
8. *TT*, IV, v, 287.
9. See Part II, the Númenor-focused material in *UT*, 165–227.
10. *TT*, IV, v, 286–87.
11. *TT*, IV, v, 280.
12. *Letters*, # 154, 293.
13. *Letters*, #181, 342.
14. *Letters*, #144, 266.
15. For Tolkien's more philosophical approach to these issues, see the dialogue "Athrabeth Finrod ah Andreth" and the essay "Myths Transformed" in *Morgoth*.
16. Anna Vaninskaya's discussion of these issues is particularly nuanced and sophisticated. *Fantasies of Time and Death: Dunsany, Eddison, Tolkien* (New York: Palgrave Macmillan, 2020), 153–68.
17. *TT*, IV, v, 286. Faramir continues on to say that the stewards were wiser than the kings because they allied themselves to the friendly Middle Men of Rohan and elsewhere. The somewhat hybrid culture that is created is less obsessed with the dread of death and more forward-looking, and hence, fertile.

18. For some thoughts on the fertility crisis in Middle-earth at the end of the Third Age, see Michael D.C. Drout, "The Influence of J.R.R. Tolkien's Masculinist Medievalism," *Medieval Feminist Newsletter* 22 (1996): 26–27.
19. *RK*, V, iv, 99–100.
20. *RK*, V, i, 24, 36; ix, 149.
21. On wraiths, see *Author*, 121–28. The Anglo-Saxons used the word *hweorfan*, "to turn," to describe what the spirit did when it left the body, and this word and *cyrran* (also "to turn") are used to translate the Latin word *conversio*, also "to turn" but in the religious sense, to convert either to Christianity or, for Christians, to a more moral form of living (i.e., entering a monastery). Thus it seems as if the Anglo-Saxons had an underlying image of *turning* being associated with spiritual change or departure. A *wraith*, then, would be a spirit that had turned the wrong way or turned too much, becoming *twisted* (a word which we still use in this sense) to evil.
22. *Letters*, #131, 216–17.
23. *S*, Akallabêth, 260. Gallant describes how "an imperial Númenórean ideology develops, which posits and privileges the hegemony of the Númenóreans, and their Dúnedain successor states, over the denizens of Middle-earth"; Richard Z. Gallant, *Germanic Heroes, Courage, and Fate: Northern Narratives of Tolkien's Legendarium* (Geneva: Walking Tree Press, 2024), 140.
24. "The fusion of the two traditions [Atlantean and Germanic] creates a unique, although always waning and mutable, ethnic identity embodied in the hegemonic polities of the successor states in exile: Arnor and Gondor." Gallant, *Germanic Heroes, Courage, and Fate*, 119.
25. *RK*, Appendix A, I, iv, 328. For discussion, see Gallant, *Germanic Heroes, Courage, and Fate*, 149–52. Gallant notes that since the reductions in lifespan and other qualities of the Númenóreans was due to the withdrawal of the gifts given at the end of the First Age, "the whole Kin-strife" [the civil war in Gondor that led to the death of many of the "great" in Gondor] is for naught, and like our own primary world, is a tragedy due to misguided racial beliefs of a biological rather than socially constructed nature," 149–52 at 149. Tolkien seems to have been remarkably consistent in his recognition of and reaction to the evils of racism despite his not having been the beneficiary of the massive contemporary academic discourse on race. See Fimi, whose discussion is comprehensive, and note that the issues have been discussed widely and Tolkien's anti-Nazi letters quoted repeatedly; Dimitra Fimi, *Tolkien, Race, and Cultural History: From Fairies to Hobbits* (New York: Palgrave Macmillan, 2009), 135–40.
26. *RK*, V, i, 27–28.
27. *RK*, V, ii, 50–51.
28. See Chapter 6, pages 229–30.
29. *Road*, 122.
30. Sandra Ballif Straubhaar, "Myth, Late Roman History, and Multiculturalism in Tolkien's Middle-earth," in *Tolkien and the Invention of Myth*, ed. Jane Chance (Lexington: University Press of Kentucky, 2004), 109; *RK*, Appendix A, I, iv, 329.
31. Gallant, *Germanic Heroes, Courage, and Fate*, 141–42; Straubhaar, "Myth, Late Roman History, and Multiculturalism," 109.
32. My emphasis. *TT*, IV, v, 287.
33. *TT*, III, ii, 38.
34. *TT*, III, vi, 110–12; *TT*, III, x, 186.
35. *TT*, III, ii, 33.
36. *TT*, III, ii, 39–41.
37. *TT*, III, vi, 120, 125.

38. *TT*, V, vi, 115–16, 119–22.
39. *RK*, V, iii, 69, 75.
40. *RK*, V, v, 104.
41. *TT*, III, vi, 121–22.
42. *TT*, III, vi, 120. Shippey notes that "freedom is not a prerogative of democracies, and . . . in free societies orders give way to discretion"; *Road*, 125. His point is that despite Rohan being a hereditary monarchy, its people still have the freedom to make decisions and rely on their own judgments to a degree that is lacking in more rule-bound societies regardless of their form of government. In other words (mine), everything is not determined purely by *who* makes the rules, but *what* those rules are and *how* the culture responds to them. Democratic societies can be just as rule-bound and oppressive of individual action and judgment as monarchies or dictatorships. Indeed, they can be worse, as we have learned to our sorrow.
43. *RK*, V, iv, 89–90.
44. *RK*, V, iv, 99–100.
45. *RK*, V, iv, 101; *RK*, VI, v, 247.
46. *RK*, V, vii, 127–28.
47. *RK*, VI, v, 247.
48. *RK*, V, vi, 118.
49. *TT*, III, vii, 144–45.
50. *RK*, V, viii, 117–18. Théoden's dying words are reminiscent of those of Thorin in *The Hobbit* (*H*, XVIII, 300–301), and this similarity is probably not a coincidence but instead evidence of the cultural links between the dwarves, with their Old Norse names, and the Germanic culture of Rohan.
51. My emphasis. *RK*, V, vii, 117–18. *RK*, V, vii, 119. Italics in original. *RK*, V, vii, 119.
52. *RK*, V, iv, 94–99.
53. *RK*, V, vii, 119.
54. *RK*, V, vii, 122.
55. *RK*, VI, v, 242.
56. Éomer is referring to Aragorn's metaphorical description of Éowyn as a white flower whose sap had been turned to ice by frost and so standing "bitter-sweet, still fair to see, but stricken, soon to fall and die." *RK*, V, viii, 142–44.
57. My emphasis. *RK*, V, iii, 76.
58. *RK*, V, viii, 143; *RK*, VI, v, 243.
59. My emphasis. *RK*, V, vi, 116. For a more detailed discussion of Éowyn's language as it evolved through Tolkien's various revisions of the scene, see my "Tolkien's Prose Style and Its Literary and Rhetorical Effects," *Tolkien Studies* 1 (2004): 132–62, particularly 152–55.
60. *RK*, V, vii, 116.
61. *RK*, V, iv, 87–90.
62. *RK*, V, iv, 97.
63. *RK*, V, iv, 94–95.
64. *RK*, V, iv, 92; *RK*, V, iv, 98–100.
65. *RK*, V, vii, 128–29.
66. *RK*, V, vii, 129.
67. *RK*, V, vii, 129–30.
68. *RK*, V, vii, 130.
69. *TT*, IV, v, 280: "I would not take this thing, if it lay by the highway. Not were Minas Tirith falling in ruin and I alone could save her, so, using the weapon of the Dark Lord, for her good and my glory. No, I do not wish for such triumphs, Frodo son of Drogo." And later, "Even if I were such a man as to desire this thing, and even

though I knew not clearly what this thing was when I spoke, still I should take these words as a vow, and be held by them." *TT*, IV, v, 289.

70. *TT*, IV, v, 289–90.
71. *RK*, V, iv, 86.
72. *RK*, V, iv, 98–99a. As Shippey notes, a ruler's insisting that he will have "naught" is even more terrifying since the advent of nuclear weapons; *Author*, 173–74.
73. *RK*, V, i, 31–32.
74. *RK*, V, vii, 129.
75. "Merry and Pippin in the middle boat were ill at ease, for Boromir sat muttering to himself, sometimes biting his nails, as if some restlessness or doubt consumed him, sometimes seizing a paddle and driving the boat close behind Aragorn's. Then Pippin, who sat in the bow looking back, caught a queer gleam in his eye, as he peered forward gazing at Frodo." *FR*, II, ix, 398. See also Sam's comments to Faramir; *TT*, IV, v, 289.
76. *FR*, II, x, 420–21.
77. By combining the information from multiple retellings of Boromir's last stand, it is possible to determine that he single-handedly kills at least twenty orcs: *FR*, II, x, 421; *TT*, III, i, 16; *TT*, III, iii, 47; *RK*, V, i, 28.
78. *TT*, III, i, 16–18, 20–22; *RK*, V, i, 27–28.
79. *TT*, III, ii, 34.
80. Or tracker-orcs merely commanded by a Nazgûl on the east bank of the river. Tolkien's synoptic chronology shows what a near thing Frodo and Sam's escape was. William Cloud Hicklin, ed. "The Chronology of *The Lord of the Rings*," *Tolkien Studies* 19 Supplement (2022): 50–55.
81. *TT*, IV, v, 274–76.
82. *TT*, III, ii, 38; *RK*, V, i, 31–32.
83. *FR*, II, x, 414–15.
84. *RK*, V, iv, 86.
85. See Gallant, *Germanic Heroes, Courage, and Fate*; Straubhaar, "Myth, Late Roman History, and Multiculturalism."
86. *FR*, II, ii, 265–66.
87. *TT*, IV, v, 279–80.
88. *RK*, V, iv, 86.
89. "to use this thing is perilous"—note the lack of any conditional or subjunctive; *RK*, V, iv, 86–87.
90. *RK*, V, iv, 87.
91. My emphases. *RK*, V, iv, 86.
92. My emphases. *FR*, II, x, 414–15.
93. Gandalf tells Denethor that if the steward had received the Ring "it would have overthrown you. Were it buried beneath the roots of Mindolluin, still it would burn your mind away." Denethor's madness inside the mausoleum of the stewards shows that those subjunctives and conditionals had become declaratives, and implies that the Ring did not have to be so close for it to affect him mentally.
94. My emphasis. *RK*, VI, i, 177.
95. Emphasis in original. *TT*, IV, ii, 241.
96. My emphases. *FR*, I, i, 42.
97. My emphases. *FR*, I, ii, 62.
98. My emphases in italics for consistency; emphases in the original are here underlined. *FR*, I, ii, 66.
99. My emphases. *RK*, VI, iii, 223.
100. *RK*, VI, i, 177.
101. *RK*, VI, ix, 303.

102. *FR*, I, v, 114–15; Hillman, 31–33; *FR*, I, ii, 62–63.
103. Plato, *The Republic*, trans. G.M.A. Grube rev. C.D.C. Reeve, in *Plato: Complete Works*, ed. John M. Cooper (Indianapolis: Hackett, 1997), 971–1223 at 1000–1001. See also John Cox, "Tolkien's Platonic Fantasy," *Seven* 5 (1984): 53–69; Frederick A. de Armas, "Gyges' Ring: Invisibility in Plato, Tolkien, and Lope de Vega," *Journal of the Fantastic in the Arts* 3, no. 4 (1994): 120–38.
104. *FR*, II, ii, 266.
105. *H*, VI, 103–5; See Hillman, 16–36, for a deeply insightful discussion of the implications of Bilbo's lie.
106. "Goblin he thought good, when he could get it"; *H*, V, 82.
107. *RK*, V, ix, 155; *RK*, Appendix B, 368–71.
108. *TT*, IV, i, 224.
109. *TT*, IV, i, 221–22.
110. For the former, see Sam's report of the Gaffer's conversation with the Black Rider (*FR*, I, iii, 85); for the latter, Bilbo's birthday speech (*FR*, I, i, 37–39), discussed above in Chapter 2, pages 80–81.
111. *WR*, 96–97.
112. Although technically he only says that at least some of the differences between the passages are likely not intentional.
113. Emphases in original. *FR*, II, x, 417.
114. *TT*, III, v, 99. Shippey explores the possibility that the second voice could be that of the Ring itself but comes to no definite conclusion; *Author*, 138–41. I agree with Hillman's closely reasoned argument that the Ring is most likely not a conscious entity (I take Gandalf's statement that it was trying to get back to its maker as a helpful analogy, like "atoms want their outermost electron shells to be filled" or "current seeks the ground"), and that the Ring contains the "strength" of Sauron but not some fragment of his consciousness; Hillman, *Pity, Power, and Tolkien's Ring*, 20–25. I would merely add that while Morgoth seemed to be able to break off pieces of his own spirit in order to give volition and seeming consciousness to dragons, wolves, and other creatures he had manufactured, Sauron is of a far lower rank as a supernatural being and possesses much less innate power. See *Morgoth*, 396–401.
115. The chronology in Appendix B reveals no obstacle to this interpretation. Gandalf sat in a high place and strove with Sauron on February 25. Frodo and Sam encounter Gollum on February 29, and Gandalf does not meet Aragorn, Legolas, and Gimli until March 1.
116. Unfortunately I did not write down the student's name when I scribbled the quote on the back of an assignment sheet in 2009.
117. *FR*, I, ii, 66; *H*, V, 86, 84, 97.
118. *TT*, IV, i, 223–25.
119. Hillman, *Pity, Power, and Tolkien's Ring*, 124.
120. *RK*, VI, i, 180.
121. *RK*, VI, iii, 221.
122. *TT*, IV, ii, 238.
123. *Treason*, 208.
124. "Supernatural" is probably incorrect as applied to Middle-earth. As Gergely Nagy argues, much of what in our world would be categorized as magic is in Middle-earth theology. Gergely Nagy, "On No Magic in Tolkien: Resisting the Representational Criteria of Realism," in *Sub-creating Arda: World-Building in J.R.R. Tolkien's Work, Its Precursors, and Its Legacies*, ed. Dimitra Fimi and Thomas Honegger (Zurich: Walking Tree, 2019), 153–75.
125. *FR*, II, vii, 381.

126. *FR*, II, vii, 381.
127. For the same idea worked out in the more formal language of philosophy and political science, see Roberto Mangabeira Unger, *Knowledge and Politics* (New York: The Free Press, 1975). And then see the devastating critique in Arthur Leff, "Memorandum: Review of *Knowledge and Politics* by R. M. Unger," *Stanford Law Review* 29 (1976–1977): 879–89.
128. Lewis wrote this in a 1959 letter to Charles Moorman. See *The Collected Letters of C.S. Lewis: Narnia, Cambridge, and Joy 1950–1963*, vol. III, ed. Walter Hooper (San Francisco: Harper San Francisco, 2007), 1049.
129. Gergely Nagy, "The 'Lost' Subject of Middle-earth: The Constitution of the Subject in the Figure of Gollum in *The Lord of the Rings*," *Tolkien Studies* 3 (2006): 57–79 at 59–60.
130. Nagy, "'Lost' Subject," 59–60. Bonniejean Christensen notes that in the first published version of *The Hobbit*, Gollum referred to himself and Bilbo as "precious"; only in the revised version did the word also apply to the Ring. "Gollum's Character Transformation in *The Hobbit*" in *A Tolkien Compass*, ed. Jared Lobdell (LaSalle, IL: Open Court, 1975), 9–28.
131. I am attempting to avoid overusing or jargonizing the term *lack*, which Nagy employs here, not as a rejection of Nagy's argument (which draws on Plato's *Symposium*), but because I want to avoid contaminating my analysis with logically incoherent and scientifically ridiculous Lacanian psychoanalysis in which *lack*—in addition to *symbolic castration*, *imaginary phallus*, *real breast*, and other quasi-Freudian obscurantist gibberish—is a term of art. In the upcoming discussion I have, at times, for purely stylistic reasons, used *lack* as a synonym, but the appearance of the word is not in any way an endorsement of Lacanian theory.
132. *FR*, I, i, 43.
133. Nagy, "Lost Subject," 61.
134. A case could be made for using *themself* as the reflexive pronoun here, but I have not figured out how to thread a passage through the ever-shifting political quagmire surrounding pronouns, and I have no desire to go down to join the corpses and light little candles.
135. *Road*, 139–40.
136. *FR*, I, ii, 64.
137. *TT*, IV, i, 222–23.
138. *RK*, V, x, 164.
139. *TT*, IV, iii, 245–46.
140. *TT*, IV, iii, 248.
141. Hillman, *Pity, Power, and Tolkien's Ring*, 140–41.
142. A character in Samuel R. Delany's *Babel-17*, the Butcher, never says *I* but instead pounds his chest with his fist in situations where the first-person pronoun is needed. Samuel R. Delany, *Babel-17* (New York: Ace Books, 1966).
143. See Daniel C. Dennett, *Consciousness Explained* (Boston: Little, Brown, 1991); and see Douglas Hofstadter, *I Am a Strange Loop* (New York: Basic Books, 2007).
144. *RK*, VI, iii, 214–15.
145. Ernest Hemingway, "A Clean, Well-Lighted Place," in *The Complete Short Stories of Ernest Hemingway* (New York: Charles Scribner's Sons, 1987), 288–91; C.S. Lewis, *The Screwtape Letters* (1942; San Francisco: HarperSanFrancisco, 2001), 60; and see *Author*, 127–28.
146. *TT*, IV, iii, 245. If, per Descartes, "I am a thing that thinks," and I am experiencing thinking, then I cannot be Nothing in any strict sense; something else must take the place held by Nothing.
147. *TT*, V, iii, 250; *TT*, V, i, 222–23.
148. See Tolkien's comments in "The Hunt for the Ring," in *Unfinished Tales*, that Sau-

ron "divined something indomitable" in Gollum, who, the narrator says, "was ultimately indomitable" because he had developed a hatred of Sauron "even greater than his terror." *UT*, 337–38. This is a good example of the "Oft evil will shall evil mar" dynamic that Tolkien uses regularly to great effect. See *TT*, III, xi, 200.

149. *RK*, V, viii, 147.
150. UT, 337.
151. The word *felt* is significant, as it is used by the narrator to describe Gollum's behavior to Frodo before the Black Gate; *TT*, IV, iii, 245.
152. Frodo's vision of a green country under a swift sunrise Hillman attributes to Sam adapting Frodo's narration of the dream he had in Tom Bombadil's house, *FR*, I, viii, 146; Hillman, *Pity, Power, and Tolkien's Ring*, 166–69.
153. *FR*, I, viii, 151.
154. *FR*, II, vii, 372.
155. *FR*, II, vii, 372–73. That whatever else Sam was offered is never stated probably makes it seem more ominous or shameful than it was (married life with Rosie Cotton? To serve Frodo perpetually?). I do not know why Tolkien chose to hide this part of Sam's thoughts, although the hesitation does contribute to the verisimilitude of his speech.
156. *TT*, IV, v, 289.
157. *TT*, IV, v, 275.
158. This is not the only time that it seems that Faramir is a mouthpiece for Tolkien's own views. See also his statements about not loving valor in arms for its own sake but for what it protects; *TT*, IV, v, 280.
159. Gandalf tells Aragorn, Legolas, and Gimli that Galadriel told him that Boromir was in peril; however, she did nothing about it at the time; *TT*, III, v, 99.
160. *UT*, 228–67.
161. *RK*, VI, vii, 268; ix, 305.
162. *RK*, VI, ix, 309.
163. See Hillman, *Pity, Power, and Tolkien's Ring*, for a very nuanced discussion of these two instances; 162–64, 199–205.
164. *Letters*, #246, 462–63, 466.
165. *TT*, III, viii, 155.
166. Edwin Muir, "A Boy's World: *The Return of the Ring [sic]* by J.R.R. Tolkien," *The Observer*, November 27, 1955, 11. Accessed July 9, 2024.
167. *Road*, 154–56 and 318–24; and *Author*, xxix–xxxii.
168. *FR*, II, vii, 380–82.

CONCLUSION: FATHERS AND SONS

1. *FR*, II, I, 245–46.
2. *MC*, 22.
3. *RK*, VI, iii, 215.
4. *RK*, VI, ix, 304
5. *Beowulf*, line 2461, my translation.
6. *OFS*, 76.
7. *OFS*, 76.
8. *RK*, V, iv, 103; vi, 123; *RK*, VI, iv, 227.
9. *MC*, 23.
10. *RK*, VI, i, 185.
11. My words here are a modification of lyrics by Gordon Sumner, "Mad About You," on Sting, *The Soul Cages* (Santa Monica: A&M Records, 1991).
12. *TT*, IV, vii, 311.

INDEX